Semantic Enterprise Application Integration for Business Processes:
Service–Oriented Frameworks

Gregoris Mentzas
National Technical University of Athens, Greece

Andreas Friesen
SAP, Inc., Germany

BUSINESS SCIENCE REFERENCE

Hershey · New York

Director of Editorial Content:	Kristin Klinger
Senior Managing Editor:	Jamie Snavely
Assistant Managing Editor:	Michael Brehm
Publishing Assistant:	Sean Woznicki
Typesetter:	Michael Brehm, Michael Killian
Cover Design:	Lisa Tosheff
Printed at:	Yurchak Printing Inc.

Published in the United States of America by
Business Science Reference (an imprint of IGI Global)
701 E. Chocolate Avenue
Hershey PA 17033
Tel: 717-533-8845
Fax: 717-533-8661
E-mail: cust@igi-global.com
Web site: http://www.igi-global.com/reference

Library of Congress Cataloging-in-Publication Data

Semantic enterprise application integration for business processes : service-oriented frameworks / Gregoris Mentzas and Andreas Friesen, editors.
       p. cm.
  Includes bibliographical references and index.
  Summary: "This book provides methods that allow for access to corporate and customer data independent of where it resides"--Provided by publisher.
   ISBN 978-1-60566-804-8 (hbk.) -- ISBN 978-1-60566-805-5 (ebook) 1. Semantic integration (Computer systems) 2. Enterprise application integration (Computer systems) 3. Service-oriented architecture (Computer science) 4. Management information systems. I. Mentzas, Gregoris, 1960- II. Friesen, Andreas. III. Title.

  TK5105.88815.S424 2010
  658'.05--dc22
                                    2009021585

British Cataloguing in Publication Data
A Cataloguing in Publication record for this book is available from the British Library.

Dedication

To Lily and Maria

Gregoris Mentzas

To Oksana, Daniel, Gregory, and Maximilian

Andreas Friesen

Table of Contents

Detailed Table of Contents

Chapter 1
Collaboration Across the Enterprise: An Ontology Based Approach for Enterprise

Aggelos Liapis, Vrije Universiteit Brussel, Belgium
Stijn Christiaens, Vrije Universiteit Brussel, Belgium

In this chapter, we will present a methodology, which has resulted in the implementation of a highly customizable collaborative environment focused to support ontology-based enterprise interoperability. An additional key issue addressed by the particular platform is the variety and number of different resources that concur to achieve a cross-enterprise business service. A second key issue is the diversity of agreed (e.g., meaning negotiation when creating online contracts) models, and the difficulty in adapting its integrated features and services to different situations.

Chapter 2

Thanasis Bouras, National Technical University of Athens, Greece
Panagiotis Gouvas, National Technical University of Athens, Greece
Gregoris Mentzas, National Technical University of Athens, Greece

If we try to increase the level of automation in enterprise application integration (EAI) scenarios, we confront challenges related to the resolution of data and message heterogeneities between interoperating services, which traditional EAI technologies are weak to solve. We propose a semantically-enriched approach for dynamic data mediation in EAI scenarios, focusing on the resolution of message level heterogeneities between collaborative enterprise services, facilitating automated data mediation during execution time by providing formal transformations of the output and input messages (of the participating services) to a common reference business data model, that is, the enterprise interoperability ontology. Moreover, we present a tool that has been developed to support the user to provide business data-related semantic annotations and XSLT transformations of the input and output message parts of collaborative enterprise services. Finally, we demonstrate the utilization of the proposed approach and toll in a real-world EAI scenario.

Chapter 3

Veronica Gacitua-Decar, Dublin City University, Ireland
Claus Pahl, Dublin City University, Ireland

Increasingly, enterprises are using service-oriented architecture (SOA) as an approach to enterprise application integration (EAI). SOA has the potential to bridge the gap between business and technology and to improve the reuse of existing applications and the interoperability with new ones. In addition to service architecture descriptions, architecture abstractions like patterns and styles capture design knowledge and allow the reuse of successfully applied designs, thus improving the quality of software. Knowledge gained from integration projects can be captured to build a repository of semantically enriched, experience-based solutions. Business patterns identify the interaction and structure between users, business processes, and data. Specific integration and composition patterns at a more technical level address enterprise application integration and capture reliable architecture solutions. We use an ontology-based approach to capture architecture and process patterns. Ontology techniques for pattern definition, extension, and composition are developed and their applicability in business process-driven application integration is demonstrated.

Chapter 4

Ingo Zinnikus, German Research Center for Artificial Intelligence (DFKI) GmbH, Germany
Christian Hahn, German Research Center for Artificial Intelligence (DFKI) GmbH, Germany
Klaus Fischer, German Research Center for Artificial Intelligence (DFKI) GmbH, Germany

In cross-organisational business interactions, integrating different partners raises interoperability problems especially on the technical level. The internal processes and interfaces of the participating partners are often pre-existing and have to be taken as given. This imposes restrictions on the possible solutions for the problems which occur when partner processes are integrated. The aim of this chapter is the presentation of a three-tier framework for managing and implementing interoperable and cross-organizational business processes. Thereby the authors want to fill the gap currently existing between processes defined on a strategic level and executed models. We describe a solution which supports rapid prototyping by combining a model-driven framework for cross-organisational business processes with an agent-based approach for flexible process execution. We show how the W3C recommendation for Semantic Web service descriptions can be combined with the model-driven approach for rapid service integration.

In service-oriented architectures (SOA), service descriptions are fundamental elements. In order to automatically execute SOA tasks, such as services discovery, it is necessary to capture and process the semantics of services. We review several Semantic Web services frameworks that intend to bring semantics to Web services. This chapter depicts some ideas from SOA and Semantic Web services and their application to enterprise application integration. We illustrate an example of logic-based semantic matching between consumer services and provided services, which are described in ontologies.

The availability of sophisticated Web service discovery mechanisms is an essential prerequisite for increasing the levels of efficiency and automation in EAI. In this chapter, we present an approach for developing service registries building on the UDDI standard and offering semantically-enhanced publication and discovery capabilities in order to overcome some of the known limitations of conventional service registries. The approach aspires to promote efficiency in EAI in a number of ways, but primarily by automating the task of evaluating service integrability on the basis of the input and output messages that are defined in the Web service's interface. The presented solution combines the use of three technology standards to meet its objectives: OWL-DL, for modelling service characteristics and performing fine-grained service matchmaking via DL reasoning, SAWSDL, for creating semantically annotated descriptions of service interfaces, and UDDI, for storing and retrieving syntactic and semantic information about services and service providers.

Chapter 7

Semantics needs to be considered in two major integration tasks. First, semantically corresponding data types that can be used for communication between components need to be identified. Second, natural language documentation needs to be studied today in order to understand component behavior, that is, dependencies between operation invocations and how semantically different outcomes of operation calls are represented in the technical output format. The approach presented in this chapter supports the two tasks as follows. First, closed frequent itemset mining (CFIM) is employed to help identifying semantically corresponding data types. Second, a formal representation for component behavior is introduced. However, as component behavior is specified during component development, but used during integration–two distinct phases involving distinct teams–we provide model transformations to ensure the consistent transfer of generic behavioral information to specific integration constraints before automated integration techniques can be applied. We applied the CFIM on the message types exposed by SAP's standard software components and show that we are able to find semantically relevant correspondences. Furthermore, we demonstrate the practical applicability of our behavioral model transformations on the basis of an SAP best practice business scenario. With the little more effort to specify behavioral information at development time in a formal way instead of in natural language, our approach facilitates the reuse of behavioral component descriptions in multiple integration projects and eases the construction of correct integrations.

Chapter 8

Andreas Friesen, SAP Research, Germany

In service-oriented business applications, B2B integration happens when a service requester invokes services of one or more service providers. Typically, there are several candidate services with similar capabilities that can be chosen by a requester in order to serve his business needs. The selection of the service to be invoked may depend on different functional and non-functional properties. The non-functional properties usually address security, reliability, performance, and so forth. The functional properties address the business process interplay at the level of the technical Web service interface and the message choreography associated with it. At the technical integration level, the description of functional and non-functional service properties has been exhaustively addressed in the scientific literature in the past. The business level however, namely, the requester's business need, the business meaning of an offered service, and the capability of a service provider to successfully perform the requested business transaction, has been rather ignored. This chapter describes a solution for service discovery and selection at the business level, that is, at the level of offered business capability of a service provider and the ability to serve a concrete requested business transaction. The proposed solution is based on semantic interpretation of offered service capabilities, contractual restrictions, business rules of the requestor specifying selection preferences, and the parameters of the run-time service request. The applicability of the proposed solution is demonstrated on a shipper-carrier integration scenario.

Chapter 9

Yildiray Kabak, Development and Consultancy Ltd., Turkey
Mehmet Olduz, Development and Consultancy Ltd., Turkey
Gokce B. Laleci, Development and Consultancy Ltd., Turkey
Tuncay Namli, Development and Consultancy Ltd., Turkey
Veli Bicer, Middle East Technical University, Turkey
Nikola Radic, European Dynamics, Greece
George Milis, European Dynamics, Greece
Asuman Dogac, Development and Consultancy Ltd., Turkey

Currently in the travel domain, most of the travel products are sold through global distribution aystems (GDSs). Since only major airline companies or hotel chains can afford to join GDSs, it is difficult for small and medium enterprises to market their travel products. In this chapter, we describe a middleware, called SATINE, to address this problem. In the SATINE middleware, existing travel applications are wrapped as Web services. Web services, as such, is of limited use because the service consumer must know all the details of the Web service like the functionality of the Web service (what it does) and the content and the structure of input and output messages. Therefore, we annotate both the service functionality and the service messages with Web ontology language (OWL) ontologies. Service functionality ontology is obtained from the "Open Travel Alliance (OTA)" specifications. Service message ontologies are automatically generated from the XML schema definitions of the messages. These local message ontologies are mapped into one or more global message ontologies through an ontology mapping tool developed, called OWLmt. The mapping definitions thus obtained are used to automatically map heterogeneous message instances used by the Web service provider and the consumer using a global ontology as a common denominator. This architecture is complemented by a peer-to-peer network which uses the introduced semantics for the discovery of Web services. Through the SATINE middleware, the travel parties can expose their existing applications as semantic Web services either to their Web site or to Web service registries they maintain. SATINE middleware facilitates the discovery and execution of these services seamlessly to the user.

The research project FUSION aims at supporting collaboration and interconnection between enterprises with technologies that allow for the semantic fusion of heterogeneous service-oriented business applications. The resulting FUSION approach is an enterprise application integration (EAI) conceptual framework proposing a system architecture that supports the composition of business processes using semantically annotated Web services as building blocks. The approach has been validated in the frame of three collaborative commercial proof-of-concept pilots. The chapter provides an overview on the FUSION approach and summarises our integration experiences with the application of the FUSION approach and tools during the implementation of transnational career and human resource management services.

The application of semantic technologies promises boosting business process management because semantic integration of business and IT is achieved. To enable the vision of semantic business process management, semantic technologies like ontologies, reasoners, and semantic Web services must be integrated in BPM tools. We extended a professional BPM tool to allow semantic business process modelling using the EPC notation. In addition, we adapted the tool's EPC to BPEL transformation to preserve the semantic annotations. By introducing a proxy service, we are able to perform Semantic Web service discovery on a standard BPEL engine. We evaluated our approach in an empirical case study, which was replicated 13 times by 17 participants from 8 different organisations. We received valuable feedback, which is interesting for researchers and practitioners trying to bring semantic technologies to end-users with no or only limited background knowledge about semantics.

Foreword

This insightful new book, published by IGI Global, lays out the history and opportunities of how semantics can be applied to solve real-world enterprise problems, such as enterprise interoperability. It fills an important void in discussions about the extended enterprise of the future, and hence comes at a timely moment as the financial and economic crisis looming in the world places a major challenge on enterprises.

In the wake of the ruin of the international monetary system established at Bretton Woods in 1944 and gradually dismantled from 1968 onwards as the world shifted from the gold-exchange standard to a de facto dollar standard, the past decade was marked by three interacting phenomena that sew the seeds of the current financial and economic crisis–a surge of liquidity around the world, a pandemic residential real estate speculation, and widespread excess leverage in all sectors of the western economies. Besides the current public policy response to the crisis, which reflects the fact that today's world leaders have learned the lessons of the Depression in the 1930's and resolved to tackle energetically the dismal consequences of the Lehman failure, companies must understand that the longer term answer to the current crisis is, more than ever, innovation and entrepreneurship.

The way out of the "doom and gloom" is a new wave of technology innovation that spurs a generation of company formation, job creation, productivity gains, and wealth accumulation. We see the first expressions of this spur with the thrust towards green technologies, nano-electronics, virtualisation, Internet of things, cloud computing, software as a service, social networking, broadband for all, and so on. Only investors and entrepreneurs can really create a future that meets the needs and expectations of our generation and the next one. But in a world where all economies are interdependent and interconnected–a phenomenon that is as irresistible as the force of gravity–investment and entrepreneurship must be joined by a third element–collaboration. Today, companies find that they must integrate production across suppliers, partners, competitors, different industries, and different continents. This requires openness and, in particular, shared standards.

To adjust to this evolution, the first step is to encourage the adoption of efficient ICT by European enterprises. For those enterprises that are ICT-oriented, including SMEs, the sharing of knowledge, products or services, the involvement in joined processes or the implantation of common integrated systems is considerably increasing as they discover the advantages of online collaboration. Additionally, our study on the Value Proposition of Enterprise Interpretability[1] research concluded that to compete effectively and build for the future, enterprises must continuously innovate and IT is the preferred vehicle towards that goal.

Interoperable enterprise collaboration tools are urgently required to support the pace of development observed. The spread and usage of today's technologies is giving many advantages to those enterprises investing in ICT but also showing us some limitations. We need to have better concepts, techniques, methods, and tools that make interoperable and collaborative enterprises a reality. Semantic interoperability, for instance, is a field that still presents various challenges and its study is absolutely essential to solve the existing problems and open the door to new possibilities.

In a very rapidly moving environment, enterprises involved in business networks and ecosystems need to align the meaning they attach to their information exchanges, ranging from fields in business documents to concepts related to process goals and activities. The semantic dimension is therefore a basis for mutual understanding and interoperability between collaborating enterprises, something happening below the layers of process interoperability and business interoperability. Essentially, semantic research tries to improve the understanding and handling of the meaning of concepts and terms used by the collaborating entities. Currently this activity is most of the time achieved manually, mainly using existing standards, and requires a painful adaptation of the processes and data exchange to the new, shared environment.

The European Commission supports the Enterprise Interoperability and Collaboration research domains since the 5th Research Framework Programme was approved. Under the "Networked Enterprise and Radio Frequency Identification (RFID)" unit, one cluster is dedicated to support the raise of Future Internet Enterprise Systems (FInES) and is driving the research to a future where European enterprises will become more competitive, efficient, and flexible. Within this cluster, various projects have proposed alternative paths to overcoming the semantic barrier using precise, computer-processable, meaning associated with each concept. They created ontology frameworks and developed various approaches, centralised or not, smoothly or highly integrated, to formalise the annotation of meaning linked to concepts. There are still many challenges to be accomplished, but the results so far are very promising.

This book has been created to put together the current knowledge on Semantics in the Enterprise Application Integration domain. The authors brought together major stakeholders in this area from Europe and other parts of the world, to develop a shared knowledge base and offer an integrated picture of the domain. It certainly represents an important contribution to this field of research and will undoubtedly be welcomed by a large community of ICT practitioners in Europe, and beyond the continent. The book provides compelling arguments, uses cases and practical solutions to one of the most important questions of our time: the relationship between technology, business, and society. It also addresses some of the most difficult issues in process and service management such as the choreography and orchestration in collaborative business processes. In this respect, it gives valuable perspectives and practical solutions towards a more sensible and responsive extended enterprise. The arguments presented are powerful and convincing for researchers, policy makers, business people, and scholars alike.

We're very proud to support this important effort of dissemination and are convinced that the readers will enjoy the discovery of its fascinating contents.

Gérald Santucci
Head of Enterprise Networking and RFID Unit

Cristina Martinez
Head of Future Internet Enterprise Systems Cluster

ENDNOTE

[1]   "Unleashing the potential of the European Knowledge Economy," published by the European Commission, 21 January 2008.

Preface

INTRODUCTION

Most enterprises contain a systemic infrastructure of several heterogeneous information technology systems, creating a complex, fuzzy network of interconnected applications, services and data sources, which is usually not well documented and expensive to maintain. Moreover, the introduction of multi-oriented, separate systems concerning enterprise resource planning (ERP), customer relationship management (CRM), supply chain management (SCM), e-business portals and B2B transactions, increases the complexity of systems integration, making the support of the interoperability among these systems a challenging task.

In this emerging business context, a clear need appears to link these former incompatible systems to improve productivity and efficiency. The solution to this need is what is called enterprise application integration (EAI), which can be defined as the use of software and architectural principles to bring together (integrate) a set of enterprise computer applications.

The goal of EAI is to integrate and streamline heterogeneous business processes across different applications and business units. We can distinguish between intra- and inter- organizational enterprise application integration. Intraorganizational EAI, commonly referred as "application to application"-integration (A2A), specifies the automated and event-driven exchange of information between heterogeneous enterprise applications and systems operating within an organization or enterprise. On the other hand, interorganizational EAI, or else B2B integration, specifies the automated and event-driven information exchange between various systems of several collaborating organizations and enterprises.

In recent years, most enterprises and organizations have made extensive investments in several EAI systems and solutions that promise to solve the major integration problem among their existing systems and resources. The business driver behind all these traditional EAI projects is to integrate processes across third-party applications as well as legacy systems to decrease the number of adapters one has to develop if connecting two systems. Traditional EAI focuses on the message-based communication of software applications interfaces, by pipelining different middleware technologies and developing various adapters, connectors, and plug-ins to provide efficient messaging support among heterogeneous systems, allowing their effective interconnection.

However, traditional EAI efforts lack an upper abstraction layer, as well as standardized architectures and implementations, making customers and end-users captive of EAI vendor-specific solutions, and creating the need for a new, high level integration for interconnecting various EAI systems with one another.

Such a need for higher level integration can be supported by exploiting recent research in service-oriented architectures and Semantic Web technologies.

Service-oriented architecture (SOA) is an approach to defining integration architectures based on the concept of a service. The goal of SOA can be described as bringing the benefits of loose coupling and encapsulation to integration at an enterprise level. In order to describe SOA, it is first necessary to define what we understand by a "service" in this context. The most commonly agreed-on aspects of the definition of a service in SOA are: services are defined by explicit, implementation-independent interfaces; services are loosely bound and invoked through communication protocols that stress location transparency and interoperability; and services encapsulate reusable business functions. After a function has been encapsulated and defined as a service in an SOA, it can be used and reused by one or more systems that participate in the architecture. Note that in contrast to reusing service implementations at runtime, the encapsulation of functions as services and their definition using interfaces also enables the substitution of one service implementation for another. For example, the same service might be provided by multiple providers, and individual service requesters might be routed to individual service providers through some intermediary agent. The encapsulation of services by interfaces and their invocation through location-transparent, interoperable protocols are the basic means by which SOA enables increased flexibility and reusability.

The purpose of the Semantic Web effort is to make the web machine processable rather than merely "human processable." The upcoming standards of the Semantic Web provide a set of concepts that can be used to annotate services and processes in a way machines can analyze. The key components of the Semantic Web technology which enable the design and development of ontologies for structuring and annotation of services and processes, include: a general-purpose language for representing information in the Web called resource definition framework (RDF); an RDF abstraction layer called RDF schema (RDFS); a language with well defined, formal semantics, built on RDF, such as the Web ontology language (OWL); and formal ontologies for marking up Web resources, used by semantically enriched service level descriptions. Enriching Web services descriptions with formally defined semantics by introducing the notion of semantic mark-up, leading towards Semantic Web services, enables machine-interpretable profiles of services and applications, realizing the vision of dynamic and seamless integration. As this semantic mark-up is machine–processable and–interpretable, the semantic profiles of Web services can be exploited to automate the tasks of discovering Web services, executing them, composing them, and interoperating with them.

The combination of SOA architectures and Semantic Web technologies supports and allows a set of essential automated services: automatic Web service discovery, involving automatic location of Web services that provide a particular functionality and that adhere to requested properties expressed as a user goal; automatic Web service composition, involving dynamic combination and aggregation of several Web services to provide a given functionality, automatic Web service invocation, involving automatic execution of an identified Web service by an agent, and automatic Web service interoperation within and across organizational boundaries.

These semantically enriched Web service oriented features can constitute the ideal solution to integration problems, as they enable dynamic, scalable and reusable cooperation between different systems and organizations.

This book presents innovative research results on the use of Semantic Web technologies and service-oriented architectures for enterprise application integration. It presents novel methods and tools, which apply semantic technologies in real-world complex systemic environments. It provides the theoretical foundations, principles, methodologies, architectures, technical frameworks, and case studies for the design and development of semantic enterprise application integration.

The audience of this book are scholars and researchers in the fields of EAI, Semantic Web technologies, interoperability, and semantic integration. The book aims to provide "food for thought" for future research. However, it also aims to address the needs of practitioners working on complex supply-chain environments, who may find within the book the foundations for new ideas in the EAI field. Graduate and post-graduate students would also find this book to be a useful reference resource.

CHAPTER OVERVIEW

Chapter 1 presents a methodology, which has resulted in the implementation of a highly customizable collaborative environment focused to support ontology-based enterprise interoperability. A key issue addressed by the particular platform is the variety and number of different resources that concur to achieve a cross-enterprise business service. A second key issue is the diversity of agreed (e.g., meaning negotiation when creating online contracts) models, and the difficulty in adapting its integrated features and services to different situations. These problems are addressed with a flexible solution, avoiding rigidity that occurs in the implementation and maintenance of existing cooperation platforms and their integration with an advanced semantic repository. The proposed platform operates at two levels: at the front end, it enables the end users to access seamless collaborative (e.g., synchronous, asynchronous and semi-synchronous) as well as individual mode tools and services to extract valuable information; at the back end, it uses a sophisticated ontology framework to support and record the collaborative work, enhancing interoperability among different enterprises and other service providers.

Chapter 2 proposes a semantically-enriched approach for dynamic data mediation in EAI scenarios, focusing on the resolution of message level heterogeneities between collaborative enterprise services and facilitating automated data mediation during execution time by providing formal transformations of the output and input messages (of the participating services) to a common reference business data model, that is, an enterprise interoperability ontology. The chapter presents a tool that has been developed to support the user to provide business data-related semantic annotations and XSLT transformations of the input and output message parts of collaborative enterprise services. Finally, it demonstrates the utilization of the proposed approach and tool in a real-world EAI scenario.

Chapter 3 discusses architecture abstractions like patterns and styles which can be used to capture design knowledge and allow the reuse of successfully applied designs, thus improving the quality of software. Knowledge gained from integration projects can be captured to build a repository of semantically enriched, experience-based solutions. Business patterns identify the interaction and structure between users, business processes, and data. Specific integration and composition patterns at a more technical level address enterprise application integration and capture reliable architecture solutions. The chapter uses an ontology-based approach to capture architecture and process patterns. Ontology techniques for pattern definition, extension, and composition are developed and their applicability in business process-driven application integration is demonstrated.

Chapter 4 introduces a three-tier framework for managing and implementing interoperable and cross-organizational business processes. The chapter aims to fill the gap currently existing between processes defined on a strategic level and executed models. It describes a solution which supports rapid prototyping by combining a model-driven framework for cross-organisational business processes with an agent-based approach for flexible process execution. It then shows how the W3C recommendation for Semantic Web service descriptions can be combined with the model-driven approach for rapid service integration.

Chapter 5 reviews several Semantic Web services frameworks that intend to bring semantics to Web services. The chapter depicts some ideas from SOA and Semantic Web services and their application to enterprise application integration. It illustrates an example of logic-based semantic matching between consumer services and provided services, which are described in ontologies.

Chapter 6 introduces an approach for developing service registries building on the UDDI standard and offering semantically-enhanced publication and discovery capabilities in order to overcome some of the known limitations of conventional service registries. The approach aspires to promote efficiency in EAI in a number of ways, but primarily by automating the task of evaluating service integrability on the basis of the input and output messages that are defined in the Web service's interface. The presented solution combines the use of three technology standards to meet its objectives: OWL-DL, for modelling service characteristics and performing fine-grained service matchmaking via DL reasoning, SAWSDL, for creating semantically annotated descriptions of service interfaces, and UDDI, for storing and retrieving syntactic and semantic information about services and service providers.

Chapter 7 considers semantics in two major integration tasks. First, semantically corresponding data types that can be used for communication between components need to be identified. Second, natural language documentation needs to be studied in order to understand component behaviour, that is, dependencies between operation invocations and how semantically different outcomes of operation calls are represented in the technical output format. The approach presented in this chapter supports the two tasks as follows. First, closed frequent itemset mining (CFIM) is employed to help identifying semantically corresponding data types. Second, a formal representation for component behaviour is introduced. However, as component behaviour is specified during component development, but used during integration–two distinct phases involving distinct teams–the chapter provides model transformations to ensure the consistent transfer of generic behavioural information to specific integration constraints before automated integration techniques can be applied.

Chapter 8 describes a solution for service discovery and selection at the business level, that is, at the level of offered business capability of a service provider and the ability to serve a concrete requested business transaction. The proposed solution is based on semantic interpretation of offered service capabilities, contractual restrictions, business rules of the requestor specifying selection preferences, and the parameters of the run-time service request. The applicability of the proposed solution is demonstrated on a shipper-carrier integration scenario.

Chapter 9 is an application in the tourism industry. Currently in the travel domain most of the travel products are sold through global distribution systems (GDSs). Since only major airline companies or hotel chains can afford to join GDSs, it is difficult for small and medium enterprises to market their travel products. This chapter describe a middleware, called SATINE, to address this problem. In the SATINE middleware, existing travel applications are wrapped as Web services. Web services, as such, is of limited use because the service consumer must know all the details of the Web service like the functionality of the Web service (what it does) and the content and the structure of input and output messages. Therefore, the chapter proposes the annotation of both the service functionality and the service messages with Web ontology language (OWL) ontologies. Through the SATINE middleware, the travel parties can expose their existing applications as semantic Web services either to their Web site or to Web service registries they maintain. SATINE middleware facilitates the discovery and execution of these services seamlessly to the user.

Chapter 10 presents the FUSION approach for supporting collaboration and interconnection between enterprises with technologies that allow for the semantic fusion of heterogeneous service-oriented business applications. The chapter provides an overview on the FUSION approach and summarises integration experiences with the application of the approach and tools during the implementation in the case of career and human resource management services.

Chapter 11 extends a professional business process management (BPM) tool to allow semantic business process modelling using the event-driven process chains (EPC) notation. The chapter presents an adaptation of the tool's EPC to business process execution language (BPEL) transformation to preserve the semantic annotations. By introducing a proxy service, it is possible to perform Semantic Web service discovery on a standard BPEL engine. The chapter presents the evaluation of the approach in an empirical case study, which was replicated 13 times by 17 participants from 8 different organisations. Valuable feedback was received, which is interesting for researchers and practitioners trying to bring semantic technologies to end-users with limited background knowledge about semantics.

Acknowledgment

We were initially motivated to edit this book when we were managing the multiyear multinational research project entitled "Business process fusion based on Semantically-enabled Service-oriented Business Applications"–code named FUSION. FUSION was a specific targeted research project partially funded by the European Commission under the Information Society Technologies programme under contract No 027385 (2006-2008).

The FUSION project aimed to promote efficient business collaboration and interconnection between enterprises (including SMEs) by developing a framework and innovative technologies for the semantic fusion of heterogeneous service-oriented business applications. Led by SAP AG, the FUSION consortium consisted of 14 partners from five European countries (Germany, Poland, Greece, Hungary and Bulgaria).

We had the opportunity to interact with many people during the development of the FUSION solution as well as during the preparation of this book. We would like to thank the European Commission for partially funding our efforts. We thank Cristina Martinez of the European Commission for her continuous support and guidance. We are also grateful to the reviewers of the project: Prof. Nada Lavrac of the Jozef Stefan Institute (Ljubljana, Slovenia), Ms. Man-Sze Li of IC Focus (London, UK) and Prof. Robert Meersman of the Vrije Universiteit (Brussels, Belgium). Their comments and recommendations have been extremely constructive and helped us shape our ideas and work

We would also like to acknowledge Julia Mosemann, Development Editor of IGI Global. We are appreciative of her interest, persistence, and feedback.

A warm thank you to our families for the support and continuous encouragement they provided us during our work on this book.

Gregoris Mentzas
National Technical University of Athens, Greece

Andreas Friesen
SAP, Inc., Germany

Chapter 1
Collaboration Across the Enterprise:
An Ontology Based Approach for Enterprise Interoperability

Aggelos Liapis
Vrije Universiteit Brussel, Belgium

Stijn Christiaens
Vrije Universiteit Brussel, Belgium

ABSTRACT

In the current competitive industrial context, enterprises must react swiftly to the market changes. In order to face this problem, enterprises must increase their collaborative activities. This implies, on the one hand, high communication between their information systems and, on the other hand, the compatibility of their practices. An important amount of work must be performed towards proper practices of standardization and harmonization. This can be defined as the concept of interoperability. Interoperability of enterprises is a strategic issue, caused, as well as enabled, by the continuously growing ability of integration of new legacy and evolving systems; in particular, the context of networked organizations of the reconciliation of the communicated business semantics is crucial to success. For this, nondisruptive reuse of existing business data stored in "legacy" production information systems is an evident prerequisite. In addition, the integration of a methodology, as well as the scalability, of any proposed semantic technological solution are equally evident prerequisites. Yet on all accounts current, semantic technologies as researched and developed for the so-called Semantic Web may be found lacking. Still, semantic technology is claimed about to become mainstream, as it is promoted by enterprise interoperation needs and increasing availability of domain specific content (for example ontologies) rather than pulled by basic technology (for example OWL) providers. In this chapter, we will present a methodology, which has resulted in the implementation of a highly customizable collaborative environment focused to support ontology-based enterprise interoperability. An additional key issue addressed by the particular platform is the variety and number of different resources that concur to achieve a cross-enterprise business service. A second key issue is the diversity of agreed (e.g., meaning negotiation when creating online contracts) models, and the difficulty in adapting its integrated features and services to different

DOI: 10.4018/978-1-60566-804-8.ch001

situations. These problems are addressed with a flexible solution, avoiding rigidity that occurs in the implementation and maintenance of existing cooperation platforms and their integration with an advanced semantic repository. The proposed platform operates at two levels: at the front end, it enables the end users to access seamless collaborative (e.g., synchronous, asynchronous, and semisynchronous), as well as individual mode tools and services to extract valuable information; at the back end, it uses a sophisticated ontology framework to support and record the collaborative work, enhancing interoperability among different enterprises and other service providers.

INTRODUCTION

Collaboration and knowledge sharing have become crucial to enterprise success in the knowledge-intensive European Community and the globalised market worldwide. In this market the trend in innovation of products and services is shifting from mere production excellence to intensive, collaborative and meaningful interoperability (De Leenheer & Meersman, 2007).

Industry and especially SMEs in Europe are under great pressures due to the increasing competition from the global market. Large companies can react in setting-up subsidiaries around the world. However, SMEs have to concentrate on setting-up cooperation and collaborations within the global market. Increasingly global supply chains are being established. Industry engaged in this cross regional supply have to handle costs, quality, trust, transactions etc. in efficient way to be competitive and at the same time be attractive for possible collaboration partners. Consequently, collaboration methods and tools have to be developed and adapted for Enterprise demands to reduce the costs for, and to handle, the worldwide collaboration processes supporting knowledge availability, persistence and sharing focusing on reducing interoperability costs in the Enterprise and collaborative business processes.

An important challenge at this point is to understand each other on different levels. This is difficult using the same language and within one culture but it becomes extremely critical between very different cultures, languages, industrial traditions, tools, laws and business rules. This constrains possible fruitful co-operations between organizations.

Enterprise modeling is used today mainly by large enterprises to clarify, analyze and implement business processes. Enterprise modeling is intended to achieve a common understanding across stakeholders. It enhances the stakeholder understanding of the co-operation however, the EM delivery need enhancing, perhaps with advanced conferencing technologies.

The availability of natural resources becomes more and more critical for the future of an enterprise, and the whole product life cycle becomes more and more the focus of interest. So interoperability is not only required in the workflow between companies during the production, but it also is a prerequisite for the whole Product Life Cycle Support (PLCS) between the various enterprises involved.

The technical support of business will be realized with the integration of smart agents/services creating the required connection between enterprises. The connections are built to meet business demands. Knowledge about, and of, enterprises will be used to facilitate interoperability dynamically during cooperation (might be temporary) e.g. a knowledge profile of an enterprises might be provided in a standard way describing which knowledge services are available as well as the conditions to access these services. Visual, easy understandable enterprise models, bridging the gaps between stakeholders and knowledge domains and providing the prerequisites for interoperability between organizations, will provide the overall picture. The research challenges are grouped from the overview across the enterprise stakeholders, the analysis of the different business facets and the configuration of the business processes by enterprise models taken into account non-functional aspects of contracting to the bridging of culture borders.

BACKGROUND

To the best of our knowledge a large portion of current research supports the view that Enterprise Interoperability must come along with considerable performance penalty (Hauguel & Viardot, 2001; IDEAS, 2003). Thus almost all of the proposed models of frameworks used to evaluate the difficulties in Enterprise Interoperability are focusing on communication, security and performance excluding the integration of a methodology focused to serve the specific cause of integration and support for legacy systems.

Casola et al. (2007) argue that despite the fact that a service provider is able to guarantee a predefined service level and a certain security level, the mere nature of interoperability and the utilisation of up to date technologies does not allow for automatic measurement of such attributes.

De Leenheer and Christiaens (2007) conceive the interoperability issue as a gap between different the social (communication between humans) and the technical (communication between machines) parts of any knowledge-sharing system. They adopt the four knowledge conversion modes described by Nonaka and Takeuchi (1995) socialization (person to person), externalization (person to machine), combination (machine to machine) and internalization (machine to person). These are described in more detail in Figure 1.

1. Interoperability of Enterprise Models

Interoperability between systems can be supported with semantic technologies by developing a shared information model for the use of different solutions (ATHENA, 2004). Semantic interoperability aims to provide the ability to bridge semantic conflicts and to create a semantically compatible information environment based on the agreed concepts between different business entities (Liapis et al., 2008).

Interoperability requires a consolidated and consistent understanding across all stakeholders, which is gathered from unstructured and incomplete views. The application of enterprise modeling promotes the common understanding of the enterprise business processes within the company and across companies (Liapis et al., 2008). The company is supported to succeed in reducing the throughput times, improving the process quality, reducing costs and therefore improving the customer satisfaction and competitiveness. To assure a correct cooperation between two or more entities it is mandatory to build an appropriate model of them (ATHENA, 2004). This can lead to a stronger amplification of all the cross-interface activities and constraints between the entities. Enterprise models illustrate the organizational business aspects as a prerequisite for the successful technical integration of IT systems or their configurations. If an IT system is not accepted by staff members, because its usefulness or is not transparent, then it quickly loses its value due to erroneous or incomplete input and insufficient maintenance. This at the end results in investment losses (Izza et al., 2006).

The enterprise models cover the knowledge of the internal processes and between organizations as well as the demand on IT support. The challenge description exemplifies the strengths, values, limitations and gaps of the application of enterprise modeling to achieve and to support

Figure 1. The gap between the social/human knowledge-sharing system and its technical "mirror" (adapted from De Leenheer and Christiaens, 2007)

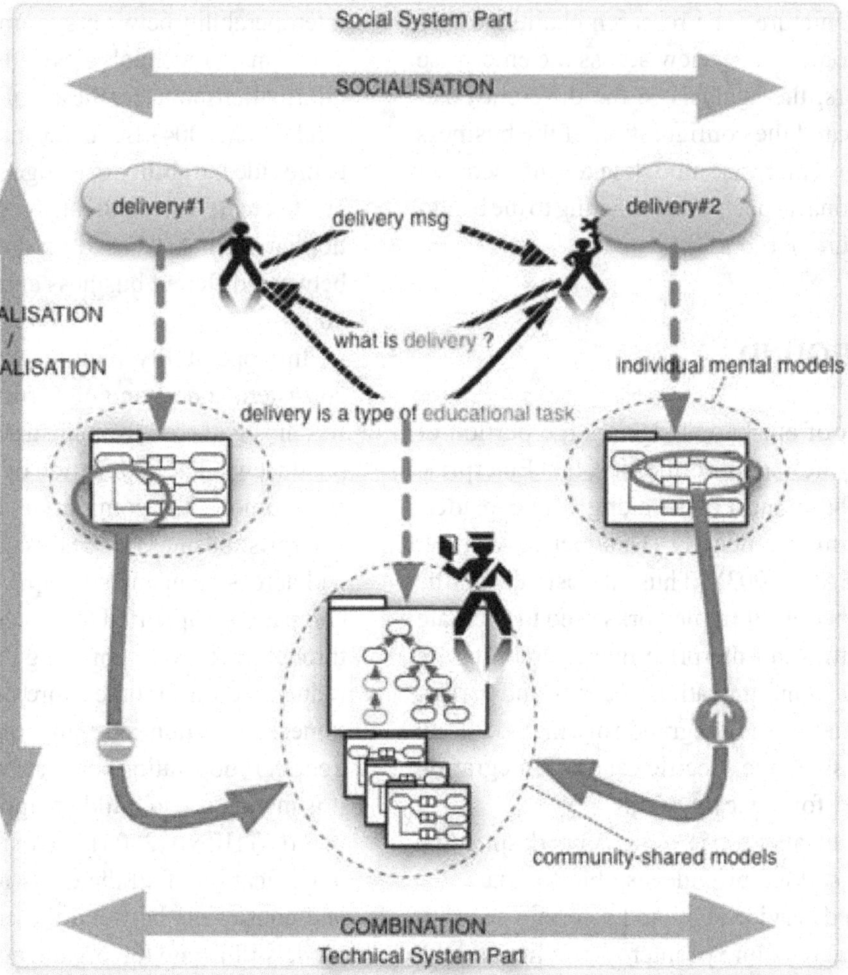

interoperability between companies and illustrates the required research topics.

- Interoperability driven by enterprise business models,
- Generic rules & services for model derived service environments,
- Interoperability of distributed enterprise models.

2. Usability of Models

The knowledge expressed in models has to be integrated into the configuration of workflows, simulation and application products. To realize the integration between the models and the executed business processes, an interoperating middleware between them and the applications, the workflow and simulations is required. This will allow a real time reaction to business changes (Izza et al., 2005).

The evolution of legacy systems and the need to migrate to or co-exist with other applications cause the requirement for a new environment of applications, information sources etc. Issues with interoperability demand that ontologies are automatically produced from several independent unstructured information bases that can be used to carry out mappings and allow information merging or application interoperability (ATHENA, 2004).

Currently there are some methods being investigated but the resources and computational power needed would appear to be excessive and not practical to use in an operational scenario (ATHENA, 2004). An interactive enterprise-to-enterprise interoperation of business must be realized.

3. Agreements and Contracting

Interoperating systems within an organization can occur without any form of governing agreement, but usually they require some form of Service Level Agreement (SLA) between departments, divisions or some form of organizational unit which states metrics for charging, and quality of service (Erl, 2005). When systems interoperate across organizations, contracts or Agreements are usually made containing some form of penalty clauses, or action to be taken when the contracted service is not provided – these may be supplemented by SLA providing the detail of the service quality agreed (Interop, 2003). Middleware mediated interoperability employing Web Services or the Grid, which includes a management function, can provide a mechanism to monitor SLA and enforce the contractual clauses to be applied when they are breached (Interop, 2003). Automatic monitoring of SLA and enforcement of contracts throughout a supply chain provides a rapid response to breaches of agreements, which in turn fosters trust between organizations as well as identifying potential financial losses. Complete

enforcement of all the terms and conditions in a contract is, as yet, infeasible, since it would require a machine understanding of legal obligations and legal interpretation, which are not yet available (Interop, 2003). However, there may be a level of monitoring and enforcement, which provides benefit in excess of the cost of implementing these management processes (Casola et al., 2007). The technical issues of representing and enforcing such SLA and contract conditions need to be resolved, to the level of methodologies for use, so that analyses can be made of the costs and benefits for different business situations to determine where the application of the technology is beneficial (European Commission, 2006).

4. SME Situation Challenges

A main challenge regarding SMEs is to change the actual situation for interoperability of SME, which is based on the force of the demand of large companies (European Commission, 2006). In most cases, SMEs tackle interoperability only if they are "commercially motivated" by large customers. Therefore, it is just a reaction of a market situation and lags behind the technical evolution of the large market players. This has to be changed into proactive acting providing interoperability actively to many customers. Based on the Enterprise Interoperability roadmap only two main aspects are relevant for SMEs (European Commission, 2006):

- Interoperability enabling cooperation between SMEs on demand (support of networking between SMEs) and
- Interoperability provided as market prerequisite for the cooperation with large companies (concurrent plug-in to different cooperation configurations).

5. Interoperability Aspects of Intercultural Cooperation

Culture diversities are a barrier between organizations and national regions to become interoperable on the enterprise level (Interop, 2003). Industry has already bilateral business links and supply chains but the effort of making systems communicate with each other on an interregional and intercontinental level is all on the shoulders of these individual enterprises. The research agenda is somehow a bit behind in the aspect of supporting these supply and value chains. Enterprises are confronted with cultural diversity when these enterprises become internationally active. Disregarding the cultural component in a situation of intercultural cooperation can and will lead to mistakes due to misunderstandings which are the result of differences in working practices, language and customs. Because of these cultural and national differences, an information system that works perfectly in one place may not work at all in another, or identical systems may find completely different uses in different situations (Brodie&Stonebraker, 1995). Hence, from a cultural standpoint, avoiding these kinds of mistakes plays a very important role for the interoperability among Enterprises and the success of business.

Since communication, knowledge and culture are intimately connected with one another, intercultural communication has to be a part of the approach. Also from multicultural coexistence to intercultural cooperation, an information system platform for building and managing a multicultural working group is a great challenge (Casola et al., 2007). Based on this platform, the intercultural teamwork management could define the rules of team members' cooperation. The vision is the availability of easy-to-use and open digital services for interregional collaboration, which bridge the intercultural and technological differences (Curtis et al., 1998). Concepts should be developed to enhance the enterprise software

application and business interoperability as well as to face the challenge of mutual intercultural understanding.

INTEROPERABILITY PROJECTS

The following projects contribute to address interoperability requirements:

1. **ATHENA** (www.athena-ip.org)**:** Advanced technologies for interoperability of heterogeneous enterprise Networks and their applications (ATHENA) aims to be the most comprehensive and systematic European research initiative in IT to remove barriers to interoperability, to transfer and apply the research results in industrial sectors, and to foster a new networked business culture.

2. **InterOP (http://interop-vlab.eu/):** InterOP aimed to extract value from the sustainable integration of these thematic components and to develop industrially significant new knowledge. Network's role was to create the conditions of a technological breakthrough to avoid that enterprise investment be simply pulled by the incremental evolution of IT offer.

3. **ABILITIES** (http://www.viewzone.org/ abilities/index.php?option=com_content&t ask=blogcategory&id=15&Itemid=14)**:** The basic goal of the present Application Bus for Interoperability In enlarged Europe SMEs (ABILITIES) proposal is: to study, design and develop a federated architecture implemented by a set of intelligent and adaptive UBL active messages (an Application Bus for EAI) and basic interoperability services, which, following the IDEAS framework and roadmap, aims at supporting SMEs EAI in e-commerce contexts, specifically in less developed Countries and less RTD intensive industrial sectors.

4. **No-REST** (http://www.no-rest.org/): The NO-REST project aims to investigate the applicability and dynamics of standards in the e-business and e-government sectors, and to develop guidelines for tools for the assessment of their performance, and of the impact they have on networked organizations.

5. **GENESiS (http://ve-forum.org/apps/pub.asp?Q=1974&T=Clusters%20and%20 Projects):** The main target of the GENESIS projcct is the research, development and initial, precompetitive application of the needed methodologies, infrastructure and middleware software components that will allow the typical, usually small and medium, European enterprise to conduct its Business transactions over Internet, by interconnecting its main transactional softwareapplications and systems with those of collaborating enterprises, banking/social insurance institutions and governmental bodies, with respect to the evolving legal and regulatory status.

6. **FUSION** (http://www.fusionweb.org/FUSION/): FUSION aims to promote efficient business collaboration within enterprises (incl. SMEs) by developing technologies for the semantic fusion of heterogeneous businesses applications. Intercultural and regulatory aspects of the enlarged Europe countries are considered instrumental in the FUSION solution.

7. **TrustCoM** (http://www.eu-trustcom.com/): TrustCoMaims in developing a framework for trust, security and contract management in dynamically evolving virtual organizations. The framework will enable secure collaborative business processing within on-demand created and self-managed, dynamic collaborative networks of businesses and governments built on top of the emerging convergence of Web Services, agent and Grid technologies.

THE NEED FOR A METHODOLOGY

According to the ISO standard, Enterprise Methodology (EM) is defined as the act of developing an enterprise model, which is a representation of what an enterprise intends to accomplish and how it operates (Curtis, 1988). More precisely, EM is the representation of the structure, the behaviour and the organization of the enterprise according to different points of views (Casola et al., 2007):

- Functional, Informational, Physical(Business), Decisional, Processes and,
- Technical, Economical, Social, Human

With two interconnected visions:

- **Global System Theory:** the global view of the enterprise which collects objectives, structure, functions, evolution of the enterprise (dynamic), links with legacy systems and features of the environment;
- **Local:** detailed description according to the concepts of activities and processes.

The role of the methodology is to represent, understand and analyze through an enterprise model, the running of an enterprise in order to improve its performance (Curtis, 1988). The role of EM in Interoperability is to define interoperability requirements and to support a solution implementation. This contributes to the resolution of interoperability problems by increasing the shared understanding of the enterprise structure and behavior. Several problems are related to interoperability and the absence of a concrete methodology to support it.

- The enterprise systems of the partners are not exchangeable (e.g., built using two different languages) or there are compatibility issues due to legacy support failure.

- The same term used by two systems does not mean the same thing (lexical ambiguity).
- Models of both enterprises show differences in practices, which are not aligned (output data of the first is semantically different to input data of the second).
- Models of both information technology (IT) systems show incompatibility in information exchange.

Based on the above issues it is almost certain that the implementation of a concrete methodology will play a significant role in interoperability, particularly in terms of analysis to target the problems, which can appear in an approach of implementation of Interoperability and how to solve these problems. Interoperability problems are either related to (i) the semantics and vocabulary used to annotate the resources; (ii) the architecture and platform; and (iii) the model of the enterprise.

The first allows having a common language; the second allows the interoperability by the technical aspects (e.g., software, hardware, net) and the third models the supply chain to allow having interoperable practices at the interfaces. To solve the problems related to ontology, we have two options: either we set up a common and global ontology in all enterprises of the supply chain but the implementation and management will be difficult and tiresome, or we set up a common ontology only at the boundaries of the enterprises. Therefore, to bring an answer to some of the enterprise interoperability problems, we need to develop a methodology, which has the following functionalities:

- To manage the evolution of enterprise with the definition of different steps;
- To manage the performance of the supply chain in its entirety. The notion of performance is very important because it allows to bring the activity and to share the information, to promote the cooperation between the function in the enterprises and between the members of the supply chain, and the will to increase the vision angle inside the supply chain;
- To model only the information, the flows and the services which, concern interoperability of the supply chain. We don't speak about boundaries of an enterprise toward another enterprise but we speak about boundaries of the supply chain. Indeed, two enterprises don't need to be completely interoperable, but they need to be interoperable at the interface. For this reason, we have to define a supply chain boundary to separate the services which collaborate from the others;
- To take into account the human aspect i.e. the communication between different people and the human psychological aspects in the evolution of their enterprise. Indeed, in the evolution management, people are often recalcitrant to change due to the conflicts involved with their current legacy systems.

THE ROLE OF COLLABORATION IN EI

Collaboration is a key factor to success in any enterprise setting, and even more so when enterprise borders have to be crossed (e.g., interoperability in the extended enterprise). According to the FRISCO report (Falkenberg et al., 1996), a community constitutes a social system, where action and discourse is performed within more or less well-established goals, norms and behavior. If collaboration within an (inter-) organizational community is to be successful, it is clear that proper communication should be in place, and that the semantics of the concepts being communicated are clear and agreed upon. Engineers or architects tasked with tying systems together need

Figure 2. Customisation of the main interface (adapted from Liapis, 2007)

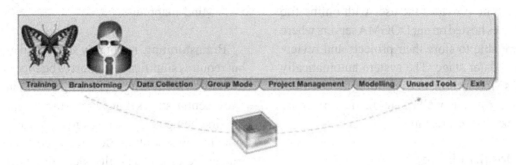

to understand each other properly in order to get maximum results out of their collaboration. Given the wide variety of design abstractions and differing terminologies, it is clear that communication in this kind of collaboration can lead to frustrating misunderstanding and ambiguities.

So far, the majority of enterprise systems have focused on the capturing and retrieval of data that is mostly unstructured, like text (in wikis, blogs forums etc.), or of a small number of predefined types, such as URLs (del.icio.us), images (Flickr), or tags (numerous sites).

Increasingly, the key features of semantically supported, collaborative tools are being applied in new contexts, and systems that work with new types of data, and with data of increasingly rich variety of content. This trend shows great promise in addressing the long-standing and difficult problem of system interoperability.

At the same time as the "Web 2.0" phenomenon has demonstrated that collaborative tools, even with very limited and informal semantic support, can dramatically increase the knowledge captured and accessible to users. The Challenge and the opportunity is to find a way to accommodate greater semantic precision while simultaneously encouraging and reaping the benefits of large-scale enterprise system collaboration on a system as well as on a community level.

In the following sections we present the tools and services of a semantically supported environment called OMOGENIA as the first of a new generation of CSCW enterprise systems.

The general architecture of the prototype is organized into the following three layers (Liapis, 2007):

- Configuration level
- Reuse level
- Reflection level

1. Configuration Level

The main attribute of the environment is the concept of customizability. It allows the user to customize the tools according to the needs of the project by simply dragging and dropping them into the categorized tabs as illustrated in figure 2 (Liapis, 2007).

2. Reuse Level

Generally, the ability to reuse heavily relies on the ability to build larger systems from smaller ones, and being able to identify and resolve common problems and conflicts between current and legacy systems (Malins et al., 2006). Reusability is often a required characteristic of collaborative environments (Liapis, 2007a). The prototype provides users with four recording mechanisms able to capture the methodology followed towards the completion of a system such as real time recording mechanisms and snapshots. In addition, the prototype provides the user with online file repositories hosted on our DOGMA servers where users are able to store their projects and review them at a later stage. The system automatically provides Meta information regarding the contributors, date, time, as well as automatic versioning and track-changes features.

3. Reflection Level

The concept behind the implementation of this prototype was to provide users with appropriate tools in order to help them reflect on their ideas. The tools were implemented and arranged in a way that a user is constantly reminded of the next step, related sources, and about past and present strategies. The prototype is designed in a way that allows participants to work collaboratively, as well as individually, simultaneously following a loosely coupled group approach. The individual tools allow users to try solutions without feeling that they are being watched or criticized. When all the participants have indicated readiness they can then begin to place components of their solutions in the collaborative space synchronously or asynchronously. All the contributions are being monitored and recorded by appropriate mechanisms providing meta-information as to the date and time the contribution took place, and the name(s) of the contributor(s).

FRONT-END OF THE PROTOTYPE

The following section presents the most significant features of the proposed prototype focusing on their architecture and contribution on the particular context.

1. Brainstorming

The proposed prototype includes the following two brainstorming techniques:

- Brainstorming
- Mind-mapping

Brainstorming, is a highly successful method, but requires significant support to be successfully used in a virtual setting (Diehl, 1987). There are two essential stages to any brainstorming process: the first being to generate as many ideas as possible (Malins et al., 2006); the second being to categorize or evaluate the ideas that have been generated (Liapis, 2007). The other technique is mind-mapping. Brainstorming through mind-maps may assist the design process by allowing the structuring of abstract concepts as well as concrete ones (Buzan, 2005).

Both tools are using the Triz[1] database and the sorting algorithms to allow users access to relevant third party online resources while brainstorming (Liapis, 2008). In addition the post it notes tool includes an integrated Really Simple Syndication (RSS) reader dedicated to scan the web for the latest technologies, approaches and events based on user input.

2. Collaborative Tools

Collaborative environments allow a virtual team or an organization to share their work, seeing what others are doing, commenting and working together. Current collaborative technology still fails to support real life collaboration (Malins and Liapis, 2007). This problem is a direct result of not looking at the dynamic aspects of work. In collaborative technology that is able to support real-life interaction processes we need to pay attention to the fact that real-life situations are dynamic and involve complex tasks (Malins et al., 2006).

Based on these grounds, we conceived the prototype as a Client server application over the Internet. Clients (user sessions) connect to a server using BSD sockets technology and TCP/IP protocol with the exception of Skype which uses peer to peer technology (P2P). TCP's reliable communication and ordering semantics greatly simplifies the system implementation offering synchronous as well as semi-synchronous (e.g., Google Docs) collaboration amongst the participants. As concerns security the environment it self encrypts every piece of information displayed through it (Liapis, 2007):

- **Voice over internet protocol (VoIP) via Skype communicator:** Skype is a free peer-to-peer VoIP Internet telephony network founded by the entrepreneurs NiklasZennström and Janus Friis. This research integrated Skype into the environment because of its ability to work almost seamlessly across network address translation processes (NATs) and firewalls.
- **Remote access via virtual network computing (VNC):** The second tool provided in the collaborative mode of the environment is a windows version of Virtual Network Computing (VNC) (Liapis, 2008). This application is an open source, cross platform project[2] developed in the engineering department of the University of Cambridge. The research has re-implemented and integrated a portable version of VNC by isolating the critical files and functionalities provided in the original application.

VNC uses the remote frame buffer protocol (RFB) to remotely control another computer. In addition it transmits the keyboard and mouse events from one computer to another. The administrator or the host of the meeting is able to tune the settings of the server customizing its performance and quality of service. For example is able to choose whether to disable participants' input, by changing their status to viewers. This feature is useful when you are presenting a solution to a distributed group as it creates an interaction protocol amongst the users (Richardson et al., 1998).

The particular technology functions under any network type local area network (LAN),

wide area network (WAN) and mobile network). In the virtual network computing (VNC), server machines supply not only applications and data but also an entire desktop environment that can be accessed from any internet-connected machine using a VNC client (Liapis, 2007a).

In contrast to many recent web based or Internet applications VNC uses a random challenge-response system to provide the basic authentication when connecting to the server (Liapis, 2008). Even though this is reasonably secure once the user is connected the traffic between the client and the server is unencrypted and therefore is unsafe for professional use (Liapis, 2007a). However VNC may be tunneled over an SSH or VPN connection which would add an extra security layer with stronger encryption (Liapis, 2008). This approach encrypts all traffic between the two machines using public key encryption techniques, making it really very difficult for anyone else to access the data. Also it is a more reliable way to penetrate strong firewalls delivering data securely and reliably (Liapis, 2008).

3. Recording Mechanisms

When a team collaborates using a groupware system its members must be coordinated in order to avoid possible conflicts (Malins et al., 2006). To preserve the integrity of the project throughout its complete lifecycle appropriate recording mechanisms should be integrated into the system (Liapis, 2007). Recording mechanisms allow participants to coordinate their work without communicating with others. This is an important characteristic as it prevents coordination breakdowns, which frequently occur during collaborative design (Malins et al., 2006). The prototype consists of four different recording mechanisms to provide participants with a verification mechanism with regards to the evolution and security of the project. In addition participants can use the outputs as a reference for future work or to review the process (Liapis, 2007):

Figure 3. DOGMA studio workbench: The modelling tool

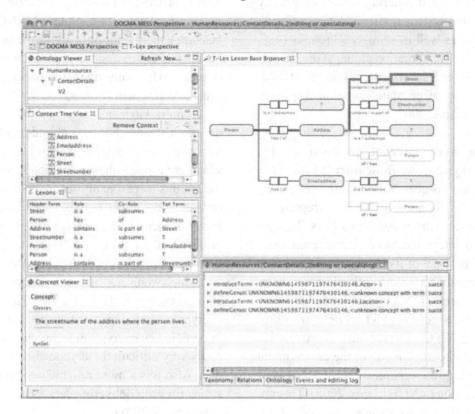

- Video and audio recording mechanism for synchronous collaborative sessions
- Automatic logging of users activity when using the environment
- Automatic file versioning
- Collaborative history mechanism in the ontology modeling tool

The outputs of these files are being saved in the file repository tool with appropriate Meta information such as date, time, and participants.

4. Ontology Management

Supporting an online team requires an advanced ontology management system, capable of mediating and sharing the contributions of the team. For a comprehensive state of the art on theories, methods, and tools for ontology management, we refer the reader to literature (e.g.,Hepp et al.,2008).

The tool illustrated in figure 3is the DOGMA Studio Workbench, which allows users to elicit and apply different ontological elements. They can browse and edit their ontologies, keep a record of different versions and share selected elements with other partners.

The Workbench is constructed according to the plug-in architecture in Eclipse. There, plug-ins, being loosely coupled ontology viewing, querying or editing modules support the different ontology engineering activities and new plug-ins continuously emerges. This loose coupling allows any arbitrary knowledge engineering community to support its own ontology engineering method in DOGMA Studio by reusing and combining these plug-ins arbitrarily. Such a meaningful combination of view/edit/query plug-ins is called a "perspective" in Eclipse.

BACK-END OF THE PROTOTYPE

As the backbone of our collaborative system, we adopted the DOGMA (Developing Ontology-Grounded Methods and Applications) framework for ontology engineering. A DOGMA inspired ontology is decomposed into a lexon-base and a layer of ontological commitments (Meersman, 1999, 2001). A full formalization of DOGMA can be found in De Leenheer et al. (2007), and an overview is given by Jarrar and Meersman (2007).

The lexon base is a pool of plausible binary fact-types that might hold in a certain domain. The lexons residing in the lexon base are not interpreted and thus reusable in different ontologies. As the lexon base can become very large, context was added to the lexons, which imposes a way of grouping the lexons in a meaningful way. This context refers to the source where the lexon was extracted from:

1. **Concept Definition Service:** Each (context, term)-pair then lexically identifies a unique concept. The concept is described by a gloss (short natural language description) and a set of synonyms. Together with the linguistic representation in the form of the lexons, DOGMA remains close to natural language, which is indispensable in communication between collaborating teams.

2. **Ontological commitment:** Any application-dependent interpretation of a set of lexons is moved to a separate layer, called the commitment layer. This layer serves as a mediator between the plausible fact types (lexons) and their axomatisation in applications. Each commitment consists of a selection of appropriate lexons and a limitation on their use through the application-specific constraints. By separating the conceptualisation (lexonbase) from the axiomatisation (commitment), this approach provides more common ground for reuse and agreements. For instance, a business rule stating that each person has exactly one address may hold for one partner's application, but may be too strong for another.

3. **Versioning:** As with all things, information systems are in constant flux. Especially in a collaborative setting, where ontology serves as a mediating instrument, we find a high and continuous need for proper versioning and evolution management. DOGMA incorporates proper support for these issues through the use of change operators, change logs and context dependencies. This includes detailed meta information such as the name of the contributor, time, date, and appropriate commentary on future changes or possible objections in a project.

Workflow

We adopt a workflow based on the DOGMA-MESS ontology engineering methodology (de Moor et al. 2006). DOGMA-MESS starts from a clear communication goal, which is translated to specific templates (knowledge artefacts at a general level). The appropriate stakeholders specialize these templates according to their own organizational views (divergence), after which they negotiate about the relevant differences in order to reach a common view (convergence). In our experiment, we were able to refine this process into several phases.

1. **Collaborative goal specification:** It is neither feasible nor relevant to consider all conflicts at once. By clearly defining a common goal (e.g., the need to exchange account information in order to enable Single Sign On), we can create a highly relevant

scope for the next steps. The goal must be specified atomically, so it cannot be further divided over a number of sub goals.

2. **Template selection:** To bootstrap the process, we have to translate the collaborative goal into an appropriate template (or set of templates), which are small conceptual models at a general level. In the ideal case, these templates can be extracted from available and proven patterns.

3. **Template specialization:** Each party then specializes the template according to the available information in their organizational model. The results of this step serve as input for the next step.

4. **Alignment:** As a result from the differences in the involved organizational specifications, a meeting must be held to resolve possible conflicts through subtle negotiation. This step can be divided over different smaller steps:

   ◦ **Lexical Grounding Step:** Where lexical conflicts are resolved and a shared schema vocabulary is built.

   ◦ **Attribution Step**: Where conflict types related to relationships are resolved.

   ◦ **Axiomatisation Step:** Where conflicts related to constraints and reference schemas are resolved.

   ◦ **Test Step:** Where the results are test for referability (Halpin, 2001), satisfiability (Jarrar&Heymans, 2007). Ideally, this includes a population test as well.

   ◦ **Operationalisation:** When consensus is reached, the results can be operationalised by choosing the appropriate operational formats (e.g., XML) and adapting the systems to send and receive the necessary messages.

FUTURE AND EMERGING TRENDS

It is clear that current teams, whether they are organisational or inter-organisational, have an increasing need for proper collaboration, especially in a distributed setting. This realization is supported by several emerging initiatives.

The IBM Eclipse team for instance bundled their experiences and lessons learnt during the development of the Eclipse framework in the Jazz project. This collaborative environment is targeted at distributed software teams and provides them with decent support for collaboration across time and location (Frost, 2007). The Jazz system, although innovative and reliable, supports only synchronous and asynchronous collaboration presenting the user with a cluttered yet fully functioning way of developing projects collaboratively. Another emerging example is Acrobat. com, which is a set of online services hosted by Adobe. They include file sharing and storage, a PDF converter, an online word processor, and web conferencing, which you can use to create and share documents, communicate in real time, and simplify working with others. The DOGMA-MESS system (Christiaens et al., 2008) provides a Meaning Evolution Support System (MESS) and platform that helps communities of practice consisting of different stakeholders from different organizations to define and evolve shared ontologies that are relevant to their joint collaboration objectives. The systems aims to make the evolution process of a collaborative community as effective and efficient as possible. A similar application is MyOntology[3], that provides wiki-based collaboration and community-driven development of ontological artefacts. The system provides a technical infrastructure for maintaining a tight coupling between an ontology and the individuals creating and using this ontology.

These moves towards collaborative environments indicate a clear trend towards a vision for the Future of the Internet, where organizations will cluster together in digital business ecosystems through tight collaboration. These collaborative environments can then support interoperability processes, which can then become pervasive in daily life and work of online communities of practice (De Leenheer and Christiaens, 2008).

CONCLUSION

Different people prefer different input mechanisms: some prefer the proper tool to capture the model immediately, while others prefer a sketch pad for quickly jotting down their understanding and ideas. As such, it is important that a collaborative environment allows for these different input mechanisms, and allows the results to be shared by the different participants.

Another conclusion is to divide collaboration projects into smaller problems so that at most 2 or 3 partners can tackle each problem. Discussing interoperability with more parties is extremely difficult.

Current teams, whether they are organisational or inter-organisational, have an increasing need for proper collaboration, especially in a distributed setting. Web conferencing services hosting group meeting combined with synchronous asynchronous and semi-synchronous collaborative tools are considered to be essential. A moderator in the form of a participant on the role of the host or an agent should keep track of the meeting using recording mechanisms as well as presenting participants with an interactions protocol when appropriate.

In this chapter we positioned the features and the underpinning technology of a collaborative platform designed to support the effective cooperation of large-scale enterprises. We outlined the key issues addressed from the specific platform such as the integration of appropriate resources that concur to achieve a cross-enterprise business service and its ability of adapting its integrated features and services according to the project needs.

REFERENCES

ATHENA. (2004). Advanced technologies for interoperability of heterogeneous enterprises networks and their applications. *FP6-2002-IST-1, Integrated Project Description of Work.*

Bennett, K. (1995, January). Legacy systems. *IEEE Software*, 19–73. doi:10.1109/52.363157

Bisbal, J., Lawless, D., Wu, B., & Grimson, J. (1999). Legacy information systems: Issues and directions. *IEEE Software*, *16*, 103–111. doi:10.1109/52.795108

Brodie, M., & Stonebraker, M. (1995). *Migrating legacy systems: Gateways, interfaces, and the incremental approach.* San Francisco: Morgan Kaufmann.

Buzan, B. T. (2005). *Definition of mind maps.* New York: St. Martin's Press.

Casola, V., Fasolino, A. R., & Mazzocca, T. (2007). A policy-based evaluation framework for quality and security in service oriented architectures. In *Proceedings of the IEEE Conference on Web Services,* (ICWS 2007).

Christiaens, S., De Leenheer, P., de Moor, A., & Meersman, R. (2008). Business use case: Ontologising competencies in an interorganisational setting. In M. Hepp, P. De Leenheer, A. de Moor & Y. Sure (Eds.), *Ontology management for the Semantic Web, Semantic Web services, and business applications, from Semantic Web and beyond: Computing for human experience.* Springer.

Curtis, B., Krasner, H., & Iscoe, N. (1988). A field study of the software design process for large systems. *Communications of the ACM*, *31*(11), 1268–1287. doi:10.1145/50087.50089

De Leenheer, P., & Christiaens, S. (2007). Mind the gap: Transcending the tunnel vision on ontology engineering. In *Proceedings of the 2nd International Conference on the Pragmatic Web,* Tilburg, The Netherlands. ACM DL.

De Leenheer, P., & Christiaens, S. (2008). Challenges and opportunities for more meaningful and sustainable Internet systems. In *Proceedings of the First Future of the Internet Symposium*, Vienna, Austria. (LNCS). Springer-Verlag.

De Leenheer, P., De Moor, A., & Meersman, R. (2007). Context dependency management in ontology engineering: A formal approach. *Journal on Data Semantics VIII*. ([]. Springer.]. *LNCS, 4380*, 26–56.

De Leenheer, P., & Mens, T. (2008). Ontology evolution: State of the art and future directions. In Hepp, et al.

De Leenheer, P., & Meersman., R. (2007). Towards community-based evolution of knowledge-intensive systems. In *Proc. on the Move Federated Conferences: ODBASE (OTM 2007)*, Vilamoura, Portugal. (LNCS 4803, pp. 989-1006). Springer.

De Moor, A., De Leenheer, P., & Meersman, R. (2006). DOGMA-MESS: A meaning evolution support system for interorganizational ontology engineering. In *Proc. of the 14th International Conference on Conceptual Structures, (ICCS 2006)*, Aalborg, Denmark. (LNCS). Springer-Verlag.

Diehl, V. (1987). Productivity loss in brainstorming groups: Toward the solution of a riddle. *Journal of Personality and Social Psychology, 53*, 497–509. doi:10.1037/0022-3514.53.3.497

Erl, T. (2005). Service-oriented architecture: Concepts, technology, and design. Upper Saddle River, NJ: Prentice Hall PTR.

European Commission. (2006). *Enterprise interoperability research roadmap*.

Frost, R. (2007). Jazz and the eclipse way of collaboration. *IEEE Software, 24*(6), 114–117. doi:10.1109/MS.2007.170

Halpin, T. (2001). *Information modeling and relational databases: From conceptual analysis to logical design*. Morgan Kaufmann

Hauguel, P. E., & Viardot, E. (2001). De la supply chain au réseau industriel. *L'expension . Management Review*, 94–100.

Hepp, M., De Leenheer, P., de Moor, A., & Sure, Y. (Eds.). (2008). *Ontology management for the Semantic Web, Semantic Web Services, and business applications*. Springer-Verlag.

IDEAS. (2003). *Project deliverable (WP1-WP7). Public reports*. Retrieved from www.ideas-roadmap.net

INTEROP. (2003). Interoperability research for networked enterprises applications and software. Network of excellence, annex 1-description of work.

Izza, S., & Vincent, L. Burlat, P., Lebrun, P., & Solignac, H. (2006). Extending OWL-S to solve enterprise application integration issues. *Interoperability for Enterprise Software and Applications Conference (I-ESA'06)*, Bordeaux, France.

Izza, S., Vincent, L., & Burlat, P. (2005). A framework for semantic enterprise integration. In *Proceedings of INTEROP-ESA'05*, Geneva, Switzerland (pp. 78-89).

Jarrar, R., & Meersman, R. (2007). Ontology engineering-the DOGMA approach. In E. Chang, T. Dillon, R. Meersman & K. Sycara (Eds.), *Advances in Web Semantic, volume 1, a state-of-the art Semantic Web advances in Web Semantics IFIP2.12*. Springer.

Klein, M. (1999). Towards a systematic repository of knowledge about managing collaborative design conflicts. In *Working Paper Series 210*. MIT Center for Coordination Science.

Liapis, A. (2007). The designer's toolkit: A collaborative design environment to support virtual teams. In *the Proceedings of IASK International Conference*, Oporto, Portugal.

Liapis, A. (2007a). Computer mediated collaborative design environments. Published doctoral dissertation, The Robert Gordon University, Aberdeen, UK.

Liapis, A. (2008). Synergy: A prototype collaborative environment to support the conceptual stages of the design process. In *Proceedings of the International Conference on Digital Interactive Media in Entertainment and Arts, DIMEA 2008*, Athens, Greece. ACM/IEEE Digital Library.

Liapis, A., Christiaens, S., & DeLeenheer, P. (2008). Collaboration across the enterprise: An approach for enterprise interoperability. *International Conference on Enterprise Information, ICEIS 2008*, Barcelona, Spain.

Malins, J., & Liapis, A. (2007). The design educator's toolkit. *Virtual Environments in Art, Design, and Education*. Dublin Institute of Technology, Dublin, Ireland.

Malins, J., Watt, S., Liapis, A., & McKillop, C. (2006). Tools and technology to support creativity in virtual teams. In S. MacGregor & T. Torres (Eds.), *Virtual teams and creativity: Managing virtual teams effectively for higher creativity*. Hershey, PA: IGI Global.

Meersman, R. (1999). The use of lexicons and other computer-linguistic tools in semantics, design, and cooperation of database systems. In Y. Zhang, M. Rusinkiewicz & Y. Kambayashi (Eds.), *Proceedings of the Conference on Cooperative Database Systems (CODAS 99)*. (pp. 1-14). Springer-Verlag.

Meersman, R. (2001). Ontologies and databases: More than a fleeting resemblance. In A. d'Atri & M. Missikoff (Eds.), *OES/SEO 2001 Rome Workshop*. Luiss Publications.

Meersman, R. (2002). Web and ontologies: Playtime or business at the last frontier in computing? In *Proceedings of the NSF-EU Workshop on Database and Information Systems Research for Semantic Web and Enterprises* (pp. 61-67).

Nonaka, I., & Takeuchi, H. (1995). *The knowledge-creating company: How Japanese companies create the dynamics of innovation*. Oxford University Press.

Oasis. (2006, August 2). Reference model for service oriented architecture 1.0, committee specification 1. Retrieved from http://www.oasis-open.org

Richardson, T., Wood, R. K., & Hopper, A. (1988). Virtual network computing. *IEEE Internet Computing, 2*(1), 1–7.

Salman, A. B., & Henning, S. (2004). *An analysis of the skype peer-to-peer Internet telephony protocol*. New York: Columbia University, Department of Computer Science.

Sheth, A. (1998). Changing focus on interoperability in information systems: From system, syntax, structure to semantics. In M. F. Goodchild, M. J. Egenhofer, R. Fegeas & C. A. Kottman (Eds.), *Interoperating geographic information systems* (pp. 5-30). Kluwer Academic Publishers.

Spyns, P., Meersman, R., & Jarrar, M. (1998). Data modelling versus ontology engineering. *SIGMOD Record, 31*(4), 12–17. doi:10.1145/637411.637413

Tomek, I., Shakshuki, E., Peng, A., Koo, A., & Prabhu, O. (2003). *FCVW-towards an eclipse-based CSCW framework*.

ENDNOTES

[1]   TRIZ is a Russian acronym for "Teoriya Resheniya Izobretatelskikh Zadatch" (Теория решения изобретательских

задач), a theory of solving inventive problems developed by Genrich Altshuller in 1946. TRIZ expands approaches developed in systems engineering and provides tools and systematic methods for use in problem formulation, system analysis, failure analysis, and patterns of system evolution (both 'as-is' and 'could be').

2   Released under the GNU Public License

3   http://www.myontology.org/

Chapter 2
Dynamic Data Mediation in Enterprise Application Integration Scenarios

Thanasis Bouras
National Technical University of Athens, Greece

Panagiotis Gouvas
National Technical University of Athens, Greece

Gregoris Mentzas
National Technical University of Athens, Greece

ABSTRACT

If we try to increase the level of automation in enterprise application integration (EAI) scenarios, we confront challenges related to the resolution of data and message heterogeneities between interoperating services, which traditional EAI technologies are weak to solve. We propose a semantically-enriched approach for dynamic data mediation in EAI scenarios, focusing on the resolution of message level heterogeneities between collaborative enterprise services, facilitating automated data mediation during execution time by providing formal transformations of the output and input messages (of the participating services) to a common reference business data model, that is, the enterprise interoperability ontology. Moreover, we present a tool that has been developed to support the user to provide business data-related semantic annotations and XSLT transformations of the input and output message parts of collaborative enterprise services. Finally, we demonstrate the utilization of the proposed approach and toll in a real-world EAI scenario.

INTRODUCTION

In the mid-1990s, a new term called enterprise application integration (EAI) was established, which introduced several methods and software components for efficiently integrating software in an enterprise. While in the past, the need for integration was driven by lower-level needs to share information among applications, today, business drivers fuel the need for integration (Vollmer & Peyret, 2005) – the need for business to respond to regulatory challenges, improve business process execution, grow

DOI: 10.4018/978-1-60566-804-8.ch002

employee productivity, and improve customer service is a hallmark driving organizations to integrate applications. In response to these new requirements, the integration market landscape is shifting. Service-Oriented Architectures (SOAs), business process management (BPM), composite applications, and other new application requirements have become the driving force in the market (Rymer et a., 2004).

The currently available enterprise application integration software address integration problems for example in the following ways (Friesen et al., 2007): a) graphically supporting the mapping of systems' interfaces to each other (e.g. SAP NetWeaver Exchange Infrastructure), b) reducing complexity using intermediate data-exchange languages (e.g. eXtensible Markup Language – XML), or c) reducing the number of connection adapters needed through the introduction of hubs (e.g. Enterprise Service Bus). These efforts entail significant costs and typically due to the "lack of automated support in defining integration, it takes a long time for a human engineer to define semantically correct integration" (Bussler, 2003).

Current industrial EAI trends and technologies, like SOA, Enterprise Bus and Web Services, are up to now quite mature. However, if we try to increase the level of automation in integration scenarios, we confront several problems and challenges (Bouras et al., 2007), such as a) data and message level heterogeneities between interoperating services, b) insufficient search and discovery of published Web Services in a common registry, and c) inadequate Web Process composition with regard to the desired functionality and operational requirements. The problem that still exists, which the traditional, syntactic EAI technologies are weak to solve, refers to the formalization and the documentation of the semantics related to the interfaces and the data structures of the deployed Web Services. This lack of formal semantics of applications and services to be integrated makes it difficult for software engineers and developers to interconnect heterogeneous applications and thus

creates obstacles in the automating EAI activities (Haller et al., 2006). There is no doubt that these needs impose the use and interpretation of semantics in EAI and that semantically enriched approaches will hopefully mitigate these problems.

In this book chapter, we present a semantically-enriched approach for dynamic data mediation in Enterprise Application Integration scenarios, based on Ontologies, Semantic Web and Semantic Web Services Technologies. Our approach, which is presented in the next section, focuses on the resolution of message level heterogeneities between collaborative enterprise services exposed from the participating business systems, facilitating automatic, dynamic data mediation during execution time by providing formal transformations of the input and output messages (of the participating Web Services) to a common reference model, i.e. an enterprise data ontology.

In addition, Section 3 provides an overview of the enterprise data ontology that we have developed and utilized as part of a multi- layered and –faceted interoperability ontology, called Enterprise Interoperability Ontology, which provides a shared, common understanding of data, services and processes within enterprise application integration scenarios.

Moreover, in Section 4, we present a tool that has been designed and developed to support the user to provide business data related semantic annotations to specific web services exposed from enterprise applications, realizing parts of their functionality. The developed tool enables the user to graphically define the required transformations of the output and input messages between web services with regard to the respective data entities (used for the annotation of these message parts) of a common ontological model. These transformations are further utilized to enable dynamic data mediation among several interconnected enterprise services, during the execution of a business process which contains these services.

Finally, we provide (in Section 5) an indicative business scenario demonstrating how our proposed approach and tool contributes to the resolution of data heterogeneities among different business, while, in Section 6, we summarize the conclusions and the future work of the research efforts presented.

THE PROPOSED DYNAMIC DATA MEDIATION APPROACH

As already stated the proposed data integration approach facilitates automatic, dynamic data mediation during execution time by providing formal transformations of the input and output messages (of the participating Enterprise Services) to a common reference model (an enterprise interoperability ontology that we developed in the Web Ontology Language – OWL). More specifically, automatic, dynamic data mediation is enabled by providing a priori mappings and transformations for all enterprise services inputs and outputs message parts (of the services' native Web Services) to a common-reference conceptual, ontological model, i.e. the data-intensive enterprise interoperability ontology.

Mappings are created between the enterprise services message elements and ontology concepts, utilizing the schemaMapping attribute to semantically annotate and associate the input and output message elements of the involved enterprise services, towards the creation of the so-called Semantic Profiles of these services, respecting the SAWSDL specification for the deployment of Semantic Web Services (Farrell & Lausen, 2007). In (Nagarajan et al., 2006), two types of mappings between enterprise services message elements and semantics have been identified: a) mappings from the Web Service message element to the ontology concept, also called the "up-cast" and/or "up-level", and b) transformations from the ontology concept to the message element, called the "down-cast" and/or "down-level".

Once these transformations are defined, two enterprise services can interoperate by reusing these mappings. Both the mappings and the message transformation occur at the instance level between the WSDL (XML) and the OWL individual.

Extending Native Web Services Interfaces with Data Semantics

As already mentioned above, the main idea behind the proposed dynamic data mediation approach is that the native descriptions (i.e. WSDL interfaces) of the standard Web Services of the involved service-oriented business applications is extended with data/information semantics. This extension process is called semantic annotation/profiling and the resulting description is the respective SAWSDL-compatible Semantic Profile.

It is obvious that, in order to solve real integration use-cases, the composed processes must also be able to execute/run. Consequently a special start event must trigger the run-time engine so as to create a process instance. The process instance works with real data which means that it communicates with real Web Services of SOA-enabled business applications. As a result, the process instance includes an invocation of one Web Service with given input data, stores the reply of this Web Service, invokes another Web Service with the stored data, and evaluates logical expressions to decide which execution branch to follow according to stored data, etc.

Because the process instances communicate to the outside world by using the semantic concepts of the common ontological reference model, the standard Web Services of the service-oriented applications can't understand them directly. To solve this, the standard Web Services are encapsulated (through the semantic annotation/profiling process) into semantically-annotated Web Services, which are directly invokable by a given process instance. These services will be referred as "mediated services".

The Web Services Profiling Walkthrough

We assume that Web Services of the service oriented business applications – called native Web services – are described by a WSDL file. This WSDL description contains the data structure (or a reference to it) of the requested input and the provided output data of operations the service provides. This structure is in the format of an XML schema definition (XSD) and is called native data structure. During the annotation process, the standard WSDL description will be extended with semantics as described in the following paragraphs.

The exact connection between the native data structure and the used ontological concepts has to be defined first. The concepts of the data-intensive interoperability ontology (i.e. the common reference model), which are the closest to native data, are identified and referenced from the extended description of the native Web Service. This results in a semantic description which is constructed by the guidelines of the SAWSDL recommendation, i.e. creation and utilization of a "modelReference" annotation mechanism pointing to a data ontological concept, for every wsdl:part of the involved Web Services.

Although one can find concepts which are very close to the native data in meaning, the syntactical differences between the concepts have to be bridged by creating and applying XSLT transformations.

The XSLT transformations are also used to handle data mismatch problems. Data mismatch problems may be caused from differences between native data structures and the selected concepts of the enterprise data ontology. This can be due to the usage of different units (e.g. when a native service uses US units whereas the Ontology concepts use metric units), different currencies, different format for the same data (for example the address, or the date is formatted in many different ways in CRP and ERP systems due to the differences between national traditions).

The created XSLT transformation code is stored at a common repository. After the transformations are present, the reference to them is added to the semantic description, i.e. the Semantic Profile, of the service.

THE ENTERPRISE INTEROPERABILITY ONTOLOGY

As we have already stated the proposed approach for dynamic data mediation is based on the definition of formal transformations of the input and output messages of the involved Web Services to a common reference model. For this purpose, we are utilizing the Data Facet of the Enterprise Interoperability Ontology (ENIO) that we have designed and developed [5]. The Enterprise Interoperability Ontology represents an explicit specification of the conceptualization of the EAI domain, and structures and formalizes the procedural and operative knowledge needed to describe and resolve the given EAI problem, providing a formal and explicit definition of the data, services and processes that exist within an application integration problem.

Overview of the ENIO Structure and Design Principles

The ENIO Ontology has a four-fold focus (Bouras et al., 2007): a) to resolve most message level heterogeneities through the formal definition of the data(-types) in the input and output messages of a service, providing a reference model of data semantics; b) to enable effective search and discovery of services through the formal representation of the capabilities and the functionality of service operators; c) to assist manual process composition through (reusable) process templates; and d) to support semi-automated process composition via the annotation of the behavioral models of collaborative EAI processes.

The above-mentioned goals of ENIO constitute

Figure 1. The ENIO conceptual structure

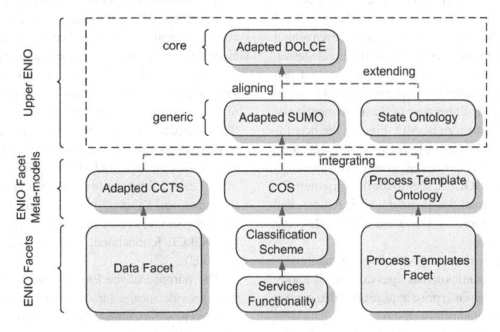

the basis for the identification of the dimensions and the structure of the ontology. We have chosen to introduce the model of an upper ontology, which covers generic and domain-independent concepts, with several, domain-related extensions that we call facets (Figure 1). We have developed a three-faceted structure for ENIO: data facet; functional facet and process facet. In the following paragraphs, we present the upper level of ENIO as well as the various facets.

We have decided to define an Upper Ontology for ENIO because: a) it provides a reference point and a framework for analyzing, harmonizing, and integrating existing ontologies and metadata standards; b) it provides a starting point, a predefined set of ontological entities and a ontology design pattern for building new, lower-level, domain ontologies; and c) a carefully engineered upper ontology, used as an ontology modelling basis, avoids the typical shortcomings, i.e. conceptual ambiguity and loose design, of commonly built ontologies (Oberle).

Based on the analysis of the characteristics of several freely available foundational ontologies

in (Oberle et al., 2006), we concluded that both DOLCE and SUMO meet most of our requirements. SUMO provides quite a rich axiomatisation that, in our case, could be a disadvantage, as in SUMO, a lot of information is represented as instances whereas other modules use concepts on the same level, concepts are instances at the same time, relations are instantiated between concepts, and some relations are even modeled as concepts (Oberle et al., 2006). Additionally, SUMO provides a rich taxonomy that can be applied fruitfully for domain ontologies. On the other hand, DOLCE is conceptually sound, and thus ideally suited for reference purposes (Oberle et al., 2006). However, it does not provide an extensive and detailed taxonomy like SUMO, and, thus, a considerable amount of additional modelling would be required.

Hence we are using in ENIO an alignment of DOLCE and SUMO that combines their advantages by including a core ontology (based on DOLCE) and a domain-independent ontology (based on SUMO) to establish the basic layers. The implementation of our upoer ENIO Ontology is based on Smart SUMO (Oberle et al., 2006). To align SUMO to DOLCE, we pruned the upper-level of the SUMO taxonomy and aligned the remaining concepts to the appropriate DOLCE categories. During the alignment, it became apparent that grasping the intended meaning of SUMO's terms is quite difficult because of the loose merging of several theories in SUMO. Finding the best fitting super-concept in DOLCE for a SUMO term was therefore non-trivial. In addition, the design patterns of DOLCE, such as the design pattern for modelling qualities of endurants via regions, had to be taken into consideration when performing the alignment.

The Data Facet of ENIO aims to formally capture the semantics of messages exchanged among collaborative enterprise applications that expose their functionality as web services. The data facet facilitates dynamic data mediation by enabling the design of mappings and XSLT transformations for all service message elements (i.e. inputs and outputs) utilizing the schemaMapping attribute as in (Nagarajan et al., 2006).

As we do not intend to re-invent the wheel, we based the ENIO Data facet on the Core Components Technical Specification (CCTS). CCTS is currently the ISO 15000-5 Technical Specification and is supported and used by more than 50 projects and initiatives (including UBL, RosettaNet, CIDX, SWIFT, OAG, etc). The meta-model of the ENIO Data Facet "ontologizes" the meta-modelling elements of CCTS, i.e. Core Components (CC), Data Types (DT), Aggregated CC (ACC), Basic CC (BCC) and Association CC (ASCC). For the population of the Data Facet, we have utilized as knowledge sources the following standards and vocabularies: the OASIS ebXML Core Components Dictionary, the RosettaNet Business Dictionary, the OAGIS specification, and the OASIS Universal Business Language.

The Functional Facet of ENIO defines the capabilities of enterprise services and provides classes for the annotation of services operators with functional semantics. This categorization of the intended functionality of the services combined with ontology-driven match-making algorithms may support efficient and effective discovery of published services in a business services registry. Furthermore, the Functional Facet of ENIO aims to assist manual process design, as the participation of a specific service in a business process composition scenario involves mainly the formal specification and shared understanding of its desired functionality. Our meta-model of the Functional Facet utilizes the Core Ontology of (Web) Services (COS)[1], which is a module of the DOLCE foundational ontology (Masolo et al., 2002).

The purpose of the Process Facet of ENIO is to provide means for defining collaborative business process templates and for annotating the states of Web Services with interior behavioural models that may be utilized in semi-automatic goal-driven composition.

For the meta-model of the ENIO Process Facet we developed a process template ontology that follows the MIT Process Handbook methodology (Malone et al., 2003) to compose reusable process templates and includes the definitions of public views of processes and their variants, e.g. the "CRM Sales Order Processing" is a variant of the public process "Sales Order Processing". Moreover, the ENIO Process Facet meta-model classifies each public view of a process under a specific category, associates them with tasks of the Functional Facet and assigns them with exactly one role, e.g. the previously mentioned public process "CRM Sales Order Processing" is classified under the "Sales and Services" category, and is associated to a task variant of the Functional Facet class "Sales" and to the "Sales Representative" role.

In addition to this, the Process Facet includes a State Ontology which extends the "State" class of DOLCE in order to describe the states of complex Web Service operations. We aim to use the State ontology in the formulation of process composition goals and in the specification of the transitions from one state to another.

The ENIO Data Facet Implementation Issues

As our goal is to provide a general reference ontology for a semantically-enriched data mediation solution for EAI scenarios, a fine-grained axiomatisation is not needed. A semi-formal ontology providing a common vocabulary with a formal taxonomy, but without detailed logical axioms is enough for our purposes. We therefore chose a common denominator of ontology features which are present in all current ontological formalisms, including but not limited to RDFS, OWL, and WSML.

The features we use are the following: concepts with formal sub-concept relation, instances with formal instantiates relation, and binary properties with single concept domain and range constraints. We have chosen OWL-DL as our implementation language because it is an already available W3C recommendation and has good tool support. Moreover, other ontology formalisms (including WSML) provide conversion utilities from and to OWL-DL. We therefore expect that ENIO can be (semi-) automatically translated into various other formats in the future, if it is needed by the target application domain.

The creation of ENIO comprised several technical tasks since already existing upper ontological models were utilized and new facet-dependent meta-models where created. First of all, DOLCE was reused as the actual upper core ontology. The first goal was the modification of SUMO so as to be aligned to DOLCE. Significant work in this field has been done in SmartWeb where a specific alignment has been proposed in (Oberle et al., 2006) and has been adopted by us.

Regarding the development of the facet-specific meta-models and their integration to the Upper ENIO Ontology, we mainly tackled three

sets of technical tasks: a) the smooth integration of COS, since it is built upon DOLCE; b) the manual creation and integration of the Process Template and the State Ontologies using the Protégé OWL API, which extended specific classes of DOLCE, i.e. the "Process" and the "State" classes; and c) the creation of the meta-model and initial population of the Data Facet utilizing the UBL/CCTS specification as a basis, which constituted the most complicated task and is discussed in the following paragraphs.

As OWL and UBL/CCTS do not respect the same meta-model formalization, we have defined a mapping between the UBL/CCTS meta-model and the OWL meta-model in order to develop a conversion utility that handles the transition from UBL/CCTS structure to OWL format. By thoroughly examining the UBL/CCTS specification, we have decided on its entities that define named classes or classes' properties and have concluded on the mapping given in Figure 2.

Specifically, the Core Component Types, the Data Types, Aggregated Component Types, and the Aggregated Business Information Entities (BIEs) define concept classes. Basic Core Components (BCCs), the Basic BIEs (BBIEs), and the Associated BIEs (ABIEs) define object properties. Moreover, the qualification of Core Components to BIEs is semantically similar to the sub-concept relation between concepts. A similar approach was proposed during the creation of the Business Data Ontology of in (Oberle et al., 2006) but it was based on CCTS ver. 1.0. The implementation has been accomplished by utilizing the UBL/CCTS published XSD schemas, we then loaded them using a java based data binder (based on the Apache Castor Library) and parsed the UBL/CCTS elements to OWL with the Protégé OWL API.

Finally we addressed three more problems (a) the fact that UBL/CCTS uses object composition instead of the typical "is-a" relation and hence we proceeded to manual modifications; (b) the fact that UBL/CCTS does not use inheritance at all, for which we identified a proper concept taxonomy

Figure 2. UBL/CCTS-to-OWL mapping

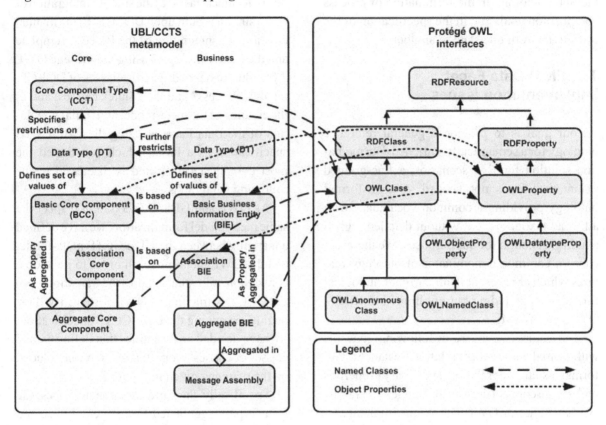

and then deleted redundant properties; and (c) in order to avoid the problems associated to the fact that the UBL/CCTS elements use various codes as references to another entity, we replaced the codes and IDs references with references to instances of the related concepts.

THE SEMANTIC ANNOTATION AND SEMANTIC PROFILING TOOL

The Need for a Tool for Facilitating Data Mediation Scenarios

The backbone of data mediation is the Private Semantic Adaptation layer (PSA). According to the 'principle' of PSA each service has a native profile and a semantically enhanced profile. The native profile is meaningful for the intra-company

communication while the semantically enhanced profile is exposed to the community and is interoperable. The task of transforming interoperable calls to native calls is undertaken by the exposed service itself. But in order to undertake such a task the Semantic Annotation and Profiling (SEAP) tool must be used.

The SEAP tool is used by the IT experts in order to make already existing exposed web services PSA enabled (interoperable). PSA enablement is the cornerstone of the Private Semantic Adaptation Layer according to which if a service is made 'PSA enabled' then other services can exchange data with this service by exchanging Ontological concepts.

PSA enablement actually pre-assumes the data, functional and behavioral annotation of the service along with the provision of information of up-casting and down-casting information. In

Figure 3. The main SEAP user interface

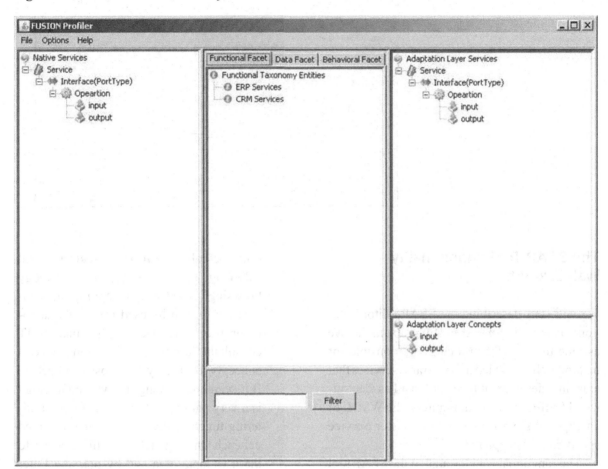

the frames of this chapter we are interested only in data mediation issues only.

After the login to SEAP the main UI is presented (Figure 3). As someone can notice the main UI comprises of 5 areas. In the left we have the Native Services Area, in the middle we have the *Ontology Browser* area and the *Ontology filtering* area, and finally in the right we have the *Adaptation Layer Services* area and the *Adaptation Layer Concepts* area. We will examine each area separately.

The *Native Services* Area is responsible for the visualization of the native services of a company. As it has been already discussed, PSA is only applied to companies that have already exposed their business logic as Web Services. These services are selected and visualized in this area.

The *Ontology Browser* area is responsible for visualizing all facets of ENIO i.e. Functional Data and Behavioral. The Ontology filtering area (also in the middle) is responsible for providing some keywords in order to sort out the visualized Ontology.

Finally in the right the *Adaptation Layer Services* are visualized. The Adaptation Layer services are actually the instantiation of services that comprise a Collaborative Business Process Template (a.k.a. CBP template in the frames of ENIO). The concepts that annotate inputs and outputs of the CBP template are visualized separately in the Adaptation *Layer Concepts* area for convenience.

Figure 4. The WSDL schematic view of exposed web service

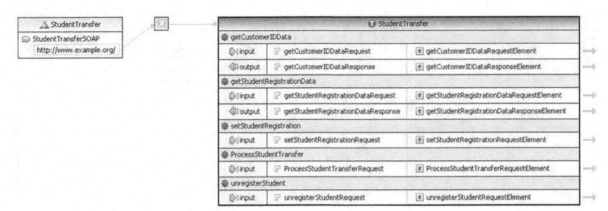

The SEAP Tool Functionality Walkthrough

We will start describing the SEAP Editor functionality utilizing a real profiling example. We assume that an IT consultant is responsible for making ENIO enabled interoperable services that exist in a department of school that has Centralized IT infrastructure. In Figure 4, the WSDL of an exposed service (a Student Transfer Service specifically) is depicted.

The functional walkthrough of the SEAP tool is listed below:

- **Ontology Selection, Loading and Visualization.** First of all, the IT consultant has to load the Ontology from the Ontology repository. After loading the Ontology all three tabs (one tab per each facet) are filled with the Ontological concepts. As presented in the Figure 5, the IT consultant can use the three different tabs to navigate through the facets of the Ontology. The Ontology is rendered as a tree in order to achieve maximum convenience during the user interaction. Both Datatype properties and Object properties are visualized. There is a completely different graphical notation model for each type of tree nodes.

- **Ontological Concept Search and Filtering.** The endmost goal of Ontology browsing is to identify an appropriate concept that has to be used during the annotation procedure. This implies that the IT consultant has to search among several concepts to identify the most appropriate. But searching among the whole Ontology is a very painful task. For this reason a filtering functionality has been implemented per each Ontology tab. By editing a term to the user input area and by pressing Filter the Ontology is automatically filtered and only relative terms are depicted. Relative terms is somehow misleading since if a concepts contains a data type property related with the user-term then this concept is also shown.

- **Web Service Description Selection, Loading and Visualization.** Once the IT consultant selects and loads a native WSDL (corresponding to an Enterprise Service) communicating with a pre-configured UDDI registry, the WSDL is visualized (Figure 5) in a descriptive manner, utilizing different visual elements for each one of WSDL building blocks, i.e. wsdl:Service, wsdl:Porttype, wsdl:Input, wsdl:Output and finally Message Part. There is no constraint to the WSDL schema

Figure 5. Multi-faceted ontology and native WSDL visualization

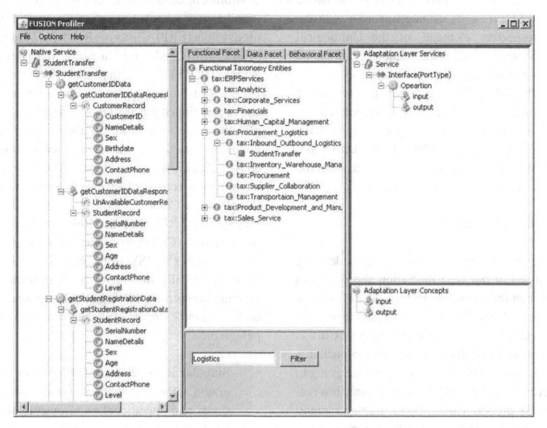

since a description with multiple Services that contain multiple Porttypes with multiple inputs/outputs can be successfully loaded.

- **Manual Add/Remove-Annotation Procedure.** The most significant task of the IT consultant is to annotate the WSDL using the concepts of the ontology that has been already loaded. The use of the SEAP tool eases this task since it eliminates the overhead of doing the annotation in the WSDL source level. Such an annotation would produce questionable results. According to the Annotation procedure that has been defined in the ENIO reference model data annotations refer to message parts, functional annotations to port types and behavioral annotations at the message part level also. Using the SEAP tool, the user is assisted during the annotation procedure since you cannot drop an Ontological concept to an irrelevant WSDL construct e.g. a functional concept to message part. After the annotation takes place, the user can easily edit its annotation by right clicking the appropriate concept.

- **Transformations Creation.** Once the data annotations are completed, the IT consultant has to provide the up- and lower- lifting information for the message parts of the selected native WSDL utilizing the so-called *Transformation Editor* of the SEAP tool that visualizes all the participating structures. Assuming the existence of a wsdl:MessagePart (e.g. CustomerRecord) that is annotated with the ontological concepts "Address" and "Customer", the IT consultant connects all elements that exist in the message part structure of the native WSDL (e.g. "CustomerRecord") with the respective elements of the Ontological Structure, selecting among predefined functions e.g. "StringConcatinate".

- **Publish.** After the annotation session is finalized, the semantically-annotated annotated is published, by creating a proxy service and forwarding the respective SA-WSDL representation to a preconfigured semantically-enriched registry.

BUSINESS USE CASE

Up to now we have examined the underlying principles of our data mediation approach and examined the use of SEAP tool. SEAP tool is a support tool, which helps IT consultants to produce interoperable services out of native services. In this section, we are going to apply our approach in a real world example. Specifically we are going to describe how our approach is applicable in a real business process called 'Stock Replenishment' that is already established in the legacy systems of GERMANOS SA in Greece.

The daily store replenishment cycle constitutes a typical case of process integration scenario. This replenishment procedure imposes that every day the franchisees have to replenish their stocks by ordering new items from the franchisor that has to invoice and deliver the items requested. The replenishment procedure involves and triggers, in all way, processes of most of the systems comprising the GERMANOS IT infrastructure, e.g. the ERP and WMS system of the Franchisor and the Retail Systems of the Franchisees. Table 1 provides the description of the most representative steps of the process.

The systemic infrastructure that supports the above-mentioned process involves enterprise applications operating in all collaboration parties, including both the franchisor (i.e. headquarters) and the franchisees (i.e. stores). The technical

environment consist of several IT systems, e.g. Retail Server-Client, Enterprise Resource Planning system (ERP), Customer Relations Management system (CRM), and Warehouse Management System (WMS), from different vendors.

The systemic infrastructure that supports the above-mentioned process involves enterprise applications operating in all collaboration parties, including both the franchisor (i.e. headquarters) and the franchisees (i.e. stores). The technical environment consist of several IT systems, e.g. Retail Server-Client, Enterprise Resource Planning system (ERP), Customer Relations Management system (CRM), and Warehouse Management System (WMS), from different vendors. More specifically, the enterprise application and systems comprising the technical environment of the example are presented in the following paragraphs:

- Singular Retail System (SRS) is an integrated software system that addresses the needs and operational requirements of intensive retail by sales companies, and constitutes the retail system of GERNANOS Retail Stores. SRS is a 3-tier application with a fat client (i.e. Retail Client) installed in each operating retail store, while the SRS Server (i.e. Retail Server) operated in Group HQ.
- SAP R/3 constitutes the corporate ERP system of the GERMANOS Group Headquarters. SAP R/3 is a client/server based application, utilizing a 3-tiered model. SAP R/3 tries to integrate all operational data and processes of the GERMANOS Group into a unified system.
- Aberon Warehouse Management constitutes the WMS system of the GERMANOS Group Headquarters. Aberon is a flexible, robust package for controlling and managing warehouses and distribution centres.

Table 1. Process steps of the stock replenishment scenario

Workflow Title	Store Order Management (Stock Replenishment)
Involved Systems	ERP, Retail System
Description	This procedure describes the steps of creating and maintaining an order from the retail store and all the appropriate administrative steps that can be performed by the headquarters.
Workflow analysis	1. Before any transaction the stock is calculated in the local warehouse
	2. Stock is automatically updated (online) in the Retail System
	3. The Retail System estimates the replenishment level of the store and proposes request for stock
	4. User performs online request for Stock to headquarters
	5. Central Warehouse Administrator checks the availability of items
	6. In case of stock existence the requested quantity is reserved. Automatically a reservation receipt is created in the retail system.
	7. The ERP locks for the appropriate recalculation of the new stock of the Central Warehouse taking into account ALL reservation requests.
	8. A new Stock statement for the Central warehouse is posted to the Retail System through a batch process.
	9. Along with stock statement exchange, headquarters produce shipping receipts/invoices to the retail store.
	10. The delivery receipt is online generated using the shipping.
	11. Process ends.
Possible Deviation 1	If ERP is already locked during online request for Stock then step 4 deviates:
Alternative Actions	4.1 request for stock is postponed
	4.2 request for stock is sent after a timeout
Possible Deviation 2	If appropriate stock is not available then Step 5 deviates:
Alternative Actions	6.2 The ERP system takes under consideration the refilling time
	7.2 User performs request for stock after a time lag
	8.2 The requested quantity is reserved. Automatically a reservation receipt is created in the Retail system.
	9.2 The ERP locks for the appropriate recalculation of the new stock of the Central Warehouse taking into account ALL reservation requests.
	10.2 A new Stock statement for the Central warehouse is posted to the Retail System though a batch process.
	11.2 Along with stock statement exchange, headquarters produce shipping receipts/ invoices to the retail store.
	12.2 The delivery receipt is generated online using the shipping.
	13.2 Process ends

We will use step 1, i.e. "*Retrieve Stock Data*" service (as involved in the visual walkthrough of the daily store replenishment procedure that occurs at GERMANOS considering the installation of the legacy systems, presented in Figure 6), in order to demonstrate our approach. According to the process a retail server which is established at the headquarters is notified by the retail clients upon the order requests. Consequently, according to our approach the exposed service '*getStockRequestforanItem*' should be transformed to an interoperable service using the SEAP tool.

More specifically, we have proceeded in the following actions:

• selection and loading the ENIO Ontology and the required native WSDLs to the

Figure 6. Business visualization of the GERMANOS "store replenishment" scenario

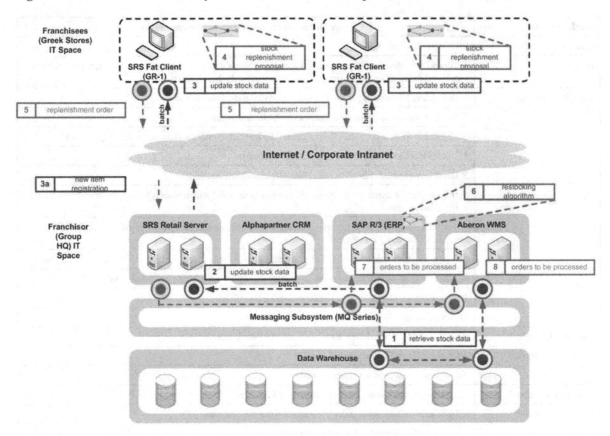

visualization component of the SEAP tool;
- identification of the ontological terms that are relevant to the visualized arguments of the loaded WSDL;
- association of the terms with the existing arguments (annotation procedure);
- provision of the up- and down- casting information i.e. the way an incoming ontological argument is transformed to a native one and vice versa.

In Figure 7, the annotation procedure is depicted (after its finalization), highlighting the ontological concepts "Address" and "Item" that are sufficient enough to cover the entire input arguments. After the annotation process, we have provided the transformation (mappings) information between the semantic concepts and the native

arguments, i.e. class "Area" and –AddressRegion etc.). In Figure 8, the mappings information between the input arguments and its annotations is depicted.

RELATED WORK

The approach presented in this book chapter is related to many research efforts conducted in areas of semantic enterprise interoperability and business application integration. For example, (Haller et al., 2005) have proposed to extend the notion of Service-Oriented Architectures by WSMO-based Semantic Web Services and showed how EAI benefits by it. On the other hand, (Izza et al., 2005) proposes an Ontology-Driven Service-Oriented Integration (ODSOI) that aims to extend the cur-

Figure 7. Semantic data annotations on a native service

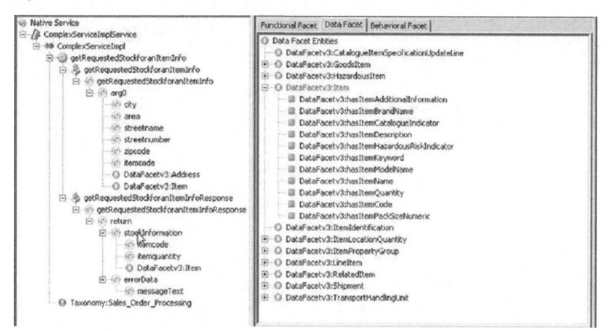

rent web services stack technology by a semantic layer offering semantic services that can define the service semantics and also perform semantic mediation in the context of EAI. Additionally, (Tektonidis et al, 2005) presents the creation of the ONAR SOA-based integration framework that enriches the semantics of the exchanged information and utilizes web ontologies to create semantic conceptualizations of the business concepts that exist inside an application. Moreover, (Anicic et al., 2006) investigates the potential of the Semantic Web technologies to support a semantic-based Enterprise Application Integration (standards architecture, providing detailed information of the support that these technologies and the underlying Description Logics (DL) formalism provide for the integration task. Finally, (Stollberg et al., 2006) presents an integrated model for mediation on the Semantic Web with special attention to Semantic Web services that is developed around the Web Service Modeling Ontology, i.e. WSMO.

CONCLUSION AND FUTURE WORK

In this book chapter, we have proposed a semantically-enriched approach for dynamic data mediation among interconnected Web Services in the framework of collaborative business processes. The proposed ontology-based approach focuses on the resolution of message level heterogeneities between collaborative enterprise services exposed from the existing, participating business systems, facilitating automatic, dynamic data mediation during execution time by providing formal transformations (up- and down- casting mappings) of the output and input messages (of the participating Web Services) to a common reference model, i.e. the Enterprise Interoperability Ontology, which constitutes a multi-layered and -faceted ontology that provides a shared, common understanding of data, services and processes within enterprise application integration cases.

Moreover, we present a tool that has been designed and developed to support the user to provide business data-related semantic annotations and the required up- and down- casting

Figure 8. Mapping information among native and semantic arguments

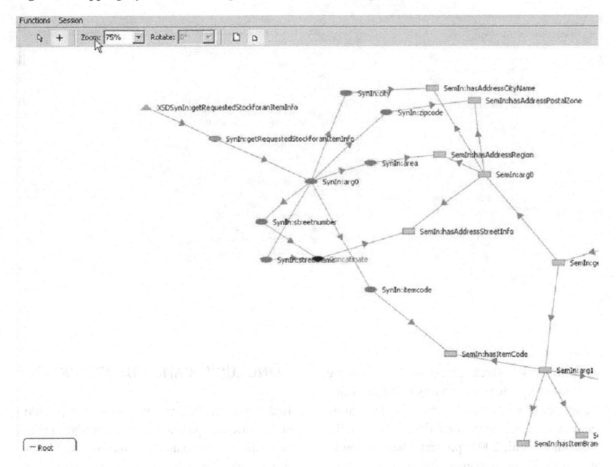

XSLT transformations of the input and output message parts of given Web Services exposed from business applications, realizing parts of their functionality.

In addition, we presented the applicability of the proposed approach in a realistic integration scenario within a franchisor-franchisees collaborative value network, comprising complex, heterogeneous systemic infrastructure. In the frame of this scenario, we have demonstrated the dynamic resolution of data heterogeneities at execution time.

In the future, we intend to generate and add a transformation repository, containing all the supported transformation types, which can be selected and reused during a service's semantic annotation and profiling process.

REFERENCES

Anicic, N., Marjanovic, Z., Ivezic, N., & Jones, A. (2006, December 28). An Aarchitecture for Ssemantic eEnterprise Aapplication Iintegration Sstandards. *International Journal of Manufacturing Technology and Management, Volume 10*, Numbers (2-3), 28 December 2006, pp. 205-226(22).

Bouras, A., & Gouvas, P. P., & G. Mentzas, G. (2007, September 3-7). ENIO: An Eenterprise Aapplication Iintegration Oontology. In the *pProceedings of the 18th International Conference on Database and Expert Systems Applications (DEXA 2007)*, 3-7 September, 2007, Regensburg, Germany, (pp. 419-423).

Bussler, C. C. (2003). "The Rrole of Semantic Web Ttechnology in Eenterprise Aapplication Iintegration", In *IEEE Data Engineering Bulletin, 26*, 2003, No. (4), pp. 62 – 68.

Farrell, J., & Lausen, H. (eEds.). (2007, January). *Semantic aAnnotations for WSDL and XML sSchema. W3C Ccandidate Rrecommendation*, January 2007. Available at:Retrieved from http://www.w3.org/TR/sawsdl

Friescn, A., & Alazeib, A. A., Balogh, A., M. Bauer, M.,A. Bouras, A., P. Gouvas, P., G. Mentzas, G., & A. Pace, A. (2007, July 23-27). Towards semantically-assisted design of collaborative business processes in EAI scenarios. In the *pProceedings of the 5th IEEE International Conference on Industrial Informatics*, July 23-27 2007, Vienna, WF-006149, (Vol.ume 2, Pagep. 779).

Haller, A., Gomez, J., & Bussler, C. (2005). Exposing Semantic Web Sservice principles in SOA to solve EAI scenarios. iIn *Workshop on Web Service Semantics, in, WWW2005*.

Haller, A., Gomez, J., & Bussler, C. (2005). Exposing Semantic Web sService principles in SOA to solve EAI scenarios. Iin *Workshop on Web Service Semantics, in, WWW2005*.

Izza, S., Vincent, L., & Burlat, P. (2005). A Uunified Fframework for Aapplication Iintegration - an Oontology-driven Sservice-oriented Aapproach. *ICEIS, 2005*(1), 165–170.

Malone, T. W. Crowston., K., & Herman, G. A. (2003). *Organizing Bbusiness kKnowledge: The MIT pProcess Hhandbook*. Cambridge, MA: MIT Press, 2003. [14]

Masolo, C., Borgo, et al. (2002, August). *The WWonderWeb Llibrary of Ffoundational oOntologies. WonderWeb Ddeliverable D17*, August 2002.

Nagarajan, M., Verma, K., Sheth, A., Miller, J., & Lathem, J. (2006). Semantic iInteroperability of Web Sservices - Cchallenges and Eexperiences. *2006 IEEE International Conference on Web Services (ICWS 2006)*.

Oberle, D. (2006). *Semantic Mmanagement of Mmiddleware, volume I of Tthe Semantic Web and Bbeyond*. Springer, 2006.

Oberle, D., Ankolekar, et al. (2006, July). *DOLCE ergo SUMO: On Ffoundational and Ddomain Mmodels in SWIntO, AIFB*,. University of Karlsruhe. July 2006.

Rymer, J., M., Gilpin, M., & K., Volmer, K. (2004). *Market Ooverview: "Integration Llandscape 2005"*. Forrester Research, Inc.

Stollberg, M., Cimpian, E., Mocan, A., & Fensel, D. (2006). A Semantic Web Mmediation aArchitecture. In *Proceedings of the 1st Canadian Semantic Web Working Symposium (CSWWS 2006)*.

Tektonidis., D., Bokma, A., Oatley, G., & Salampasis, M. (2005). ONAR: An oOntologies-based Sservice-Ooriented Aapplication Iintegration fFramework,. *I-ESA'05*, Geneva, Switzerland.

Vollmer, K., & H., Peyret, H. (2005). *Topic Ooverview: "Application Iintegration Ssolutions"*. Forrester Research, Inc.

ENDNOTE

[1]   Core Ontology of (Web) Services (COS). Available at http://cos.ontoware.org/

Chapter 3
Ontology–based Patterns for the Integration of Business Processes and Enterprise Application Architectures

Veronica Gacitua-Decar
Dublin City University, Ireland

Claus Pahl
Dublin City University, Ireland

ABSTRACT

Increasingly, enterprises are using service-oriented architecture (SOA) as an approach to enterprise application integration (EAI). SOA has the potential to bridge the gap between business and technology and to improve the reuse of existing applications and the interoperability with new ones. In addition to service architecture descriptions, architecture abstractions like patterns and styles capture design knowledge and allow the reuse of successfully applied designs, thus improving the quality of software. Knowledge gained from integration projects can be captured to build a repository of semantically enriched, experience-based solutions. Business patterns identify the interaction and structure between users, business processes, and data. Specific integration and composition patterns at a more technical level address enterprise application integration and capture reliable architecture solutions. We use an ontology-based approach to capture architecture and process patterns. Ontology techniques for pattern definition, extension, and composition are developed and their applicability in business process-driven application integration is demonstrated.

1 INTRODUCTION

Software applications are built or acquired to provide specialised functionality required to support business processes. If new activities and applications are created and integrated into existing business processes and infrastructures, new architecture and information requirements need to be satisfied. Enterprise Application Integration (EAI) aims to link separate applications into an integrated system

DOI: 10.4018/978-1-60566-804-8.ch003

driven by business models and the goals they implement.

Business process management (BPM) aims to improve productivity, product quality, and operations of an enterprise. BPM encompasses methods, techniques, and tools to support the analysis, design, implementation and governance of operational business processes. Processes models have a critical role in the redesign of business processes. However, business analysts and software developers often face difficulties managing challenges such as discovering, modelling, and understanding business processes in the context of their implementation through software applications.

Increasingly, enterprises are using Service-Oriented Architecture (SOA) as an approach to EAI. SOA has the potential to bridge the gap between business and technology and to improve the reuse of existing applications and the interoperability with new ones. Software services are the building blocks of SOA. They can be composed to provide more complex functionality and to automate business processes. However, if applications are created without a structured architectural design, integrating these into a coherent architecture closely aligned with the business processes becomes a significant challenge. Business processes do not map one-to-one to service architecture processes. This gap has turned out to be difficult to approach systematically and to automate.

Abstraction and knowledge representation are principles that can address these challenges. Architecture abstractions like patterns and styles capture design knowledge and allow the reuse of successfully applied designs, thus improving the quality of software. Abstraction is a central driver in software engineering approaches; at the business level the reuse of successfully business designs is equally important. The development of integrated enterprise-wide application architectures is a continuous process. To improve the process and overall quality, the experience of analysts, architects and developers should be captured and reused. Knowledge gained from integration projects should be captured to build a repository of semantically enriched, experience-based pattern solutions.

Reusing proven solutions in a semantically enriched form reduces costs and development time and ensures coherently integrated and architected application systems aligned with business processes. Using patterns enables architects to implement successful application integration solutions.

- Business patterns identify the interaction and structure between users, business processes, and data.
- Architectural patterns at a technical level address enterprise application integration and capture reliable architecture solutions.

A framework is required that can capture architectures and patterns as models and that can integrate representations from the different perspectives of business and software technology. We use an ontology-based approach to capture process and architectural patterns. A set of ontology-based pattern languages and techniques is developed and its applicability in business process-driven enterprise application integration demonstrated. A number of benefits of an ontology-based solution can be identified:

- enhanced extensibility through a taxonomical framework,
- alignment with ontology-based domain models and integration frameworks,
- use of ontologies as a semantical modelling notation,
- exploitation of the logical aspect of ontologies to infer additional knowledge from facts asserted in ontologies,
- use of ontologies as a formal reasoning framework to support architecture activities such as discovery and matching.

We outline the background in terms of SOA and ontology approaches in Section 2. Our proposed architecture framework is presented in Section 3, including a scenario that serves as an application context in which our solution is demonstrated. In Section 4, we introduce our ontology-based service modelling notation and look at pattern modelling and matching. Section 5 investigates transformations. Finally, we discuss our results and future trends, before ending with some conclusions.

2 BACKGROUND

SOA is the context of this work. In this section, we provide some background on SOA frameworks and how ontology technology has been utilised to support SOA, in particular in the context of enterprise integration.

2.1 SOA and Ontology Support for SOA Frameworks

SOA frameworks provide methodological guidelines, modelling support, and tools to develop service-oriented architectures. A service architecture design relates two domains that have their own modelling representation and dynamics regarding changes, i.e. the business domain and the software application domain. A SOA framework must provide an integrated modelling solution for both domains.

Successful, proven designs documented in the form of software design patterns have been widely used by software architects to develop software systems with improved quality (Gamma, Helm, Johnson, and Vlissides, 1993; Bass, Clements and Kazman, 2003). Similarly, business patterns provide proven designs for process models and informational models that help business analysts in creating business models (Fettke and Loos, 2006). An architectural framework must provide support to work with pattern descriptions and allow the incorporation of patterns into designs.

Ontologies are means of knowledge representation, defining so-called shared conceptualisations. Ontologies are frameworks for terminological definitions that can be used to organise concepts in a domain. Simple examples of ontologies are taxonomies, i.e. classification schemes used for example to classify animals or plants into hierarchies. Combined with a terminological logic such as description logic (Baader, McGuiness, Nardi, and Schneider, 2003), we obtain a framework for specification, classification, and reasoning in an application domain. The Semantic Web is an initiative for the Web that builds up on ontology technology (Daconta, Obrst and Smith, 2003). XML is the syntactical format. RDF – the Resource Description Framework – is a triple-based formalism (subject, property, object) to describe entities. OWL – the Web Ontology Language – provides additional logic-based reasoning based on top of RDF.

A specific application of ontologies in SOA are service ontologies – which have demonstrated the benefits of ontologies for software composition (Payne. and Lassila, 2004). WSMO (Lara, Stollberg, Polleres, Feier, Bussler, and Fensel, 2005), OWL-S (OWL-S Coalition, 2002) and the Semantic Web Services Framework SWSF (Semantic Web Services Language (SWSL) Committee, 2006) are the predominant service ontologies. Service ontologies are ontologies to describe Web services, aiming to support their semantics-based discovery in Web service registries. The Web Service Process Ontology WSPO (Pahl, 2007) is also a service ontology, but its focus is description and reasoning about service composition and service processes. The FLOWS ontology in SWSF comprises, like WSPO, process modelling.

Our work can be seen in the context of model-driven development (MDD). We can link our integration framework to two of the MDA model layers proposed by the OMG – computation-independent and platform-independent. The need for a specific MDD solution for the services context is a concern. The ubiquity of Web services and the existence of standardised and accepted platform and modelling technology justify this requirement. An OMG initiative to define and standardise an ontology metamodel (ODM) allows the integration of SOA-related ontologies with OMG standards (Object Management Group, 2003). ODM provides mappings to OWL-DL and also a UML2 profile for ontologies. We use ontologies instead of the Unified Modelling Language UML – the OMG suggestion – for modelling. ODM, however, is a standard addressing ontology description, but not reasoning. The reasoning component, which is important in our framework, would need to be addressed in addition to the standard.

2.2 Related Work

Several methodologies for service architecture design and development have been proposed in the past few years from industry and academia (Erl, 2004), (Papazoglou and van den Heuvel, 2006), (Erradi, Anand, and Kulkarni, 2006). Even though these methodologies provide useful guidelines, they do not propose techniques or tools to automate activities during the design process. They also require advances on modelling support for semantic and behavioural aspects of both business and software domains. In (Aalst, Beisiegel, Hee, Konig and Stahl, 2007), behaviour relies on the modelling richness of the process language used and the description of messaging protocols at component model level. Semantic aspects are not considered.

Architecture transformations are the main architectural concerns in the implementation of an architecture design. Traceability among elements of an architecture is an important property for architecture modification and evolution.

- Traceability between software components and relevant business elements of an enterprise has been exploited (Bernus, Nemes and Schmidt, 2003). In (Steen, Strating,

Lankhorst, Doest and Iacob, 2005), the authors discuss the relevance and impact of service orientation to enterprise architectures. Traceability between services is used to align different views and to analyse the impact of changes in one view. Even though modelling support for traceability is provided, the architectural description of services in the different views is introduced at a high level.

- In (Dijkman and Dumas, 2004), a multi-view point approach for service-oriented design is introduced. The authors focus on interrelations of viewpoints at service and service composition level to allow consistency between different parties designing an inter-organisational service-based architecture. The views involve interface behaviour, provider behaviour, choreography, and orchestration. They formalise the views from a control flow perspective in terms of Petri nets. Traceability between views enables the static verification of the consistency of composite services.

Expert design knowledge expressed as patterns is often neglected in most architecture design frameworks. Analogously to patterns, styles are architectural abstractions that constrain the types and relations among elements of a design. In (Papazoglou and van den Heuvel, 2006), the advantages of using reference models to guide the definition of normalised business functions are discussed. In (Baresi, Heckel, Thöne and Varro, 2006), an architectural style-based approach to SOA modelling and design is presented. Service architectures models are refinements of business architectures. The refinement of specific business scenarios into service architectures is based on the refinement of a generic business-level style into a service architecture style.

Some developments have started to exploit the connection between ontologies and layered architectural modelling. In (Djurić, 2004), an

MDA-based ontology architecture is defined. This architecture includes aspects of an ontology metamodel and a UML profile for ontologies. A transformation of the UML ontology to OWL is implemented. The work by (Gašević, Devedžić, and Djurić, 2004; Djurić, 2004) and the OMG (Object Management Group, 2003a; Object Management Group, 2003b), however, needs to be carried further to address the ontology-based modelling and reasoning of service architectures. In (Pahl, 2008), we have presented work on semantic model-driven development of Web service architectures that integrates a service ontology framework into an MDA-framework in order to achieve higher degrees of automation. In (Zdun and Dustdar, 2007) and (Foster, Mukhija, Uchitel, and Rosenblum, 2008), MDD approaches to integrate process-driven SOA models are proposed. Beside meta-modelling support, Zdun and Dustdar use software design patterns for the integration of services and the business processes using them. To introduce patterns into the MDD approach, they propose pattern primitives as an intermediate abstraction to formally model informal design patterns. A pattern language for process-oriented integration of services is provided. However, the integration of business-level and service-based architectures needs to be further addressed in the context of Web-based ontology technology.

A natural application of ontologies in architecture design would focus on structural aspects of the architecture. In (Pahl, Giesecke and Hasselbring, 2007), an ontology-based approach for modelling architecture styles is presented. The authors introduce operators for style modification and combination between styles. Relations between quality requirements and style modelling are investigated. This work, however, is not adequately applicable to service process modelling and patterns as process-style abstractions. Grønmo et.al. (Grønmo, Jaeger, and Hoff, 2005) introduce – based on ideas from (Djurić, 2004) – an ontology-based service and service process modelling approach. Starting with a UML profile

based on activity diagrams, services are modelled. These models are then translated into OWL-S.

3 AN ARCHITECTURE FRAMEWORK FOR SOA-BASED EAI

A layered architecture for service-centric enterprise application integration is the backbone of our proposed framework. This framework shall now be introduced. We also introduce a case study that illustrates the main challenges of business process and architecture integration.

The problems of application integration in terms of modelling aspects, but also architecture and transformation issues need to be addressed:

- Modelling aspects. Modelling different views such as information hierarchy, behaviour, and semantics needs to be represented in an integrated framework.
- Architecture aspects. Architecture description and architecture abstractions in terms of patterns and styles are central. Reusable architecture design knowledge can be captured in the form of patterns.
- Transformation issues. Essentially, vertical transformations from business to software architectures are of relevance. Business aspects need to be mapped to services. A synchronisation between the respective model aspects is required.

3.1 Model Alignment and Traceability

Enterprise application integration aims to link separate applications into an integrated system driven by business models and the goals they implement. A central problem of applications integration is maintaining alignment between business and technical dimensions involved. Consistence between the dimensions can be improved through explicitly connecting the modelling elements of the EAI problem with elements of the architecture solution through traces. Change management and traceability are important aspects of IT system and business alignment. Two viewpoints need to be considered:

- Business View: Two main models describe the business dimension of the EAI problem: process models and domain models. While business process models capture the dynamics of the business, domain models capture structural relations between business concepts.
- Applications View: An application architecture represents a system composed of several software applications. Application architectures at enterprise scale normally grow in a decentralised way and involve different technologies, paradigms of development and modelling notations.

In order to provide traceability support to the views and elements involved in the integration problem, we develop an architectural approach that supports explicit traces between elements from different layers in a layered architecture. An explicit traceability model maintains the dependencies between elements of the integration problem and its service-centric solution. Traces provide flow dependency information among services that define the technical services composition. A pattern-driven transformation technique between the layers is the solution (Gacitua-Decar and Pahl, 2008b). Ontology support provides the necessary semantic integrity.

3.2 Layered Architecture

Our integration solution is structured based on a layered architecture called LABAS (Layered Architecture for Business, Applications and Services) (Gacitua-Decar and Pahl, 2008a). LABAS contains different layers capturing the business view, the applications architecture view and the view of the service-based integration solution.

From a modelling point of view, an ontology-based meta-model will later define the common constructs among the different layers and provide the modelling support for the transformation from business to software levels. Figure 1 shows the LABAS layers.

- *Business Modelling Layer*. The Business Modelling Layer (BML) is a container for the elements of the process model and the domain model. BML represents the business context of the integration problem. We use BPMN to model business processes and a basic ontology to represent domain information model entities.
- *Application Architecture Layer*. The Application Architecture Layer (AAL) is a container for the application components supporting the business processes in BML. AAL is organised as a process-wide applications architecture. Applications might be owned by different process roles in the BML. In order to describe an AAL model in architectural terms, we adopt the component and connector view (Garlan and Schmerl 2006), which describes a software system as a set of components. Each component has a set of ports with interfaces, which enables the interaction with other components through connectors.
- *Business-Application Intermediate Layer*. The Business-Application Intermediate Layer (BAIL) provides a consolidated view of the integration problem. The aim behind jointly modelling the business and applications views is to derive an integration solution from BAIL models. The consolidated model integrates the models through a traceability model. The integrated models are the business process model, the domain model and the application architecture model. Traces between process steps and domain model elements, and between domain model elements and application

Figure 1. Layered Integration Architecture Framework. (© 2008, Veronica Gacitua-Decar. Used with permission.)

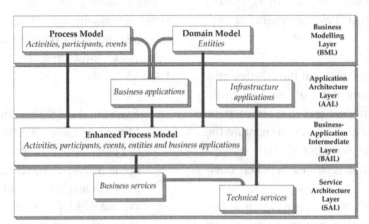

components are the core elements that consolidate the business and application views of the integration problem.

- *Service Architecture Layer.* The Service Architecture Layer (SAL) provides a service-based integration view. It is a container for software services. These services, organised in a service architecture (Alonso, Casati, Kuno, and Machiraju, 2004) implement the integration solution. We use a process-centric component and connector view (Allen and Garlan, 1997) to represent AAL elements.

We propose an incremental transformation from business models into service architecture descriptions to design the solution to the process and applications integration problem. The transformation is supported by architectural abstractions (patterns) and techniques allowing patterns manipulation. The pattern-based techniques provide support to business analysts and software architects to incrementally design the service architectures. The main supported activities encompass:

- *Business model augmentation* involves the addition of patterns into business models.

Pattern instantiation techniques support this activity.

- *Business and technical service identification* involves the analysis of business models and their relation with the supporting applications in order to identify the services of the architecture solution – using pattern identification and matching.
- *Incremental business model to service architecture transformation* generates, step-by-step, an architecture solution to the business and applications integration problem. This activity is supported by pattern-based transformation templates that represent predefined transformation steps.
- *Service architecture augmentation* incorporates SOA patterns to provide solutions to technical issues such as communication, security, and distribution of services.

3.3 Application Scenario

We illustrate the modelling, integration and transformation needs to solve a business process and enterprise application integration problem through an application scenario. It serves us as requirements elicitation tool for the ontological framework and acts as a framework to demon-

Figure 2. Loan Management Process. (© 2008, Veronica Gacitua-Decar. Used with permission.)

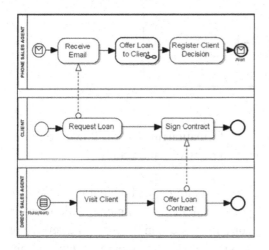

strate where and how ontology-based techniques are beneficial.

The case study looks at the proposed framework within a scenario of integrated financial network services from an application perspective. Figure 2 describes three actors and their processes involved in loan request and approval activities.

The business scenario is a simplified process for loan management in a bank. The process starts when a client requests a loan by email. A phone bank's agent from a call centre calls the client to present an offer. The agent registers the relevant information regarding the client acceptance. If the client accepts the offer and the amount of money involved in the loan is sufficient to meet the sales goals of the bank, then a business alert is triggered. The alert triggers the visit of a direct bank's agent located near the client. This agent visits the client with the objective of signing a contract.

The business scenario describes a situation where individual processes from different parties have to be integrated – a central problem we aim to address. The consequence at technical level is an enterprise application integration problem. In order to demonstrate how to solve the business process and enterprise application integration problem, we detail the *offer loan to client* activ-

ity from the business process shown in Figure 2. Then, we sketch the steps followed for the rest of the activities. Finally, we discuss how all the described steps accomplish the goal of solving the integration problem.

- The *offer loan to client* activity is performed by a bank agent, who calls clients to explain the conditions of a loan. The agent requires information of the client's funds, contact information and the available offer (loan). The amount of money and conditions of the loan depends on the goals that the bank agents have to meet.

- The *offer loan to client* activity consists of three more fine-grained process steps. The process steps, the domain model elements involved, and the applications supporting the activity are shown in Figure 4. Note that the model from Figure 4 is at the Business-Application Intermediate Layer (BAIL) and adds traces between elements from the Business Modelling (BML) and Applications Architecture Layer (AAL).

Loan-to-Client is a common pattern that is instantiated in the loan management process. We assume that the structure and process steps of the *offer loan to client* activity are described in a business pattern catalogue as the *Loan-to-Client* pattern (see Figure 3). In the scenario here, matching of a business pattern is done straightforward by inspection of the process model and a business pattern catalogue.

The central architectural problem of integration is addressed through the BAIL. As indicated in Figure 1, it merges aspects from the BML and the AAL. On the technical level, the applications involved with the *offer loan to client* activity are a mail server application (EMAIL_MNG), a customer relation management application (CRM), an application managing the client's bank account (BANK_ACC), and two applications managing the information of sales and plans of the bank

Figure 3. Loan-to-Client Pattern. (© 2008, Veronica Gacitua-Decar. Used with permission.)

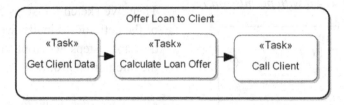

(SALES and PLANNING, respectively). The available operations from the applications that support to the process are shown in the application interfaces at the bottom of Figure 4. The link between the AAL application interfaces (bottom), BML information elements (middle) and the BML process (top) is created through traces modelled by the software architect.

BAIL elements need to be transformed to SAL representations. The *Loan-to-Client* pattern has an associated transformation template, i.e. a collection of rules that guide the process transformation. The transformation template has a description of the business process pattern, the transformation and the associated service description. The business service description from the transformation template is pre-established, and the application-centric service description is generated for each specific application through a set of transformation rules. The following outlines the applied transformation rules:

- process patterns (as boundaries) to service ports: as default an implementation for the common pattern in the form of a service or service process is assumed – e.g. the abstract Loan-to-Client pattern is mapped to a respective technical service,

- applications to (legacy) systems: existing applications represented at the AAL layer are mapped to legacy application service providers (legacy participant) – e.g. BANK-ACC, CRM, SALES or PLANNING,

- business actors to business service providers (service participant): business actors provide business services that might be implemented through composition of services provided by legacy participants,

Figure 4. Enhanced Business Process at Business-Applications Intermediate Layer BAIL. (© 2008, Veronica Gacitua-Decar. Used with permission.)

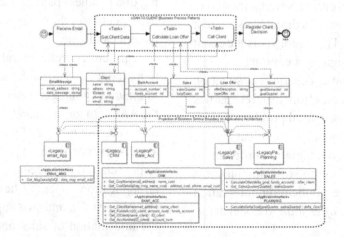

Figure 5. SAL Applications architecture. (© 2008, Veronica Gacitua-Decar. Used with permission.)

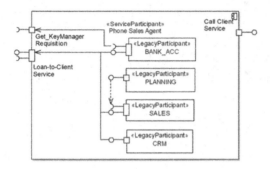

- process steps to service operations: operation-based mapping including in/output and pre/postconditions – e.g. the steps to get client data, calculate loan offer and call client, which are mapped to (legacy) component operations exposed as services.

The transformation from the BAIL layer (Figure 4) to the SAL layer maps business processes to service architecture elements. Figure 5 shows the application transformation result. It integrates legacy components as services into the SAL architecture. The Loan-to-Client pattern is implemented as a separate service that encapsulates the corresponding workflow internally. Figure 6 shows the process pattern and the associated composed service description. We have detailed one of the pattern activity steps to indicate that patterns are often used at a high level of abstraction. If needed, planning approaches can be used to determine the low-level flow (McIlraith and Son, 2002).

4 PATTERNS MODELLING AND MATCHING USING A SERVICE PROCESS ONTOLOGY

We present our ontology-based architectural framework in this section. This framework supports, in addition to behavioural specification and modelling of processes through a process pattern ontology, also pattern matching and layered transformation through refinement techniques and meta-modelling and structural connectivity through an architectural pattern ontology – see Figure 7.

We distinguish two types of patterns, representing different architectural perspectives:

- Process patterns are workflow patterns, i.e. behaviour is the main focus. These are behaviour-oriented patterns that represent common process building blocks.
- Architectural patterns are structurally oriented patterns that focus on structural service connectivity. They define architectural styles and that have a direct link to quality attributes.

These patterns occur at different levels of abstraction (business process and services architectures), possibly based on different notations. An integrative mechanism with rigorous formal semantics is provided through ontologies. For both, we define suitable ontology languages and techniques. We introduce the ontological tools based on the structure imposed by our architectural approach:

- behaviour through process ontologies in the context of description and modelling,
- refinement in the context of pattern matching,
- connectivity through architectural patterns in the context of transformations.

An ontology-based process-centric service architecture language is the central tool that supports modelling needs arising in our integration framework. The challenge of incorporating ontology technology to enrich architecture abstractions and architecture integration is to find a language that satisfies two criteria: firstly, to integrate business and technology-level descriptions and, secondly,

Figure 6. SAL-level process for the Loan-to-Client Pattern. (© 2008, Veronica Gacitua-Decar. Used with permission.)

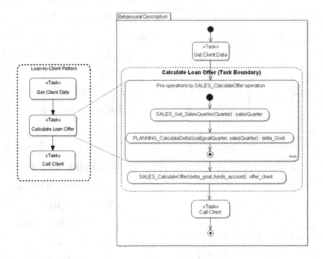

to support pattern formulation, identification and matching for service processes. Ontology languages can provide the required language. Various models are used in the development process, such as a computation-independent business domain models that captures the characteristics of the application domain and a platform-independent, but technology-oriented architecture models that describe the service-based software system in abstract terms.

Figure 7. Ontology-based Semantic Architecture Framework. (© 2008, Veronica Gacitua-Decar. Used with permission.)

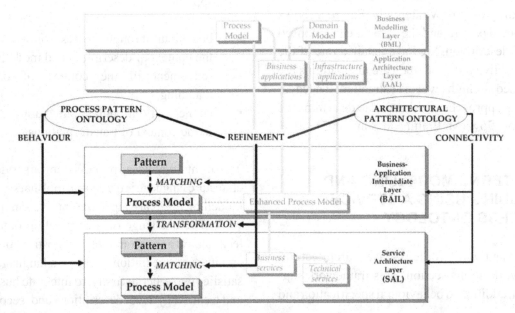

4.1 A Service Process Ontology

The ontological modelling of services is our central concern. We need to look at how these models are used in the business process-driven software development. We can use Semantic Web-based ontologies to formalise and axiomatise business and service processes, i.e. to make statements about processes and to reason about them. Description logic, which is used to define OWL, is based on concept and role descriptions. Concepts represent classes of objects; roles represent relationships between concepts. Concept descriptions are based on logical combinators (negation, conjunction) and hybrid combinators (universal and existential quantification).

We first present a common ontology-based process modelling language, before explaining its application to BPMN, which is the main language for the BML and BAIL. Ontologies are a description of concepts and their relationships. Our solution is based on the service process ontology WSPO. WSPO is based on an extension of description logics. In particular, a rich role expression sublanguage is added to model service processes (Pahl, 2007). Service composition in Web- and other service-oriented environments is interaction. Services are considered as independent concurrent processes that can interact (communicate) with each other. Central in the composition are the interaction connectivity of services and the abstract effect of individual services.

An intuitive approach to represent process interaction behaviour in an ontological form is to consider services as central concepts. We, however, propose a approach that is particularly suitable for the abstract description of service *effects* and service process *connectivity* (Plasil and Visnovsky, 2002). Our objective is to represent services based on inherent notions of state and state transition. States of the systems are the central concepts; transitions (service) are represented as roles, see Figure 8. Service executions lead from old (pre)states to new (post)states, i.e. the service is represented as a role or relationship in an ontological sense (a rectangle in the diagram). For instance, we could specify that a customer may check his/her account balance, or, that a transfer of money must result in a reduction of the source account balance. Usually, relationships in ontologies are used to express static properties, but they can also be seen as accessibility relationships between states of a system. We introduce a basic set of role expressions (composed ontological relationships) as service *connectors* for sequential composition $R;S$, iteration $!R$, choice $R+S$, and concurrency $R \times S$ into a basic ontology language to describe processes. These are common operators in process algebras. Using this language, we can express ordering constraints for services. For instance,

Login; !(BalanceEnq + Transfer)

is a role expression describing a connector process of an online banking user starting with a login, then repeatedly executing balance enquiry or money transfer.

The transitional *connector* roles are complemented by more descriptional *effect* roles. The effect is a contract-based specification of invariants, pre- and postconditions describing the obligations of users and providers. For instance, *preCond* associates a precondition to a prestate; *inSign* associates the type signatures of possible service parameters. Some properties, such as the service name, remain invariant. A logical *effect* specification focussing on safety is

positive(balance) -> Transfer . reduced(balance)

saying that if the account balance is positive, then money can be transferred, resulting in a reduced balance. Here, *Transfer* is the service; *positive(balance)* and *reduced(balance)* are pre- and postcondition, respectively. These conditions are concept expressions. *Transfer* causes a system to transfer from a prestate *pre* to a poststate *post*.

We use a connection between description logic and dynamic logic – a modal logic for the

Figure 8. A Service Process Ontology. (© 2008, Claus Pahl. Used with permission.)

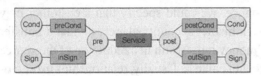

description of programs and processes based on operators to express necessity and possibility (Kozen and Tiuryn, 1990) – to address safety (necessity of behaviour) and liveness (possibility of behaviour) aspects of service process behaviour. The idea behind this is that roles can be interpreted as accessibility relations between states, which are central concepts of process-oriented software systems. We have investigated this from a theoretical perspective in (Pahl, 2007). Although we have introduced an extended role expression sublanguage, the combination of operators still remains decidable.

A more complex example shall illustrate the description of service processes in terms of offered individual services and the connectivity.

```
process BankAccount
   service
      Login
(no:int,user:string): bool
      CheckAcc (dest:int): bool
      Logout (no:int): void
      Balance (no:int): real
      Lodgement
(no:int,sum:real): void
Transfer
(no:int,dest:int,sum:real): void
   connector
      Login; !(Balance+Lodgement
+(Transfer×CheckAcc)); Logout
```

We assume that the bank account process uses services provided elsewhere, such as login, logout and the check-account function:

```
process AccountRegistry
   service
      export CheckAcc (no:int):
bool
   connector
      !CheckAcc

process LoginServer
   service
      export Login
(no:int,user:string): bool
      export Logout (no:int):
void
   connector
      !(Login+Logout)
```

This describes a central online banking process, defined in the *BankAccount* process, that uses (or imports) other services to fulfil its tasks, i.e. *BankAccount* is a client of *AccountRegistry* and *LoginServer*.

Domain models complement the process models at the BML layer. Domain models often form the starting point for software development. Central concepts of a domain have to be identified and described in their properties (as relationships to other concepts). For the banking sector, we identify concepts such as account or account user (which are static objects) and account login, lodgement, and transfer (which are dynamic activities or processes). The capture of these objects and processes is particularly important. Processes for instance are described in terms of the objects they process. The resulting model is a semantic net consisting of (two types of) concepts and roles relating these concepts. A taxonomy, a basic ontology providing a structured vocabulary, shall form the domain model for this investigation.

4.2 A Semantic BPMN Enhancement

BPMN is a standard notation to model business processes that is especially suitable for business analysts. In order to describe processes, the no-

Figure 9. A Semantic BPMN Extension. (© 2008, Claus Pahl. Used with permission.)

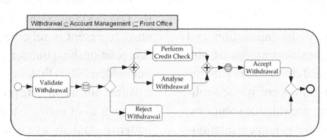

tation provides constructs to represent business events, process steps, elements that control the order of the process steps and elements that groups the previous constructs into organisational roles. It allows the representation of processes owned by one organisation, but also of shared processes between two or more organisations. BPMN allows hierarchical modelling of processes. It provides support to model information flow between process steps.

The provided modelling constructs in BPMN do not support domain modelling. In order to provide traceability between the informational view and the process views at business level, and subsequently at software levels, we have extended BPMN to allow traces with domain model elements and application components through an ontology-based model. The traces provide flow dependencies information among services that guide the technical services composition. Figure 9 shows an extract of the semantic extension of the BPMN notation. Central to ontologies at this layer is the intrinsic specification of process behaviour in the ontology language itself. Behaviour specifications based on the descriptions of necessity and possibility are directly accessible to logic-based methods; behaviour-related inference of service properties is possible. Using the service ontology model from the previous section, we add to BPMN:

- the description of effects as pre/post-conditions, which includes guard conditions that

allows acceptance to be decided if a check has been performed successfully:

PerformedCreditCheck() = true -> Accept Withdrawal . WithdrawalAccepted()

- a domain model taxonomy that relates concept terms used in the process model to the domain ontology – here *Withdrawal*, *AccountManagement* and *FrontOffice* are BML-level information element organised into a hierarchy:

Withdrawal ⊑ AccountManagement ⊑ FrontOffice

- textual representation (and formal semantics) of processes in terms of the connector-based role language, which would result in

Validate Withdrawal ;
(((Perform Credit Check + Analyse Withdrawal) ; Accept Withdrawal)
× Reject Withdrawal)

We have only considered core BPMN constructs here in order to illustrate the principles of ontology-based process modelling. We will consider further concepts later on.

4.3 Process Patterns

Business patterns identify the interaction and structure between users, business processes, and data. Specific integration and composition patterns at a more technical level address enterprise application integration and capture reliable solutions. Patterns as abstractions of quality implementations are discussed from two perspectives:

- ontology-based business pattern representation to capture common business domain and process solutions; business patterns identification guides the services definition;
- ontology-based SOA pattern representation to capture quality IT and software architecture solutions; SOA patterns instantiation improves architecture designs.

The pattern identification and matching process is based on ontology-based matching.

Process patterns are essentially common workflow patterns. These can be operator-oriented, e.g. a multi-choice pattern that allows the selection of a number of options instead of an exclusive selection based on the basic choice operator (Aalst, Hofstede, Kiepuszewski, and Barros, 2003). The other category consists of application context-oriented and often more complex patterns derived from the business context. The bank account process has a common set of account usage activities at its core that can be represented in the form of a pattern:

```
process AccountProcess
  service
     Balance (no:int): real
     Lodgement
(no:int,sum:real): void
     Transfer
(no:int,dest:int,sum:real): void
  connector
     Balance+Lodgement+Transfer
```

Patterns are formulated in the same way as the process connectors. The abstraction that patterns represent is reflected through a subsumption relationship (Baader, McGuiness, Nardi and Schneider, 2003) that we expect to hold between a pattern and a concrete process. Using subsumption instead of instantiation allows us to capture pattern instantiation (e.g. for the operator-oriented ones), but also pattern refinement (e.g. for the domain-specific ones). Process model elements can belong to more than one pattern.

The aim of the pattern support is to identify occurrences of known patterns in a business process. This matching requires technical support, in particular for the formal effect and connector descriptions. Service-based software systems are based on a central state concept; additional concepts for auxiliary aspects such as the pre- and poststate-related descriptions are available. Services are behaviourally characterised by transitional connector roles (state changes) and descriptional roles (auxiliary state descriptions).

The identification of patterns in processes can be implemented based on a graph-theoretic approach, focusing on graphs as the structural backbone of ontologies. The algorithms are based on a graph-centric approach and they consider the restricted vocabulary of different vertical business domains and hierarchical pattern matching. The validation of matching can be based on techniques such as refinement.

In order to support process pattern matching at the SOA level through ontology technology, we need to extend the ontology language. We can make statements about service processes, but we cannot refer to the data elements processed by services. The role (or relationship) expression sublanguage needs to be extended by *names* (representing data elements) and parameters (which are names passed on to services for processing). We can make the bank account *Transfer* service description more precise by using a data variable (*sum*) in pre- and postconditions and as a parameter:

Figure 10. A Semantic SOA Process Model Example. (© 2008, Claus Pahl. Used with permission.)

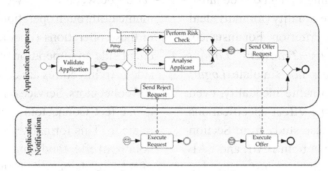

balance >= sum -> Transfer(sum) . balance = balance@pre – sum

decreasing the pre-execution *balance* by *sum*. (Pahl, 2007) describes the ontological details of the names inclusion in service process ontologies. An illustration of adding a *PolicyApplication* data item is presented in Figure 10. This also indicates the intended distributed nature of the application into interacting Request and Notification processes.

4.4 A Technique for Process Pattern Matching

A matching technique needs to be supported by a comparison construct. We already mentioned a refinement notion as a suitable solution. Simulation is the other notion that we apply. This definition, however, needs to be based on the support available in description logics. Subsumption is here the central inference technique. Subsumption is the subclass relationship on concept and role interpretations. We define two types of matching. These correspond to the two role types – effect and connector:

- Service effect (semantics). For individual services, we define a refinement notion based on the design-by-contract principle, i.e. weaker preconditions (allowing a service to be invoked in more states) and stronger postconditions (improving the results of a service execution). For example

true -> Transfer(sum) . balance = balance@pre – sum

matches, i.e. refines

balance >= sum -> Transfer(sum) . balance = balance@pre – sum

as it allows *balance* to be negative due to a weaker, less restrictive precondition *true*.

- Process connector (structure and behaviour). For service processes, we define a simulation notion based on sequential process behaviour. A process matches another process if it can simulate the other's behaviour. For example, the expression

Login; !(BalanceEnq+Transfer); Logout
matches, i.e. simulates
Login; !BalanceEnq; Logout

since the *Transfer* service can be omitted. The provider needs to be able to simulate the process pattern requested by a potential user. Our constructive support for subsumption determination is based on a simulation notion for complex role expressions of the ontology language (Pahl, 2007).

Both forms of matching are sufficient criteria for subsumption between the respective constructs. Matching of effect descriptions is the prerequisite for the assembly of services in architectures and the composition of services to processes. Matching guarantees the proper interaction between composed services in the actual process.

If necessary, a matching variant can be introduced that includes name equality (for individual services) as a matching criterion. For instance, *Login; !(BalanceEnquiry+Transfer); Logout* does not match, i.e. does not simulate *Login; !BalEnq; Logout* due to name inequality, even if the respective semantic effect specifications match. In terms of the case study from Section 3.3, this allows patterns at both BAIL and SAL to be modelled and matched against respective processes (Figure 7).

5 TRANSFORMATIONS AND ALIGNMENT

Structured, pattern-based transformations are the solutions to the IT alignment and traceability problem in relation to business architecture models. Not only functionality, but also the quality of implementations is critical to achieve business goals associated to business models. Therefore, we discuss quality in the context of architectural patterns.

5.1 Metamodels and Structural Connectivity

In order to define the transformation between business and technology layer – more concretely between BAIL and SAL layer – we define metamodels for each layer. The metamodels are captured as an architectural pattern language. At the core of the transformation definition is an architecture metamodel ontology that defines the central architectural concepts. These concepts are five core types of architectural elements:

Architecture, Service, Connector, Effect, Operation

These are derived from a general concept called *Element* that captures all architectural notions. Services and connectors are core elements of architecture descriptions. Services encapsulate computation and connectors represent communi-

cation between the services. Services can communicate through operations. Connectors connect to these operations (operation activation on the client side and operation execution of the server side). Architectures are compositions of services and connectors. Services are described in terms of their effect. Connectors refer to the operations they relate to. This formalises at metamodel level the notions of effect and connectivity. The vocabulary of the five elements is formally defined in terms of a simple logical formulation.

$Service \sqcup Connector \sqcup Effect \sqcup Operation \sqcup Architecture \sqsubseteq Element$

and

$Architecture = \exists\ hasPart\ .\ (Service \sqcup Connector \sqcup Effect \sqcup Operation)$

$Service = Element \sqcap \exists\ hasInterface\ .\ Effect$

$Connector = Element \sqcap \exists\ hasInterface\ .\ Operation$

The predicates *hasPart* and *hasInterface* are predefined relationships between architecture elements. An architecture has parts such as service, connector, effect or operation. The existential qualifier describes that these components might exist. In terms of architecture models, these elements are types, i.e. meta-level constraints for a concrete architecture.

5.2 Architectural Patterns and Quality

Defining a process or a pattern is actually done by extending the basic vocabulary of the metamodel layer from the architecture ontology. Again, we use the subsumption relationship rather than instantiation. This allows us to keep all descriptions at one ontological level, thus simplifying the language framework. This metamodel defines the structural elements of processes. Their semantics and process behaviour are defined through the service process ontology. This approach also allows us to introduce the specific types that form an architectural pattern by defining its structural connectivity, which explains a link to quality considerations. The approach shall be illustrated using the hub-and-spoke architectural pattern. This pattern abstracts a system that manages a composition from a single location, the hub. We start with an extension of the hierarchy of architecture types in order to introduce style-specific services and connectors:

HubSpokeService $\sqsubseteq$ *Service* and *HubSpoke* $\sqsubseteq$ *Connector*

A standard connector, *HubSpoke*, connects hubs and spokes. Further constraints could limit the number of hubs to one:

HubSpokeArchitecture = =1 hasPart. Hub

with *HubSpokeArchitecture* $\sqsubseteq$ *Architecture*. Spokes can be instantiated in any number. These new elements shall be further detailed and restricted to express their semantics. *Hub* and *Spoke* connectivity through input and output ports is defined as follows:

Hub = =10 *hasOperation* $\sqcap$ $\exists$ *hasOperation* . *Input*

Spoke = =1 *hasOperation* $\sqcap$ $\exists$ *hasOperation* . *Output*

This explains that hubs receive up to 10 incoming requests from spokes. A spoke is only connected to one hub. *Hub* and *Spoke* are services of a hub-and-spoke architecture. Each of these services is characterised through the number and types of operations using so-called predicate restrictions on a numerical domain and the usual concept descriptions. The expression $\leq n$ is used to express *hasOperation*.$(n \mid n \leq 1)$. In addition to these structural conditions that define connections between the service types, a number of semantic constraints can be formulated. Disjointness requires the services to be truly different: *Hub* $\sqcap$ *Spoke* $= \bot$; completeness requires hub-and-spoke services to be made up of only the two specified types: *HubSpokeService* = *Hub* $\sqcup$ *Spoke*.

We define an architectural pattern to be a subtype of the architecture type.

PipeFilterPattern $\sqsubseteq$ Architecture

PipeFilterPattern = $\exists$ *hasPart*.

(PipeFilterService $\sqcup$ *PipeFilterConnector* $\sqcup$

Operation)

Architectural patterns can be linked to quality attributes. Some of the advantages of the hub-and-spoke architectural pattern for Web service implementations in terms of quality aspects are, according to (Barrett, Patcas, Murphy and Pahl, 2006):

- Composition is easily maintainable, as composition logic is all contained at a single participant, the central hub.
- Low deployment overhead as only the hub manages the composition.
- Composition can include externally controlled participants. Web service technologies, for instance, would enable the reuse of existing service components.

The main disadvantages of this architectural pattern are:

- A single point of failure at the hub provides poor reliability and availability.
- A communication bottleneck at the hub results in restricted scalability. SOAP messages have considerable overhead for message deserialisation and serialisation.
- The high number of messages between hub and spokes is sub-optimal.

Quality is important to achieve business goals and this quality link can be the driver to select and enforce suitable patterns.

5.3 Transformation Templates

We return to the transformation problem, which we address using pattern-dependent transformations. During the design of service-centric architecture solutions for the EAI problem, business process models are annotated with information of matched business patterns. Matched business patterns define the boundaries of coarse-grained and business-centric services. Each matched pattern has a predefined transformation providing a process-centric service description. A set composed of the pattern, the transformation and the associated service description is named *transformation template*. Similar ideas are presented in (Baresi, Heckel, Thöne and Varro, 2006). While they follow a structural view, we use a process-centric view.

Transformation templates are the building blocks of an incremental transformation from the enhanced business process models (BAL) that contextualise the integration problem into a service-centric solution (SAL) aligned with the business and applications levels. A transformation template refines an enhanced business process model into a service architecture description. Each element's type from an enhanced business process description has a refined version as an element of a service architecture. Particular transformation templates are defined through transformations at metamodel level. The main refinements of elements from BAIL to elements of the service architecture are shown in Table 1. It addresses mappings between the main architectural elements:

- Service & Operation: mapping of service boundaries (pattern-based abstractions)
- Behaviour: mapping of processes and their elements
- Connectivity: mapping of process connectors
- Effect: mapping of in- and output elements and associated effect specifications

The relations among BAIL elements are preserved by the transformation. These relations provide information about the flow dependencies between business services.

Service implementations are constrained by the applications supporting the business processes. Traces between business model elements and applications support the refinement of business services into more concrete services based on the functionality of the applications (Figure 4). The refinement of service connectivity processes and patterns is verifiable through subsumption – available for both the process and the architecture connectivity ontology. Corresponding theory has been developed in (Pahl, 2007).

As Figure 4 shows, the transformation template defined based on the mappings in Table 1 addresses the process models only. Another important component of transformation is the application model. Applications are existing system components that provide business and infrastructure support for the implementation of the SAL design. Central aspects defining their transformation that reflect AAL elements shall be outlined:

- Capabilities (abstraction). An application operation can be traced to a process step in a business process service boundary. In order to provide output and postconditions, an application component traced to a process step might depend on other application components. Those components are also part of the mapping to SAL.
- Behaviour (process elements). Process-centric descriptions of application component capabilities are derived from a refinement of the described process in a business process service boundary. New inputs, outputs, preconditions and postconditions from the technical view in BAIL are introduced to the business view at the same layer. They are mapped to a refined business service interface protocol, which considers constraints from the applications.
- Effects (in/outputs and pre/postconditions). Inputs and preconditions of the application component operations are traced back to business process steps within a business process service boundary. Inputs and preconditions of interface operations of the application participant's interfaces and the outputs and postconditions of the

Table 1. Mapping at Metamodel Level for Transformation Templates.

BAIL (business-oriented)	SAL (business-oriented)
Service & Operation: Abstraction	
Process pattern (business process service boundary)	*Business process-centric service* (port operations)
Behaviour: Process elements	
Process description of business process service boundary	Business *service interface protocol*
Process steps of a business process service boundary	*Business process-centric service interface operation*
Connectivity: Connector elements	
Sequence flow	*sequence orchestration connector* (sequential composition within a specific business service provider)
Message flow	*Sequence choreography connector* (sequential composition of business services)
Gateways XOR, OR, AND	*Exclusive choice* ($\oplus$), *choice* (+), *concurrency* ($\times$) *connectors*, respectively
Indication of *Loop* in a process step or sequence flow connection to an "upstream" process step.	*Iteration connector* (!) for operations associated with process steps of the loop framed by the sequence flow connection to an "upstream" process step.
Effect: In/outputs, pre/postconditions	
Inputs and preconditions of the inbound business process step of a business process service boundary. • Inbound business process step is the initial process step(s) framed by the business service boundary defined by a business process pattern. • Inputs are defined by domain model elements traced with process steps. • Preconditions are defined for each process step.	*Inputs and preconditions* of business process-centric service. Respective elements of business process-centric services: • identified service • input elements • preconditions
Outputs and postconditions of outbound business process step of a business process service boundary. • Outbound business process step is the final process step(s) framed by the business service boundary defined by a business process pattern. • Outputs are defined by domain model elements traced with process steps. • Postconditions are defined for each process step.	*Outputs and postconditions* of business process-centric service. Respective elements of business process-centric services: • identified service • output elements • postconditions

application operations are traced to the business process steps within a business process service boundary.

• Connectivity (connector elements). Process-centric application component connectors (sequential composition, iteration, choice, and concurrency) are mapped to sequential composition (;), iteration (!), choice (+), exclusive choice ($\oplus$) and concurrency ($\times$), respectively.

Several model-driven development approaches have followed a strategy of direct translation from business modelling constructs to software constructs, e.g. direct transformation from BPMN to BPEL constructs. However, business models could contain sections that cause deadlocks and other problems for the process execution (Koehler, Hauser, Küster, Ryndina, Vanhatalo, and Wahler, 2008). In LABAS, the transformation from business models to service architectures is based on pattern-based transformation templates. An advantage of using transformation templates is that they can be designed to provide error-free transformations. Nevertheless, this requires an initial step to refine the business process model to match the business model section of the transformation template. In (Ouyang, Dumas, Hofstede, and Aalst, 2007), a control-flow pattern approach for BPMN-to-BPEL translation is presented. The transformation templates in LABAS follow a similar approach, but also consider application domain-specific patterns. The transformations can be semi-automated where the tool takes the burden of carrying out the transformation and the software architect determines, based on a automated pattern discovery, the relevant patterns to be applied and preserved.

6 DISCUSSION

We use an ontology-based notion of patterns to link business processes and service architectures. Our survey of SOA methodologies and tools has identified this as a weakness in current enterprise modelling. As mentioned in the background section, current support for service architecture definition from business process neglects this aspect. Often, only reference models for specific domains are suggested to map business processes onto architectures. In many cases, these are geared towards a provider's tool landscape. In order to achieve an independent, automatable solution, a more structured and systematic approach to architecture integration needs to be taken.

An ontology-based framework needs an initial investment. Clearly, the benefits that we outlined in the Introduction and the beginnings of the technical sections, needs to make the additional efforts acceptable. In our approach, we expect architectures and patterns to be formulated explicitly, in a notation based on ontologies. We have addressed this concern through the following measures:

- a profile for UML activity diagrams is available, described in (Pahl, 2008), which shields the ontology notation and would not require specific expertise from a developer or software architect who is familiar with a common, de-facto standard such as UML – this reduces the skills gap that developers might face;

- higher degrees of automation in terms of service and pattern identification, architecture generation, and architecture traceability – this provides direct return on investment in terms of the explicit architecture specification;

- maintenance support through explicit and documented traces between business processes and service architectures – this is the benefit from investing into explicit pattern identification and transformation.

A central aim of this chapter is to identify the weaknesses in state-of-the-art in business process-driven SOA and demonstrate potential of ontologies in this context. Our contribution in this respect is a framework consisting of an architectural model (LABAS), an ontology language for service process description based on (WSPO) and techniques for pattern modelling, matching and transformation. Although a full development environment implementing these languages and techniques is still in progress, prototype components for this environment demonstrate central benefits. In particular we have worked on a Jena-based tool to process ontologies, combined with the FaCT description logic reasoner; a range of pattern identification algorithms that detect existing patterns in process descriptions based on different degrees of matching; and a transformation tool that extracts connectivity and process aspects from an architecture model and generates a Web service process (in WS-BPEL and WSDL).

These efforts have supported so far the feasibility of the approach and demonstrate that essential development steps can be automated – either fully or embedded into an interactive process with the developer. A specific aspect that we have already mentioned and that contributes to automation is decidability. Our past investigations into the theoretical aspect confirm that the ontology language presented is decidable. However, extensions or variations of the language might change this property, and consequently impact the automation degree. Another aspect in addition to automation is usability. The critical component is the service process ontology, which might cause problems for developers for two reasons: firstly, unfamiliarity with ontologies in general and, secondly, the fact that a non-standard interpretation (or use) of ontological modelling is applied (processes as roles). To overcome this, and increase the usability, we have developed an extension of UML based on a profile for UML activity diagrams.

7 FUTURE TRENDS

A number of developments will affect the application, but also further research and development of the proposed framework. In particular, we discuss improved maintenance (traceability), support for process ontologies, and model-driven development concerns (transformation customisation) here:

- Traceability Automation. A semantically enhanced solution for Enterprise Application Integration for business processes in service-oriented environments needs to provide a framework that links business and service processes. Consequently, the need to look at service modelling and process transformation emerges. Explicit traces were a key suggestion. However, to fully support traceability and to possibly derive traces automatically, more work needs to be done in terms of ontology integration and mapping, which our use of domain process patterns and architectural pattern ontologies demonstrates.
- Service and Process Ontologies. While ontology-based frameworks to describe structural, static knowledge has been widely explored, the representation of behaviour is less well advanced. In particular, the reasoning support has focused on static relationships such as subsumption and composition. However, representing dynamics directly would require the interpretation of relationships as dynamic dependencies, denoting for example state change. The WSPO framework, which we have used here, is a step in this direction. WSPO and SWSF/FLOWS are more recent process-oriented service ontologies that reflect the need to address composition ontologically. However, this work also demonstrates challenges. For instance, decidability is difficult to achieve, but a necessity for automated support.
- Customisation of Transformations. In terms of transformation, we have focussed on traceability and preservation. However, model-driven development as an emerging software development approach demonstrates the need to address the customisation of transformation in order to deal with specific requirements in terms of for example quality, platform, or language. In particular, directly quality-driven transformation is a promising idea that would allows resulting architectures to be tailored towards selected quality criteria. We have indicated how patterns and qualities can be linked, but more work is needed to influence quality in complex multi-pattern systems.

8 CONCLUSION

Knowledge representation and management is increasingly important in all aspects of information technologies. Knowledge can play a particularly central role in the context of EAI and service-oriented software development. The emergence of the Web as a development and deployment platform for software emphasises this aspect. We have structured a knowledge space based on different ontological techniques for service and application integration in service-oriented architectures. Processes and their behavioural properties and patterns as abstractions were the primary aspects.

We have developed a process-oriented, layered architecture based on an ontological model. The composition of process-oriented services based on ontological descriptions is a central activity. While some of the underlying techniques, for instance for matching, are already used in areas such as component-based software development, it is necessary to used widely accepted languages and techniques specific to the Web platform for Web services-based software development. Explicit, machine-processable knowledge is the key to future automation of development and integration activities. In particular, ontologies have the potential to become an accepted format that supports such an integration and automation endeavour for the SOA platform. Comprehensive tool support for all integration activities, however, remains difficult to achieve. We have demonstrated here the benefit of ontology techniques to support selected activities in the SOA-driven EAI context.

REFERENCES

Aalst, W. M. P., Beisiegel, M., Hee, K. M. V., Konig, D., & Stahl, C. (2007). An SOA-based architecture framework. *International Journal of Business Process Integration and Management*, *2*(2), 91–101. doi:10.1504/IJBPIM.2007.015132

Aalst, W. M. P., Hofstede, A. H. M., Kiepuszewski, B., & Barros, A. P. (2003). Workflow patterns. *Distributed and Parallel Databases*, *14*(1), 5–51. doi:10.1023/A:1022883727209

Allen, R., & Garlan, D. (1997). A formal basis for architectural connection. *ACM Transactions on Software Engineering and Methodology*, *6*(3), 213–249. doi:10.1145/258077.258078

Alonso, G., Casati, F., Kuno, H., & Machiraju, V. (2004). *Web services–concepts, architectures, and applications*. Berlin, Germany: Springer-Verlag.

Baader, F., McGuiness, D., Nardi, D., & Schneider, P. P. (Eds.). (2003). *The description logic handbook*. Cambridge, UK: Cambridge University Press.

Baresi, L., Heckel, R., Thöne, S., & Varro, D. (2006). Style-based modeling and refinement of service-oriented architectures. *Software and Systems Modeling*, *5*(2), 187–207. doi:10.1007/s10270-006-0001-4

Barrett, R., Patcas, L. M., Murphy, J., & Pahl, C. (2006). Model driven distribution pattern design for dynamic Web service compositions. In *International Conference on Web Engineering ICWE06* (pp. 129-136). Palo Alto: ACM Press.

Bass, L., Clements, P., & Kazman, R. (2003). *Software architecture in practice* (2nd edition). *SEI Series in Software Engineering*. Boston, MA: Addison-Wesley.

Bernus, P., Nemes, R., & Schmidt, G. (2003). *Handbook on enterprise architecture (international handbooks on information systems)*. Heidelberg, Germany: Springer-Verlag.

Coalition, O. W. L.-S. (2002). DAML-S: Web services description for the Semantic Web. In I. Horrocks & J. Hendler (Eds.), *Proceedings of the First International Semantic Web Conference ISWC 2002.* (LNCS 2342, pp. 279–291). Berlin, Germany: Springer-Verlag.

Daconta, M. C., Obrst, L. J., & Smith, K. T. (2003). *The Semantic Web*. New York: Wiley.

Dijkman, R. M., & Dumas, M. (2004). Service-oriented design: A multiviewpoint approach. *International Journal of Cooperative Information Systems (IJCIS). Special Issue on Service Oriented Modeling, 13*(4), 337–368.

Djurić, D. (2004). MDA-based ontology infrastructure. [ComSIS]. *Computer Science and Information Systems, 1*(1), 91–116. doi:10.2298/CSIS0401091D

Erl, T. (2004). *Service-oriented architecture: Concepts, technology, and design*. Upper Saddle River, NJ: Prentice Hall.

Erradi, A., Anand, S., & Kulkarni, N. (2006). SOAF: An architectural framework for service definition and realization. *Proceedings of the IEEE International Conference on Services Computing* (pp. 151-158). IEEE Computer Society.

Fettke, P., & Loos, P. (2006). *Reference modeling for business systems analysis*. Hershey, PA: IGI Publishing.

Foster, H., Mukhija, A., Uchitel, S., & Rosenblum, D. (2008). A model-driven approach to dynamic and adaptive service brokering using modes. *Proceedings of 6th International Conference on Service Oriented Computing ICSOC 2008* (pp. 558-564).

Gacitua-Decar, V., & Pahl, C. (2008a). Pattern-based business-driven analysis and design of service architectures. *Proceedings of the 3rd International Conference on Software and Data Technologies* (pp. 252-257).

Gacitua-Decar, V., & Pahl, C. (2008b). Service architecture design for e-businesses: A pattern based approach. *Proceedings of the 9th International Conference on Electronic Commerce and Web Technologies EC-Web08*. (LNCS 5183, pp. 41-50). Berlin, Germany: Springer-Verlag.

Gamma, E., Helm, R., Johnson, R. E., & Vlissides, J. M. (1993). Design patterns: Abstraction and reuse of object-oriented design. *Proceedings of the 7th European Conference on Object-Oriented Programming* (pp. 406-431). Berlin, Germany: Springer-Verlag.

Garlan, D., & Schmerl, B. (2006). Architecture-driven modelling and analysis. *Proceedings of the Eleventh Australian Workshop on Safety Critical Systems and Software-SCS '06* (pp. 3-17). Melbourne, Australia: Australian Computer Society, Inc.

Gašević, D., Devedžić, V., & Djurić, D. (2004). MDA standards for ontology development–tutorial. In *4th International Conference on Web Engineering ICWE2004*, Galway, Ireland. Retrieved on December 9, 2008, from http://afrodita.rcub.bg.ac.yu/~gasevic/tutorials/ICWE2004/

Grønmo, R., Jaeger, M. C., & Hoff, H. (2005). Transformations between UML and OWLS. In A. Hartman & D. Kreische (Eds.), *Model-driven architecture–foundations and applications*. (LNCS 3748, pp. 269–283). Berlin, Germany: Springer-Verlag.

Koehler, J., Hauser, R., Küster, J., Ryndina, K., Vanhatalo, J., & Wahler, M. (2008). The role of visual modeling and model transformations in business-driven development. (ENTCS 211, pp. 5-15). Amsterdam, The Netherlands: Elsevier Science Publishers B. V.

Kozen, D., & Tiuryn, J. (1990). Logics of programs. In J. van Leeuwen (Ed.), *Handbook of theoretical computer science, vol. b* (pp. 789–840). Amsterdam, The Netherlands: Elsevier Science Publishers.

Lara, R., Stollberg, M., Polleres, A., Feier, C., Bussler, C., & Fensel, D. (2005). Web service modeling ontology. *Applied Ontology, 1*(1), 77–106.

McIlraith, S., & Martin, D. (2003). Bringing semantics to Web services. *IEEE Intelligent Systems*, *18*(1), 90–93. doi:10.1109/MIS.2003.1179199

McIlraith, S., & Son, T. C. (2002). Adapting golog for composition of Semantic Web services. *Proceedings of the Eighth International Conference on Principles of Knowledge Representation and Reasoning* (pp. 482-493).

Object Management Group. (2003a). *MDA model-driven architecture guide v1.0.1. OMG*. Retrieved on September 9, 2008, from www.omg.org/docs/omg/03-06-01.pdf

Object Management Group. (2003b). *Ontology definition metamodel-request for proposal (OMG Document: as/2003-03-40). OMG*. Retrieved on September 9, 2008, from http://www.omg.org/docs/ad/03-03-40.pdf

Ouyang, C., Dumas, M., Hofstede, A. H. M., & Aalst, W. M. P. (2007). Pattern-based translation of BPMN process models to BPEL web services. [JWSR]. *International Journal of Web Services Research*, *5*(1), 42–62.

Pahl, C. (2007). An ontology for software component matching. *International Journal on Software Tools for Technology Transfer (STTT) . Special Edition on Foundations of Software Engineering*, *9*(2), 169–178.

Pahl, C. (2008). Semantic model-driven development of Web service srchitectures. [IJWET]. *International Journal of Web Engineering and Technology*, *4*(3), 386–404. doi:10.1504/IJWET.2008.019540

Pahl, C., Giesecke, S., & Hasselbring, W. (2007). An ontology-based approach for modelling architectural styles. *First European Conference on Software Architecture ECSA 2007* (pp. 60-75). Berlin, Germany: Springer-Verlag.

Papazoglou, M. P., & van den Heuvel, W. J. (2006). Service-oriented design and development methodology. *Int. J. of Web Engineering and Technology*, *2*(4), 412–442. doi:10.1504/IJWET.2006.010423

Payne, T., & Lassila, O. (2004). Semantic Web services. *IEEE Intelligent Systems*, *19*(4), 14–15. doi:10.1109/MIS.2004.29

Plasil, F., & Visnovsky, S. (2002). Behavior protocols for software components. *ACM Transactions on Software Engineering*, *28*(11), 1056–1075. doi:10.1109/TSE.2002.1049404

Semantic Web Services Language (SWSL) Committee. (2006). *Semantic Web services framework (SWSF)*. Retrieved on September 9, 2008, from http://www.daml.org/services/swsf/1.0/

Steen, M. W. A., Strating, P., Lankhorst, M. M., Doest, H. W. L., & Iacob, M. E. (2005). In Z. Stojanovic & A. Dahanayake (Eds.), *Service-oriented enterprise architecture. Service-oriented software system engineering: Challenges and practices* (pp. 132-154). Hershey, PA: Idea Group.

Zdun, U., & Dustdar, S. (2007). Model-driven and pattern-based integration of process-driven SOA models. *International Journal of Business Process Integration and Management*, *2*(2), 109–119. doi:10.1504/IJBPIM.2007.015135

Chapter 4
Agent–Driven Semantic Interoperability for Cross–Organisational Business Processes

Ingo Zinnikus
German Research Center for Artificial Intelligence (DFKI) GmbH, Germany

Christian Hahn
German Research Center for Artificial Intelligence (DFKI) GmbH, Germany

Klaus Fischer
German Research Center for Artificial Intelligence (DFKI) GmbH, Germany

ABSTRACT

In cross-organisational business interactions, integrating different partners raises interoperability problems especially on the technical level. The internal processes and interfaces of the participating partners are often pre-existing and have to be taken as given. This imposes restrictions on the possible solutions for the problems which occur when partner processes are integrated. The aim of this chapter is the presentation of a three-tier framework for managing and implementing interoperable and cross-organizational business processes. Thereby the authors want to fill the gap currently existing between processes defined on a strategic level and executed models. We describe a solution which supports rapid prototyping by combining a model-driven framework for cross-organisational business processes with an agent-based approach for flexible process execution. We show how the W3C recommendation for Semantic Web service descriptions can be combined with the model-driven approach for rapid service integration.

INTRODUCTION

Today's enterprises operate in a dynamic environment which is characterized by global outsourcing,

shrinking product life-cycles, and unstable demand. To prosper in this environment, enterprises face a growing need to share information and to collaborate at all levels of the value chain. As organizations are gradually transforming into "networked organiza-

DOI: 10.4018/978-1-60566-804-8.ch004

tions", interoperability becomes the main challenge to realize the vision of seamless business interaction across organizational boundaries.

In cross-organisational business interactions, the most desirable solution for integrating different partners would suggest to integrate their processes and data on a rather low level. However, the internal processes and interfaces of the participating partners are often pre-existing and have to be taken as given. Furthermore, in cross-organisational scenarios partners are typically very sensitive about their product data and the algorithms that process it. In many cases, private processes are only partially visible and hidden behind public interface descriptions (Schulz & Orlowska, 2004). This imposes restrictions on the possible solutions for the problems which occur when partner processes are integrated.

Service-oriented architectures (SOA) (Erl, 2005) are today's favourite answer to solve interoperability issues. It enables partners to offer the functionality of their systems via a public service interface (e.g. as WSDL[1] description) and hide the sensitive parts behind it. A very important second advantage of SOA is the possibility of a loose coupling of partners. New partners can enter the system with little effort whereas obsolete partners are able to leave it easily. Especially in the case where e.g. additional smaller non-Original Equipment Manufacturers (OEM) are integrated in a sales process, the system needs to become robust against temporary unavailable partners.

Despite the advantages of a SOA, several difficulties arise especially in the case where the systems of the partners have evolved independently for several years:

- The philosophies of the systems differ, e.g. one partner service uses a strict sequential run through the product space whereas another service allows e.g. randomly browsing through the products and product features.
- The granularity of operations of the various partner services differs.

- Non-functional aspects such as exception handling, session management, transactional demarcation, which differ from partner to partner, supersede the core functionality of the services.
- Structural differences in the payload data of the exchanged messages stemming from data models used by the different partners' sites are present.
- Semantical and pragmatic misunderstandings of the exchanged messages may arise due to different tagging of business data, different conventions, protocols etc.

These are typical interoperability problems occurring in cross-organisational scenarios which require SOA-based solutions. The European FP6 project ATHENA (Advanced Technologies for interoperability of Heterogeneous Enterprise Networks and their Applications) provided a comprehensive set of methodologies and tools to address interoperability problems of enterprise applications in order to realize seamless business interaction across organizational boundaries.

A core idea in the ATHENA project was to bring together different approaches and to combine them into a new framework: a modelling approach for designing collaborative business processes (CBP), a *model-driven* development framework for SOAs and an *agent-based* approach for flexible execution (see Figure 1). For modelling SOAs a platform independent metamodel for SOAs (PIM-4SOA, Benguria et al., 2006) was developed in ATHENA. It turned out that these approaches fit nicely together, as e.g. the PIM4SOA metamodel and the agents' metamodel bear a striking resemblance to each other.

The agent paradigm can be considered as promising approach to executable SOA in a nice manner. Several agent-based programming platforms exist to implement agent systems that offer different advantages when executing SOA. For the purpose of improving the interoperability between those platforms, we investigated a plat-

Figure 1. ATHENA approach for model-driven development of collaborative business processes

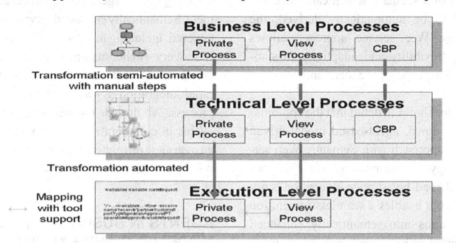

form independent modelling language for MAS called PIM4Agents (Hahn, 2008) that provides a link to existing programming languages based on the principles of model-driven development.

Combining Semantically Enhanced Service-Oriented Architectures with Model-Driven Development of Agent Systems

In principle, the model-driven development approach allows specifying a custom-tailored workflow which incorporates the practical experience of business analysts and developers. Despite the rather static nature of many business scenarios, points or situations of choice occur, where the specific partners which deliver a specific task, e.g. a carrier service, can be selected at design or even at execution time, thus allowing a certain degree of flexibility in business service provisioning if semantically-enriched information is available. However, since the existing standards for business services lack *semantics*, the meaningful integration of services exclusively relies on human business domain experts (Kaiser, 2007). In contrast, Semantic Web service technology adds expressivity to existing Web service standards by introducing well-formed semantics, which simple

Web service descriptions are lacking, and envisages the automated and meaningful composition of complex business services through logic-based reasoning upon their semantic annotations. However, in many real-world cases of business process modeling among contracted and trusted business partners, the fully automated coordination of partly unknown business Web services, as envisaged by the Semantic Web service community, is neither adequate nor efficient in practice.

This short discussion already reveals that both approaches—model-driven development as well as Semantic Web services—have their pros and cons when used to integrate external, outsourced business services. However, the commonality that both approaches envision intelligent agents to be key enabler for service composition and coordination results in the following statements:

- *Agent technology* makes both concurrent technologies, *model-driven development* and *Semantic Web services*, more convergent to realize efficient and meaningful agent-based coordination of pervasive business services in practice
- It is possible to harness the benefits of both for this purpose. While a modelling approach is necessary for capturing complex

aspects of a scenario which cannot be expected to be automatically derived, the Semantic Web service approach allows adding flexibility and adaptivity to standard business process execution.

The chapter shows in detail that the combination of a top-down, agent-based model-driven development approach with Semantic Web service technology for business service discovery and, eventually, ad-hoc service invocation is not only feasible but enables a seamless integration of agent systems into semantically enhanced service-oriented architectures. In previous work we already demonstrated how agent technologies can be integrated with a model-driven approach to system design (Kahl et al., 2006) and standard approaches to the design of service-oriented architectures (Fischer, Hahn & Madrigal-Mora, 2007). In the following, we describe our end-to-end tool chain which supports a model-driven approach, including metamodels based on Ecore format, a graphical editor for visually designing the artefacts and model-to-model and model-to-text transformations for generating executables. Based on the current work in FP7 projects COIN[2] and SHAPE[3], we show that a seamless integration of Semantic Web services with agent technologies enables semantic enterprise application integration.

Structure of the Book Chapter

The structure of this chapter is the following: We introduce and discuss the key concepts and technologies used. A methodology for agent-based, model-driven development of SOAs will be presented as outlined in (Kahl et al., 2006) and (Zinnikus, Hahn & Fischer, 2008). Then, the scenario of a pilot application of the ATHENA approach to interoperability is introduced. We discuss the interoperability problems to be solved, followed by a section in which a platform independent metamodel for multiagent systems based on (Hahn 2008) is introduced, as well as

mappings to an agent-based execution environment. Semantically enhanced service integration is covered, including the usage of Semantic Service Discovery (matchmaking) for flexible service provisioning and the usage of SAWSDL for rapid integration of services into a collaborative process. We discuss the advantages of applying agents in collaborative business scenarios, give an overview on related work and close the chapter with a summary and an outlook.

AGENTS IN BUSINESS PROCESS MODELLING AND EXECUTION

Partners in inter-organizational collaborations are autonomous, socially cooperating and co-ordinating by exchanging information (sending messages) and share a need to adapt to changing environments. Thus, they display features which are often attributed to *agents*.

There is still an ongoing debate about exactly which properties characterise agents, but the following definition has found common consent:

An agent is an encapsulated computational system that is situated in some environment, and that is capable of flexible, autonomous action in that environment in order to meet its design objectives (Wooldridge, 1997).

In this definition **flexible** requires the agent to exhibit pro-active, reactive, and social behaviour. We can therefore define the **key** properties of agents as:

- **autonomy**: agents are clearly identifiable problem solving entities — with well-defined boundaries and interfaces — which have control both over their internal state and over their own behaviour.
- **reactivity**: agents are situated (embedded) in a particular environment, i.e. they receive inputs related to the state of their environment through sensors. They then respond in a timely fashion, and act on the

environment through effectors to satisfy their design objectives.

- **pro-activeness**: agents do not simply act in response to their environment, they are designed to fulfill a specific purpose, i.e. they have particular objectives (goals) to achieve. Agents are therefore able to exhibit goal-directed behaviour by **taking the initiative** and opportunistically adopting new goals.
- **social ability**: agents are able to cooperate with humans and other agents in order to achieve their design objectives.

Agent-oriented **interactions** usually occur through a **high level (declarative) agent communication language**. Consequently, **interactions are conducted at the knowledge level**, that is, the semantic level (Newell, 1982), in terms of which goals should be followed, at what time, and by whom. In most cases, agents act to achieve objectives either on behalf of individuals/companies or as part of some wider problem solving initiative. Thus, when agents interact there is typically some underpinning organizational context. This context defines the nature of the relationship between the agents.

Drawing these points together, the essential concepts of agent-based computing are: agents are capable of highly autonomous behaviour, representing **encapsulations of computational entities and functions, high level inter-actions and organizational relationships within a society of agents** situated **in their environment**.

In cross-organizational business scenarios, interactions are based on message exchanges. Here, messages must convey the semantics of data (the intension and extension of expressions used), as well as their pragmatics (the interpretation of information in different contexts). In one context, a specific message, e.g. a *purchase order*, must be followed by a *confirm* message, in another context a reject message may be allowed. Hence, for specifying interactions, protocols define the admissible sequences of messages. Agent-oriented research has adopted insights from speech act theory (Searle, 1969) and proposed the FIPA (Foundation for Intelligent Physical Agents) protocol and communicative act specification (FIPA, 2000).

Agent and multiagent systems (MAS) research can be seen as branch of Artificial Intelligence (AI). One of the most influential textbooks on AI even considers agent-oriented research as encompassing the subfields of AI (Russell & Norvig, 1995). The Semantic Web initiative on the other hand emerged from AI and is at least in parts motivated by ideas of agent-oriented research (Hendler, 2001). The Semantic Web builds on results from AI, in particular Description (and other) Logics, as theoretical foundation. Basic reasoning tasks such as subsumption and consistency checking of expressions are used e.g. as technique in Semantic Web service matchmaking (for a survey of service matchmaking techniques, see Klusch, 2008). However, in business scenarios, instance checking is more important, e.g. realization, which finds the most specific concept an individual object is an instance of; and retrieval, which finds the individuals in the knowledge base that are instances of a given concept, e.g. retrieving all instances of the concept *Customer* which have a *validCreditCard*. These can all be accomplished by means of instance checking, which itself, from the perspective of Description Logics, is reducible to consistency checking.

Agents and Service-Oriented Architectures

SOAs as an architectural style for distributed systems have steadily been gaining momentum over the last few years and are now considered as mainstream in enterprise computing. Compared to earlier middleware products, SOAs put a stronger emphasis on loose coupling between the participating entities in a distributed system. The four fundamental tenets of Service Orientation capture the essence of SOAs: explicit boundaries, autonomy of services, declarative interfaces, data formats and policy-based service description.

Web Services are the technology that is most often used for implementing SOAs. Web Services are a standards-based stack of specifications that enable interoperable interactions between applications that use the Web as a technical foundation (Booth, 2004). The emphasis on loose coupling also means that the same degree of independence can be found between the organisations that build the different parts of an SOA. The teams involved only have to agree on service descriptions and policies at the level of abstraction prescribed by the different Web Service standards.

Web services are supported by a stack of Internet standards (HTTP, XML, SOAP, WSDL, and UDDI) which needed to be complemented by a process layer, since business scenarios are process-driven. The term process-driven emphasizes the importance of process models created on the preliminary engineering layer. At the execution layer, these models are used for process orchestration. *Orchestration* in this context describes the composition of business objects in a process flow. In detail, it defines a complex interaction between business objects, including business logic and execution order of the interactions. Without orchestrating business objects, the overall context between the single process steps would be lost. Collaboration partners must be enabled to access data and applications in an easy and secure way. *Choreographies* on the other hand define collaborations between interacting parties.

The similarities between agent architectures and SOAs have already been recognized (e.g. Singh & Huhns, 2005). There is a still ongoing discussion about the relation between Web services and agents (Dickinson & Wooldridge, 2005; Payne, 2008). A crucial feature of agents is, in our view, the use of an *explicit* and, in most cases publicly available, i.e. not "mental" *representation* of entities in the collaboration (services, contracts, protocols) for reasoning and decision-making.

WSDL is e.g., an explicit, publicly available (if stored in a UDDI registry) representation about technical aspects of a service, but it can hardly be used for reasoning or decision-making. Its main purpose is to support the (mainly manual) integration of a service. The Semantic Web initiative took up this challenge and developed a set of formalisms for semantic markup of services and other entities.

In the vision of Semantic Web services (Studer, Grimm & Abecker, 2007), creating semantic markup of Web services makes them machine understandable and use-apparent. Based on that, agent technologies can be developed that exploit this semantic markup to support automated Webservice composition and interoperability. Driving the development of the markup and agent technology are the automation tasks that semantic markup of Web services will enable — in particular, service discovery, execution, and composition and interoperation.

Several proposals for semantically enhanced service descriptions were submitted for standardisation, namely, OWL-S (Martin et al., 2004), WSMO (de Bruijn et al. 2005) and SAWSDL (Farrell & Lausen, 2007), which has just reached the status of a proposed recommendation within W3C. SAWSDL extends the de-facto standard for service description (WSDL) by annotating elements in a service description and providing schema mappings for transformation of data. The annotation of elements can be used for service discovery whereas the mapping information can be used for invocation of a service. It is this latter feature which makes SAWSDL an interesting candidate for service integration, because, based on a well established standard (WSDL), a service provider can supply its partners not only with a syntactical description of her service interface via a WSDL file, but additionally with the information required for ad-hoc invocation of his service.

In our approach, we use a model-driven approach for the integration of existing services and, by using SAWSDL service descriptions, show how a SAWSDL description of partner services can be used to accelerate the integration process.

Model-Driven Development and EAI

The Object Management Group's (OMG) Model-Driven Architecture (MDA) (Object Management Group, 2006; Kleppe, Warmer & Bast, 2003) promotes the production of models with sufficient detail that they can be used to generate executable software. In a model-driven development process, three fundamental models are distinguished: a computation-independent model (CIM), a platform-independent model (PIM) and a platform-specific model (PSM). A CIM is a model which describes the area of application and contains no details of the technical aspects of the system. CIM models are analysis models of applications. An analysis model is derived from reality with the goal of a better understanding. A PIM is a model which represents a platform with a specific degree of independence from implementation details, in order to be usable for different execution platforms of a similar kind. The PIM models are application design models. A PSM is a model that instantiates a PIM and provides it with details, which are specific to a certain kind of execution platform. MDA supports the transformation from reusable models to executable software.

Artefacts generated with the model-driven approach are normally only used at design-time. In order to really display agent-like behaviour, participants in an interaction need explicit representations of activities (processes, protocols, negotiations) and entities (services, contracts) for decision-making and reasoning. Thus, the availability and usage of such explicit representation for decision-making during runtime is a crucial and distinguishing feature of agent-behaviour also in SOAs and business contexts.

EAI is, in general, a design-time problem. The main goal is to achieve a dependable execution of business processes within and across organizational boundaries and frictionless information exchange. In contrast, agent-like behaviour in agent-oriented systems is displayed during runtime, when adaptive decisions and behaviour is required. However, for agents in order to communicate and cooperate, basic interoperability issues have to be resolved already during design-time. Solutions for common message formats and pragmatics, data semantics and transportation issues have to be provided in advance.

When integrating partners into a collaborative process, interoperability problems occur on a syntactical as well as on a semantical level (Omelayenko & Fensel, 2001). For solving the interoperability problems related to service and process integration, the Semantic Web initiative proposed to harness formalized knowledge representation, i.e. ontologies, for aligning heterogeneous models.

Agent research contributes significantly to solving these problems with techniques and methodologies. Model-driven, agent-based systems combined with Semantic Web technology furthermore help to design inter-organizational workflows such that there is local autonomy without compromising the consistency of the overall process.

METHODOLOGY

Business process modeling is a complicated process and it is obvious that different modeling approaches have their strengths and weaknesses in different aspects due to the variety of their underlying formalisms. There are many well-known problems regarding process modeling methodologies, such as the classic tradeoff between expressivity of the modeling language and complexity of model checking. Some languages offer richer syntax sufficient to express most relevant business activities and their relationships in the process model, while some provide more generic modeling constructs which facilitate efficient verification of the process model at design time.

The successful modeling and implementation of collaborative business processes (CBP) requires a clear understanding of the common processes across all stakeholders involved. There is also a need for a structured approach towards mapping internal (private) business processes of an enterprise onto a CBP. Ideally, the implementation of CBPs starts on a strategic level using enterprise models to identify business structures between and within companies as well as their interrelations. The main target is to achieve a common agreement between all stakeholders (process owners). Based on this agreement an interim level between design and execution (process engineering level) is used to perform a detailed execution-oriented modeling and evaluation in a platform independent way.

The approach consists of three steps: (1) create a common understanding of the inter-organizational workflow by specifying the shared public workflow, (2) partition the public workflow over the organizational entities involved, and (3) for each organizational entity: create a private workflow which is a subclass of the relevant part of the public workflow.

Following this approach, designing SOAs top-down, starting from the enterprise level, involves several different stakeholders within and between enterprises. In order to support the various views pertinent to these stakeholders, we have defined a Model-driven Development (MDD) framework. The MDD framework partitions the architecture of a system into several *visual* models at different abstraction levels subject to the concerns of the stakeholders. This allows important decisions regarding integration and interoperability to be made at the most appropriate level and by the best suited and knowledgeable people. The models are also subject for semi-automatic model transformations and code generation to alleviate the software development and integration processes.

In order to fill the gap currently existing between processes defined on a strategic enterprise level and executed models (cf. Fig. 1), we present

a three-tier framework for managing and implementing interoperable and cross-organizational business processes. Though it is possible to execute CBPs with the help of traditional means, e.g. communicating workflow engines or e-business protocols like RosettaNet, the use of agents for implementation seems to offer various advantages. The approach in this chapter describes the conceptual preparation of CBPs independent of specific techniques used for execution. However, the authors consider the potentials of their execution offered by agents in comparison to other state of art techniques like WS-BPEL engines.

The three levels are similar to the different types of models used in model-driven architectures (Object Management Group, 2006). However, as the focus is specifically on modelling CBPs, different names are chosen for the three levels in order to distinguish this approach from the general approach of model-driven architectures (i.e. CIM, PIM and PSM):

Collaboration Strategy: This level represents the business view on the cooperation and describes the interaction of the partners. The CBPs modeled on this level allow analyzing business aspects like costs, involved resources etc.

Process Engineering: This level provides a more detailed view on the CBP representing the complete control flow of the process. Also the message exchange between single tasks is modeled on this level and can thereby be analyzed. However, the control flow and the message exchange are specified in a platform independent manner. This supports reuse of the process models as the models on this level can be ported to various means of execution.

Process Execution: On this level the CBP is specified in the modeling language of a concrete business process engine. It is extended with platform specific interaction information, e.g., concrete message formats sent or received during CBP execution or the specification of particular data sources providing data during process execution.

The second dimension deals with the question of hiding sensitive information in a collaborative scenario. Within the framework we distinguish private knowledge, which is internal to a company, from local knowledge, which still is confidential but is necessary for implementing the collaboration and should be shared bilaterally. In contrast to private and local knowledge, global knowledge is essential for all companies (e.g. if a company leaves the network or a product is not available anymore) and should be accessible for all partners of the network.

SCENARIO

In 2002, due to new laws in EU legislation, the market of car distribution changed fundamentally. Instead of being limited to selling only one brand, vending vehicles of different brands under one roof was facilitated. Dealers now can reach a broader audience and improve their business relations for more competitiveness. As a consequence, many so-called *multi-brand dealers* have appeared.

Today, multi-brand dealers are confronted with a huge set of problems. Rather than having to use the IT system of one specific car manufacturer, multi-brand dealers are now faced with a number of different IT systems from their different manufacturers. One specific problem is the integration of configuration, customization and ordering functionality for a variety of brands into the IT landscape of a multi-brand dealer.

In this chapter, the business cases we are looking at are such multi-brand dealers. Multi-branding seamlessly offers products of different brands in one coherent sales process. This establishes a certain level of comparability among products of different brands and provides added value to the customers, thus strengthens the competitiveness of multi-brand dealers. However, multi-branding calls for an increased level of interoperability among the dealer on one side and the different manufacturers on the other side.

Today, however, systems for car configuration and order processing of different car manufacturers are isolated systems and not integrated into the dealer specific IT landscape. Thus, multi-brand dealers are faced with a simple multiplication of IT systems to support their pre-sales, sales and after-sales processes. As a consequence, one of the desired advantages of multi-branding, namely to seamlessly offer cars of different car manufactures and to establish comparability among the different products is seriously put at stake. We rather observe the phenomenon of what we call *early brand selection*, i.e. a customer has to choose his desired brand at the beginning and then go all the way through its brand-specific product configuration and order process. Changing the brand later means starting the process all over from the beginning.

We describe an integrated scenario, where multi-brand dealers use services provided by the different car and non-OEM manufactures and plug them into an integrated dealer system.

The desired to-be-scenario with its general architecture is depicted in Figure 2. The systems of the different car and non-OEM manufacturers are integrated via an integrator component. This integrator enables the dealer to access the software of the manufacturers in a uniform manner. The chapter will focus on the manufacturer integration and present the model-driven, agent-based integration approach for cross-organizational processes modeling.

For the service integrator, the generated process models are executed as software agents on Jack (JACK Intelligent Agents, 2006), an agent platform based on the BDI-agent theory (belief-desire-intention, Rao & Georgeff, 1991). In the following, we will describe this approach in detail.

Figure 2. Overview over the architecture of the solution

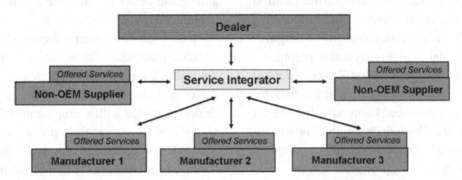

INTEROPERABILITY ISSUES

As can be seen from the description of the scenario, the setting includes a complex interaction between the partners. The design of such a scenario implies a number of problems which have to be solved:

- the partners expect and provide different data structures (data heterogeneity)
- the different partners (may) expect different atomic protocol steps (service granularity)
- changing the protocol and integration of a new partner should be possible in a rapid manner (scalability)
- the execution of the message exchange should be flexible, i.e. in case a partner is unavailable or busy, the protocol should nevertheless proceed

These are typical interoperability problems occurring in cross-organisational scenarios which in our case have to be tackled with solutions for SOAs. A core idea in the ATHENA project was to bring together different approaches and to combine them into a new framework: a modelling approach for designing collaborative processes, a model-driven development framework for SOAs and an agent-based approach for flexible execution.

Data heterogeneity is tackled with transformations which are specified at design-time and executed at run-time by transforming the exchanged messages based on the design-time transforma-

tions. Transformations can be defined horizontally, e.g. between two different XML schemas, or vertically, e.g. between a representation on the ontological level and the concrete data structure of a service (i.e. again an XML schema). Here, issues concerning semantic integration become prevalent. As we will see, vertical transformations between a common ontology and the local data formats of the partners are a possibility to introduce flexibility into a collaborative process. Semantic Web services provide the necessary ingredients for this step.

The problem of different service granularity, which is itself an aspect of semantic integration, is solved by specifying a collaborative protocol which allows adapting to different service granularities. Adaptation to different service granularity is done on a PIM level by abstracting from differences in the concrete details of service invocation.

Scalability is envisaged by applying a model-driven approach: the protocol is specified on a platform-independent level so that a change in the protocol can be made on this level and code generated automatically. Finally, flexibility is achieved by applying a BDI agent-based approach. BDI agents provide flexible behaviour e.g. for exception-handling (service failures) in a natural way (compared to e.g. BPEL4WS where specifying code for faults often leads to complicated, nested code).

MODEL-DRIVEN PROTOCOL MEDIATION AND THE COMMON DATA MODEL

Process and Protocol Mediation

When the interaction protocol that a given service provides does not match the interaction protocol it is expected to provide, there are basically two options: (1) modify the service to suit the new expected interaction protocol; or (2) mediate between the interaction protocol of the service as it is, and the interaction protocol as it should be. The former option is usually not suitable because the same service may interact with other services that rely on the interaction protocol that the service currently provides. In other words, the same service may participate in different collaborations such that in each of these collaborations a different interaction protocol is expected from it. Thus, mediation between the *provided interaction protocol* of a service, and the various interaction protocols that are expected from it (i.e., the *required interaction protocols*), is generally unavoidable. A manufacturer M_1 may expect one message from the service integrator whereas a manufacturer M_2 expects a two-step invocation with a loop involved (see Figure 3 for a mediation of different service granularities from the viewpoint of the service integrator).

This issue has been widely studied in the area of software components where it is known as *adaptation*. Since services are expected to participate in collaborations driven by process models, behavioural mediation is a prominent requirement. Some work has been done in this area both in the components and services community (e.g. Benatallah et al., 2005), but there is still no overarching framework and supporting tools for behavioural service mediation are missing.

For integrating consortial partners and their services, partners define the shared process as well as the Common Data Model (CDM) together. The CDM defines the application domain on an intensional level. In the CDM, representation of data is done on the ontological level.

Most of the work on component adaptation focuses on structural mediation (i.e., mediating different structural interfaces and specifically, between different data types). Roughly speaking, two alternatives are possible, analogous to the local-as-view vs. global-as-view distinction (Lenzerini, 2002): the common data structure is defined independently from the local data model of each partner. Each partner then defines a (local) mapping from the common data model to the local model. The main advantage of this approach is scalability, i.e. the number of mappings which have to be specified is reduced from $m \cdot n$ (in the case of m partners interacting directly with n partners) to $m + n$ (Fensel et al. 2001).

The mapping in turn can be executed (at runtime) either by the consumer of the service or the partner service itself. The first solution is the one preferred by Semantic Web service approaches, e.g. SAWSDL where the service provider describes the mapping to e.g. XML Schema. The mapping is used by a service consumer who invokes the service. The second solution means that the service consumer always sends the same message (e.g. a SOAP message) to a partner service and does not care about the local data model. This is reasonable if specifying as well as testing the mapping is tedious and the mapping underlies many changes.

In a global-as-view approach, the common data model is defined as view on the local data models of the partners. A disadvantage of this approach is that the integration of a new partner requires changing the common data model.

PIM4AGENTS, A METAMODEL FOR AGENT-BASED SYSTEMS

For modelling MAS and in particular the protocol and the common data model, we developed a platform independent modeling language for MAS

Figure 3. Behaviour model for adapting to different service granularity

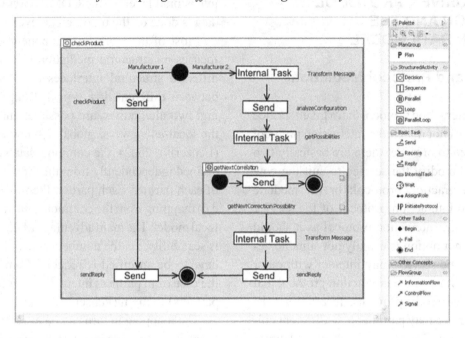

called domain-specific language for multiagent systems (DSML4MAS). The abstract syntax of this language is defined by a platform independent metamodel for MAS called PIM4Agents which uses the ontology definition metamodel (ODM) (Kendall, 2006) for describing the common data model.

The PIM4Agents (Hahn, Madrigal-Mora & Fischer, 2008; Hahn, 2008) that defines the abstract syntax of modelling language for multiagent systems is a visual platform-independent model that specifies multiagent systems in a technology independent manner. It represents an integrated view on agents in which different components can be deployed on different execution platforms. The PIM4Agents metamodel defines modelling concepts that can be used to model six different aspects or views of an agent system that are listed below:

- **Agent aspect** describes single autonomous entities, the capabilities they have to solve tasks and the roles they play within the MAS. The agent aspect is centered on the concept of *Agent*, the autonomous entity capable of acting in the environment. An *Agent* has access to a set of Resources from its surrounding *Environment*. These *Resources* may include information or ontologies the *Agent* has access to. Furthermore, the *Agent* can perform particular *DomainRoles* that define in which specific context the *Agent* is acting and *Behaviours* that define how particular tasks are achieved. Furthermore, the *Agent* may have certain *Capabilities* that represent the set of *Behaviours* the *Agent* can possess. In addition to the various agent types, the system designer can define which *AgentInstances* conforming to its particular agent type are created at run-time.

- **Organization aspect** describes how autonomous entities cooperate within the MAS and how complex organizational structures can be defined. An *Organization* defines the social structure *Agents* can take part in. The *Organization* is a special kind of *Agent* and can therefore perform *DomainRoles* and have *Capabilities* which can be performed by its members. In addition to the *Agent* properties, an *Organization* may have its own internal *Protocols* specifying (i) how the *Organization* communicates with other *Agents* be them atomic *Agents* or complex *Organizations* and (ii) how organizational members are coordinated.

- **Role aspect** covers feasible specializations of the *Role* concept (i.e. *DomainRoles* used to partition the organizational space and *Actors* used to define the message exchange within *Protocols*) and how they could be related to each other. The *Role* specifies the responsibilities of the *Agent* in terms of (i) *Capabilities* and *Resource* that need to be provided by the *Agents* and (ii) *Capabilities* and *Resource* that are provided to the *Agent* performing this *Role*.

- **Interaction aspect (see**Figure 4**)** describes how the interaction between autonomous entities or organizations takes place. Each interaction specification includes the *Actors* involved and in which order *ACLMessages* are exchanged between these *Actors* in a protocol-like manner. Furthermore, a

Protocol refers (i) to a set of *TimeOuts* that define the time constraints for sending and receiving *ACLMessages*, (ii) to a set of *MessageScopes* that defines the *Messages* and their order how these arrive, and (iii) to a set of *MessageFlows* that specify how the exchange of *ACLMessages* is processed.

- **Behavioural aspect** (see Figure 5) describes how *Plans* are composed by complex control structures and simple atomic tasks like sending or receiving a *Message* and how information flows between those constructs. A *Plan* specifies the agents' internal processes. It represents a super class connecting the agent aspect with the behavioural aspect. Informally, a *Plan* refers to a set of *Flows*, be them *ControlFlows* or *InformationFlows* that are contained in the plan description. These different specializations of *Flow* link *Activities* to each other, either defining the control flow or information flow.

- **Environment aspect** contains any kind of *Resource* (i.e. *Service, Object*) that is dynamically created, shared, or used by the *Agents* or *Organizations*, respectively.

Figure 4. The metamodel (part) reflecting the interaction aspect of PIM4Agents

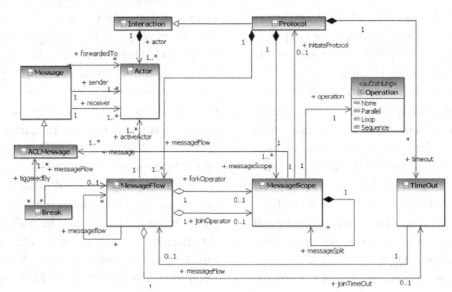

Figure 5. The metamodel (part) reflecting the behavioural aspect of PIM4Agents

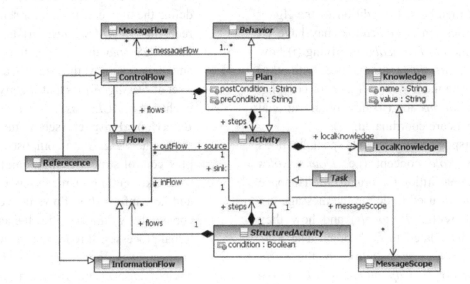

- **Deployment aspect** describes the run-time agent instances that are involved and how these are assigned to the organization's roles. In particular, this aspect deals with the kind of *AgentInstances* that exist in the running systems and how these instances are bound to the particular *DomainRoles* through the concept *DomainRoleBinding* and Actors through the concept of ActorBinding.

The concrete syntax of DSML4MAS (Warwas & Hahn, 2008) is specified using the Graphical Modeling Framework (GMF) that provides the fundamental infrastructure and components for developing visual design and modeling surfaces in Eclipse. For generating a graphical editor, a mapping between the concepts of the abstract syntax and their particular notation that should be used within the created editor is defined. To reduce the complexity of the generated design, GMF support to distinguish between several diagrams with the graphical editor. For our purpose, for each aspect of PIM4Agents (i.e. agent, organization, behaviour, protocol, environment) we defined a diagram. Furthermore, we have one additional diagram for

modelling the binding between *DomainRoles* of an *Organization, AgentInstances* and *Actors* of a *Protocol*. Changes made in one diagram are propagated to all other diagrams.

CODE GENERATORS, MODEL-DRIVEN MULTIAGENT SYSTEMS

Model transformations are one of the key mechanisms within MDD. Basing on code generation templates, the model is transformed to executable code that may optionally be merged with manually written code. One or more model-to-model as well as a model-to-text transformation steps could be necessary for code generation. The implementation of model-to-model transformations is done using the Atlas Transformation Language Language ATL) (Jouault & Kurtev, 2006) that again bases on the Ecore meta-metamodel. In the context of our approach, we developed model transformations to two target languages (i.e. *Jack* and *JADE* (Bellifemine et al., 2005)). The main motivation for choosing the mentioned AOPLs is their different view on agent systems. Whereas *Jack* bases on principles of the Belief-Desire-Intention

(BDI, cf. Rao & Georgeff, 1991) architecture, *JADE* focuses on the compliance with the FIPA specifications for interoperable intelligent MASs and thus concentrates on interaction aspects. A mapping from the PIM4Agents's concepts to the concepts of the different execution platform demonstrates that the concepts of the PIM4Agents can be considered as platform independent. We focus in this chapter on the PIM4Agents to *Jack* transformation. For detailed information regarding the PIM4Agents to *JADE* transformation, we refer to Hahn, Madrigal-Mora & Fischer (2008). In the remainder of this section, several mapping rules are discussed that transfer the PIM4Agents metamodel to the metamodel of *Jack* (JackMM). For detailed information regarding JackMM and the model transformation we refer to Fischer, Hahn & Madrigal-Mora (2007).

Via model-to-model transformations, PIM-4Agents models can be transformed into underlying platform-specific models such as *Jack* or *JADE*. The business protocol between dealer (dealer software), integrator and manufacturers is specified as PIM4Agents protocols (see Figure 6 and Figure 7). For the interaction between service integrator and manufacturers, the messages *request_*checkProduct and *request configureCar*

are sent from *ServiceIntegrator* to *Manufacturer1* and *Manufacturer2*. These both actors reply by sending an answer message. The interaction protocol in Figure 7 represents a contract-net style conversation between *ServiceIntegrator* and the *ServiceProvider's* specializations *Part1* and *Part2*. Note that several *AgentInstances* can be bound to the same *Actor*. If a *Message* is sent to an *Actor*, the *Message* is actually sent to each *AgentInstance* bound to the particular *Actor* in parallel.

In order to execute collaborative processes specified on the PIM-level, the first step consists of transforming PIM4Agents models to agent models that can be directly executed by specific agent execution platforms. In our case, the Jack Intelligent agent framework is used for the execution of BDI-style agents. The constructs of the PIM4Agents metamodel are mapped to BDI-agents represented by the *Jack* metamodel (JackMM).

The partner models are transformed to a *Jack* agent model with the model-to-model transformation developed in the ATHENA project. The following sketch outlines the generic *metamodel* mappings (see Figure 9).

The source and target concepts of the *Organization2Team* mapping rule nicely corresponds

Figure 6. Interaction Model (Service Integrator - Manufacturer part)

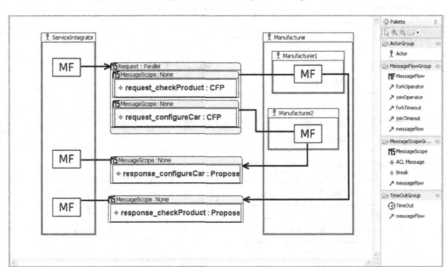

Figure 7. PIM4agents interaction model (service integrator - parts provider)

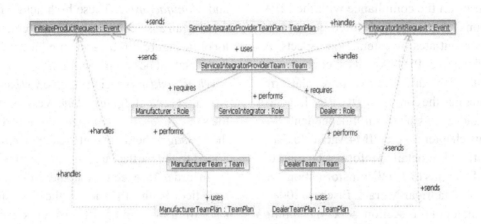

to each other as both (i) make use of an internal behavior that specifies how their members are coordinated and (ii) require and perform roles. The *Behavior* as well as the *Roles* could thus be easily mapped from the PIM4Agents to Jack through the mappings *Plan2TeamPlan* and *Role2Role*. The only difference between both metamodels is the manner in which interactions are defined, i.e. the interaction in the PIM4Agents is defined by

a *Protocol* whereas JackMM defines the interaction between entities in an event-driven manner without explicitly specifying a protocol.

Hence, the organization *ServiceIntegrator* in Figure 6 is mapped to the corresponding team ServiceIntegrator, The team makes use of the roles *Dealer* and *Manufacurer* required by the organization in which it participates.

The *Team2TeamPlan* mapping rule transfers

Figure 8. Jack model generated from PIM4Agents (part)

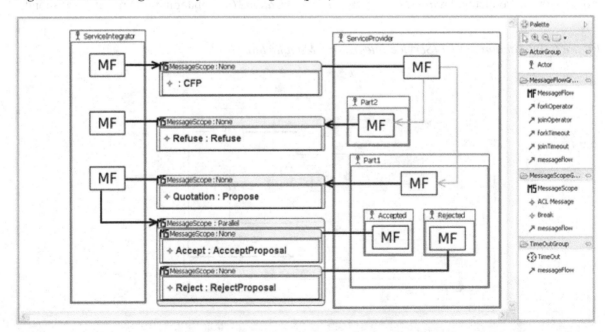

the information how a combined service is orchestrated into a corresponding *TeamPlan*. Finally, each *Message* defines inside a PIM4Agents model is mapped to an *Event* in JackMM by applying the *Message2Event* mapping rule. In the Jack platform, *events* are the means of communication between *agents*.

In this service-oriented setting, the partners provide and exhibit services. Partner (manufacturer etc.) services are described as WSDL interfaces. The WSDL files are used to generate integration stubs for the integrator. We use a model-driven approach for mapping WSDL concepts to agent concepts, thereby integrating agents into an SOA and supporting rapid prototyping.

The process integrator and the manufacturers are modelled as Web services. Their interface is described by WSDL descriptions publishing the agent platform as Web service. In the pilot, only the process integrator is executed by Jack agents which are wrapped by a Web service, whereas the manufacturers and other partner services are pure Web services. However, this is no restriction since the approach also allows generating the necessary artefacts for the other participants as well.

For integrating Web services into the Jack agent platform, we map a service as described by a WSDL file to the agent concept *Capability* which can be conceived of as a module. A capability provides access to the Web services via automatically generated stubs. A capability comprises of plans for invoking the operations as declared in the WSDL (it encapsulates and corresponds to commands such as invoke and reply in BPEL4WS).

Applying these transformations, a PIM4Agents model can be automatically transformed into a PSM model, e.g. the Jack model illustrated in Figure 8. The PSM model is then serialized into Jack artefacts, e.g. *Teams*, *Events* (Messages), *Team Plans* (see Figure 9) and *Beliefs* which can be further modified if necessary. For modifying generated artefacts, the Jack development environment provides a graphical modelling tool which allows visual design of agents, plans and other constructs (Figure 10). It has to be noted, however, that changes on the PSM level may affect the PIM level and should be done carefully in order to avoid inconsistencies.

It should be stressed that these model transfor-

Figure 9. PIM4Agents and WSDLMM to JackMM transformation

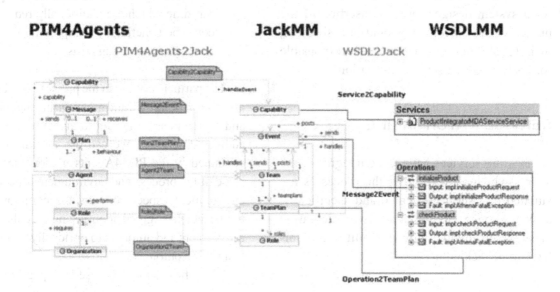

Figure 10. Generated Jack team plan for ServiceIntegrator

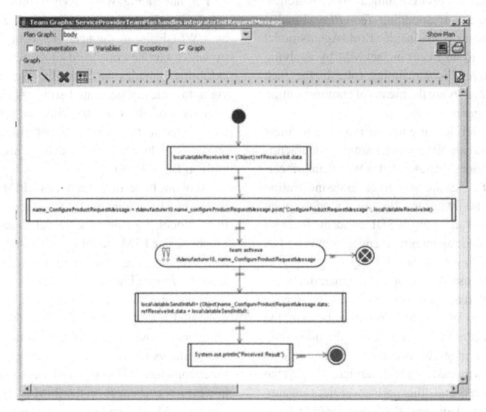

mations and the respective code generation can be done automatically if (i) the PIM4Agents model is defined properly and (ii) the WSDL descriptions are available. The only interventions necessary for a system designer are the insertion of the proper XSLT transformations and the assignment of the capabilities to the agents/teams responsible for a specific Web service invocation.

SERVICE MATCHMAKING

As existing services have to be integrated, the agents which are executing the processes are situated in a service-oriented and specifically, a Web service environment. Two integration tasks which involve interoperability problems have to be tackled:

- integrate services which are "fixed" i.e. known in advance when the process is specified.
- Provisioning services at design time or even run-time which are additionally required or could be beneficial for improving the overall result or reducing costs.

The partner services in the previous section are assumed to be known and given during the analysis and design phase. In order to discover and select additional services, we can use the information contained in the PIM4Agents model, especially those of the process and environment aspect. The environment aspect contains the common data model which is agreed upon among the collaborating partners and amounts to or (ideally) conforms to a shared ontology.

It can furthermore be used to specify search

requests for potentially usable services. In our automotive scenario, there are a number of standards which can form the basis for the environment model (e.g. STAR standard for automotive retail industry). The concepts of the standard and their relation to each other are either integrated into the common data model or used as annotation of the data model. If the local data model of the partners differs from the common model, the local partner is responsible for defining a mapping from the common model to the local model. If we assume that other external services use the same vocabulary for their service description (or their annotation), the concepts can be used to formulate service requests and search for relevant services which offer the required functionality. This assumption of a shared vocabulary among actors is reasonable, since in our scenario product data underlies strong standardization pressure.

In order to do that, we have to collect the description about a required service from the model, i.e. service operation, input and output of the service as well as pre- and post-conditions of the tasks. In fact, this information about the service requirements is sufficient to formulate a query (at design time) to a semantic matchmaker, e.g. for an OWL-S, a WSMO, or a SAWSDL matchmaker (see Figure 11).

If a plan step, e.g. a Task involves a message exchange with an external partner, the requirements which the external partner must fulfil can be derived from the PIM model. The pre- and post-conditions of a task and the message refer to the input and output parameters which the external service must provide. Since pre- and post-conditions as well as input and output are the main features a matchmaker uses for checking service compliance, the service requirement contained in the PIM model can be transformed into service requests by using the pre- and post-conditions of a task (for WSMO) or input and output concepts (for OWL-S or SAWSDL) of a message sent to a specific service. For matchmaking, we use the OWL-S (Klusch, Fries & Sycara, 2006) and WSMO matchmaker (Kaufer & Klusch, 2006).

Since the OWL-S matchmaker essentially takes the service profile as requirement, we generate an OWL-S service description with a profile. An OWL-S matchmaker request consists of an OWL-S service description, including a service

Figure 11. Integration process of external services

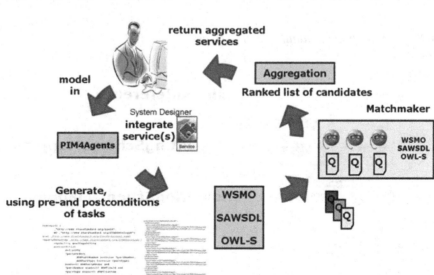

profile with input and output concepts referring to a shared ontology. In WSMO, a *Goal* describes the requested functionality of a required service.

Discovered services can be integrated at design time either by using the grounding contained in the service descriptions or by directly integrating the service using its WSDL description as described above.

SEMANTICALLY ENHANCED INTEGRATION OF PARTNER PROCESSES

The integration of partners as previously described is based on the assumptions that partners provide their service description in a WSDL format and that the mapping between heterogeneous data formats is specified especially for integrating the partner service at a pre-defined place in the process. However, a more flexible way of integrating is required if a SOA should tap its full potential. Therefore, a service description which supports flexible integration has to contain additional mapping information for mediating different data structures.

If we assume, as mentioned above, that partners or other external services use the same

vocabulary for their service description (or their annotation), the concepts can be used to annotate service descriptions and specify a mapping from the global data structure to the partner services and vice versa.

The Semantic Web standard SAWSDL is a suitable candidate for improving the integration process described in the previous section. It enables semantic annotations for Web services not only for discovering Web services but also for invoking them. It is open enough to allow for annotation with arbitrary 'models', i.e. ontologies, embodied in the common data model. Furthermore, SAWSDL contains references to a *liftingSchemaMapping* and a *loweringSchemaMapping* (see Figure 12). A *liftingSchemaMapping* takes as input XML data (that adheres to a given XML schema) and produces semantic data (that adheres to a semantic model, in our case the global data model) as output. The application of a *loweringSchemaMapping* has the reverse effect.

More precisely, the following extensions are used for annotation:

- **modelReference:** A modelReference points to one ore more concepts with equally intended meaning expressed in an arbitrary semantic representation language. They

Figure 12. SAWSDL annotation of manufacturer service

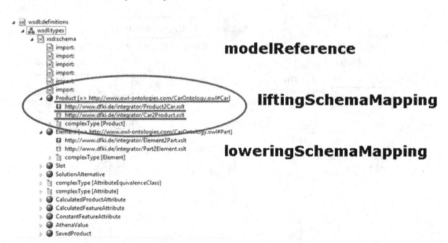

are allowed to be defined for every WSDL and XML Schema element, though the SAWSDL specification defines their occurrence only in WSDL interfaces, operations, faults as well as XML Schema elements, complex types, simple types and attributes. The purpose of a model reference is mainly to support automated service discovery.

- **liftingSchemaMapping:** Schema mappings are intended to support automated service execution by providing rules specifying the correspondences between semantic annotation concepts defined in a given ontology (the "upper" level) to the XML Schema representation of data actually required to invoke the Web service using SOAP (the "lower" level), and vice versa. A liftingSchema-Mapping describes the transformation from the "lower" level in XML Schema up to the ontology language used for semantic annotation.

- **loweringSchemaMapping:** The reference tag loweringSchemaMapping describes the transformation from the "upper" level of a given ontology to the "lower" level in XML Schema.

Both mappings can be used to facilitate the integration steps described in the previous section. Partners annotate their WSDL with mappings to and from the common data model and produce a corresponding SAWSDL description. The transformation to Jack models can still be done according to the model-driven approach. The XSLT transformations which were necessary for each integration task can now be isolated and embedded into the service description. This allows reusing the service description at different steps inside and outside of the collaboration. Annotating an existing WSDL description of a service for integration is an additional effort for a partner; however, the advantage is reusability of a service description if the collaborative process changes.

Issues with SAWSDL

SAWSDL is agnostic to semantic representation languages and to domain knowledge used for annotation. This can be an advantage, but in certain cases the resulting uncertainty is a drawback. The publisher of a SAWSDL web service has to know in advance which ontologies might be used by potential service consumers. In completely open settings, this is not feasible. However, in collaborative settings, the domain ontologies used by partners are known in advance and can be covered by a SAWSDL description. An interesting concept is the notion of a *Business Ecospace* which is enhanced with semantic technology. In a Business Ecospace, partners which enter the Ecospace would publish their local domain knowledge which can in turn by used by service providers to allow new partners to integrate and use their services in a seamless manner.

ADVANTAGES OF AGENT-BASED PROCESS EXECUTION

Agentis[4], in a whitepaper, states three main advantages of the agent-based approach to business processes:

- *Rapid development:* By using high levels of abstraction to represent business logic, users can design their application much faster, without having to translate business activities into actual code; in addition, by eliminating the need to code links between sub-processes, development time grows linearly with additional processes instead of exponentially. This allows users to develop process libraries that are comprised of tens of thousands of processes if needed, thus increasing the customization of the system.

- *Agility and incremental deployment:* business sub-processes are self-contained, with their own objectives, context and logic. They can be added, deleted or changed without worrying about interdependencies with other sub-processes, resulting in high responsiveness to the business environment.

- *Run-time scalability:* by breaking down processes into small sub-processes that can be executed independently, the runtime can use massively parallel processing techniques, resulting in a very high number of concurrent users and number of process state changes per second. In addition, only the necessary end-to-end process is created dynamically at runtime, based on the service objectives and the service context, which allows for an almost infinite number of configurations, critical for highly customized applications.

In the following we will briefly discuss advantages of applying BDI-agents in a service-oriented environment. In order to compare an agent-based approach with other standards for Web service composition, the distinction introduced by Yang, Heuvel & Papazoglou (2002) between *fixed*, *semi-fixed*, and *explorative composition* is useful. Fixed composition can be done with e.g. BPEL4WS, but also by applying BDI agents. Semi-fixed composition might also be specified with BPEL4WS: partner links are defined at design-time, but the actual service endpoint for a partner might be fixed at run-time, as long as the service complies with the structure defined at design-time. Late binding can also be done with the Jack framework. The service endpoint needs to be set (at the latest) when the actual call to the service is done. Explorative composition is beyond of what BPEL4WS and a BDI-agent approach offer (at least if they are used in a 'normal' way). To enable explorative composition, a general purpose planner might be applied which dynamically generates, based on the service descriptions stored in a registry, a

plan which tries to achieve the objective specified by the consumer (Sirin et al., 2004).

It might seem as if BPEL4WS and BDI-style agents offer the same features. However, there are several advantages of a BDI-style agent approach. An important question is how the availability of a partner service is detected. This might be checked only by actually calling the service. If the service is not available or does not return the expected output, an exception will be raised. BPEL4WS provides a fault handler which allows specifying what to do in case of an exception. Similarly, an agent plan will fail if a Web service call raises an exception, and execute some activities specified for the failure case. However, the difference is that a plan is executed in a context which specifies conditions for plan instances and also other applicable plans. The context is implicitly given by the beliefs of an agent and can be made explicit. This means that in a given context, several plan instances might be executed, e.g. for all known services of a specific type, the services are called (one after another), until one of the services provides the desired result. An exception in one plan instance then leads to the execution of another plan instance for the next known service.

Additionally, BDI-style agents provide the possibility of 'meta-level reasoning' which allows choosing the most feasible plan according to specified criteria. Similarly, if for a specific goal several plan types are feasible, an agent executes one of these plans and, in case of a failure, immediately executes the next feasible plan to achieve the desired goal. The BDI-agent approach supports this adaptive behaviour in a natural way, whereas a BPEL4WS process specification which attempts to provide the same behaviour would require awkward coding such as nested fault handlers etc.

Furthermore, since it is in many cases not possible to fully specify all necessary details on the PIM level, a system engineer must add these details on the PSM level. Hence, *customizing the composition* is facilitated since the different plans clearly structure the alternatives of possible actions. Since the control structure is implicit, changes in a plan do not have impact on the control structure, reducing the danger of errors in the code. Another advantage is that *extending* the behaviour by adding a new, alternative plan for a specific task is straightforward. The new plan is simply added to the plan library and will be executed at the next opportunity.

Finally, business process notations allow specifying unstructured processes. To execute these processes with BPEL, unstructured process descriptions normally are transformed to block-structured BPEL processes. In doing so, most approaches restrict the expressiveness of processes by only permitting acyclic or already (block-) structured graphs (Mendling, Lassen & Zdun, 2005). In the case that any unstructured processes shall be executed, an approach like described in Ouyang et al. (2006) has to be followed. The idea is to translate processes with arbitrary topologies to BPEL by making solely use of its Event Handler concept. The result is again cumbersome BPEL code, whereas the Jack agent platform naturally supports event-based behaviour.

RELATED WORK

Agent-Based Representation and Enactment of Business Processes

In recent years, agents were proposed for enacting workflows and business processes. This category is especially interesting in the context of the agent-driven EAI, viewing business processes in an agent-based way (Singh & Huhns, 1999; Singh, 2004; Petrie & Bussler, 2003). The topic gains increasingly more interest in the semantic web and knowledge management communities.

Agent-oriented approachs were previously already considered for workflow and process management. *ADEPT* (Jennings et al., 2000) was one of the seminal projects which developed agent-

technology for business processes. It provided the conceptualization and implementation of an agent-based system for managing corporate-wide business processes. The ADEPT philosophy was founded upon two key notions: (i) developing responsibility for provisioning and managing the business; and (ii) making the problem-solving components reactive and proactive so they can respond to unexpected situations.

For assessing different approaches to business process management and enactment the nature of the processes have to be taken into account. While the traditional workflow systems have been designed for routine tasks, e.g., administrative office processes, more flexibility is needed in business processes that comprise actions performed by customers, or that span multiple companies. Here, agent- and rule-based approaches may be more adequate. The most flexibility is probably needed in very knowledge-intensive tasks (e.g., decision making) which can only be coarsely modeled in traditional workflow systems, resulting in a low level of system support.

In the pre-SOA and Semantic Web era, several approaches came up with ideas similar to current technologies. Webflow (Grasso et. al., 1997) complements conferencing and document sharing systems on the WWW by executing business processes that involve coordinating people, documents, and software objects. Nissen (2000) proposes a design of a set of agents to perform activities associated with the supply chain process in the area of E-Commerce. In Stormer & Knorr (2001), agents have been used as part of the infrastructure associated with the WfMS itself in order to create an agent-enhanced WfMS. Zeng et. al. (2001) propose an approach that combines agents with workflows to effectively integrate cross-enterprise workflows. Agents are used to encapsulate (i.e., wrap) services which are able to execute workflow tasks. Based on the requirements of tasks, the system searches for agents with matching capabilities. The relevant agents are used to execute the tasks which are dynamically composed by the system in order to provide the whole service. However, based on the Web service technology stack, the configuration task is simplified as Semantic Web technologies become available: Web Services as well as EAI infrastructures increasingly provide simpler data access, too. Furthermore, modelling languages and standards are now available which facilitate mutual understanding of process and data descriptions.

Recent approaches take these new trends into account. Savarimuthu et. al. (2005) discuss how an agent-based architecture can be used to bind and access Web services in the context of executing a workflow process model. They use an example from the diamond processing industry to show how an agent architecture can be used to integrate Web services with WfMSs. Blake & Gomaa (2005) describe an adaptation of software agents as a possible solution for the composition and enactment of cross-organizational services. Their approach details design aspects of an architecture that would support this evolvable service-based workflow composition. The internal coordination and control aspects of such an architecture is addressed. These agent developmental processes are aligned with industry-standard software engineering processes. In the context of the SUPER project under the EU 6th Framework Programme Information Society Technologies Objective (contract no. FP6-026850), efforts were made to integrate BPEL4WS and Semantic Web services (Nitzsche et al., 2007). This is an ongoing work which is similar to our effort, but until now it is not clear how adaptive, agent-like behaviour can be based on the integration of Semantic Web services into BPEL processes.

Agents, Web Services and Model-Driven Development

Apart from the wealth of literature about business process modelling, enterprise application integration and SOAs, the relation between agents and SOAs has already been investigated.

Several approaches already exist to integrate Web services into agent systems. Singh & Huhns (2005) cover several important aspects, Vidal, Buhler & Stahl (2004) propose the application of agents for workflows in general. Greenwood & Calisti (2004) and Dickinson & Wooldridge (2005) present a technical and conceptual integration of an agent platform and Web services. However, the model-driven approach and the strong consideration of problems related to cross-organisational settings have not been investigated in this context. Furthermore, our focus on tightly integrating BDI-style agents fits much better to a model-driven, process-centric setting than the Web service gateway to a JADE agent platform considered by e.g. Greenwood & Calisti.

Cabri, Leonardi & Puviani (2007) provide an overview of agent-based modelling approaches for enterprises. Penserini et al. (2006) describe the TROPOS methodology for a model-driven design of agent-based software systems. However, the problems related to integration of agent platforms and service-oriented architectures are beyond their focus. Endert et al. (2007) map BPMN models to BDI agents but do not consider an integration of agents and Web services.

SUMMARY AND OUTLOOK

In this chapter, we presented a pilot developed within the EU project ATHENA in the area of multi-brand automotive dealers. For its realization, several integration problems on different levels had to be solved. We described a solution which supports rapid prototyping by combining a model-driven framework for cross-organisational service-oriented architectures with an agent-based approach for flexible process execution. The model-driven approach can be extended using Semantic Web service descriptions for service integration. We argued that agent-based SOAs provide additional advantages over standard process execution environments.

From a research transfer point of view, the following lessons could be learned:

- Evidently, a model-driven approach is a step in the right direction as design-time tasks are separated from run-time tasks which allows performing them graphically. Moreover, it is easier to react to changes of the different interacting partners as only the models have to be adapted but not the run-time environment.
- A model-driven, agent-based approach offers additional flexibility and advantages (in general and in the scenario discussed) when agents are tightly integrated into a service-oriented framework.
- The PIM4Agents metamodel is expressive enough for modelling service requirements which can be used for Semantic Web service discovery.

For further enhancing the capabilities of agents, the already existing formalisms for describing entities in a collaboration have to be extended. This concerns service descriptions, but also descriptions of data models, contracts, protocols and negotiations. Furthermore, the connection between metamodels and ontologies should be strengthened. The integration of metamodels for agents, processes and services would allow generating the still necessary transformations in an automatic way, thus fulfilling the far reaching vision of the Semantic Web.

REFERENCES

Bellifemine, F., Bergenti, F., Caire, G., & Poggi, A. (2005). JADE-a java agent development framework. In R. Bordini, M. Dastani, D. J., & A. El Fallah Seghrouchni (Eds.), *Multiagent programming: Languages, platforms, and applications, volume 15 of multiagent aystems, artificial societies, and simulated organizations* (pp. 125–147). Berlin, et al.: Springer.

Benatallah, B., Casati, F., Grigori, D., Motahari-Nezhad, H., & Toumani, F. (2005). Developing adapters for Web services integration. In *Proceedings of the International Conference on Advanced Information Systems Engineering (CAiSE)*, Porto, Portugal (pp. 415-429). Springer Verlag.

Benguria, G., Larrucea, X., Elvesæter, B., Neple, T., Beardsmore, A., & Friess, M. (2006). A platform independent model for service oriented architectures. In *2nd International Conference on Interoperability of Enterprise Software and Applications (I-ESA 2006)*.

Blake, M. B., & Gomaa, H. (2005, July). Agent-oriented compositional approaches to services-based cross-organizational workflow. *Decision Support Systems*, 40(1), 31–50. doi:10.1016/j.dss.2004.04.003

Booth, D., Haas, H., McCabe, F., Newcomer, E., Champion, M., Ferris, C., & Orchard, D. (2004). *Web services architecture*. Tech. Rep. W3C Working Group.

Bouras, A., Gouvas, P., & Mentzas, G. (2007). ENIO: An enterprise application integration ontology. In *18th International Conference on Database and Expert Systems Applications (DEXA 2007)* (pp. 419-423).

Buhler, P., & Vidal, J. M. (2005). Towards adaptive workflow enactment using multiagent systems. *Information Technology and Management Journal, Special Issue on Universal Enterprise Integration*, 61–87.

Cabri, G., Leonardi, L., & Puviani, M. (2007). Service-Oriented Agent Methodologies. In *5th IEEE International Workshop on Agent-Based Computing for Enterprise Collaboration (ACEC-07)*.

de Bruijn, J., Bussler, C., Domingue, J., Fensel, D., Hepp, M., Keller, U., et al. (2005). *Web service modeling ontology (WSMO). W3C member submission*. Retrieved on June 3, 2005, from http://www.w3.org/Submission/WSMO/

Dickinson, I., & Wooldridge, M. (2005). Agents are not (just) Web services: Considering BDI agents and Web services. In *AAMAS 2005 Workshop on Service-Oriented Computing and Agent-Based Engineering (SOCABE)*, 2005.

Endert, H., Hirsch, B., Küster, T., & Albayrak, S. (2007, May 14). Towards a mapping from BPMN to agents. In J. Huang, R. Kowalczyk, Z. Maamar, D. L. Martin, I. Müller, S. Stoutenburg, & K. Sycara (Eds.), *Service-oriented computing: Agents, semantics, and engineering. AAMAS 2007 International Workshop, SOCASE 2007*, Honolulu, HI (pp. 92-106).

Erl, T. (2005). *Service-oriented architecture: Concepts, technology, and design*. Prentice Hall International.

Farrell, J., & Lausen, H. (2007). Semantic annotations for WSDL and XML schema. W3C proposed recommendation. Retrieved on July 5, 2007, from http://www.w3.org/TR/sawsdl/

Fensel, D., Ding, Y., Omelayenko, B., Schulten, E., Botquin, G., Brown, M., & Flett, A. (2001). Product data integration for B2B e-commerce. *IEEE Intelligent Systems, 16*(4), 54–59. doi:10.1109/5254.941358

FIPA. (2000). *FIPA communicative act library specification. Specification, Foundation for Intelligent Physical Agents*. Retrieved from www.fipa.org

Fischer, K., Hahn, C., & Madrigal-Mora, C. (2007). Agent-oriented software engineering: A model-driven approach. *International Journal of Agent-Oriented Software Engineering, 1*(3/4), 334–369. doi:10.1504/IJAOSE.2007.016265

Grasso, A., Meunier, J., Pagani, D., & Pareschi, R. (1997, May). Distributed coordination and workflow on the World Wide Web. *Computer Supported Cooperative Work, 6*(2-3), 175–200. doi:10.1023/A:1008652312739

Greenwood, D., & Calisti, M. (2004). Engineering Web service-agent integration. *2004 IEEE International Conference on Systems, Man and Cybernetics, 2*, 1918–1925.

Hahn, C. (2008). A platform independent agent-based modeling language. In *Proceedings of the Seventh International Conference on Autonomous Agents and Multiagent Systems (AAMAS)* (pp. 233-240).

Hahn, C., Madrigal-Mora, C., & Fischer, K. (2008). A platform-independent metamodel for multiagent systems. *International Journal on Autonomous Agents and Multi-Agent Systems*. The Netherlands: Springer.

Hahn, C., Madrigal-Mora, C., Fischer, K., Elvesæter, B., Berre, A. J., & Zinnikus, I. (2006, September 19-20). Metamodels, models, and model transformations: Towards interoperable agents. *Multiagent System Technologies, 4th German Conference, MATES 2006*, Erfurt, Germany. (LNCS 4196, pp. 123-134). Springer.

Hendler, J. (2001). Agents and the Semantic Web. *IEEE Intelligent Systems, 16*(2), 30–37. doi:10.1109/5254.920597

Intelligent Agents, J. A. C. K. (2006). *The agent oriented software group (AOS)*. Retrieved from http://www.agent-software.com/shared/home/

Jennings, N. R., Faratin, P., Norman, T. J., O'Brien, P., Odgers, B., & Alty, J. L. (2000). Implementing a business process management system using ADEPT: A real-world case study. *Int. Journal of Applied Artificial Intelligence, 14*(5), 421–465. doi:10.1080/088395100403379

Jouault, F., & Kurtev, I. (2006). Transforming models with ATL. In *Satellite Events at the MoDELS 2005 Conference*. (LNCS 3844, pp. 128–138). Springer.

Kahl, T., Vanderhaeghen, D., Ziemann, J., Zinnikus, I., Loos, P., & Fischer, K. (2006). Agent-supported cross-organizational business process management and implementation. *International Transactions on Systems Science and Applications, 1*(4), 369–374.

Kaiser, M. (2007). Toward the realization of policy-oriented enterprise management. *IEEE Computer, 40*(11), 57–63.

Kaufer, F., & Klusch, M. (2006). WSMO-MX: A logic programming based hybrid service matchmaker. In *4ᵗʰ European Conference on Web Services (ECOWS '06)* (pp. 161–170).

Kendall, E. (2006). The ontology definition metamodel-an MDA-based framework for semantic interoperability. *Semantic Technology Conference*, San Jose, CA.

Kleppe, A., Warmer, J. B., & Bast, W. (2003). *MDA explained—the model driven architecture: Practice and promise.* Addison-Wesley.

Klusch, M. (2008). Semantic Web service coordination. In M. Schumacher, H. Helin, & H. Schuldt (Eds.), *CASCOM-intelligent service coordination in the Semantic Web.* Birkhäuser: Verlag, Springer.

Klusch, M., Fries, B., & Sycara, K. (2006). Automated Semantic Web service discovery with OWLS-MX. In *AAMAS '06: Proceedings of the Fifth International Joint Conference on Autonomous Agents and Multiagent Systems* (pp. 915–922). New York:ACM Press.

Koehler, J., Hauser, R., Küster, J., Ryndina, K., Vanhatalo, J., & Wahler, M. (2006). The role of visual modeling and model transformations in business-driven development. In *Fifth International Workshop on Graph Transformation and Visual Modeling Techniques.*

Lenzerini, M. (2002). Data integration: a theoretical perspective. In *PODS '02: Proceedings of the Twenty-first ACM SIGMOD-SIGACT-SIGART Symposium on Principles of Database Systems* (pp. 233–246). New York: ACM Press.

Martin, D., Burstein, M., Hobbs, J., Lassila, O., McDermott, D., McIlraith, S., et al. (2004). OWL-S: Semantic markup for Web services. W3C member submission. Retrieved on November 22, 2004, from http://www.w3.org/Submission/OWL-S/

Mellor, S. J., Scott, K., Uhl, A., & Weise, D. (2004). *MDA distilled.* Addison-Wesley.

Mendling, J., Lassen, K., & Zdun, U. (2005). *Transformation strategies between block-oriented and graph-oriented process modelling languages.* Tech. Rep. JM-200510 -10. TU Vienna.

Newell, A. (1982). The knowledge level. *Journal of Artificial Intelligence, 18*(1), 87–127. doi:10.1016/0004-3702(82)90012-1

Nissen, M. E. (2000). Supply chain process and agent design for e-commerce. *33ʳᵈ Hawaii International Conference on System Sciences,* Maui, HI.

Nitzsche, J., van Lessen, T., Karastoyanova, D., & Leymann, F. (2007). BPEL for Semantic Web services (BPEL4SWS). In *Proceedings of the 3ʳᵈ International Workshop on Agents and Web Services in Distributed Environments AWeSome '07- On the Move to Meaningful Internet Systems, OTM 2007 Workshops.*

Object Management Group. (2006). *MDA guide, Object Management Group, Inc., final adopted specification.*

Omelayenko, B., & Fensel, D. (2001). A two-layered integration approach for product information in B2B e-commerce. In K. Madria & G. Pernul (Eds.), *Proceedings of the Second International Conference on Electronic Commerce and Web Technologies (EC WEB-2001).* (LNCS 2115, pp. 226–239). Springer-Verlag.

Ouyang, C., Dumas, M., Breutel, S., & ter Hofstede, A. H. M. (2006, June 5-9). Translating standard process models to BPEL. In *Advanced Information Systems Engineering, 18th International Conference, CAiSE 2006,* Luxembourg (pp. 417–432). Springer.

Payne, T. R. (2008). Web services from an agent perspective. *IEEE Intelligent Systems, 23*(8).

Penserini, L., Perini, A., Susi, A., & Mylopoulos, J. (2006, June 5-9). From stakeholder intentions to software agent implementations. In *Advanced Information Systems Engineering, 18th International Conference, CAiSE 2006,* Luxembourg (pp. 465–479). Springer.

Petrie, C., & Bussler, C. (2003). Service agents and virtual enterprises: A survey. *IEEE Internet Computing,* 58–78.

Rao, A. S., & Georgeff, M. P. (1991). Modeling rational agents within a BDI architecture. In J. Allen, R. Fikes, & E. Sandewall (Eds.), *2nd International Conference on Principles of Knowledge Representation and Reasoning (KR91)* (pp. 473-484). San Mateo, CA: Morgan Kaufmann Publishers Inc.

Russell, S., & Norvig, P. (1995). *Artificial intelligence: A modern approach.* Upper Saddle River, NJ: Prentice Hall.

Savarimuthu, B. T. R., Purvis, M., Purvis, M. K., & Cranefield, S. (2005). Integrating Web services with agent based workflow management system (WfMS). *IEEE/WIC/ACM International Conference on Web Intelligence,* 471- 474

Schulz, K., & Orlowska, A. (n.d.). Facilitating cross-organisational workflows with a workflow view approach. *Data & Knowledge Engineering, 51*(1), 109–147. doi:10.1016/j.datak.2004.03.008

Searle, J. R. (1969). *Speech acts.* Cambridge, UK: Cambridge University Press.

Singh, M. P. (2004). Business process management: A killer app for agents? In *Proceedings of the Third International Joint Conference on Autonomous Agents & Multiagent Systems (AAMAS) 2004* (p. 26).

Singh, M. P., & Huhns, M. N. (1999). Multiagent systems for workflow. *International Journal of Intelligent Systems in Accounting Finance & Management, 8,* 105–117. doi:10.1002/(SICI)1099-1174(199906)8:2<105::AID-ISAF163>3.0.CO;2-#

Singh, M. P., & Huhns, M. N. (2005). *Service-oriented computing-semantics, processes, agents.* John Wiley & Sons, Ltd.

Sirin, E., Parsia, B., Wu, D., Hendler, J., & Nau, D. (2004). HTN planning for Web service composition using SHOP2. *International Semantic Web Conference 2003, 1,* 377–396.

Stormer, H., & Knorr, K. (2001). AWA-eine architektur eines agentbasierten workflow-systems. In H. H. Buhl, A. Huther & B. Reitwiesner (Eds.), *Tagungsband 5. Internationale Tagung Wirtschaftsinformatik (WI2001)* (pp. 147–160).

Studer, R., Grimm, S., & Abecker, A. (2007). *Semantic Web services: Concepts, technologies, and applications.* New York: Springer.

Vidal, J., Buhler, P., & Stahl, C. (2004). Multiagent systems with workflows. *IEEE Internet Computing, 8*(1), 76–82. doi:10.1109/MIC.2004.1260707

Warwas, S., & Hahn, C. (2008). The concrete syntax of the platform independent modeling language for multiagent systems. In *Proceedings of the International Workshop on Agent-based Technologies and Applications for Enterprise Interoperability (ATOP 2008),* Estoril, Portugal.

Wooldridge, M. (1997). Agent-based software engineering. *IEE Proceedings. Software, 144*(1), 26–37. doi:10.1049/ip-sen:19971026

Yang, J., Heuvel, W., & Papazoglou, M. (2002). Tackling the challenges of service composition in e-marketplaces. In *Proceedings of the 12th International Workshop on Research Issues on Data Engineering: Engineering E-Commerce/E-Business Systems (RIDE-2EC 2002),* San Jose, CA.

Zeng, L., Ngu, A., Benatallah, B., & O'Dell, M. (2001, January 29-February 1). An agent-based approach for supporting cross-enterprise workflows. In *Proceedings of the 12th Australasian Database Conference,* Gold Coast, Queensland, Australia. *ACM International Conference Proceeding Series, 10,* 123-130. Washington, D.C.: IEEE Computer Society.

Zinnikus, I., Hahn, C., & Fischer, K. (2008). A model-driven agent-based approach for the integration of services into a collaborative business process. In *Proceedings of the Seventh International Conference on Autonomous Agents and Multiagent Systems (AAMAS)* (pp. 241-248).

ENDNOTES

[1]   Web Service Description Language

[2]   Enterprise Collaboration & Interoperability (http://www.coin-ip.eu/)

[3]   Semantically-enabled Heterogeneous service Architecture (http://www.shape-project.eu/)

[4]   http://www.agentissoftware.com/en/index.jsp

Chapter 5
The Semantic Side of Service-Oriented Architectures

Catarina Ferreira da Silva
University of Lyon 1, France

Paulo Rupino da Cunha
University of Coimbra, Portugal

Parisa Ghodous
University of Lyon 1, France

Paulo Melo
University of Coimbra and INESC Coimbra, Portugal

ABSTRACT

In Service-Oriented Architectures (SOA), service descriptions are fundamental elements. In order to automatically execute SOA tasks, such as services discovery, it is necessary to capture and process the semantics of services. We review several Semantic Web Services frameworks that intend to bring semantics to Web Services. This chapter depicts some ideas from SOA and Semantic Web services and their application to enterprise application integration. We illustrate an example of logic-based semantic matching between consumer services and provided services, which are described in ontologies.

INTRODUCTION

A new paradigm of information systems design – the service-oriented architecture (SOA) – has been consistently gaining acceptance. It is an architectural paradigm aiming at dealing with business processes distributed over a large landscape of former and newer heterogeneous systems that are under the control of different owners (Josuttis, 2007). The goal of SOA is to structure large distributed systems based on the abstractions of business rules and functions.

In SOA approach, traditional business logic is extracted from inside silo applications and exposed as reusable services. These, in turn, can be easily composed into higher-level business processes using graphical tools. Changes become much easier and the gap between needs and IT support is narrowed. The organizations become more agile and flexible.

DOI: 10.4018/978-1-60566-804-8.ch005

However, some challenges remain in assembling business processes from services. Business processes carry semantics, which are usually neither explicitly nor formally expressed. To represent semantic content in an explicit way can be a hard task because it requires domain experts to formalise the implicit knowledge about services or processes. Still, representing semantics explicitly through formal ontologies of products, processes or services, may help describe, compose and match services, such as between consumer-required services and provider-specified services.

The concepts of SOA may be applied to provide for several tasks, and among those the ones usually associated with Enterprise Application Integration (EAI). Web Services and SOA technology can be used to support EAI tasks, like process modelling, process execution, message routing, transformation and delivery among systems (Haller, Gomez & Bussler, 2005). The use of a common representation for data (usually XML) however does not preclude mismatches between systems, and while syntactic and structural mismatches may be solved using common Web Service standards, semantic mismatches are usually solved in an ad-hoc fashion. Similarly, process modelling using common tools does not guarantee the easy or automatic selection of adequate services (from a pool of common or domain-specific services).

This chapter intends to explain how semantically SOA and its technologies can be used to perform some integration tasks. The goal is more to depict some ideas from SOA and Semantic Web Services and their application to EAI than to provide new research. On the practical side, we show how we can use formal domain ontologies to describe and to match services. We review several semantic web services frameworks that intend to bring semantics to Web Services. We discuss the loose coupling aspect of SOA regarding semantic enrichment of Web Services description. Then we illustrate our approach related to the discovery of services in the context of a product catalogue using semantic web services represented in OWL-S.

We then use a logic-based matchmaker to detect if services match. The use of reasoning is intended to be a consistent way to verify matching services.

BACKGROUND

By nature, all large systems are heterogeneous, *i.e.* they lack uniformity. These systems were initially developed with different purposes, and evolved towards accretions of different platforms, programming languages and even middleware. SOA paradigm aims at dealing with heterogeneous systems in a decentralised way as much as possible. Decentralisation helps to obtain loose coupling. SOA key technical concepts are services, loose coupling and interoperability. We briefly describe these three concepts below.

Although several definitions exist, in short, a service is an information technology (IT) representation of self-contained business functionality.

Loose coupling minimises dependencies and thus helps scalability, flexibility and fault tolerance. When dependencies are reduced, modifications have minimised effects and the systems still run when part of them are down. When problems occur, it is important to decrease their effects and consequences. Josuttis (2007) elaborates on several strategies to apply loose coupling.

The ISO/IEC 2382-01 (1993) states that interoperability is the capability to communicate, execute programs, or transfer data among various functional units in a manner that requires the user to have little or no knowledge of the unique characteristics of those units. Thus, interoperability enables systems to communicate, understand each other and exchange information. Syntactic and structural interoperability is already set up with transformations, for instance, using standards like XML and XML Schema and associated tools. Syntactic and structural transformations are used to convert schema representations into a target format. Approaches that target at enhancing interoperability based on structure and on syntax can only produce improvements when a certain conceptual homogeneity between graphs to compare exists. Solving mismatches on the semantic level, *i.e.* to come up to semantic interoperability, is a complex accomplishment. More and more semantic resources are available, for instance within the Web, that are as many different cognitive viewpoints over application domains.

Particularly, semantic interoperability is the ability to exchange information and use it, ensuring that the precise meaning of the information is understood by any other application that was not initially developed for this purpose ("European Interoperability Framework, " 2003). Semantic interoperability enables systems to process the information produced by other applications, *i.e.* use it isolated or combined with their own information, in a meaningful way. Therefore, semantic interoperability is an important requirement for improving communication and productivity.

Although many SOA definitions include the term Web Services, these are one possible way to realize a SOA infrastructure by using a specific implementation strategy (Josuttis, 2007). Anyway, web services are emerging as the de facto standard for SOA implementations. However, web services related technologies deal with almost exclusively syntactic and structural aspects of information and lack of semantics considerations.

Traditionally, services are described using XML language (Bray, Paoli & Sperberg-Mc-Queen, 2006), for instance with the Web Services Description Language, WSDL (Christensen, Curbera & Meredith, 2001) or its second version, WSDL 2.0 (Chinnici, Moreau & Ryman, 2007). This language specifies a format to define service interfaces, *i.e.* the technical aspects of calling web services. It can describe two different aspects of a service that are its signature, particularly service name and service parameters, and its binding and deployments details, such as protocol and location. Although WSDL 2.0 provides the ability to extend WSDL files, the underlying XML language does not enable to convey precise and unambiguous

semantics. This means a WSDL file is not enough to manage the whole service contract.

According to Haller, Gomez & Bussler (2005) determining the semantics for services interfaces means to define the concepts as well as the relationships between them through ontologies. According to frequently quoted Gruber (1993) an ontology is a formal explicit specification of a shared conceptualization. Thus, an ontology defines a common agreement upon terminology by providing a set of concepts and relationships among the set of concepts. In order to capture semantics of relations and of concepts, an ontology generally also provides a set of axioms, which means expressions in a logical framework.

Representational techniques being developed for the Semantic Web can be used to capture and process semantics. Some of these techniques ground on XML language, bringing other complementary language constructors. From the W3C, the Semantic Web Activity group ("W3C Semantics," 2004) recommends specific languages such as Resource Description Framework, RDF (Beckett, 2004), Resource Description Framework Schema, RDF(S) (Brickley & Guha, 2004) and Web Ontology Language, OWL (McGuinness & Van Harmelen, 2004). Particularly, OWL includes three sublanguages: OWL-lite, OWL-DL, and OWL full. The first two, but not the third, correspond to decidable description logics (Baader, Calvanese & McGuinness, 2003). Decidability implies that fundamental questions about an ontology are guaranteed to be answerable, such as the question of subsumption. A specific class A subsumes another class B when it is a superclass of a class B.

In the domain of Semantic Web Services, the research community proposed several structured service description languages. Examples of these languages are Semantic Markup for Web Services, OWL-S[1] (Martin, Burstein & Hobbs, 2004) and Web Service Modelling Language, WSML[2] (De Bruijn, Lausen & Polleres, 2005) which have formal logic semantics groundings. Another outcome in this domain is the Semantic Annotations for WSDL and XML Schema, SAWSDL[3] (Farrell & Lausen, 2007), a W3C 2007's recommendation, which does not have any formal semantics. In this chapter, we briefly survey these approaches and languages hereafter.

Haller, Gomez & Bussler (2005) state that the usage of semantic web services and semantic SOA can help overcome the limitations of traditional SOA. This can be done by facilitating the matching of semantically similar operations in different systems, by supporting service mediation through ontology adaptation (for both process mediation and data mediation, according to the definitions of Fensel & Bussler (2002)) and by providing the standard Web Services communication mechanisms for system and process-independent communication.

To support these tasks and increase the automation in EAI, Bouras et al. (2007) proposed ENIO, an ontology that permits shared understanding of data, services and processes within B2B integration scenarios while Izza, Vincent & Burlat (2006) proposed OSDOI, a framework for EAI evolution using semantic Web Services.

Semantic Annotations for WSDL and XML Schema (SAWSDL)

SAWSDL approach (Farrell & Lausen, 2007) proposes a set of extension attributes for the WSDL and XML Schema definition languages that allows description of additional semantics of WSDL components. The SAWSDL specification defines how semantic annotation is accomplished using references to semantic models, such as ontologies. It provides mechanisms by which concepts from these semantic models, typically defined outside the WSDL document, can be referenced from within WSDL and XML Schema components using annotations. SAWSDL defines the following three extensibility attributes to WSDL 2.0 elements for their semantic annotation:

- A modelReference extension attribute; This is used to specify the association between a WSDL or XML Schema component and a concept in some semantic model. It is used to annotate XML Schema type definitions, element declarations, and attribute declarations as well as WSDL interfaces, operations, and faults. In terms of the WSDL 2.0 component model, a SAWSDL model reference is a new property.

- liftingSchemaMapping and loweringSchemaMapping extension attributes, that are added to XML Schema element declarations and type definitions for specifying mappings between semantic data and XML. Particularly, lifting schema mapping transforms XML data into instances of a semantic model, and lowering schema mapping does the opposite, it transforms semantic model instances into XML data. This SAWSDL schema mapping intends to address post-discovery issues when using Web services, such as how to overcome structural mismatches between the semantic model and the service inputs and outputs.

Hereafter we discuss some limitations and advantages of this approach. Quoting from the example section[4] of the SAWSDL recommendation: "Practice has shown that it is a very hard task to create XSLT or XQuery transformations that take arbitrary RDF/XML as input." As so, to lower schema mappings, they use XML technologies combined with an RDF query language like SPARQL to pre-process the RDF data. Thus, using SAWSDL implies the need to rely on outside software to solve semantic heterogeneities. In real applications, this task is probably assigned to external mediators.

As some OWL sublanguages bring more constraints and expressivity than RDF, a reference model defined in OWL has to be pre-processed with OWL specific tools as well. Regarding lowering schema mapping, transformations from OWL to XML can cause information loss, since XML is a less expressive language. Thus, we think using only SAWSDL may not be the best choice when the available reference model is defined in OWL.

Again, quoting from the SAWSDL recommendation: "Semantics in the scope of this specification refers to sets of concepts identified by annotations."[5] As stated by Klusch (2008a), the main criticism of SAWSDL is that it has no formal semantics and is a mere syntactic extension of WSDL.

Nevertheless, SAWSDL is less complex than OWL-S or WSML in the sense it only adds three basic constructs to connect XML WSDL representations to outside metadata information. As so, SAWSDL is convenient for applications and domain reference models that do not need the complexity or expressivity of OWL-S or WSML languages. To support SAWSDL some software is being developed, such as Lumina[6] and Radiant[7], both part of the METEOR-S project.

Web Service Modelling Language (WSML)

WSML[8] (De Bruijn, Lausen & Polleres, 2005) is a formal language for the semantic markup of web services. It is used to describe a semantic web service in terms of its functionality (service capability), imported ontologies and interface to enable access. WSML syntax mainly derives from F-logic. It also has a normative human-readable syntax, an XML and RDF syntax. WSML comes in five variants that are WSML-Core, WSML-DL, WSML-Flight, WSML-Rule and WSML-Full.

"A WSML service capability describes the state-based functionality of a service in terms of its precondition (conditions over the information space), postcondition (result of service execution delivered to the user), assumption (conditions over the world state to met before service execution), and effect (how does the execution change the world state). Roughly speaking, a WSML service capability consists of references to logical expressions in a WSML variant that are named by the scope (precondition, postcondition, assumption, effect, capability) they intend to describe." (Klusch, 2008a, p. 47).

The Web Service Modelling Ontology (Roman, Lausen & Keller, 2004), WSMO uses the WSML as the underlying representation language. WSMO defines four main modelling components: ontologies, goals, services and mediators. WSMO goals represent the objectives of the service requester to be fulfilled when consulting a Web Service. The provider side declares the service capability within a web service declaration. WSMO mediators should help matching goals and capabilities.

Haller, Gomez & Bussler (2005) propose a specific SOA architecture that applies WSMO framework and uses a specific execution environment, Web Service Execution Environment, WSMX[9] (Zaremba & Oren, 2005). In this environment, they need specific adapters to transform external messages into the WSML compliant format understood by WSMX, and mediators that perform tasks such as translation between ontologies.

Major criticism of WSML concern the lack of formal semantics of its service interface and the lack of principled guidelines for developing the proposed types of WSMO mediators for services and goals in concrete terms (Klusch, 2008a). WSML complete connection with W3C standards, such as WSDL and SAWSDL, is missing. To make up for this seems to be an ongoing work.

To support WSML some software is being developed, such as the WSML service editor associated with the WSMO studio[10], WSML-DL and WSML-Rule reasoner and the WSML validator. For instance, the SUPER[11] project uses WSMO as the underlying ontology.

Figure 1. Top level of OWL-S 1.1 service ontology. (adapted from Martin, Burstein & Hobbs, 2004)

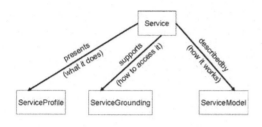

Semantic Markup for Web Services (OWL-S)

Based on OWL, Martin, Burstein & Hobbs (2004) propose OWL-S also known as OWL for Services. OWL-S currently supersedes DAML-S (Burstein, Ankolenkar & Paolucci, 2003) and intends to add precise semantics to service description and not to replace WSDL description or other existing and useful descriptions. In order to link OWL-S to WSDL some attributes are added to WSDL extensions, thus connecting both languages and generated files. For instance, maps were specified between OWL-S parameters and WSDL message parts.

OWL-S consists in three parts: the *service profile*, the *process model* (captured by the *ServiceModel* class, Figure 1) and the *grounding* (through the *supports* property referring to the *ServiceGrounding* class, Figure 1). The service profile sets out what a service does and is used to advertise the service. The process model aims at describing how the service is used, *i.e.* gives a detailed description of a service's operation. The grounding provides details on how to interact with a service, via messages.

The service profile intends to allow service providers to advertise their service and service requesters, also known as service consumers, to specify what capabilities they expect from the service they need. In OWL-S 1.0, a service profile includes functional parameters that are hasInput,

hasOutput, precondition and effect (known colloquially as IOPEs), as well as non-functional parameters such as serviceName, serviceCategory, qualityRating, textDescription, and meta-data about the service provider. Inputs and Outputs parameters specify the data transformation produced by processes. Here a process means a specification of the ways a client may interact with a service. Therefore a process can generate and return new information based on information it is given and the world state. Information production is described by the inputs and outputs of the process. A process can produce a change in the world and this transition is described by the preconditions and effects of the process. Preconditions specify facts required prior to the execution of the service. Effects are the expected result from the successful execution of the service. In OWL-S 1.1, the IOPE parameters are specified in the process model with unique references to these definitions from the service profile (Figure 2).

The semantics of each input and output parameter is defined as an OWL concept formally specified in a given ontology, while preconditions and effects are represented as logical formulas that can be expressed in any appropriate logic (rule) language such as KIF, PDDL, and SWRL. In fact, the formal representation of the execution behaviour associated with the process model constructs related to preconditions and effects can not be adequately expressed in OWL-DL.

Quoting (Martin, Burstein & Hobbs, 2004): "The Profile of a service provides a concise description of the service to a registry, but once the service has been selected the Profile is useless; rather, the client will use the Process Model to control the interaction with the service. Although the Profile and the Process Model play different roles during the transaction between Web services, they are two different representations of the same service, so it is natural to expect that the input, output, precondition, and effects of one are reflected in the IOPEs of the other."[12] In OWL-S 1.1, the process model also specifies IOPEs of all

Figure 2. Structure of the OWL-S 1.1 service profile. (adapted from Martin, Burstein & Hobbs, 2004)

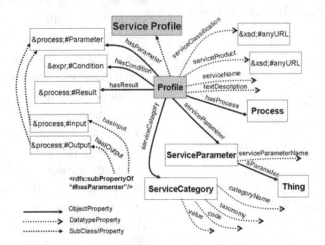

processes that are referenced in the profiles of the respective services.

An OWL-S process model describes the composition (choreography and orchestration) of one or more services. Composite processes are hierarchically defined workflows, consisting of atomic, simple and other composite processes. These process workflows are constructed using a number of different control flow operators that are Sequence, Unordered (lists), Choice, If-then-else, Iterate, Repeat-until, Repeat-while, Split, and Split+Join (Figure 3).

The grounding of a service specifies the details of how to access the service. These details have mainly to do with protocol and message formats, serialization, transport, and addressing. Martin, Burstein & Hobbs (2004) exemplify a grounding of OWL-S services in WSDL: each atomic process is mapped to a WSDL operation, and inputs and outputs are mapped to respectively named XML data types of corresponding input and output messages.

Regarding limitations of OWL-S approach, Klusch (2008a) argues that:

Figure 3. Top-level structure of the OWL-S 1.1 process model. (adapted from Martin, Burstein & Hobbs, 2004)

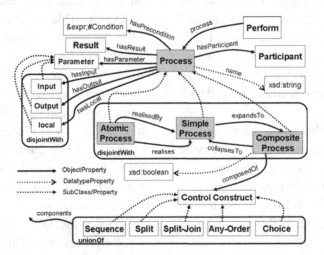

- OWL-S has limited expressiveness of service descriptions, which corresponds to that of its underlying OWL-DL;
- The static and deterministic aspects of OWL-DL may limit OWL-S expressiveness, particularly regarding the specification of some conditional effects;
- In contrast to WSDL, an OWL-S process model cannot contain any number of completely unrelated operations;
- The semantics of the OWL-S process model is missing.

Yet, OWL-S benefits from a large support from the community. Several software and applications were developed and are being developed for this language and ontology of semantic service descriptions, such as the OWL-S editor, the OWL-S API[13] and OWL-S service matchmakers, like OWLS-UDDI[14], OWLSM12[15] and OWLS-MX13[16], to name a few.

Moreover, OWL-S grounds its success on existing W3C Web standards such as WSDL and semantic web languages like OWL. It does not seem to us that the choice of SAWSDL as a W3C recommendation can endanger the future adoption of OWL-S as a W3C Semantic Web Services standard because both languages have different goals and are appropriate to different technological situations.

According to Klusch (2008a), neither OWL-S nor WSML provide any agreed formal standard workflow-based semantics of the service process model (orchestration and choreography). Alternatively, for abstract service descriptions grounded in WSDL, the process model can be intuitively mapped to BPEL orchestrations with certain formal semantics. In the EU project SUPER, an extension for BPEL, named sBPEL, is proposed which allows a process to interact with Semantic Web Services (Bhiri et al., 2008). We do not detail sBPEL further because it is out of the scope of this chapter.

LOOSE COUPLING AND SEMANTIC WEB SERVICES

Independently of specific SOA infrastructure or public registries of services, at some moment in SOA lifecycle it is necessary to match service request descriptions with available service descriptions, in order to verify if the latter corresponds to service consumer needs. This kind of task is common in inter-EAI where it is assumed that a market for services exists and to find the service best suited to the required task is needed, but it can also be present in intra-EAI situations where a company comprises sub-units that evolve individual solutions (even if service-enabled) in partial isolation. To automate this task as much as possible, both consumer and provider service descriptions have to be precisely described, such as within ontologies of services.

Loose coupling usually leads to a situation where only a few fundamental and stable concepts, attributes and data types are defined as a common data model or ontology. However, there will always be ontologies for the same domain created by different communities around the world. Thus, services are described in different ontologies. Therefore, it is necessary to provide the means of finding semantic similarities between them, *i.e.* by aligning the service ontologies. Mediators can do this task, for instance within an Enterprise Service Bus (ESB), that can help a service call performed by a consumer to find the service provider that can process this request. Josuttis (2007) details functionalities of ESB.

Aligning ontologies means discovering a collection of binary mappings between concepts of these ontologies (Ferreira da Silva, 2007; Kalfoglou & Schorlemmer, 2003). Keeping ontology consumer services separated from ontology provider services serves loose coupling.

If we try harmonizing the different ontologies by introducing a common ontology inside the ESB, for instance by merging the input ontologies instead of aligning them, we will easily disable the effect of loose coupling. Moreover, since in dynamic runtime environments the partners, *i.e.* service consumers and service providers, are not known beforehand, to build a merged ontology during design time does not seem feasible or worthy.

ALIGN SEMANTIC SERVICES

Mappings are frequently a manual task (Grau et al., 2005). However, some approaches try to bring about automation in order to help the complex and tedious mapping task, especially when reference models, such as ontologies, are huge. For instance, CtxMatch-2.1 (Bouquet, Serafini & Zanobini, 2006) incorporates a DL-based reasoner to find mappings and to align ontologies. Klusch (2008b) classifies semantic matchmaking techniques, and their associated tools, as logic-based, non-logic-based and hybrid:

- Non-logic-based matching applies techniques such as graph matching, data mining, linguistics, or content-based information retrieval to exploit semantics that are either commonly shared (in XML namespaces) or implicit in patterns or relative frequencies of terms in service descriptions;
- Logic-based semantic matching of services like those written in the service description languages OWL-S and WSML exploit standard logic inferences;
- Hybrid matching refers to the combined use of both types of matching.

Klusch (2008b) states hybrid matchmaker, based on syntactic matching techniques, produce better results than only logic-based matchmaker under certain conditions (that are not specified), as resulted of the first experimental evaluation of the performance of hybrid semantic service matchmakers OWLS-MX (Klusch, Fries & Sycara, 2006) and iMatcher2 (Kiefer & Bernstein, 2008).

In our viewpoint, the choice of the matchmaker depends on the context, particularly on the ontologies and service descriptions at hand. For instance, if only logic-based semantic service descriptions are available, then it seems inappropriate to apply non-logic-based or hybrid matching.

Each of the implemented Semantic Web service matchmakers supports only one of the many existing Semantic Web Service description formats. Refer to Klusch (2008b) for more information. Very few matchmakers ignore the structured Semantic Web Service description formats, using monolithic descriptions of services in terms of a single service concept written in a given DL. In such case, semantic matching directly uses DL inferencing, such as performed by Pellet (Sirin, Parsia & Cuenca Grau, 2007) and Racer (Li & Horrocks, 2004).

Currently, most Semantic Web Service matchmakers perform service profile rather than service process model matching. Service profile matching determines the semantic correspondence between services based on the description of their profiles. Semantic matching of service process models, in general, is very uncommon.

DISCOVERY OF SEMANTIC WEB SERVICES IN A CATALOGUE OF PRODUCTS

To illustrate our approach, we take a hypothetical situation of services discovery. On one hand, an online catalogue of electrical products includes electrical connectors among other products. These products are described in ontologies and also by service descriptions. The ontology describing design information of an electrical connector included in the catalogue is represented in Figure 4.

The service descriptions were previously created using the OWL-S editor plugin (Elenius, Denker & Martin, 2005) within the Protégé tool, and were then manually associated to each product

Figure 4. Graphical representation of the first connector, arcs represent non-hierarchical properties

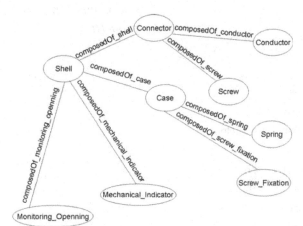

of the catalogue. In order to describe services we use OWL-S because the ontologies of products were already defined using OWL.

On the other hand, an agent in charge of the electrical plan of a civil engineering building needs detailed design information about an electrical connector for which the main design information is represented in Figure 7. As so, this agent requests a service that looks for information detail about an electrical connector. Figure 9 represents part of its service description. This service looks for the information of an electrical connector, the definition of which matches information in the associated ontology.

Figure 4 shows the main ontological classes and non-hierarchical properties, while Figure 5 shows the definition of the "Connector" concept. Protégé ontology development tool (Noy & McGuinness, 2001) is used to display the connector OWL representations.

According to this ontology, the Connector concept comprises other products' concepts, namely: "Conductor", "Screw" and "Shell". In other words, the "Connector" concept is necessarily and sufficiently defined using existential and universal restrictions by the following parts (1) to (3):

Figure 5. Definition of the first connector using Protégé ontology development tool

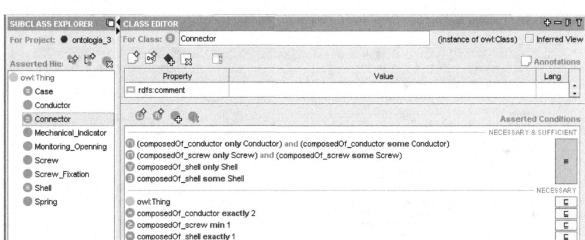

Figure 6. List of properties defined for the first connector product

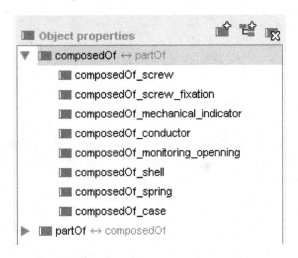

Figure 7. Graphical representation of the second connector, arcs represent non-hierarchical properties

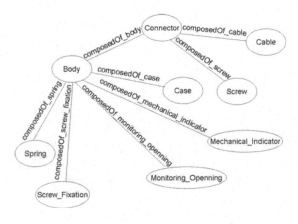

1. $\forall$composedOf_conductor.Conductor $\sqcap$ $\exists$ composedOf_conductor.Conductor
2. $\forall$composedOf_screw.Screw $\sqcap$ $\exists$ composedOf_screw.Screw
3. $\forall$composedOf_shell.Shell $\sqcap$ $\exists$ composedOf_shell.Shell

Figure 6 shows the object properties hierarchy of the first electrical connector.

The ontology of the agent in charge of the electrical plan describes a different electrical connector (Figure 7). In this one, the "Connector" concept is composed by the concepts "Cable", "Screw" and "Body".

Figure 8 shows the necessary and sufficient definition, as shown in Protégé tool.

Box 1. shows part of the service description of the agent that requests design information about an electrical connector.

The matching can be obtained using a logic-based semantic matchmaker for OWL-S, such as the OWLSM (Jäger et al., 2005) matchmaker and OWLS-UDDI (Paolucci et al., 2002), that focuses on Input/Output-matching. This can detect if the inputs and the outputs of both service description of the requestor and of the provider match. If this is the case, then the ESB calls a DL inference engine, such as Pellet, in order to compare both electrical connector ontological definitions.

Figure 8. The second hierarchical representation of the connector classes and their definition

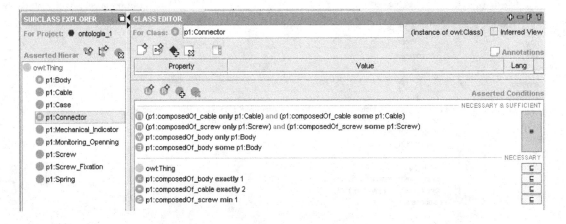

Figure 9. Display of the Pellet inference engine result

```
<!-- Service description of the service requestor, the civil engineering agent -->
<service:Service rdf:ID="ElecConnectorFinderService">
        <service:presents rdf:resource="#ElecConnectorFinderProfile"/>
        <service:describedBy rdf:resource="#ElecConnectorFinderProcess"/>
        <service:supports rdf:resource="#ElecConnectorFinderGrounding"/>
</service:Service>
<!-- Profile description -->
<Finder:ElecConnectorInfoService rdf:ID="ElecConnectorFinderProfile">
        <service:presentedBy rdf:resource="#ElecConnectorFinderService"/>
        <profile:serviceName xml:lang="en">ElecConnector Finder</profile:serviceName>
        <profile:textDescription xml:lang="en">This service looks for the
information of an Electrical Connector, the definition of which matches
information in the ontology.</profile:textDescription>
        <profile:hasInput rdf:resource="#ElecConnectorDefinition"/>
        <profile:hasOutput rdf:resource="#ElecConnectorInfo"/>
</ Finder:ElecConnectorInfoService > (...)
```

In this case, as shown in Figure 9, both electrical connector definitions are compared and no inconsistencies are detected by Pellet. Several parts of both connector definitions match, such as "conductor" and "cable". This information is returned to the requestor service, the one of the agent in charge of the electrical plan of a civil engineering building.

FUTURE TRENDS

One future trend concerns the problem of dealing with incomplete and uncertain information about services and user preferences for service discovery. As so, approximated matching, applying for instance possibility and fuzzy theories, calls further investigation.

Another trend is related to other aspects a service consumer may take into account in order to decide for a provided service. All service aspects that are important to a service consumer in the decision process should be inputs of a reasoning process. For instance, the specification of the level of expected service during its term, *i.e.* the Service Level Agreement, should be part of a formal service description in order to be accounted for when matching service ontologies.

CONCLUSION

Overall, the main goal of representing Semantic Web Services is to enable automation of SOA tasks, including fostering Enterprise Applications Integration, and that is why we need ontologies of services and tools enabling to reason on service semantics. We review several semantic web services frameworks that intend to bring semantics to Web Services. We describe an example of product catalogue to detect if consumer and provided services match, where services are described in ontologies using OWL-DL and OWL-S. The semantic matching detection is logic-based.

REFERENCES

W3C Semantic Web Activity. (2004). Retrieved on July 19, 2005, from http://www.w3.org/2001/sw/

Baader, F., Calvanese, D., & McGuinness, D. (2003). *The description logic handbook: Theory, implementation, and applications*. Cambridge University Press.

Battle, S., Bernstein, A., & Boley, H. (2005, September). *Semantic Web services framework (SWSF) overview version 1.0. W3C member submission.* Retrieved on June 26, 2006, from http://www.daml.org/services/swsf/1.0/overview/

Beckett, D. (Ed.). (2004, February 10). *RDF/XML syntax specification (revised). W3C recommendation.* Retrieved on February 15, 2004, from http://www.w3.org/TR/2004/REC-rdf-syntax-grammar-20040210/

Bhiri, S., Stein, S., Norton, B., & Dimitrov, M. (2008, September). *Semantic BPM tutorial.* Milan, Italy.

Bouquet, P., Serafini, L., & Zanobini, S. (2006). Bootstrapping semantics on the Web: Meaning elicitation from schemas. *Proceedings of the World Wide Web Conference* (pp. 505-512).

Bouras, A., Gouvas, P., Kourtesis, D., & Mentzas, G. (2007). Semantic integration of business applications across collaborative value networks. In L. Camarinha-Matos, H. Afsarmanesh, P. Novais & C. Analide (Eds.), *Establishing the foundation of collaborative networks: Vol. 243. IFIP International Federation for Information Processing* (pp. 539-54). Boston: Springer. DOI:10.1007/978-0-387-73798-0_58

Bray, T., Paoli, J., & Sperberg-McQueen, C. (Eds.). (2006, August 16). *Extensible markup language (XML) 1.0 (fourth edition). W3C Recommendation.* Retrieved on August 27, 2006, from http://www.w3.org/TR/2006/REC-xml-20060816/

Brickley, D., & Guha, R. V. (2004, February 10). *RDF vocabulary description language 1.0: RDF schema. W3C Recommendation.* Retrieved on May 6, 2004, from http://www.w3.org/TR/2004/REC-rdf-schema-20040210/

Burstein, M., Ankolenkar, A., & Paolucci, M. (2003). *DAML-S: Semantic markup for Web services. The DAML Services Coalition.* Retrieved on January 27, 2004, from www.daml.org/services/daml-s/0.9/daml-s.html

Chinnici, R., Moreau, J. J., & Ryman, A. (2007, June 26). *Web services description language (WSDL) version 2.0 part 1: Core language. W3C Recommendation.* Retrieved on October 27, 2007, from http://www.w3.org/TR/2007/REC-wsdl20-20070626

Christensen, E., Curbera, F., & Meredith, G. (2001, March 15). *Web services description language (WSDL) 1.1. W3C Note.* Retrieved on May 5, 2003, from http://www.w3.org/TR/2001/NOTE-wsdl-20010315

De Bruijn, J., Lausen, H., & Polleres, A. (2005, June). The Web service modeling language WSML: An overview. DERI Tech. Rep. 2005-06-16. Retrieved on January 23, 2006, from http://www.wsmo.org/wsml/wsml-resources/deri-tr-2005-06-16.pdf

Elenius, D., Denker, G., & Martin, D. (2005). The OWL-S editor-a development tool for Semantic Web services. *Proceedings of the 2nd European Semantic Web Conference* (ESWC), Heraklion, Greece.

European Interoperability Framework for pan-European eGovernment services. (2003). Retrieved on June 17, 2005, from http://ec.europa.eu/idabc/servlets/Doc?id=19528

Farrell, J., & Lausen, H. (Eds.). (2007, August 28). *Semantic annotations for WSDL and XML schema (SAWSDL). W3C Recommendation.* Retrieved on July 15, 2008, from http://www.w3.org/TR/2007/REC-sawsdl-20070828/

Fensel, D., & Bussler, C. (2002). The Web service modeling framework WSMF. *Electronic Commerce Research and Applications, 1*(2), 113–137. doi:. doi:10.1016/S1567-4223(02)00015-7

Ferreira da Silva, C. (2007). Découverte de correspondances sémantiques entre ressources hétérogènes dans un environnement coopératif. Doctoral dissertation n° 281-2007, Villeurbanne, Université Claude Bernard Lyon 1.

Gruber, T. R. (1993). A translation approach to portable ontology specifications. *Knowledge Acquisition*, *5*, 199–220. doi:10.1006/knac.1993.1008

Haller, A., Gomez, J. M., & Bussler, C. (2005, May). *Exposing Semantic Web service principles in SOA to solve EAI scenarios*. Paper presented at the WWW 2005 Conference, Chiba, Japan.

ISO/IEC 2382-01. (1993). *Information technology–vocabulary–part 1: Fundamental terms*. International Standard Organisation.

Izza, S., Vincent, L., & Burlat, P. (2006). A framework for semantic enterprise integration. In D. Konstantas, J.-P. Bourrières, M. Léonard & N. Boudjlid (Eds.), *Interoperability of enterprise software and applications* (pp. 75-86). London: Springer. DOI:10.1007/1-84628-152-0_8

Jäger, M. C., Rojec-Goldmann, G., Liebetruth, C., Mühl, G., & Geihs, K. (2005). Ranked matching for service descriptions using OWL-S. *Proceedings of 14 GI/VDE Fachtagung Kommunikation in Verteilten Systemen KiVS*, Kaiserslautern.

Josuttis, N. M. (2007). *SOA in practice*. Sebastopol, CA: O'Reilly. ISBN-10: 0-596-52955-4

Kalfoglou, Y., & Schorlemmer, M. (2003). Ontology mapping: The state of the art. In P. McBurney & S. Parsons (Eds.), *The Knowledge Engineering Review Journal*, *18*(1), 1–31. UK: Cambridge University Press. DOI: 10.1017/S0269888903000651

Kiefer, C., & Bernstein, A. (2008). The creation and evaluation of iSPARQL strategies for matchmaking. *Proceedings of European Semantic Web Conference*. Springer.

Klusch, M. (2008a). Semantic Web service description. In M. Schumacher, H. Schuldt & H. Helin (Eds.), *CASCOM: Intelligent service coordination in the Semantic Web. Whitestein series in software agent technologies and autonomic computing* (pp. 59-104). Basel: Birkhäuser. DOI: 10.1007/978-3-7643-8575-0_4

Klusch, M. (2008b). Semantic Web service coordination. In M. Schumacher, H. Schuldt & H. Helin (Eds.), *CASCOM: Intelligent service coordination in the Semantic Web. Whitestein series in software agent technologies and autonomic computing* (pp. 31-57). Basel: Birkhäuser. DOI:10.1007/978-3-7643-8575-0_3

Klusch, M., Fries, B., & Sycara, K. (2006). Automated Semantic Web service discovery with OWLS-MX. *Proc. 5th Intl. Conference on Autonomous Agents and Multiagent Systems* (AAMAS), Hakodate, Japan. ACM Press.

Li, L., & Horrocks, I. (2004). A software framework for matchmaking based on Semantic Web technology. *International Journal of Electronic Commerce*, *8*(4), 39–60.

Martin, D., Burstein, M., & Hobbs, J. (2004, November 22). *OWL-S: Semantic markup for Web services. W3C Member Submission*. Retrieved on February 16, 2005, from http://www.w3.org/Submission/2004/SUBM-OWL-S-20041122/

McGuinness, D. L., & Van Harmelen, F. (Eds.). (2004, February 10). *OWL Web ontology language overview. W3C Recommendation*. Retrieved on February 15, 2004, from http://www.w3.org/TR/2004/REC-owl-features-20040210/

Noy, N. F., & McGuinness, D. L. (2001). Ontology development 101: A guide to creating your first ontology. *Semantic Web Working Symposium 2001*.

Paolucci, M., Kawamura, T., Payne, T. R., & Sycara, K. (2002). Semantic matching of Web services capabilities. *Proceedings of the 1st International Semantic Web Conference (ISWC2002)*.

Roman, D., Lausen, H., & Keller, U. (2004). *Web service modeling ontology (WSMO). WSMO final draft*. Retrieved on November 15, 2005, from http://www.wsmo.org/2004/d2/v1.0/

Sirin, E., Parsia, B., & Cuenca Grau, B. (2007). Pellet: A practical OWL-DL reasoner. *Journal of Web Semantics: Science, Services, and Agents on the World Wide Web*. In E. Wallace (Ed.), *Software engineering and the Semantic Web, 5*(2), 51-53.

Zaremba, M., & Oren, E. (2005). *WSMX execution semantics. WSMX working draft D13.2 v0.2*. Retrieved on March 7, 2006 from [REMOVED HYPERLINK FIELD]http://www.wsmo.org/2005/d13/d13.2/v0.2/2005022/

ENDNOTES

1 http://www.w3.org/Submission/OWL-S
2 http://www.wsmo.org/TR/d16/d16.1/ v0.21/20051005/
3 http://www.w3.org/TR/sawsdl/
4 http://www.w3.org/TR/2007/REC-sawsdl-20070828/#Example
5 http://www.w3.org/TR/2007/REC-sawsdl-20070828/#Terminology
6 http://lsdis.cs.uga.edu/projects/meteor-s/ downloads/Lumina/
7 http://lsdis.cs.uga.edu/projects/meteor-s/ downloads/index.php?page=1
8 http://www.wsmo.org/TR/d16/d16.1/ v0.21/20051005/
9 http://sourceforge.net/projects/wsmx/
10 http://www.wsmostudio.org/download. html
11 http://www.ip-super.org/content/ view/70/72/
12 http://www.w3.org/Submission/2004/ SUBM-OWL-S-20041122/#4
13 http://projects.semwebcentral.org/projects/ owl-s-api/
14 http://projects.semwebcentral.org/projects/ mm-client/
15 http://projects.semwebcentral.org/projects/ owlsm/
16 http://projects.semwebcentral.org/projects/ owls-mx/

Chapter 6
Supporting Semantically Enhanced Web Service Discovery for Enterprise Application Integration

Dimitrios Kourtesis
South East European Research Centre (SEERC), Research Centre of the University of Sheffield and CITY College, Greece

Iraklis Paraskakis
South East European Research Centre (SEERC), Research Centre of the University of Sheffield and CITY College, Greece

ABSTRACT

The availability of sophisticated Web service discovery mechanisms is an essential prerequisite for increasing the levels of efficiency and automation in EAI. In this chapter, we present an approach for developing service registries building on the UDDI standard and offering semantically-enhanced publication and discovery capabilities in order to overcome some of the known limitations of conventional service registries. The approach aspires to promote efficiency in EAI in a number of ways, but primarily by automating the task of evaluating service integrability on the basis of the input and output messages that are defined in the Web service's interface. The presented solution combines the use of three technology standards to meet its objectives: OWL-DL, for modelling service characteristics and performing fine-grained service matchmaking via DL reasoning, SAWSDL, for creating semantically annotated descriptions of service interfaces, and UDDI, for storing and retrieving syntactic and semantic information about services and service providers.

INTRODUCTION

Service-oriented computing is emerging as the dominant paradigm for enterprise computing and is changing the way business software applications are architected, developed, delivered, and consumed. The model of Service Oriented Architecture (SOA) and its manifestation through Web service technology standards promise to alleviate many of the barriers that stand on the path to Enterprise Ap-

DOI: 10.4018/978-1-60566-804-8.ch006

plication Integration (EAI) and become enablers for business agility in the modern enterprise.

In a service-oriented landscape where contemporary technologies are employed, the integration of a set of enterprise applications (such as ERP, CRM, or WMS), is typically performed by composing the reusable Web services that are exposed by the individual applications into service orchestrations which are encoded in the popular WS-BPEL language -Web Services Business Process Execution Language- (Alves, et al., 2007). A BPEL orchestration is essentially an executable program that specifies how a set of services exposed by different applications should be coordinated in order to realise a specific business process, such as order fulfilment or stock replenishment. By deploying the service orchestration on a BPEL execution engine, the fulfilled business process is externalised as a normal Web service on the corporate network, which means that it can be consumed by client applications or re-composed in new Web service orchestrations.

Web Service Discovery for Enterprise Application Integration

During the phases of construction and maintenance of a service orchestration, the business process expert needs to search and discover Web services that are suitable for carrying out each of the key activities/functions in the workflow of the envisaged business process. The Web services that will finally be selected and included in the orchestration, among the tens or hundreds of services that may potentially be available on the corporate network, have to match a number of requirements. Depending on the application domain and the type of business process that the orchestration seeks to realise, these requirements may involve functional or non-functional aspects of service operation.

In every occasion, however, an essential requirement that needs to be satisfied is the integrability of the Web service on the basis of the

input and output messages that are defined in the service's interface. The ability of a Web service to be integrated in a service orchestration depends on whether proper data flow and thus proper communication can be established among the two. More specifically, proper data flow can be achieved only if the amount of data which the BPEL orchestration provides as input when it invokes a service are sufficient with regard to the amount of data that the service expects to receive, and at the same time, the amount of data that the service produces as output are sufficient with regard to the amount of data that the orchestration expects to obtain. If this condition holds, integration can be made possible even if the schema definitions of the business objects to be exchanged by the two parties along input and output messages are not identical (the heterogeneity can be overcome by applying some data mediation/transformation process).

Undeniably, in a fully SOA-enabled business application ecosystem with tens or hundreds of deployed Web services, the task of manually searching and identifying services that satisfy the above requirements for integrability can become extremely resource-intensive and error prone. This is why the existence of intelligent automated Web service discovery mechanisms that can address these needs is considered a core challenge for increasing the levels of efficiency and automation in EAI.

Web Service Discovery with UDDI

The need for efficient search and discovery of services was the original motivation behind the development of the Universal Description, Discovery and Integration (UDDI) specification as a standardised way to catalogue and discover reusable Web services (Clement, Hately, von Riegen, & Rogers, 2004). The UDDI specification was the result of an industry-driven standardisation effort led by the OASIS consortium, and its scope was not limited to providing support for EAI alone, but for a much wider range of use cases. Primarily due to the active promotion of the standard by the enterprise software industry, UDDI quickly became one of the core standards in the Web service technology stack and an integral part of every major SOA vendor's technology strategy (see IBM WebSphere UDDI Registry, Oracle Service Registry, SAP Enterprise Services Registry, Microsoft Windows Server 2003 Enterprise UDDI Services, etc).

The UDDI specification standardises an XML-based data model for storing descriptive information about Web services and their providers, and a Web service-based application programmatic interface for publishing this information to the registry and performing discovery queries. Web service advertisements are represented as records in the registry. In order to describe the functionality of some service, its respective record contains references to external descriptions of technical specifications or to classification schemes which are developed and maintained by either third-party actors (e.g. standardisation bodies), or by service providers themselves. Numerous such references can be used for representing different aspects of a Web service's functional and non-functional properties. For the purpose of being generic, the UDDI standard does not prescribe any specific method, formal or informal, for creating these specifications and classification schemes. Overall, services advertised in UDDI registries can be searched by prospective service consumers based on one of the following criteria: i) the service's declared conformance to some technical specification, where matching is evaluated against a provided specification identifier, ii) the service's attributed categorisation within a classification system, where matching is evaluated against a provided category title, and iii) the service's name, where matching is evaluated against a provided keyword search term.

The fundamental problem with the UDDI description and discovery mechanism outlined above is that despite the fact that the available service descriptions are machine-processable, they lack the formal rigour and machine-understandable semantics that would make them amenable to logic-based reasoning and automated processing. As a result, UDDI registries cannot offer the kind of fine-grained service matchmaking functionality that would be required for supporting automated integrability-oriented service discovery in the context of EAI. With today's state of practice, a developer in a typical EAI scenario still needs to retrieve the service-related artefacts referenced by a UDDI service advertisement (and most importantly the WSDL document) and inspect them manually, in order to decide if the advertised service can be interoperable with other services assembled in a service orchestration.

Semantically-Enhanced Web Service Discovery

In order to increase the levels of automation in EAI and overcome the problem of ambiguity that currently hinders automated service discovery, service characteristics need to be described in a formal, machine-understandable manner that is amenable to processing within semantically-enhanced service registries. The use of Semantic Web technologies to represent service properties and the introduction of semantic matchmaking functionality in service registries (primarily UDDI) has been the focus of numerous works in recent years, generally within the field of Semantic Web Services (SWS) research. The vision in SWS research (Martin, Domingue, Brodie, & Leymann, 2007; Martin, Domingue, Sheth, Battle, Sycara, & Fensel, 2007) is to bring semantics into the realm of Web service specifications in order to not only enable fully automated service discovery, but facilitate the automation of a broad array of design-time and run-time activities in service-oriented computing.

In this chapter we present a new approach for developing service registries that build on the UDDI standard and offer semantically-enhanced

Web service publication and discovery capabilities. The approach aspires to promote efficiency in EAI in a number of ways, but primarily by automating the task of evaluating service integrability on the basis of the input and output messages that are defined in the Web service's interface. Overall, the semantically-enhanced service registry combines three existing standards from the domains of Web service technologies and Semantic Web technologies to address its objectives: OWL-DL (McGuinness & van Harmelen, 2004), for modelling service characteristics and performing fine-grained service matchmaking via Description Logic reasoning, SAWSDL (Farrell & Lausen, 2007), for creating semantically annotated descriptions of service interfaces, and UDDI (Clement, Hately, von Riegen, & Rogers, 2004), for storing and retrieving syntactic and semantic information about services and service providers. The approach that we put forward has been applied and validated during the development of the FUSION Semantic Registry[1], a semantically-enhanced service registry that has been utilised in research project FUSION[2] and is released as open source software.

The organisation of the chapter is as follows. Section 2 introduces the background to the discussed topic, outlines a set of requirements for Semantic Web Service discovery in the context of EAI, and provides a detailed review of related research works that focus on semantic enhancements to UDDI registries. Section 3 presents our approach for describing service characteristics in order to support integrability-oriented service discovery with the FUSION Semantic Registry. Section 4 presents an overview of the FUSION Semantic Registry architecture and its application programming interfaces. Section 5 provides a walkthrough of the core activities performed during service publication, while section 6 provides a walkthrough of the activities performed during service discovery. Lastly, section 7 summarises the key points presented in this chapter, presents an overview of how our work compares with other related works, and provides an outlook to future research directions.

BACKGROUND AND RELATED WORK

In this section we briefly introduce Semantic Web Services (SWS) as the background to the discussed topic and outline some fundamental requirements for Semantic Web Service discovery in the context of EAI. We also provide a detailed review of related research works which employ SWS technologies in order to provide enhancements for UDDI-based service registries, and contrast each of these works with the requirements set for discovery in the context of EAI. Note that a detailed discussion on how the related works that are presented here compare to our own solution and to the overall requirements is not provided here, but placed in appropriate sections throughout the chapter and finally summarised in the end of the chapter.

Semantic Web Service Description Frameworks

The domain of Semantic Web Services is positioned at the intersection of Semantic Web technologies and Web service technologies and has been a distinct research theme since 2001 (McIlraith, Son, & Zeng, 2001). The vision in SWS research is to bring formal logic-based semantics into Web service technology standards such that service characteristics can be explicated in an unambiguous, computer-interpretable manner that facilitates the automation of a broad range of activities, primarily discovery, composition, execution and mediation. The core idea is that by using formal representation schemes to describe Web service characteristics, service-related artefacts can be automatically processed by specialised tools through logic-based inference and automated reasoning.

Evidently, the degree of automation that can be achieved depends on the expressiveness and overall capabilities of the semantic representation formalism that is employed for this purpose. Recent years have seen the development of numerous such formalisms for representing service characteristics, termed SWS description frameworks. The most prominent proposals towards a standardised SWS framework have been OWL-S (Martin, et al., 2004), WSMO (Bruijn, et al., 2005), and WSDL-S (Akkiraju, et al., 2005). The latter provided the foundation for the development of SAWSDL (Farrell & Lausen, 2007) which was eventually ratified by the W3C in 2007 and is currently the only standard in the area of SWS.

Requirements for Semantic Web Service Discovery in the Context of EAI

The application of Semantic Web Service technologies for enhancing various aspects of Enterprise Application Integration has been investigated in numerous works (Bussler, 2003); (Haller, Gomez, & Bussler, 2005); (Preist, Esplugas-Cuadrado, Battle, Grimm, & Williams, 2005); (Anicic, Ivezic, & Jones, 2006); (Izza, Vincent, & Burlat, 2006). One of the most recent research efforts in this direction was that of project FUSION, an EU-funded collaborative research project undertaken by a consortium of industrial and academic partners that was coordinated by SAP. FUSION focused on improving the efficiency of business process integration within and across enterprises by leveraging SWS technologies for achieving interoperability among service-oriented business applications (Alazeib, et al., 2007). The project delivered a complete reference framework and a methodology for semantics-based EAI, a reference implementation of the proposed framework, and a validation of the overall approach through three pilot studies on intra- and inter-organisational integration.

The introduction of semantics to Web service discovery is an essential requirement for realising the Semantic EAI approach that is put forward by FUSION. In general, the development of a semantically-enhanced service registry is an undertaking that encompasses the following research challenges.

- Firstly, devising means for describing service advertisements and service requests in a formal, semantically-rich and machine-understandable form that captures their salient properties and allows for comparing them in an automated way through logic-based inferencing.
- Secondly, developing a service registry that augments the typical functions of UDDI registries by introducing a reasoning mechanism that can process the semantic service descriptions and carry out automated matchmaking among service advertisements and requests.

As a general rule, it would also be desirable to address these requirements in a way that promotes the use of open standards and open source software, such as in the languages to be used for encoding the semantic descriptions of services and in the technologies to be used for the development of the registry.

Beyond the above definition of research challenges which is broad and application-independent, the context of Enterprise Application Integration gives rise to some more specific requirements that must be overcome for effective service discovery, as the FUSION project has demonstrated.

Firstly, concerning the description of service advertisements and requests, the context of EAI imposes some requirements with regard to the type of service properties that need to be described, and consequently, imposes requirements with regard to the ontology language and the ontology structure that is employed for capturing them.

More specifically, a fundamental criterion that must be considered in Web service discovery for EAI, as already mentioned in the introduction, is the integrability of a service on the basis of the input and output messages that are defined in its interface. During matchmaking we need to be able to evaluate if the amount of data that the service consumer (i.e. the BPEL orchestration) can provide as input to a service are sufficient with regard to the amount of data that the service expects to receive, and vice versa for the outputs. Therefore, the input and output data parameters of a service that are defined in WSDL (Christensen, Curbera, Meredith, & Weerawarana, 2001) using XML Schema Definitions (XSD) are regarded as salient properties of that service that need to be semantically represented. Consequently, a critical requirement that is placed on the ontology language in which the schemata of input and output parameters are to be represented, is that it should be expressive enough to allow the preservation of the semantics of arbitrarily complex XML Schema Definitions.

Secondly, concerning the design and implementation of the service registry, the context of EAI places some important requirements with regard to the matchmaking function and the capabilities of the underlying reasoning mechanism. To enable automated discovery, the registry must employ logic-based inferencing for the purpose of matchmaking among service requests and advertisements, on the basis of the ontological representations of their I/O data schemata. For that reason, it is a requirement that the registry's inference engine can perform sound and complete reasoning at a level of expressiveness that is equivalent to that of the ontology in which the I/O data schemata are represented. In addition, since the I/O-based matchmaking function evaluates service suitability on the basis of the service's interface, i.e. only from a technical point of view, it would be desirable for the registry to provide an auxiliary semantic matchmaking function that assesses the suitability of a Web service for some given process task from a business point of view. As demonstrated in the FUSION project, but also in other related works that are presented next, an intuitive way in which this could be achieved is through category-based indexing and searching, whereby each service is assigned a category from some taxonomy of business areas/activities which designates the intended functionality of that service. This auxiliary matchmaking function can significantly improve the results of service discovery by filtering out advertised services that happen to have integrable interfaces because their inputs and outputs match the specifications of the request, but are nevertheless performing business tasks irrelevant to the needs of the requestor (e.g. consider the functionality of CreateOrder vs. CancelOrder).

Note that the above discussion of requirements for the description of service properties and the design and implementation of the service registry is only a brief outline. A more detailed analysis of the motivation behind these requirements and how they are addressed in our approach and implementation is provided later in the chapter.

Related Work on UDDI-Based Semantic Service Registries

The use of SWS frameworks for representing discovery-related service properties and facilitating semantically-enhanced matchmaking in Web service registries has been investigated in numerous research works. In recognition of the fact that UDDI is a widely endorsed Web service technology standard with extensive support by the industry, the vast majority of these works has focused on combining these SWS frameworks with UDDI-based service registries, rather than proprietary registry back-ends. The rationale behind this decision is that the best way to promote the adoption of Semantic Web technologies is by enhancing today's widely-endorsed technology standards with semantics whenever appropriate and where feasible, instead of trying to introduce new standards. In this review we confine ourselves to works that seek to promote semantically-enhanced service matchmaking specifically in relation to the open standard of UDDI, and in addition, works that are not only theoretic but come with a proof-of-concept system implementation.

Paolucci, Kawamura, Payne, & Sycara (2002) from Carnegie Mellon University were the first to propose that discovery in UDDI registries can be significantly enhanced by introducing semantic matchmaking among service descriptions. The paper presents a matchmaking algorithm able to recognise various degrees of matching among a request and an advertisement that are described with DAML-S (the precursor of OWL-S), by applying subsumption reasoning on the ontological representations of their inputs and outputs. The authors also propose to integrate a matchmaking engine that realises this approach inside the UDDI registry and provide a mapping between DAML-S Profiles and the UDDI data model. Subsequent work by the same group (Srinivasan, Paolucci, & Sycara, 2005) proposes a revised mapping between OWL-S Profiles and the UDDI data model, and an improved version of the matchmaking algorithm from Paolucci et al (2002). Since the SWS framework that is adopted in this work is OWL-S, the ontology language in which input and output parameters are to be represented is OWL. As will be shown later in the chapter, the OWL language includes the dialect of OWL-DL which appears to be sufficiently expressive for representing XSD structures, so the requirement for ontological expressivity that we described earlier could be satisfied. Moreover, in the implementation of their semantic service registry the authors employ an inference mechanism that relies on standard Description Logic reasoners like Pellet and Racer which are known to perform sound and complete reasoning over knowledge-bases encoded in OWL-DL.

The divergence of this work with regard to the requirements that we outlined in the previous section is very small and can be found in the following. Firstly, the introduction of the OWL-S matchmaker in the UDDI registry necessitates the modification of the UDDI server's API which is a practice that conflicts with the standard. Secondly, the approach described in the papers lacks an auxiliary semantic matchmaking method such as category-based matchmaking for complementing the I/O-based matchmaking (although the implemented OWL-S/UDDI matchmaker tool apparently supports classification-based search). Thirdly, the implementation of the OWL-S/UDDI matchmaker is freely available in binary form[3] but the source code is not released in order to be adapted and extended with regard to our set requirements.

A research work by a different group at IBM that expands the approach introduced by Paolucci et al. (2002) is presented in Akkiraju, Goodwin, Doshi, & Roeder (2003). The authors present a method to improve the effectiveness of service discovery in UDDI based on a two-stage service discovery process which combines syntactic category-based search via the standard UDDI search mechanism, and semantic I-O-based search via logic-based inferencing. They also propose extensions to the specification of the UDDI inquiry and publish API in order to support automatic service composition based on DAML-S service descriptions. The main idea is that if no single matching service can be found for a submitted service request, the registry could attempt to construct a sequential composition of Web services that fulfils the request by chaining the output of one service to the inputs of another. The authors report that they have implemented and tested a registry that realises this approach using DAML-S v0.7 for the service descriptions, DAML+OIL for the representation of the domain ontology in which inputs and outputs are defined, DAMLJESSKB for performing inferencing, and IBM's implementation of UDDI version 2.0 for the registry back-end.

The above described work does not match all of the previously outlined requirements, because of the following reasons. Firstly, the category-based matchmaking method is not a semantic one, and as already explained this has several limitations. Secondly, it is unclear whether the expressivity of DAML+OIL would be sufficient for representing arbitrarily complex XSD schemata of service inputs and outputs, and moreover, it is unclear whether the ontology expressiveness supported by the DAMLJessKB inference engine would suffice for reasoning over such representations. Thirdly, similarly to the approach of Paolucci, Kawamura, Payne & Sycara (2002), this work proposes the modification of the UDDI server's API with non-standard functions. Lastly, the reported implementation of the semantically-enhanced UDDI registry has not been made publicly available, although some of the ideas and functionality seem to have been incorporated in the subsequent release of IBM alphaworks Semantic Tools for Web Services[4], which is a set of Eclipse plug-ins (closed source) for semantic matching and composition of Web services that does not rely on UDDI as the registry back-end.

Another approach for developing OWL-S-based semantically-extended UDDI registries is presented in Luo, Montrose, Kim, Khashnobish, & Kang (2006). The key feature of the proposed solution is that relationships among ontology concepts which are encoded in OWL are resolved at the time of publication and indexed in UDDI in a way that enables purely syntactic querying at the time of discovery using the standard UDDI API. An OWL2UDDI transformation method is presented for analysing ontologies encoded in OWL and representing associations among equivalent concepts, parent concepts, and child concepts into the UDDI data model, such that queries for some concept would also return related concepts that have been determined through reasoning at the time of indexing. The modules for publishing and query processing are placed on the client-side and as a result no modifications to the UDDI server implementation or interface are mandated.

This work diverges from our stated requirements because of the following reasons. Firstly, as explained by the authors, the approach covers only a portion of the vocabulary in the OWL language, and thus has a rather limited expressivity capacity that would not suffice for preserving the semantics of arbitrarily complex XML Schema Definitions. For example, it cannot cope with property restrictions within definitions of OWL classes. Secondly, the approach does not address I/O-based matchmaking specifically, but rather, it is said to support a generic matchmaking process that compares OWL-S Profiles of service advertisements and service requests as whole entities, using one-to-one semantic property annotation matching. As a result, it is unclear whether the system that the authors have implemented takes the principle of subsumption asymmetry among inputs and outputs into consideration (i.e. that for a match to exist, the output of the advertised service must be a subtype of the output specified in the service request, and the input specified in the service request must be a subtype of the input of the advertised service). Lastly, the paper reports a proof-of-concept implementation of the approach but the authors have not made it publicly available.

An approach by the LSDIS group at the University of Georgia Athens based on the WSDL-S specification is introduced in Sivashanmugam, Verma, Sheth, & Miller (2003) and elaborated in Li, Verma, Mulye, Rabbani, Miller, & Sheth (2006). In the first of these two works the authors present a theoretical approach for publishing WSDL-S service descriptions that have been semantically annotated with references to concepts defined in an ontology. The paper presents a WSDL-S to UDDI mapping for storing the semantic annotations and facilitating subsequent discovery of Web service operations based upon them. A discovery algorithm is defined which first selects the services using ontological concepts representing the functionality of operations (i.e. a form of categorisation), and then uses inputs and outputs to prune the search. The service requestor can initiate the discovery by creating a semantic request template that specifies the desired functionality (i.e. category), inputs, and outputs, by references to ontological concepts. In the subsequent work of Li et al (2006) the authors describe the way in which Web service descriptions can be annotated, published and discovered using Radiant and Lumina, a pair of graphical tools integrated with the METEOR-S Web Services Discovery Infrastructure (Verma, Sivashanmugam, Sheth, Patil, Oundhakar, & Miller, 2005) which supports scalable publication and discovery in peer-to-peer networks of distributed registries.

The approach by the LSDIS group is very close to the requirements that we have set in the previous section. The only exception concerns the requirement of sufficient ontological expressivity for the representation of service message parameters and for reasoning, which is however an essential requirement for integrability-oriented service discovery. The theoretic approach that is described in the papers is generic and does not prescribe any particular ontology language for creating semantic representations of inputs and outputs or categories of functionality, neither any specific reasoner for reasoning over these representations. However, the implementation of the approach which is available as open source software with METEOR-S[5] assumes the availability of OWL ontologies and implements an OWL reasoner based on the Jena API. The problem with ontology expressivity lies in the processing capabilities of Jena, because according to its documentation[6], Jena rule-based reasoners are able to provide semantic entailments only for OWL ontologies using the vocabulary of the OWL-Lite dialect, and some constructs from the more expressive dialect of OWL-DL. In order to mitigate the effects from this lack of processing power Jena implements the DIG description logic reasoner interface for connecting to external reasoners, but this does not suffice to overcome the issue, since

it is known that some OWL-DL constructs cannot be expressed in the DIG "tell" language, and some desirable queries are not possible. Overall, it appears that the ontology expressivity supported by the Jena-based reasoner would not suffice for reasoning over representations of arbitrarily complex definitions of XSD schemata of service input and output message parameters.

A number of service discovery engine prototypes have also been developed in the context of the WSMX Working Group[7] for supporting the three different discovery approaches that are put forward in WSMO, i.e. keyword-based discovery, lightweight semantic discovery based on WSML-Rule and WSML-DL, and heavyweight semantic discovery based on WSML-Flight (Keller, Lara, Polleres, Toma, Kifer, & Fensel, 2004). The specific works however do not offer themselves for direct comparison with the other approaches presented above, as they do not attempt to provide semantic enhancements to UDDI but rather stand as independent WSMX environment components that are not meant to be integrated with UDDI registries.

INTEGRABILITY-ORIENTED DESCRIPTIONS OF SERVICE PROPERTIES

As mentioned in the previous section, semantically-enhanced publication and discovery of services in UDDI-based registries encompasses two main objectives. Firstly, describing service advertisements and service requests in a machine-understandable form that captures their salient characteristics and allows for comparing them in an automated way. Secondly, augmenting the typical functions supported by UDDI registries (i.e. storing syntactic metadata about services and their providers) with the addition of a mechanism for semantic service indexing and matchmaking. This section of the chapter discusses the first objective. More specifically, we first describe what are the salient service characteristics (functional and non-functional properties) that are modelled in order to support integrability-oriented service discovery with the FUSION Semantic Registry, and subsequently, we analyse how these characteristics are captured in a suitable semantic representation formalism.

Service Properties for Integrability-Oriented Service Matchmaking

The Semantic Web Services research literature features an abundance of different approaches for service matchmaking. Each of them is intended to address a specific set of requirements and therefore focuses on a different set of service properties, functional or non-functional ones. The set of service characteristics that the FUSION Semantic Registry considers during matchmaking is a combination of functional and non-functional properties and represents the minimum amount of information that would be needed for determining if some advertised service is capable of performing some task and at the same time is syntactically and semantically interoperable with the service consumer, i.e. with the BPEL orchestration that invokes the service and consumes its output.

Functional Properties of Web Services: Inputs and Outputs

As already mentioned in the introduction, in integrability-oriented service matchmaking we need to detect if interoperability at the level of data can be guaranteed among an advertised service and its prospective consumer, such that proper data flow and communication can be established among the two. In the context of FUSION, but also in most of the approaches for Semantic Enterprise Application Integration, the service consumer is an executable Web service orchestration encoded in WS-BPEL. The WS-BPEL-encoded orchestration is essentially a controller program that is itself exposed as a Web service and whose purpose is to specify how a set of Web services exposed by different enterprise applications should interoperate to realise a specific business process. What we therefore seek to determine in our integrability-oriented service matchmaking is if some advertised service can be safely integrated in this executable orchestration.

The instance data to be used at run-time by the executable BPEL orchestration for invoking the advertised service may have originated from a previous step in the process (i.e. from some other Web service participating in the orchestration), may have resulted from numeric calculations or string manipulations within the BPEL code, or may have been provided to the controller service from the external environment (i.e. from the system that triggered the execution of the BPEL orchestration). Similarly, the instance data that the BPEL controller service will receive as output from the invoked service may later on be fed into some other Web service taking part in the orchestration, may be used for performing internal calculations that affect control flow, or may be returned by the controller service to the environment. Data-level compatibility among the inputs and outputs of Web services participating in an orchestration and the orchestrator service itself is therefore an essential requirement for guaranteeing communication and composability (Kourtesis & Paraskakis, 2008a; Kourtesis & Paraskakis, 2008b).

In plain terms, in order to assert this notion of data-level compatibility we need to ensure that the data that the controller BPEL service is able to provide upon invocation are sufficient with regard to the input data that the advertised service expects to receive, and conversely, the output data that the advertised service produces are sufficient with regard to the data that the controller service expects to receive. We use the term *sufficient* to denote that the data schemata of the two parties may not necessarily be identical for integration to be possible. Rather, it would suffice to assert that the service consumer can provide *at least* the amount of data that the advertised service expects to receive, and at the same time, the advertised service can generate *at least* the amount of data that the consumer (i.e. the controller service) expects to obtain. If this can be asserted, then it is safe to assume that a transformation from the more informative data schema to the least informative one can be obtained in a straightforward manner (manually or semi-automatically) and therefore data flow in the business process can be made possible.

This relates directly to the notions of covariance and contravariance applied in the context of function subtyping and safe substitution, which have been studied in detail within type-theory and object-oriented programming research (Simons, 2002). If we attempt to draw parallels with service-orientation, we could say that in order to substitute a service request with a service advertisement the first must be shown to subsume the latter (i.e. the request must be more generic than the advertisement). In other words, the advertisement must be proven to be a subtype, or special case, of the request. For this subsumption ordering to hold, the subsumption relation among the input types of the request and the input types of the advertisement must be contravariant (i.e. the advertisement input types must subsume the request input types), while the subsumption among their output types must be covariant (i.e. the request output types must subsume the advertisement output types). In practical terms, if a data parameter subsumes another, it means that the one which is subsumed is more specific and thus more informative than the one which subsumes it.

Evaluating this type of compatibility is particularly meaningful in cases where two enterprise applications share a data model specification as a basis for exchanging interoperable business objects or electronic documents, but are not obliged to instantiate or make use of all schema attributes for every entity defined in that model. As a result, the case may arise where the developers of different applications have chosen to instantiate the schema attributes of a base entity in different

ways, thus arriving to only partially overlapping and effectively incompatible definitions of data parameters that nevertheless carry the same name. This is also a typical situation when working under the assumption of a shared base ontology that can be specialised and customised for niche application domains through subclassing and applying restrictions on class definitions, as in the case of FUSION (Bouras, Gouvas, & Mentzas, 2008). Different developers may choose to extend a base ontology concept in different ways, thus creating potential interoperability problems. Figure 1 illustrates an example case in which the base concept of FUSIONAddress (depicted in the middle column) has been specialised in two different ways, for modelling the data spaces of two different enterprise applications.

Although System1_Address and System2_Address are subclasses of the same concept (FUSIONAddress), interoperability can be guaranteed only when information flows from System2 to System1, and not the other way around. This is because the schema of System2_Address is more informative than the schema of the latter. To illustrate this, let us assume that we wished a BPEL orchestration controller to consume some service exposed by System2, which required to be provided with address information as input (e.g. in order to calculate the cost of shipping some item). If the controller service had obtained this address information in a previous step from System1 we would have an impedance mismatch problem, because System2 expects to receive data for the hasDistrict and hasFloor attributes that are not part of System1_Address, thus rendering integration impossible. On the contrary, if we wished to feed address-related data retrieved from System2 into System1 then a transformation function (within the BPEL code or externally via XSLT) could be provided to take care of the mapping.

The overall integration-oriented principle of asserting that the consumer is able to provide *at least* the amount of input data expected by the advertised service, and vice-versa for outputs, can

Figure 1. Mismatch at the level of data schema among System1 and System2 due to different ontology class restrictions (adapted from Kourtesis & Paraskakis, 2008b)

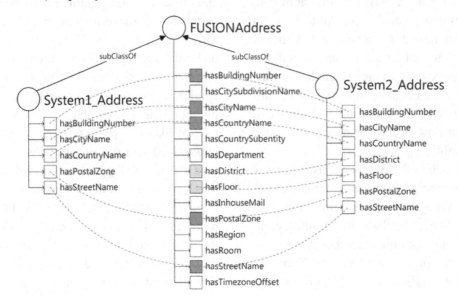

also be applied to evaluating compatibility at the service message level. The request and response messages of service operations have their own schema definitions and may be made up of multiple data parameters. For instance, let us assume that some advertised service expects to receive an address, a purchase order, and a product description as part of the request message for invoking one of its operations, but the prospective service consumer (i.e. the BPEL controller service) cannot obtain the product description data from any other participating service or from the external environment. Inevitably, it would be impossible to integrate the specific advertised service into the orchestration.

In order to evaluate the compatibility among inputs and outputs in an automated way and perform integrability-oriented service matchmaking we need to describe the data schema for input and output parameters in an ontological manner. Since the schemata of Web service inputs and outputs are defined using XSD, the ontological formalism to be used for encoding definitions of inputs and outputs should be sufficiently expressive to facilitate modelling of arbitrarily complex XSD

schemata as those found in WSDL inputs and outputs, while retaining decidability to enable automated processing.

Based on recent research works on transformations from XML/XSD to OWL (Bohring & Auer, 2005) (Garcia & Gil, 2007) it appears that the minimum level of expressiveness that would be required for representing XSD constructs in OWL while preserving the intended semantics would be that of the OWL-DL dialect. OWL-DL is one of the three dialects of the W3C standard Web Ontology Language (OWL) and is termed "DL" due to its direct correspondence with Description Logics. The other two dialects are OWL-Lite, which is less expressive than OWL-DL due to its restricted vocabulary[8], and OWL-Full, which is more expressive than OWL-DL because it does not restrict the OWL vocabulary, but consequently cannot be used as the basis for inferencing that is sound and complete. In contrast to the other dialects, OWL-DL can be applied in cases where the need for expressiveness is accompanied by the need for computational completeness (guaranteeing that all valid entailments will be computed) and decidability (guaranteeing that all computations will finish in finite time) for the purposes of automated reasoning (McGuinness & van Harmelen, 2004).

More specifically, the need for OWL-DL arises because the OWL-Lite vocabulary does not suffice for expressing the semantics of some important XSD constructors which are frequently used within WSDL documents for defining the structures of input and output messages. For example:

- The semantics of the xsd:choice compositor (which is equivalent to an XOR) can only be expressed in OWL through boolean combinations of the owl:intersectionOf, owl:unionOf and owl:complementOf constructors. However, the expressivity of OWL-Lite does not suffice because the use of owl:unionOf and owl:complementOf are not allowed. These constructors are allowed only in OWL-DL and OWL-Full.

- The semantics of the xsd:enumeration constraint (which is placed within an xsd:restriction to limit the content of an XML element to a set of acceptable values) can be expressed in OWL using the owl:oneOf constructor. Similarly to the case above, the expressivity of OWL-Lite is not sufficient because owl:oneOf is not allowed in this dialect, in contrast to OWL-DL and OWL-Full.

- The semantics of the xsd:minOccurs and xsd:maxOccurs indicators (which specify the number of times an XML element can be found in a document) can be expressed with the owl:minCardinality and owl:maxCardinality constructors. In contrast to OWL-DL and OWL-Full, the vocabulary of OWL-Lite restricts the use of the owl:maxCardinality and owl:minCardinality constructors to cardinality values of 0 or 1, and therefore does not allow expressing arbitrary numbers for the occurrence of XSD elements.

Once an OWL-DL-encoded representation is available for the service inputs and outputs, compatibility among advertisements and requests can be evaluated through standard subsumption reasoning with a Description Logics reasoner. The FUSION Semantic Registry utilises Pellet for this purpose, as will be discussed later in the architecture section. Our matchmaking algorithm, returns a positive match among a service advertisement and a service request if the input concept associated with the advertisement subsumes the input concept of the request (i.e. the first is equivalent or less informative than the second, as happens with System1_Address which subsumes System2_Address in Figure 1), and the output concept associated with the request subsumes the output concept of the advertisement (the latter is equivalent or more informative than the first).

Non-Functional Properties of Web Services: Categorisation

Non-functional properties also play an important role in service discovery, and are increasingly attracting the interest of the Semantic Web Services research community as an important area of study. Non-functional properties may relate to quality of service (QoS), policy compliance, adherence to technical standards or protocols, or categorisation within a classification system. The only type of non-functional property that is taken into account for matchmaking by the FUSION Semantic Registry is the latter, i.e. the categorisation of a service advertisement with regard to some semantically represented classification system, in order to designate the functionality of that service and assist in simple tasks like browsing through advertisements and performing coarse-grained filtering during matchmaking.

Classification systems facilitating this form of categorisation have been used in the industry for a long time. Some of the most known classification systems are the United Nations Standard Products and Services Code (UNSPSC), the North Ameri-

Figure 2. Excerpt from the taxonomy of business functions that is part of the FUSION ontology

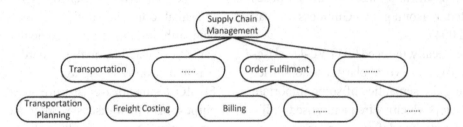

can Industry Classification System (NAICS), the MIT Process Handbook (MPH), and the enhanced Telecom Operations Map (eTOM). A number of classification systems have been also built on top of information interchange models such as the Open Travel Alliance (OTA), and the Open Financial Exchange (OFX).

As an example, consider the taxonomy illustrated in Figure 2, which is an excerpt from the taxonomy of business functions that is part of the FUSION Ontology. Let us assume that a service request is classified under Supply Chain Management, and that some advertisement is classified under Freight Costing. As seen from the diagram, Freight Costing is a subcategory of Transportation that is itself classified under Supply Chain Management. A semantic representation of this taxonomy and a suitable matchmaking mechanism allows detecting that the service advertisement matches the request, since the category of Supply Chain Management services is more generic than the Freight Costing services category.

Intuitively, the end goal in categorisation-level matching within the FUSION Semantic Registry is to determine if the semantic categorisation class attributed to some service request is equivalent, more specific, or more generic than the one specified in some service advertisement. In OWL-DL terms, in order to have a positive match, the categorisation class associated with a request must subsume the categorisation class of an advertisement (i.e. the first must be equivalent or more generic than the second).

Semantic Representation of Service Characteristics in FUSION

By using a semantic representation formalism to express the above presented characteristics of Web services, providers and requestors create definitions of service capabilities that are automatically processable through reasoning and logic-based inference. In turn, this facilitates fine-grained service matchmaking for supporting integrability-oriented service discovery, and effectively, for increasing the levels of automation in EAI. As already said in the background section, the extent to which this can be achieved depends on the semantic representation formalism that is adopted for this purpose.

Although the FUSION reference framework is abstract and does not prescribe the use of any specific Semantic Web Service description framework, the tools that comprise the reference implementation of the FUSION System, including the FUSION Semantic Registry, utilise SAWSDL. In contrast to developing Web service descriptions at a high conceptual level and then linking these specifications to concrete Web service interfaces that are described in WSDL (as proposed in OWL-S and WSMO), the approach that SAWSDL puts forward is bottom-up: the WSDL documents are to be enriched with annotations that capture machine processable semantics by pointing to concepts defined in externally maintained semantic models. This approach has numerous advantages, but the most important one is that SAWSDL can be agnostic to the knowledge representation formalism one

Figure 3. Fragment of FUSION ontology used for modeling service requests and advertisements

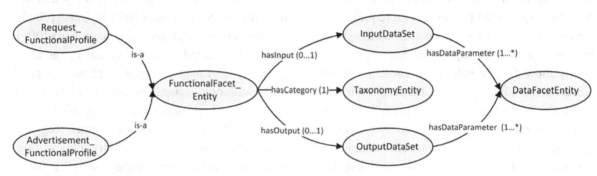

adopts for modelling service characteristics.

The semantic model that serves as the basis for creating, storing, and reasoning upon representations of service characteristics in the FUSION project is the FUSION Ontology (Bouras, Gouvas, & Mentzas, 2007), which has been encoded in OWL-DL. Its multi-faceted structure reflects different types of concepts necessary for modelling a service: the data structures a service exchanges through input and output messages (data semantics), the functionality categorisation of a service with regard to a taxonomy of business functions (classification semantics), and the behaviour it may expose within a complex and stateful process execution (behavioural semantics). As we already mentioned the latter is not employed in the context of service discovery within FUSION.

In order to represent the functional and non-functional service properties that are of interest for matchmaking in the FUSION Semantic Registry, one needs to create a so-called Functional Profile, and define its key attributes in terms of references to the abovementioned FUSION Ontology. As presented in Kourtesis and Paraskakis (2008b) and also illustrated in Figure 3, a Functional Profile is expressed as a named OWL class that is attributed a set of three different OWL object properties:

- **hasCategory:** associates a FunctionalProfile with exactly one TaxonomyEntity concept from the service

classification taxonomy that is part of the FUSION Ontology, to represent the service's categorisation.

- **hasInput:** associates a FunctionalProfile with an InputDataSet concept, in order to represent the set of data parameters that a service expects to receive and consume. The cardinality of this property is zero in the case of an *out-only* Message Exchange Pattern (MEP), or one, in the case of an *in-out* MEP.

- **hasOutput:** associates a FunctionalProfile with an OutputDataSet concept, in order to represent the set of data parameters that a service will produce if invoked. The cardinality of this property is zero in the case of an *in-only* MEP, or one, in the case of an *in-out* MEP.

Finally, each InputDataSet and OutputDataSet concept is associated with one or more DataFacetEntity concept(s) through a hasDataParameter object property, in order to represent the individual data parameters which are exchanged as part of the whole set of inputs or outputs (e.g. address, purchase order, product description, etc).

Depending on the perspective from which the Functional Profile is viewed, the provider's or the requestor's, we can make a distinction among Advertisement Functional Profiles (AFPs) and Request Functional Profiles (RFPs). The first are created automatically by the FUSION Semantic registry at the time of service publication, while the latter are created by the service requestor at the time of discovery (or even at an earlier stage to be used as service request templates).

To allow for the automated construction of Advertisement Functional Profiles (AFPs) in the FUSION Semantic Registry, service providers need to augment the WSDL interfaces of their provided services with semantic annotations, as per the SAWSDL specification. According to the SAWSDL annotation conventions that apply in FUSION, the semantics of a Web service's input and output data should be captured by adding modelReference annotations to the appropriate <xs:element> entities under <wsdl:types>, while functionality categorisation semantics should be captured via modelReference annotations on <wsdl:portType> entities.

ARCHITECTURE OF THE FUSION SEMANTIC REGISTRY

In the previous section we described the salient service characteristics (functional and non-functional properties) that should be modelled to support integrability-oriented service discovery, and analysed how these characteristics are captured in a suitable semantic representation formalism. This section of the chapter discusses the technical aspects of our approach for augmenting UDDI-based service registries with semantic matchmaking extensions. We provide an overview of the architecture that we employed in the development of the FUSION Semantic Registry and an outline of the programmatic interfaces that it exposes.

A distinctive characteristic of the FUSION Semantic Registry architecture is that it can augment the search facilities of a UDDI registry without mandating any modifications to the standardised UDDI registry API as required by the approach of Akkiraju et al (2003) and without requiring to tamper with the implementation of the UDDI registry at source code or configuration level in

order to integrate the matchmaking mechanism as required by the approach of Akkiraju et al (2003), Paolluci et al (2002), and Srinivasan et al (2005). This is considered an important advantage compared to other approaches, as it allows adopters of this solution to use their existing or preferred UDDI server implementation (e.g. IBM WebSphere UDDI Registry, Oracle Service Registry, SAP Enterprise Services Registry, etc) without performing any changes, thus encouraging uptake of such technology by end users.

As illustrated in Figure 4, we propose an architecture where the UDDI server stands independently to the semantically-enabled service registry modules and works as a back-end. The FUSION Semantic Registry exposes two specialised Web service APIs to the client for publication and discovery functions, and is responsible for performing the associated SAWSDL parsing, OWL ontology processing, and DL reasoning operations. Approaches based on this principle of accommodating semantic processing functions without imposing any changes to the UDDI server implementation or interface have been also proposed in other works (Pokraev, Koolwaaij, & Wibbels, 2003; Colgrave, Akkiraju, & Goodwin, 2004; Luo, Montrose, Kim, Khashnobish, & Kang, 2006).

The UDDI module that is depicted in Figure 4 can be any UDDI server implementation that complies with the UDDI v2 or v3 specification, although the FUSION Semantic Registry has been developed and tested using Apache jUDDI[9]. The OWL KB module is a typical OWL ontology with RDF/XML serialisation that the Semantic Registry uses for storing the Advertisement Functional Profiles it generates at the time of service publication, as will be explained in the next section of the chapter. In the centre of the figure is the actual FUSION Semantic Registry, a J2EE Web Application that complies with the Java Servlet 2.4 specification and can be deployed on any compatible container implementation, such as Apache Tomcat.

Figure 4. Semantic registry architecture (adapted from Kourtesis & Paraskakis, 2008a)

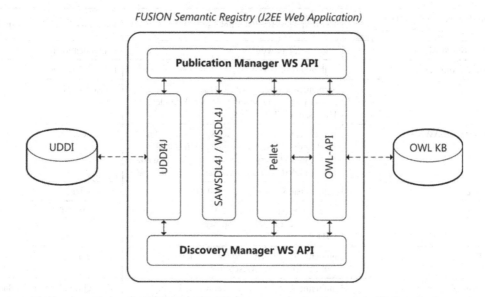

The Publication Manager module of the FUSION Semantic Registry provides a Web service API to the user for adding, removing, or updating Web service advertisements, as well as adding, removing, or updating descriptions of service providers. A list of the Web service operations exposed by the Publication Manager and the parameters of the respective request and response messages is provided in Table 1.

The Discovery Manager module provides a Web service API for retrieving a specific service advertisement or service provider record via its key, discovering a set of services or service providers through keyword-based for terms contained in their names, and most importantly, discovering a set of services based on a Request Functional Profile. A list of the Web service operations exposed by the Discovery Manager and the parameters of the respective request and response messages is provided in Table 2.

The dependencies that the Publication Manager and Discovery Manager modules have on the third-party components depicted in the centre of Figure 4 are examined in the following sections, along with the overviews of the semantic service publication and discovery processes.

SERVICE PUBLICATION PROCEDURE

As detailed above, the Publication Manager Module provides a Web service API to the user for adding, removing, or updating descriptions of Web services, as well as adding, removing, or updating descriptions of service providers. This section of the chapter focuses on the most important of these functions, the process of publishing a semantically-enhanced service description (addService).

Apart from the authentication token, the publication query that initiates the publication process includes the following parameters: (i) the service provider ID (every service advertisement is associated to exactly one service provider that is identified by a UUID key), (ii) a URL pointing to the SAWSDL document that describes the service, (iii) an optional service name, and (iv) an optional free text description. The process that follows based on this input comprises a number of phases that are presented in the following subsections.

Table 1. Publication manager Web service API

Publication Manager Web Service Operation	Request Message Parameters	Response Message Parameters
initiatePublicationSession	username, password	authenticationToken
terminatePublicationSession	authenticationToken	terminationSuccess
addService	authenticationToken, serviceName, serviceFreeTextDescription, serviceProviderU-UID, sawsdlURL	serviceUUID
addServiceWithoutSAWSDL	authenticationToken, serviceName, serviceFreeTextDescription, serviceProviderUUID, sawsdlURL, hasCategoryAnnotationURI, hasInputAnnotationURIList, hasOutputAnnotationURIList	serviceUUID
removeService	authenticationToken, serviceUUID	serviceRemovalSuccess
modifyService	authenticationToken, serviceUUID, serviceName, serviceFreeTextDescription, serviceProviderU-UID	serviceModificationSuccess
addServiceProvider	authenticationToken, serviceProviderName, serviceProviderFreeTextDescription	serviceProviderUUID
removeServiceProvider	authenticationToken, serviceProviderUUID	serviceProviderRemovalSuccess
modifyServiceProvider	authenticationToken, serviceProviderUUID, serviceProviderName, serviceProviderFreeText-Description	serviceProviderModificationSuccess

Table 2. Discovery manager Web service API

Discovery Manager Web service operation	Request message parameters	Response message parameters
getAllServiceProviderUUIDs	-	List of all service provider keys (UUIDs)
doKeywordSearchForServiceProviders	keyword	List of all service provider keys (UUIDs)
getServiceProviderDetails	serviceProviderUUID	serviceProviderName, serviceProvider-FreeTextDescription, listOfProvidedServiceUUIDs
getAllServiceUUIDs	-	List of all service keys (UUIDs)
doKeywordSearchForServices	Keyword	List of all service keys (UUIDs)
doSemanticSearchForServices	requestFunctionalProfileURI, serviceProviderUUID	List of all service keys (UUIDs)
getServiceDetails	serviceUUID	serviceName serviceFreeTextDescription, locationOfSAWSDLDocument, serviceProviderUUID, categoryAnnotationURI, listOfInputAnnotationURIs, listOfOutputAnnotationURIs, listOfMatchingRFPURIs

Phase 1: Parsing of the Service SAWSDL Document

The first step that the Publication Manager performs is to retrieve the SAWSDL document from the specified URL and parse it to extract the semantic annotations it contains. As discussed in section 2, WSDL interfaces are augmented with potentially multiple modelReference annotations on <xs:element> entities, in order to capture the data semantics of the service (consumed inputs or produced outputs), and a single modelReference annotation on <wsdl:portType> entities to capture its functionality categorisation semantics. At the time of this writing the current implementation of the Semantic Registry SAWSDL parser relies on the WSDL4J[10] and SAWSDL4J[11] libraries to create an in-memory representation of the SAWSDL document and extract the URIs of the ontological concepts being referenced by the modelReference annotations.

Phase 2: Construction of a UDDI Advertisement

The next step in the publication process is to map the information that was provided as part of the publication query (i.e. the service name, free text description, and service provider's UUID) and the information that was extracted by parsing the SAWSDL document (i.e. input, output, and category annotation URIs), into a UDDI service advertisement. Communication between the FUSION Semantic Registry and the UDDI server for this purpose is facilitated by

UDDI4J[12]. As illustrated in Figure 5, this mapping requires creating a uddi:businessService entity and instantiating the values of its uddi:name, uddi:description, and uddi:businessKey attributes, as well as a uddi:categoryBag that includes one uddi:keyedReference entity for every extracted annotation URI.

In order to support the representation of syntactic properties and binary relations among WSDL entities in UDDI, Colgrave & Januszewski (2004) introduced a number of Canonical tModels that should be registered in a UDDI server installation before publication and discovery of WSDL documents (i.e. during the UDDI server's deployment). The FUSION Semantic Registry extends this idea and makes use of pre-registered canonical tModels (see Table 3) for representing the different types of semantic annotations that can be placed on SAWSDL documents (input, output, or category annotations). Depending on the type of semantic information being modelled, each uddi:keyedReference entity should point to the appropriate canonical tModel (Input Annotation tModel, Output Annotation tModel, or Category Annotation tModel). As depicted in

Figure 5. SAWSDL to UDDI mapping (adapted from Kourtesis & Paraskakis, 2008a)

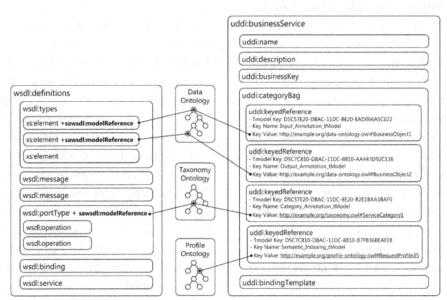

Table 3. Sample pre-registered canonical tModels for facilitating indexing in the registry

tModel Key	Name
uuid:7CB6D040-0F32-11DD-9040-B5988DE060A3	Category_Annotation_tModel
uuid:7CB94140-0F32-11DD-8140-8AB199A03241	Input_Annotation_tModel
uuid:7CBB8B30-0F32-11DD-8B30-A33C65E2A5DF	Output_Annotation_tModel
uuid:7CBB8B30-0F32-11DD-8B30-D549BB31EB3E	Semantic_Indexing_tModel

Figure 5, an additional canonical tModel is used for indexing service advertisements with respect to the Request Functional Profiles that they can readily satisfy (Semantic Indexing tModel), but the uddi:keyedReference entities that point to this tModel are created at a later stage in the publication process.

Phase 3: Generation of Advertisement Functional Profile and Matchmaking

The next step in the publication process is to create an Advertisement Functional Profile (AFP) based on the extracted semantic annotations and add it to the registry's internal OWL Knowledge Base (KB) with the help of the OWL API library[13]. The construction of the AFP follows the modelling conventions analysed in section 3. Once the AFP has been constructed, the Pellet DL reasoner[14] is used for performing an "eager" semantic classification of the new AFP against all known Request Functional Profiles (RFPs). The purpose of this classification procedure is to identify RFPs representing service requests that the newly added service advertisement can readily satisfy.

We refer to this classification procedure as "eager" since it takes place at publication-time. In contrast, a "lazy" classification procedure would not have taken place before the actual need for matchmaking arises during discovery-time. This approach is placing an inevitable overhead on the time required to complete the publication of a service advertisement, but it substantially reduces the time required to perform matchmaking at

discovery-time, so it is considered particularly beneficial.

In order to claim that the new service advertisement (AFP) can satisfy a pre-registered service request (RFP), three conditions must be checked independently and be asserted:

1. the InputDataSet concept associated with the RFP must be subsumed by the InputDataSet of the AFP,
2. the OutputDataSet of the RFP must subsume the OutputDataSet of the AFP,
3. the TaxonomyEntity concept associated with the RFP must subsume the TaxonomyEntity of the AFP.

Phase 4: Indexing of Semantic Matching Results in the UDDI Registry

The last step in the publication process is to map the semantic matchmaking information that resulted from the publication-time matchmaking algorithm described above into the UDDI service advertisement. This requires retrieving the advertised uddi:businessService entity and its associated uddi:categoryBag from the UDDI server, and creating one uddi:keyedReference for every RFP that the service matches with. What this essentially achieves is indexing the service advertisement with respect to all service requests it can readily satisfy. As depicted in Figure 5, uddi:keyedReference entities should be made to point to the canonical tModel used for this purpose (the Semantic Indexing tModel), and the URI of each RFP should be specified as the Key Value of the uddi:keyedReference. When this step is completed, a new semantic service advertisement has been created, registered with the UDDI registry, and is available for discovery.

SERVICE DISCOVERY PROCEDURE

As presented previously, the Discovery Manager module provides a Web service API for retrieving service advertisements or service provider records via their unique keys, discovering sets of services or service provider records through keyword-based search, and most importantly, discovering sets of services based on a Request Functional Profile that represents the requirements of the service consumer. This latter type of semantic matchmaking functionality is the focus of this section.

The discovery query that initiates the semantic matchmaking process comprises two elements: (i) a URI pointing to some Request Functional Profile (RFP), and (ii) an optional UUID designating the preferred service provider, i.e. the company, business unit, or specific business application that should expose the service. The RFP that the URI points to may be defined within an ontology that is shared by service providers and service requestors alike (i.e. be a reusable RFP defined in the FUSION Ontology), or within some third-party ontology that imports and extends the shared ontology (i.e. be a custom-built and non-shared RFP). Depending on which of the two cases holds, the algorithm would follow a different discovery path. Resolving the location of the ontology in which the RFP is identified is therefore the first step in the discovery process.

If the RFP is defined in the shared FUSION Ontology the Discovery Manager will look for service advertisements indexed in UDDI with a reference to that RFP. This means looking for services with AFPs that have matched the requested RFP during the "eager" publication-time classification. To re-

trieve such advertisements the Discovery Manager places a simple syntactic matchmaking query to the UDDI server, looking for uddi:businessService entities having a uddi:categoryBag that contains a uddi:keyedReference which points to the Semantic Indexing tModel, and moreover, has a Key Value that is equal to the URI of the RFP.

Since the matchmaking and indexing process is repeated every time a new RFP is created and added to the shared ontology, the UDDI server's semantic matching index is bound to always be accurate and up to date. This means that if some service advertisement matches some RFP which is defined in the shared ontology, the registry is guaranteed to have this association indexed in the UDDI server, and be able to instantly retrieve the advertised service.

Due to the shared ontology assumption that is made in the context of FUSION, this is the most typical type of discovery querying envisaged for the FUSION Semantic Registry, and is also the simplest and fastest type of matchmaking possible. Since the time-consuming process of subsumption reasoning and hierarchy classification has been already performed at publication-time, the computational complexity of discovery-time matchmaking for RFPs defined in a shared ontology is essentially as low as that of a conventional UDDI server. In other words, the use of semantics does not impose any noteworthy overhead compared to syntactic matchmaking.

If the RFP is defined in a non-shared ontology the Discovery Manager would need to load that ontology into memory and perform a complete semantic matchmaking process among the specified RFP and all AFPs stored in the OWL-KB. The conditions that need to be checked in order to assert that a service advertisement can satisfy the request are the same as the ones defined for publication-time matchmaking.

The result of the discovery process, regardless of the ontology in which the RFP is defined, is a list of UUID keys corresponding to advertisements of services that comply with the matchmaking criteria modelled in the RFP. If a service provider UUID has been also specified in the discovery query, the UDDI server will restrict the result set to only those services offered by the specified provider.

CONCLUSIONS AND OUTLOOK

The availability of sophisticated Web service discovery mechanisms is an essential prerequisite for increasing the levels of efficiency and automation in Enterprise Application Integration. In a contemporary service-oriented business application ecosystem, the integration of a set of different applications is typically realised by creating executable specifications of how the Web services that these applications expose should be orchestrated in order to fulfil a particular business process. The outcome of the integration procedure is a set of executable business processes, each of which invokes a number of Web services in the order dictated by the underlying business logic, assigning the output of one service into the inputs of others, and where necessary, applying transformations from the data representation of one service provider to that of another. Therefore, an essential criterion for selecting services that are suitable for composition, among the tens or hundreds of Web services potentially available, is the integrability of a service on the basis of the input and output messages that are defined in its interface. The description and discovery mechanism of contemporary UDDI-compliant service registries is not sufficiently sophisticated and fine-grained to address the above criterion for service selection, and thus cannot support automated service discovery in the context of EAI. The fundamental problem is that the service descriptions available in UDDI lack the machine-understandable semantics that would make them amenable to automated processing.

In this chapter we presented an approach for developing service registries which build on UDDI

and offer semantically-enhanced Web service publication and discovery capabilities by employing Semantic Web Service technologies. Our approach aspires to promote efficiency in EAI in a number of ways, but primarily by automating the task of evaluating Web service integrability on the basis of the input and output messages that are defined in a service's interface. The approach that we put forward has been applied and validated during the development of the FUSION Semantic Registry, a semantically-enhanced service registry that has been utilised in research project FUSION and is released as open source software. Our solution places emphasis on the use of open standards and has been realised by combining three prominent standards from the area of Web Services and the Semantic Web: OWL-DL, for modelling salient service characteristics and performing fine-grained service matchmaking via Description Logic reasoning, SAWSDL, for creating semantically annotated descriptions of service interfaces, and UDDI, for storing and retrieving syntactic and semantic information about services and service providers. To the best of our knowledge the work presented in this chapter represents the first attempt to combine these three standards into a comprehensive and openly available solution.

Our approach has been specifically tailored to support Semantic Web Service discovery in the context of EAI according to the requirements that we outlined in Section 2 and explained in detail in Section 3. The following table provides a comparison among our work and other related works that we have reviewed in this chapter, on the basis of some features that are central to our work and stem from the above mentioned requirements. As already stated, we confine ourselves to evaluating works that seek to promote semantically-enhanced service matchmaking specifically in relation to the open standard of UDDI, and in addition, works that are not only theoretic but come with a proof-of-concept system implementation.

As can be seen from the table, all of the related works address the problem of matchmaking based

Table 4. Comparison with related works

	FUSION Semantic Registry	(Sivashanmugam et al, 2003) (Li et al, 2006)	Akkiraju et al, 2003	(Paolluci et al, 2002) (Srinivasan et al, 2005)	(Luo et al, 2006)
Matchmaking based on inputs and outputs?	+	+	+	+	+/-
Ontological expressiveness for I/O at OWL-DL level?	+	-	-	+	-
Sound and complete reasoning at OWL-DL level?	+	-	-	+	-
Matchmaking based on service categorisation?	+	+	+	+	+/-
Loose coupling with UDDI registry?	+	+	-	-	+
Support for SAWSDL standard?	+	-	-	-	-
Semantic regstry rleased as open source software?	+	+	-	-	-

on service inputs and outputs, and most of them also cater for categorisation-based matchmaking. Nevertheless, it appears that only our work and the work described in Paolucci et al (2002) and Srinivasan et al (2005) meet the requirement for ontology language expressiveness that would be sufficient for representing arbitrarily complex XSD schemata of service inputs and outputs, in conjunction with the ability to perform sound and complete reasoning at the same level of expressiveness. Moreover, in our attempt to promote the use of open standards our work is one of the few that have been designed for loose-coupling with the UDDI registry, and thus do not necessitate any modifications to the UDDI server's API or to its internal logic. As already mentioned this is considered an advantage compared to other approaches, as it allows adopters to use their existing UDDI server implementation without performing any changes, thus encouraging uptake of SWS technology by end users. Lastly, the semantically-enhanced service registry that was developed by the LSDIS group (Sivashanmugam et al, 2003; Li et al, 2006) and the FUSION Semantic Registry are currently the only implemented systems that are made publicly available as open source software, and our registry is at the time of this writing the only available service registry that supports the newly ratified SAWSDL specification, which is the only standard in the SWS area.

Using the presented approach and registry implementation as the foundation for our future work, we plan to expand into Web service discovery based on behavioural service descriptions, considering service preconditions and effects, and discovery based on non-functional properties of services, considering aspects such as compliance to policies and business rules and adherence to Service Level Agreements. The scope of the registry can be expanded by the addition of repository functions for handling semantic metadata, and its functionality can be augmented to include the validation of services through registry-based functional testing (Kourtesis, Ramollari, Dranidis, & Paraskakis, 2008). These extensions would be steps towards investigating the application of semantic technologies in a wider context of Service Lifecycle Management and towards the development of a theoretical and technological approach for supporting SOA Governance through the realisation of semantically-enhanced registry and repository solutions.

REFERENCES

Akkiraju, R., Farrell, J., Miller, J., Nagarajan, M., Schmidt, M., Sheth, A., et al. (2005). *WSDL-S: Web service semantics. W3C member submission.*

Akkiraju, R., Goodwin, R., Doshi, P., & Roeder, S. (2003). A method for semantically enhancing the service discovery capabilities of UDDI. *Workshop on Information Integration on the Web,* Acapulco, Mexico.

Alazeib, A., Balogh, A., Bauer, M., Bouras, A., Friesen, A., Gouvas, P., et al. (2007). Towards semantically-assisted design of collaborative business processes in EAI scenarios. *5th IEEE International Conference on Industrial Informatics (INDIN 2007)* (pp. 779-784). Vienna, Austria.

Alves, A., Arkin, A., Askary, S., Barreto, C., Bloch, B., Curbera, F., et al. (2007). *Web services business process execution language version 2.0.* OASIS Standard.

Anicic, N., Ivezic, N., & Jones, A. (2006). An architecture for semantic enterprise application integration standards. In D. Konstantas, J. P. Bourrières, M. Léonard & N. Boudjlida (Eds.), *Interoperability of enterprise software and applications* (pp. 25-34). London: Springer-Verlag.

Beyer, D., Chakrabarti, A., & Henzinger, T. (2005). Web service interfaces. *14th International Word Wide Web Conference (WWW 2005)* (pp. 148-159), Chiba, Japan.

Bohring, H., & Auer, S. (2005). Mapping XML to OWL ontologies. *13th Leipziger Informatik-Tage Conference (LIT 2005)* (pp. 147-156).

Bouras, A., Gouvas, P., & Mentzas, G. (2007). ENIO: An enterprise application integration ontology. *18th International Conference on Database and Expert Systems Applications* (pp. 419-423), Regensburg, Germany.

Bouras, T., Gouvas, P., & Mentzas, G. (2008). Dynamic data mediation in enterprise application integration. In O. Cunnigham & M. Cunnigham (Eds.), *Collaboration and the knowledge economy: Issues, applications, and case studies, e-challenges e-2008 conference* (pp. 917-924), Stockholm, Sweden.

Bruijn, J., Bussler, C., Domingue, J., Fensel, D., Hepp, M., Keller, U., et al. (2005). *Web service modeling ontology (WSMO).* W3C member submission.

Bussler, C. (2003). The role of Semantic Web technology in enterprise application integration. *A Quarterly Bulletin of the Computer Society of the IEEE Technical Committee on Data Engineering, 26*(4), 62–68.

Christensen, E., Curbera, F., Meredith, G., & Weerawarana, S. (2001). *Web services description language (WSDL) version 1.1. W3C note.*

Clement, L., Hately, A., von Riegen, C., & Rogers, T. (2004). *Universal description, discovery, and integration version 3.0.2.* OASIS Standard.

Colgrave, J., Akkiraju, R., & Goodwin, R. (2004). External matching in UDDI. *2004 IEEE International Conference on Web Services (ICWS'04)* (pp. 226 - 233), San Diego, CA.

Colgrave, J., & Januszewski, K. (2004). *Using WSDL in a UDDI registry version 2.0.2. OASIS UDDI specification TC technical note.*

Farrell, J., & Lausen, H. (2007). *Semantic annotations for WSDL and XML schema. W3C recommendation.*

Garcia, R., & Gil, R. (2007). Facilitating business interoperability from the Semantic Web. In W. Abramowicz (Ed.), *BIS 2007.* (LNCS 4439, pp. 220-232). Berlin/Heidelberg: Springer.

Haller, A., Gomez, J., & Bussler, C. (2005). Exposing Semantic Web service principles in SOA to solve EAI scenarios. *14th International World Wide Web Conference (WWW 2005),* Chiba, Japan.

Izza, S., Vincent, L., & Burlat, P. (2006). A framework for Semantic enterprise integration. In D. Konstantas, J. P. Bourrières, M. Léonard, & N. Boudjlida (Eds.), *Interoperability of enterprise software and applications* (pp. 75-86). London: Springer-Verlag.

Keller, U., Lara, R., Polleres, A., Toma, I., Kifer, M., & Fensel, D. (2004). *WSMO D5.1-WSMO Web service discovery (v0.1). WSML working draft.*

Kourtesis, D., & Paraskakis, I. (2008). Combining SAWSDL, OWL-DL, and UDDI for semantically enhanced Web service discovery. In S. Bechhofer, M. Hauswirth, J. Hoffmann & M. Koubarakis (Eds.), *ESWC 2008.* (LNCS 5021, pp. 614-628). Berlin/Heidelberg: Springer.

Kourtesis, D., & Paraskakis, I. (2008). Web service discovery in the FUSION semantic registry. In W. Abramowicz & D. Fensel (Eds.), *BIS 2008.* (LNBIP 7, pp. 285-296). Berlin/Heidelberg: Springer.

Kourtesis, D., Ramollari, E., Dranidis, D., & Paraskakis, I. (2008). Discovery and selection of certified Web services through registry-based testing and verification. In L. Camarinha-Matos & W. Pickard (Eds.), *Pervasive collaborative networks, IFIP 283/2008* (pp. 473-482). Boston: Springer.

Lécue, F., Salibi, S., Bron, P., & Moreau, A. (2008). Semantic and syntactic data flow in Web service composition. *2008 IEEE International Conference on Web Services (ICWS '08)* (pp. 211-218), Beijing, China.

Li, K., Verma, K., Mulye, R., Rabbani, R., Miller, J., & Sheth, A. (2006). Designing Semantic Web processes: The WSDL-S approach. In J. Cardoso & A. Sheth (Eds.), *Semantic Web services, processes, and applications* (pp. 161-193). Springer.

Luo, J., Montrose, B., Kim, A., Khashnobish, A., & Kang, M. (2006). Adding OWL-S support to the existing UDDI infrastructure. *2006 IEEE International Conference on Web Services (ICWS'06),* Chicago, IL.

Martin, D., Burstein, M., Hobbs, J., Lassila, O., McDermott, D., McIlraith, S., et al. (2004). *OWL-S: Semantic markup for Web services. W3C member submission.*

Martin, D., Domingue, J., Brodie, M., & Leymann, F. (2007). Semantic Web services, part 1. *IEEE Intelligent Systems, 22*(5), 12–17. doi:10.1109/MIS.2007.4338488

Martin, D., Domingue, J., Sheth, A., Battle, S., Sycara, K., & Fensel, D. (2007). Semantic Web services, part 2. *IEEE Intelligent Systems, 22*(6), 8–15. doi:10.1109/MIS.2007.118

McGuinness, D., & van Harmelen, F. (2004). *OWL Web ontology language overview. W3C recommendation.*

McIlraith, S., Son, T., & Zeng, H. (2001). Semantic Web services. *IEEE Intelligent Systems, 16*(2), 46–53. doi:10.1109/5254.920599

Paolucci, M., Kawamura, T., Payne, R. T., & Sycara, K. (2002). Semantic matching of Web service capabilities. In I. Horrocks & J. Hendler (Eds.), *The Semantic Web-ISWC 2002.* (LNCS 2342, pp. 333-347). Berlin/Heidelberg: Springer-Verlag.

Pokraev, S., Koolwaaij, J., & Wibbels, W. (2003). Extending UDDI with context aware features based on semantic service descriptions. *2003 International Conference on Web Services (ICWS'03)* (pp. 184-190), Las Vegas, NV.

Preist, C., Esplugas-Cuadrado, J., Battle, S. A., Grimm, S., & Williams, S. K. (2005). Automated business-to-business integration of a logistics supply chain using Semantic Web services technology. In Y. Sure, W. Nejdl, C. Goble, G. Antoniou, P. Haase, S. Staab, et al. (Eds.), *The Semantic Web– ISWC 2005* (pp. 987-1001). Berlin/Heidelberg: Springer.

Simons, A. J. (2002, November-December). The theory of classification, part 4: Object types and subtyping. In R. Wiener (Ed.), *Journal of Object Technology*, 27-35.

Sivashanmugam, K., Verma, K., Sheth, A., & Miller, J. (2003). Adding semantics to Web services standards. *2003 International Conference on Web Services (ICWS'03)* (pp. 395-401), Las Vegas, NV.

Srinivasan, N., Paolucci, M., & Sycara, K. (2005). An efficient algorithm for OWL-S based semantic search in UDDI. In J. Cardoso & A. Sheth (Eds.), *Semantic Web services and Web process composition.* (LNCS 3387, pp. 96-110). Berlin/Heidelberg: Springer-Verlag.

Verma, K., Sivashanmugam, K., Sheth, A., Patil, A., Oundhakar, S., & Miller, J. (2005). METEOR-S WSDI: A scalable P2P infrastructure of registries for semantic publication and discovery of Web services. *Journal of Information Technology Management*, 6(1), 17–39. doi:10.1007/s10799-004-7773-4

ENDNOTES

[1] http://www.seerc.org/fusion/semanticregistry/

[2] http://www.fusion-strep.eu/.

[3] http://www.daml.ri.cmu.edu/matchmaker/inst-mm.htm

[4] http://www.alphaworks.ibm.com/tech/ws-sem

[5] http://lsdis.cs.uga.edu/projects/meteor-s/downloads/Lumina/

[6] http://jena.sourceforge.net/how-to/dig-reasoner.html

[7] http://www.wsmx.org/

[8] http://www.w3.org/TR/2004/REC-owl-features-20040210/#s2

[9] http://ws.apache.org/juddi/

[10] http://sourceforge.net/projects/wsdl4j

[11] http://knoesis.wright.edu/opensource/sawsdl4j/

[12] http://uddi4j.sourceforge.net/

[13] http://owlapi.sourceforge.net/

[14] http://pellet.owldl.com/

Chapter 7
Light–Weight Semantic Integration of Generic Behavioral Component Descriptions

Jens Lemcke
SAP Research, Germany

ABSTRACT

As stated by the Aberdeen group, integration costs 40% of a company's IT budget today. The difficulty of integration arises because the description of software components–in service-oriented architectures (SOA) predominantly done by XML schema definition (XSD) and the Web service definition language (WSDL)–is on the technical level. The technical description neglects important detail of the intended usage of software components, which is also referred to as their semantics. Particularly, semantics needs to be considered in two major integration tasks. First, semantically corresponding data types that can be used for communication between components need to be identified. Second, natural language documentation needs to be studied today in order to understand component behavior, that is, dependencies between operation invocations and how semantically different outcomes of operation calls are represented in the technical output format. The approach presented in this chapter supports the two tasks as follows. First, closed frequent itemset mining (CFIM) is employed to help identifying semantically corresponding data types. Second, a formal representation for component behavior is introduced. However, as component behavior is specified during component development, but used during integration–two distinct phases involving distinct teams–we provide model transformations to ensure the consistent transfer of generic behavioral information to specific integration constraints before automated integration techniques can be applied. We applied the CFIM on the message types exposed by SAP's standard software components and show that we are able to find semantically relevant correspondences. Furthermore, we demonstrate the practical applicability of our behavioral model transformations on the basis of an SAP best practice business scenario. With the little more effort to specify behavioral information at development time in a formal way instead of in natural language, our approach facilitates the reuse of behavioral component descriptions in multiple integration projects and eases the construction of correct integrations.

DOI: 10.4018/978-1-60566-804-8.ch007

INTRODUCTION

The integration of different business partners' IT systems is an essential task to improve the agility of a company and thus facilitate its success in a more and more dynamic business environment. Unfortunately, the task of business integration is extremely expensive. As stated by the Aberdeen group, it consumes about 40% of a company's IT budget (Kastner and Saia, 2006). We address two main cost drivers in this chapter.

1. An inherent prerequisite for complex workflow integration is enumerating the potential communications between the IT systems that were independently developed and are now to be integrated. This task is based on the semantic similarity of the participant's message types. The **identification of semantic correspondences** is one of the two by far most work-intense tasks in IT system integration besides the actual design of the collaborative business process (Küster et al., 2007, Pistore et al., 2005d).

2. The behavioral capabilities of IT systems – in this chapter we focus on dependencies of operation invocations – are usually documented in natural language. The integration of IT systems into complex workflows must properly utilize the IT systems with respect to their capabilities. This means that a team of consultants has to **interpret the natural language documentation** in order to properly create the complex workflow. Interpretation of natural language is ambiguous and cannot be stored for the repeated use of the IT systems in subsequent integration projects.

We base the solution of the above mentioned challenges in the context of the Web services architecture (Krafzig et al., 2004). That means we assume the existence of WSDL-based Web service descriptions and XSD-based message type descriptions. We address the challenges in the following ways.

1. We employ closed frequent itemset mining (CFIM) to identify semantically similar message types. This task serves two purposes. First, identified semantically similar types are not necessarily technically identical. Thus, types being technically incompatible require either to be changed to become interoperable or an appropriate adapter needs to be constructed if the identified types are later used for communication. Second, identified semantically similar types can be used for communication between multiple components or IT systems. This information is one prerequisite for process integration in the following step.

2. We propose a *methodology* to manage behavioral information throughout a component's lifecycle: When a component is built, writing a technical documentation in natural language is replaced by formally describing the generic behavior of components – this is in our approach done by drawing a state transition system (STS). When a component is integrated with others, the specific role the component plays in that integration is derived in a model-driven way from its generic behavior. As no interpretation of natural language is necessary any more, ambiguity is gone and the unambiguous component's capability description can be reused in subsequent integration projects.

As connotated, we *instantiate* the methodology by introducing one possible syntax and semantics of behavioral models and by defining the necessary transformations of behavioral models for each step in the methodology.

3. As an integration of software components must be executable to be effective, we define the execution semantics of behavioral

models and the generated integration using the abstract state machine (ASM) formalism. Having this, we can transform the integration to an existing executable language, such as BPEL. As also the description of services is done via WSDL in our approach, existing SOA infrastructure can be used at run time. We call our approach "light-weight" as *semantic* information is only minimally used where needed during design time and the execution of the properly created integration remains totally *"syntactic"*.

The approach presented in this chapter is inspired by and uses concepts of the following EU-funded research projects. We adopt the standpoint of the ATHENA project where a company's business process can be separated to an internal process and a view process. View processes of different companies can be combined to a collaborative business process (see Greiner 2007).

Unlike the ATHENA project, which merely provided tools to support manual modeling, the completed project DIP and its successor SUPER focus on automating as many tasks as possible with the heavy use of semantic Web technology. That is also the aim of the work presented in this chapter. However, the consequence of the intensive use of semantic Web technology in DIP and SUPER is that not only at design time, but also at run time, semantic-aware engines are required which becomes a burden for the deployment of semantic concepts in existing scenarios using existing technology.

In contrast to that, the FUSION project aimed at applying the results from, amongst others, DIP and ATHENA in a light-weight manner. Semantic technologies were only introduced where needed and especially only for design-time artifacts. Orchestrations generated with FUSION technology would still be deployable on existing Web services infrastructure such as Web application servers and BPEL execution engines.

The MOST project ("Marrying Ontologies and Software Technology") started in 2008 and aims at combining the achievements in the area of semantic Web services, such as carried out in the projects DIP, SUPER, and FUSION, with the current developments in the area of software technology, such as Model-Driven Software Development (MDSD).

This chapter advances parts of the work performed in FUSION and prepares them to be applied in the context of MOST. In particular, the process composer we reference in this chapter was developed in FUSION, as well as the explication of behavioral information using behavioral models and SA-WSDL. A prerequisite for process composition in FUSION was manually enumerating all allowed, potential communications between components. We advance the automation of this task by the CFIM (point 1 above) in this chapter. Finally, we integrate the FUSION composer in the software development lifecycle by providing a methodology (point 2 above) to consistently transform behavioral models. We preserve the feature that the composition result can be deployed on existing infrastructure as it was possible in FUSION also for the transformations in our new method presented in this chapter (point 3 above).

The rest of this chapter is structured as follows.

In the introductory part, we first introduce a running example to demonstrate the steps of our solution later. Afterwards, we present background information of the technical artifacts and their currently predominant representations relevant in the area of integration in service-oriented architecture, i.e. amongst others: XML schema definition (XSD), Web service definition language (WSDL), and business process execution language (BPEL).

After that introduction, we name problems that arise today with respect to using the representations for integration, and we provide our understanding of the source of the problem—the missing seman-

Figure 1.

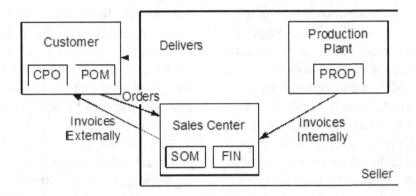

tics in data, operation, and integration representations. During that discussion, we provide formal definitions of semantics in the different areas. In the subsequent section, we review how existing approaches try to cope with the issues of missing semantics and where they fall short.

After stating the issues, we provide our solutions that respect semantics for process integration. We begin with an architectural overview of our solution and then cover its parts individually, which are semantic message alignment, semantic process design, and semantic process execution.

We conclude with a summary.

INTRODUCING THE RUNNING EXAMPLE

In this chapter, we introduce SAP's best practice business process "cross-company-code sales order processing" to demonstrate the findings of this chapter. SAP's Best Practices (http://www.sap.com/bestpractices) are a collection of standard configurations for SAP systems. The aim of the best practices is to shorten the time needed to implement an SAP solution in a business with standard processes.

The integration process cross-company-code sales order processing depicted in Figure 1 consists of two participants – the notation of the graphics

is taken from SAP Best Practices documentation which can be found under the link above.

1. Customer.
2. **Seller.** The seller is further split to its divisions
   ° sales center and
   ° production plant.

In business terms, each division has a unique company code. Therefore, cross-company-code sales order processing means the selling procedure involves multiple departments. The business process of cross-company-code sales order processing works as follows. A customer orders goods from the sales organization of their vendor, or seller. The vendor has a distribution plant that belongs to a different company code. The goods are delivered from the distribution plant directly to the customer. But the customer receives their invoice from the sales organization. Intercompany billing takes place between the two company codes. Thus, the business process of the seller locally communicates with the three components sales order management (SOM), invoicing (FIN), and production (PROD).

Following the premise of this chapter, we assume that customer and seller are companies willing to cooperate. It is common for a company purchasing goods to execute a local purchasing process. Therefore, in addition to the cross-company-code sales order processing best practice business process, we assume that the customer follows a complex purchasing business process locally. The business process of the customer involves the creation of a purchase order and its approval by an appropriate person. This functionality is distributed to the two components create purchase order (CPO) and purchase order management (POM).

The challenges for the participants in our example are to identify the messages used by CPO and POM that have correspondences in SOM, FIN, and PROD in order to correctly integrate the components. Our solution is to use a data mining technique to identify semantically correlating messages.

Further, it is a challenge to identify how the desired collaborative sales business process as it lives in the heads of the business process experts can be implemented using the capabilities of the components. Mostly, a strict top-down modeling leads to a theoretically great business process that may pose an ordering of process steps that contradicts the capabilities of the components. Contrarily, a strict bottom-up approach might lead to optimal partial business processes in each department, but it is not ensured that customer, sales center, and production plant consistently evolve in the case of exceptional behavior. For example, upon a purchase order cancellation from the customer, it must be ensured that the sales center and, if production already started, also the production plant, coherently cancel their operations. Our solution chooses the ways in the middle in that component capabilities are captured "bottom up" during component design time and integration requirements are created "top down" during integration design time. Model-to-model and model-to-code transformations transform component capabilities to concrete, executable integration logic while observing the integration requirements.

Finally, let's assume that the sales center needs to implement a change to its local procedure due to a law change after the integration with the customer and the production plant has been completed – and maybe was productive quite some time. Currently, the sales center would alter the explicit implementation of its local procedure. However, local change often has an impact on the collaborative process. It is now a challenge to maintain consistency among the processes of all departments. Our solution to this is not to make integration code explicit. Rather, the specification, or the semantics, of the integration may be altered which directly ensures the consistent adaptation of the whole collaborative business process.

TECHNICAL ARTIFACTS INVOLVED IN PROCESS INTEGRATION

We continue the introductory part of this chapter by presenting background information of the technical artifacts and their currently predominant representations relevant in the area of integration in service-oriented architecture. In particular, we cover:

- representation of data,
- representation of operations, and
- representation of integration.

Representation of Data

For the definition of data types, the prevailing method in Web services architectures is XML schema. XML schema is a language to describe the structure of a set of XML documents that validate against the schema. We refer to an XML document also as a hierarchical type because XML schema allows for the construction of complex types by an arbitrary nesting of other complex and simple types.

In this chapter, we work with an abstraction of

XML schema which we call "hierarchical type" definition. This abstraction allows omitting the many technical details of the language which are not considered in our approach. A hierarchical type consists of a hierarchy of elements of either simple or complex type having names. We formalize this as follows.

- **Hierarchical type schema.** Let CT be a set of complex types, ST a set of simple types, N a set of names, Δ a relation of types and elements where the type is said to directly contain the element, then a hierarchical type schema H is a tuple defined as seen in Figure 2.

- **Sub element.** Let $H = \langle CT, ST, N, \Delta \rangle$ be a hierarchical type schema. An element $c = \left(n_c, t_c \right)$ is called a direct sub element or direct child of an element $e = \left(n_e, t_e \right)$ with respect to H, if and only if (see Figure 3)

Representation of Operations

In the context of Web services architecture, operations are represented using the Web services description language (WSDL). WSDL is an XML grammar for describing network services as collections of communication endpoints, called ports, capable of exchanging messages (see Christensen et al., 2001). The abstract definition of endpoints and messages is separated from their concrete deployment in the network or data format bindings. This allows the abstract definition and reuse of messages, port types, and operations. Roughly, A WSDL file contains the definition of a service. A service consists of operation definitions. Each operation definition consists of message type definitions. And each message type definition consists of data type definitions – predominantly done using the XML schema definition language (XSD).

Figure 2.

$$\mathcal{H} := \langle CT, ST, N, \Delta \rangle$$
$$T = CT \cup ST \text{ (hierarchical types)}, \quad CT \cap ST = \varnothing$$
$$E = N \times T \text{ (elements)}$$
$$\Delta : \ T \times E$$

Figure 3.

$$(t_e, (n_c, t_c)) \in \Delta \quad (n_e, n_c \in N, \ t_e \in CT, \ t_c \in CT \cup ST)$$

Representation of Integration

There are multiple approaches to represent the integration of Web services. The way we represent integration in our approach shares the basic concepts with these languages.

- **Business process execution language (BPEL).** This language can be directly used in conjunction with WSDL. The WSDL descriptions of Web services can be used in BPEL to execute operations of the Web services. Variables can be defined to store the results of Web service operations and to feed information as input to Web service operations.

- **Business process modeling notation (BPMN).** This language has a less concrete scope than BPEL. BPMN is mostly used as a solely graphical notation to document the flow of a business process. In contrast to BPEL, BPMN consists of the notion of manual tasks.

- **UML activity diagram (AD).** This language is mainly used to document the implementation of a software component. This may indeed be understood as an integration of services as well. However, neither human tasks may be represented nor connections to existing WSDL descriptions can be connected to a UML AD.

- **Event-driven process chain (EPC).** This language is mostly used for modeling business processes of an organization. It has the target to support business experts with it basic modeling constructs, which are events, functions, and connectors that are combined in a directed graph.
- **Petri Nets.** This is a mathematical modeling language that consists of places, transitions, and directed arcs. Petri Nets have precise execution semantics. The few modeling constructs allow in combination to mimic the behavior of more complex flow constructs that are represented in other languages like BPMN as explicit nodes, such as exclusive choice and parallel flow. This results often in a larger net than would have been achieved with another modeling language.

All languages highlighted above provide means to express control flow and data flow between activities. Therefore, they provide constructs to express sequential, synchronized parallel, and alternative execution.

SEMANTICS THAT INFLUENCE PROCESS INTEGRATION

After the introductory part, we now turn to arising issues with respect to using the representations presented before for integration, and we provide our understanding of the source of the problem—the missing

- message semantics,
- process semantics, and
- integration semantics.

During this discussion, we provide formal definitions of semantics in each area. But before we start with the specific definitions, we provide the more general definition of ontology which is closely connected to semantics in the area of the semantic Web, as ontology refers to the explication of semantics in the context of the semantic Web.

The term ontology has been widely used by many communities using different definitions. The origin of the term ontology is in philosophy. Here, ontology means the science of being (see Rosenkrantz, 1998). Ontology discovers approaches to sort out what things and what kinds of things exist. In computer science, the term ontology is used to refer to one understanding of the things in the world. As one computer program is a model, by definition it only works on a subset of the world (Stachowiak, 1973). Therefore, the ontology it utilizes needs only describe parts of the whole set of existing things. Other programs may describe a different set of things needed for their purposes, and again other programs may use a different conceptualization to categorize existing things as there were more than one basic category proposals in philosophy as well. For the sake of computing with ontologies, Gruber (1995), Staab and Studer (2004) introduce a definition of ontology as "a formal, explicit specification of a shared conceptualization."

In this chapter, the following definition of the term ontology better represents our approach as its focus lies on consensus knowledge in a community rather than on requiring a correct conceptualization. We understand ontology as

"a set of vocabulary definitions that expresses a community's consensus knowledge about a domain." (Gruber, 1995)

Message Semantics

XML schema can be understood as a means to ease data type definition. Unfortunately, ease of definition leads to a multitude of types developed to capture similar objects for similar purposes. It is essential for semantic process integration to semantically align type definitions beforehand. Although semantic alignment brings many advantages when it comes to collaboration, it is very rarely reached in computer science. In contrast, we repeatedly observe certain situations of lacking alignment in integration scenarios. In the following, common situations of misalignment are systematically presented based on the concept of the semiotic triangle (Ogden and Richards, 1923), which we also explain below.

At least part of the reason for ambiguity is that objects (such as o, p) are referred to by terms (such as x, y). The research fields of linguistics and semiotics have revealed that this facilitates misunderstanding of the objects, because there is actually no direct connection between a term and an object. Rather, both are connected via a concept (such as c) that the term stimulates in the imagination of a human peer or in the implementation of a computer. The concept that is connected to a data type defines the semantics of the data. These relations, shown in Figure 4, are called the semiotic triangle.

Whereas a term can be used to refer to multiple types of objects and an object may be referred to by multiple terms, a concept is always unique.

The different potential interrelations between objects, terms and concepts are depicted in Figure 5. We are going to separately address all these cases. But before, we give a systematic overview over situations of lacking alignment.

- **Redundancy / synonym vs. parallel.** A

Figure 4.

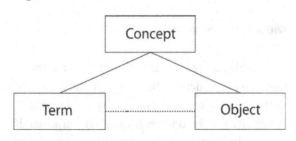

known object o once called "x" may be referred to as "y" at another time or in another place. This may be an indication that x and y are just two synonymous denotations for the same concept (c). Vice versa, x and y may indeed denote disjoint concepts and just happen to be materialized by an object o' equal to o (g).

- **Inconsistency vs. false friend.** We could furthermore come across two situations where the first time the term "x" is used to address an object "o", and a second time "x'", equivalent to x, refers to an object "p". Again, it might be the case that o and p are two different materializations of x in different contexts (b). Conversely, this case might be an indication that x is inconsistently used; once to refer to o, and another time to refer to p (f).

- **Clean repetition vs. illusive friend.** Finally, we observe a very cumbersome situation when an object o is once called x, and at another time or in another place an object o', equal to o, is also called x', equal to x. This might of course indicate that when we observe o' being referred to as x', that this happens with the same background as when o was called x (a). However, it might also be the case that in the first place term x was used to reference o but the second time just the same term x' was used to refer to an equally appearing object o' which indeed might be totally different from o (e) in its use or in its meaning in the second context.

- **Clean distinction vs. heterogeneity.** We may also observe the opposite to the previous when in the first place x is used to refer to o, and in the second place p is called y. On the one hand, this might indicate that o and p are completely different and thus the different terms x and y are used to refer to them (h). On the other hand, it might also be the case that x and y are just the same terms for the same thing, which, unfortunately, is heterogeneously materialized at the two distinct observations as o and p (d).

Process Semantics

There are two main challenges with contemporary Web service descriptions: the gap between technical and semantic representation, and a lack of information on operation interdependencies.

- **Technical representation vs. semantic meaning.** A Web service description as provided by the prominent technology WSDL describes what is needed to technically

invoke a Web service. Although a WSDL document describes the types of operations, its parameters and their detailed structure, it lacks to state the different potential meaning of an operation for a business process. It is very common that such information is hidden in specific values of a message. Thus, a different instantiation of the abstract message type "purchase order" may actually once be a purchase order request, another time a purchase order acceptance, and a third time a purchase order cancellation, depending on, e.g., a type code field part of the purchase order message (see Fensel and Bussler, 2002).

- **Operation interdependencies.** The

Figure 5. Possible semiotic triangles for two repetitive observations

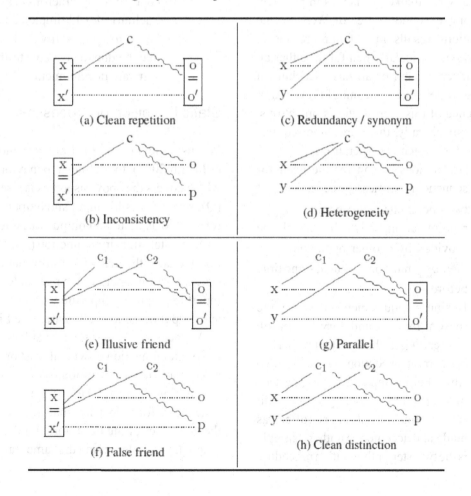

(a) Clean repetition

(b) Inconsistency

(c) Redundancy / synonym

(d) Heterogeneity

(e) Illusive friend

(f) False friend

(g) Parallel

(h) Clean distinction

second challenge of Web service descriptions for integration is that there is no machine-interpretable information with formal semantics on how different operations included in the description may depend on each other. For example, an online purchasing system may provide three Web services: login, search and order. Whereas the system does not care whether the customer directly orders without search for products, it may indeed care that a customer is logged into the system already before they pose an order. The current take on this matter is that Web services are said to be stateless. That means that a Web service may be invoked at any time without breaking the system. However, this definition does not say how a Web service may successfully be invoked. Whereas in practice, a wrong execution order of Web service operations results in a failure response, this is not particularly helpful for either an automated system or an unskilled human trying to generate a meaningful execution sequence of this Web service's operations. More specifically, there are three requirements for sequencing operations.

1. An obvious reason for the need for sequencing is a message dependency of two operations. If an operation $o_{receive}$ requires an input which can only be provided by another operation o_{send}, then o_{send} must be executed some time before $o_{receive}$.

2. Business requirements may be the reason for a mandatory operation sequencing although technically a concurrent execution would be possible. For example, a buying service may state that it would give its credit card information only after an offer was made and accepted. Another example is the two-step authorization procedure

where a purchase order before being issued first needs to be checked by a representative of the financial department and subsequently, depending on the amount, also by the representative's manager. The business reason for sequencing is clearly to reduce the amount of authorization requests that hit the financial department representative's manager.

3. Finally, the most profound reason for the need to sequence at the interface level is that a Web service may be implemented in a way that the invocation of operations in the wrong order will always fail. There does not even need to be any reason for this—it is enough that the implementation cannot cope with any other invocation order. Such an inflexible implementation may be due to a poor software design which may be due to cost constraints during software development.

Static Definition of Processes

We use the notion of Lemcke and Friesen (2007a;b;2008) to define a behavioral model which covers the above aspects via a set of states (Q), a set of possible input and output messages, referred to as input and output variables (Σ and Z), and a state transition function (δ). The definition includes the behavioral information via the state transition function. We restrict to describe a bipartite graph. By bipartite we mean that input and output transitions alternate. (see Figure 6)

We also refer to a state with at least one leaving output transition or with at least one entering input transition as operation.

Multiple input transitions leaving the same state stand for a decision that is determined by the consumer of the behavioral model. Multiple output transitions leaving the same state stand for behavior out of the consumer's sphere of influence. We refer to this as non-deterministic behavior.

In order to be able to identify a single behavioral model in a set of behavioral models, we introduce a set of identifiers (ID). Each identifier from the set ID identifies exactly one behavioral model. We use the superscript notations Q^{bm}, Σ^{bm}, Z^{bm}, q_0^{bm}, δ^{bm}, δ_{in}^{bm}, and δ_{out}^{bm} to refer to the components of the behavioral model identified by $bm \in ID$ when reference otherwise would be ambiguous.

We explicitly refuse business logic encoded into behavioral models, because this is an implementation detail that should only appear in the implementation of a behavioral model but not in the behavioral model itself. This means that the behavioral model does not contain the information how the implementation decides which of the output alternatives will be given for a specific input. In related workflow specification languages, like BPEL or BPMN, explicit conditions can be specified that examine data contained in messages. In our approach, we explicitly forbid the examination of messages because this would make the behavioral model dependent on the complete message type. Instead, we only allow the behavioral model to refer to an abstraction of the data transported in a message by allowing differentiating the explicit output alternatives.

As behavioral models do not contain business logic, messages whose content influences subsequent behavioral models must be classified into different variables. We are hence only interested in a variable's status rather than its value and introduce the varState function. (see Figure 7)

Example

The behavior of the customer's and the seller's IT systems can be described using the presented formalism. The customer's purchasing business process locally communicates with the two components as depicted in the figure below. In the

Figure 6.

$$\mathcal{BM} := \langle Q, \Sigma, Z, \delta, q_0 \rangle$$
$$q_0 \in Q$$
$$\delta = \delta_{in} \cup \delta_{out}$$
$$\delta_{in} : Q \times (2^\Sigma \setminus \{\varnothing\}) \to Q$$
$$\delta_{out} : Q \times (2^Z \setminus \{\varnothing\}) \to Q$$

Figure 7.

$$\text{varState} : \{ (bm, v) \mapsto status ; \ bm \in \text{ID}, v \in (\Sigma^{bm} \cup Z^{bm}),$$
$$status \in \{\text{undef}, \text{initialized}, \text{processed}\} \}$$

picture, we display state transition systems by using boxes to represent states and directed arcs to represent transitions. Text above a state transition system denotes the component it is related with. Text next to an arc names the communicated data type. Direction of communication is identified by the use of smaller ($<$) and greater-then signs ($>$). The closed side of the greater/smaller sign pointing towards the arc denotes input, pointing away from the arc denotes output.

1. **Create purchase order (CPO).** This component consists of a user interface that allows entering the goods a human needs to order. When the user is done, the system outputs a purchase order (PO). In order to update the user about the status of the order, the component may either receive a failure notification (FAIL) or a positive notification (DONE).

2. **Purchase order management (POM).** This component is capable to perform two functions.

   a. A given purchase order is approved or declined by a representative of the finance department. Therefore, the component takes a purchase order (PO) as an input and may communicate an approval (APR) or rejection message (REJ) in response.

b. In the case a purchase order was approved, the purchase order management component handles the payment of the ordered goods once an appropriate invoice was received. Therefore, the final operation of this component is to accept an invoice (INV).

The business process of the seller locally communicates with three components as depicted in Figure 8.

1. **Sales order management (SOM).** The sales order is the counterpart of the buyer's purchase order at the seller's site. As both purchase order and sales order share a lot of similar fields, in, e.g., an SAP system, a sales order can be constructed from a purchase order (PO). The first component of the seller is thus capable to receive a purchase order and output the newly derived sales order (SO) for local use. The sales order is used to keep track of the selling process. When the selling process is done, a sales order becomes closed. In the seller's component of our example, this is expressed by a second operation taking a delivery (DEL) and an invoice (INV) as inputs. The sales order

management component is located at the sales center department of the seller.

2. **Invoicing (FIN).** Similar to the sales order, a "delivery" (DEL) is used to keep track of the activities to prepare the final shipment of goods. These activities normally include the picking of the goods from storage, packing the goods, labeling the package, and posting the goods issue. After posting the goods issue, a delivery can be used to generate an invoice from its data. Therefore, the invoicing component in our example takes as input a delivery and outputs an invoice (INV). Additionally, an incoming invoice can be paid by the invoicing component. Therefore, another one-way operation takes an invoice as an input. No ordering of both operations is prescribed. This means that the component's implementation can cope with any sequential invocation of both operations. Determining the operations' sequence in this case means adding further business logic and depends on their use in an integration scenario. The invoicing component is part of the seller's sales center, too.

3. **Production (PROD).** The production component is part of the seller's production plant department. For simplicity, we assume that this component has a single operation that receives a sales order (SO) as an input and returns a delivery (DEL) and an invoice

Figure 8.

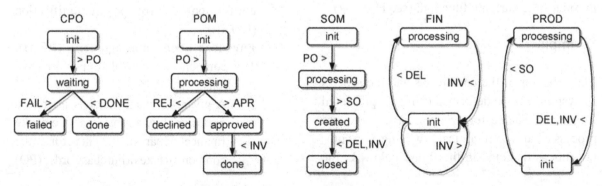

(INV) upon completion. We thus abstract from the complex local communication that manages the production procedure.

Execution Semantics of Processes

For the definition of the operational semantics of the state transition system, Lemcke and Friesen (2007a;b;2008) use the abstract state machine (ASM) formalism.

ASM is a specification for software systems and a method for software system design. Börger and Stärk (2003) claim the ASM notation to be intuitive to technicians as it reads like pseudo-code over abstract data. We abstain from exposing business experts to a notation like ASM. We use ASM just to define the semantics of behavioral models. Business experts would only see the graphical representation of behavioral models.

The main concept of an ASM is the transition rule of the form **if** *<condition>* **then** *<updates>* which transforms abstract states. The condition is an arbitrary predicate logic formula without free variables, whose interpretation evaluates to true or false. The updates are a set of assignments of the form $f(p_1, ..., p_n) := v$ that take place con-

currently. An update is to be understood as the definition of the value of the function f with the parameters $p_1, ..., p_n$ to v. $f(p_1, ..., p_n)$ is also called location. The set of all locations makes up the abstract state of an ASM. The condition of a transition rule checks for properties of the current state of the ASM. A rule is called active if its condition evaluates to true. The run of an ASM is defined as the parallel firing of all active rules. Firing means a state transition where the following state is equivalent to the current state after applying the update assignments of the active rules.

There are two additional constructs to group rules of common form. The first states the concurrent execution of multiple rules: **forall** *<x>* **with** *<ψ>* **do** *<R>*, where usually *x* has unbound occurrences in R. The second states the non-deterministic execution of one rule out of R: **choose** *<x>* **with** *<ψ>* **do** *<R>*.

The complete, formal execution semantics of ASM may be found in Börger and Stärk (2003). Due to the execution semantics, the readable ASM pseudo-code may be used for formal software specification as it allows formally proving properties of the specified software system. The ASM

Figure 9.

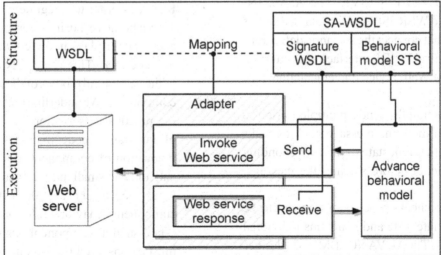

Figure 10.

$$\text{SEND}(bm) \equiv \ \text{do forall} \ \{ \ (\ I, s_{\text{post}} \ ) : \ (\ s_{\text{pre}}, \ I, \ s_{\text{post}} \ ) \in \delta_{\text{in}}^{bm} \ \}$$
$$\text{if bmState}(bm) = s_{\text{post}}$$
$$\text{and varState}(bm, i_1) = \text{initialized and} \dots$$
$$\text{and varState}(bm, i_{|I|}) = \text{initialized then}$$
$$\text{INVOKEWS}(bm, I)$$
$$\text{forall } i \in I \text{ do varState}(bm, i) := \text{processed}$$
$$\text{where}$$
$$i_x \in I, \ x = 1 \dots |I|$$

Figure 11.

$$\text{RECEIVE}(bm) \equiv \ \text{do forall} \ \{ \ (s_{\text{pre}}, O) : \ (s_{\text{pre}}, O, s_{\text{post}}) \in \delta_{\text{out}}^{bm} \ \}$$
$$\text{if bmState}(bm) = s_{\text{pre}} \text{ and WSRESPONSE}(bm, O) \text{ then}$$
$$\text{forall } o \in O \text{ do varState}(bm, o) := \text{initialized}$$
$$\text{where}$$
$$o_x \in O, \ x = 1 \dots |O|$$

method supports rigorous software design as its formal grounding allows the formal definition of refinement as detailed in Börger (2003).

With the short introduction to ASM, we are now prepared to express the execution semantics of a behavioral model in terms of ASM. The following picture expresses our perspective about how existing information artifacts involved in the structural and execution world (such as WSDL and Web service implementation) can be extended by a semantic layer on top (represented using SA-WSDL). (see Figure 9)

A Web service interface is abstracted by the ASMs SEND and RECEIVE. The ASMs IN-VOKEWS and WSRESPONSE contained access the adapters that connect the semantic definitions with the technical WSDL interface and thus with the underlying Web service implementation. (see Figure 10)

SEND potentially sends multiple variables that belong to the same message, and it checks for the correct current state of the corresponding behavioral model before sending the message. (see Figure 11)

RECEIVE checks a behavioral model to be in an appropriate state and maintains individual variable states. The ADVANCEBM ASM defines

Figure 12.

$$\text{ADVANCEBM}(bm) \equiv \ \text{do forall} \ (\ s_{\text{pre}}, \ V, \ s_{\text{post}} \ ) \in \delta^{bm}$$
$$\text{if bmState}(bm) = s_{\text{pre}}$$
$$\text{and varState}(bm, v_1) = \text{initialized and} \dots$$
$$\text{and varState}(bm, v_{|V|}) = \text{initialized then}$$
$$\text{bmState}(bm) := s_{\text{post}}$$
$$\text{where}$$
$$v_x \in V, \ x = 1 \dots |V|$$

the actual behavior of a behavioral model based on its state transitions. (see Figure 12)

Integration Semantics

As elaborated before, BPM faces the challenge to overcome semantic, syntactic and implementation heterogeneities. Business process management systems support the design, execution, and monitoring of business processes. The only manual part is the design of business processes, which in fact is a relevant research topic as a multitude of research publications in the area of process integration indicate. The challenges of business process design involve multiple integration participants, whose IT systems must coherently evolve during the execution of a business process. We adopt the view of the research projects named in the introduction, and perceive the following four aspects relevant in this respect.

1. **Roles.** In order to integrate participants of a collaborative business process, the role each partner plays in the collaboration has to be defined. This is actually a restriction of the behavioral models of the participating components. We underline this statement by the practical observation that a large part of integration code manages the correct invocation of component model methods, and only a small part is actual business logic (see Küster et al., 2007). A company's component behavioral information is being established at component design time and must be observed for each integration with

partners. This information needs to be re-engineered for each integration project at integration design time, if no proper reuse mechanism is in place.

2. **Provided behavior.** An integration can be required to serve an external interface. This is the case when the collaborative business process itself is provided as a service to others. In this case, the external interface can consist of operations and a restriction on the sequences the operations may be invoked to function properly. Thus, a provided behavior can be seen as an additional role. However, the provided behavior is differently perceived when seen as a role model – from the provider's perspective – and when seen from a consumer's perspective. We denote the provider's perspective by B^{-1} for a consumer's perspective B of a provided behavior. A more formal definition of the correspondence of both views follows in the main part of this chapter.

3. **Allowable communication.** A prerequisite for the integration of complex processes is enumerating the allowable communications between the IT systems to be integrated. This is one of the two by far most work-intense tasks in IT system integration besides the actual design of the collaborative business process Küster et al. (2007), Pistore et al. (2005d). In fact, this information is a restriction to the semantic correspondences on the data integration layer. However, this information is not stored today. It resides in the heads of experts who know what the potential connections are or they detect them from looking at the message types.

4. **Goals.** All participants have to coherently pursue some common goal in the collaborative process. Such a goal may either exclusively concentrate on the desired outcome of the process, or also state acceptable recovery outcomes.

a. **Desired outcome as a goal.** Commonly pursuing a goal means that all participants have to cooperate in a way that activities required by a later process step have been executed by a participant in a former process step. Here, activities includes operation interdependencies discussed before with the addition that such interdependencies can now span multiple participants, and with the difference that only interdependencies that affect the business goal need to be considered. Cross-participant operation interdependencies are inherent to business integration, as the reason for interoperation is to achieve a common business goal by combining the capabilities of the partners. A collaborative business process must have the potential to achieve the business goal when executing the process.

b. **Goal includes recovery outcomes.** Correctly treating recovery outcomes becomes important as soon as operations in a process have side effects—that is they change the state of the world—which is the standard case in business processes. For example, consider a process step that takes money from someone's bank account and books a flight ticket for them. This shall, for example, only happen in the case where another process step successfully rented a hotel room for the requester. Here it is important that the participating process steps are either all completed or none of them. This behavior is also known as transactionality. We are able to specify transactionality by explicitly stating the desired as well as the undesired but acceptable outcomes of a business process. We aim to cover with our definition especially transactionality in long-running business processes. We claim that obliging a process to either end in a desirable state for all participants or to take corrective actions when not all participants end in a desirable state can also be understood as transactionality.

c. A sub problem of transactionality is called exception handling. Exception handling is ensuring transactionality in the presence of undesired IT system responses that may hinder the achievement of the primary business goal. Some analysts say that 80% of integration development time goes into exception handling (see http://www2.sys-con.com/itsg/virtualcd/WebServices/archives/0307/sherman/index.html). Undesired system responses may result from

- non-deterministically observable system implementations, such as a flight booking service may either respond positively or negatively;

- faulty implementation exceeding the system's interface contract, for example, a system proposing to always accept a reservation, but at execution time responds with a decline message; or

- system failure on a lower level, for example due to hardware failure or break-down of a network connection, for example, the invoker of the flight-booking service does not receive its answer in the case the network connection dropped.

Common practice proposes to handle issues on the level they occur. As business process management relies on the contracts Web service descriptions provide, the issues of faulty imple-

mentation and system failure are out of the scope of this chapter.

The role, provided behavior, allowable communication, and the goal define the intention, that is, the requirements or the semantics, of integration. In contrast to the semantics of integration, a concrete integration consists of a subset of the allowable communications plus an ordering that defines the execution of the integration. We define a correctness relation between integration requirements and a concrete integration in the following section.

Static Definition of Integration

For the roles and provided behavior part of integration semantics, we use behavioral models, which were explained before.

Before defining communication between different behavioral models, we need some prerequisite definitions. Since we now have to refer to behavioral models and their variables in a global manner, we need to add a unique identification to each such statement. We thus introduce two sets that uniquely identify states and variables of specific behavioral models. (see Figure 13)

Correspondingly, we define a possible communication as a tuple of a globally unique output variable of one behavioral model and a globally unique input variable of another behavioral model. (see Figure 14)

Based on the state and variable assignment definitions, a concrete communication can be defined as a copy rule (Lemcke and Friesen, 2007a;b;2008). (see Figure 15)

The following is an example for a copy rule stating to copy the value of PO from the create

Figure 13.

$$\mathcal{B} := \{ bm \mapsto bmState : bm \in \mathrm{ID}, bmState \in Q^{bm} \}$$
$$Variable := \{ (bm, v) : bm \in \mathrm{ID}, v \in (\Sigma^{bm} \cup Z^{bm}) \}$$

Figure 14.

$$\mathcal{A} := \{ ((bm_1, o), (bm_2, i)) : bm_1, bm_2 \in \text{ID},$$
$$bm_1 \neq bm_2, o \in Z^{bm_1}, i \in \Sigma^{bm_2} \}$$

Figure 15.

$$C := \langle S, A \rangle, \ S \subseteq \mathcal{B}, \ A \subseteq \mathcal{A}$$

purchase order component to the purchase order management component when POM's behavioral model is in the initial state and CPO's execution has started, denoted by CPO's behavioral model being in state waiting. (see Figure 16)

The goal part of integration semantics must include the notion of recovery goals. We thus define the correctness of a composition based on the states that all participating behavioral models can potentially reach in the end of the execution of the integration. Such a set of states is called Goal. We differentiate between primary goals (P) and recovery goals (R). Both types of goals are used to describe the requirements of a correct integration (Γ). We define an integration to be correct if and only if it has the following properties.

- Each execution results in a system state that is part of the composition goal.
- There must be a theoretic execution that leads to a system state defined as one of the primary goals.

By this definition, we ensure transactionality of the behavioral models. Thus, one has the possibility to specify that either all behavioral models have to reach a successful state or no behavioral model must reach a successful state.

Figure 16.

$$c_3 = (\{(\text{CPO}, \text{waiting}), (\text{POM}, \text{init})\},$$
$$\{((\text{CPO}, \text{PO}), (\text{POM}, \text{PO}))\})$$

Example

We now define the integration semantics for the customer's purchasing procedure and the seller's sales order processing in our cross-company-code sales order processing scenario:

1. **Purchasing procedure.** The role models of the components to participate in the integration equal the component models displayed before.

The externally observable interface (CUST)—or the provided behavioral model—of the customer's purchasing procedure consists of:

a. sending a purchase order (PO) and
b. expecting an invoice (INV) or a failure notification (FAIL) in response.

The provider view consists of the opposite transitions:

a. A purchase order is received.
b. An invoice or a failure notification is given in response.

The allowable communication between the roles is defined as shown in Figure 17.

As for the composition goal, a desired final state is reached when CPO has received DONE, POM has received INV, and CUST[1] sent INV. It is an acceptable recovery goal that:

- CPO receives FAIL when POM sent REJ and CUST[1] is still in its initial state, and
- CPO receives FAIL when POM sent APR

Figure 17.

$$((CPO, PO), (POM, PO)),$$
$$((POM, REJ), (CPO, FAIL)),$$
$$((CUST^{-1}, FAIL), (CPO, FAIL)),$$

$$((CPO, PO), (CUST^{-1}, PO)),$$
$$((POM, APR), (CPO, DONE)),$$
$$((CUST^{-1}, INV), (POM, INV))$$

but did not receive INV and $CUST^{-1}$ sent FAIL.(see Figure 18.)

A correct concrete integration of the components is given by the copy rules shown in Figure 19.

2. **Sales order processing.** The role model corresponding to the SOM component equals the component model. For the invoicing component, we sequence and unfold the two components. We place the operation taking a delivery and returning an invoice in the sequence before the one-way operation that takes an invoice.

Through the sequencing, we introduce business logic that will be completed by the subsequent variable assignments. In particular, we use the first operation to create the invoice for the customer. The second operation pays the intercompany bill from the production plant.

The production component's behavioral model becomes unfolded to yield the role model.

For simplicity, the sales order processing does not involve any non-determinism in contrast to the purchasing procedure. Thus, the externally observable interface (SELR)—or the provided behavioral model—of the seller's business process first expects a purchase order (PO) and answers with an invoice (INV). Consequently, the provider's view of the provided behavioral model first sends a purchase order and afterwards expects an invoice as input.

The allowable communications between the role models are given in Figure 20.

As we consider a simplified process for the seller whose execution may not fail, we only need to define a primary goal and no recovery goals. The desired final state is reached when

- $SELR^{-1}$ has received INV,
- SOM received DEL and INV,
- FIN received INV, and

Figure 18.

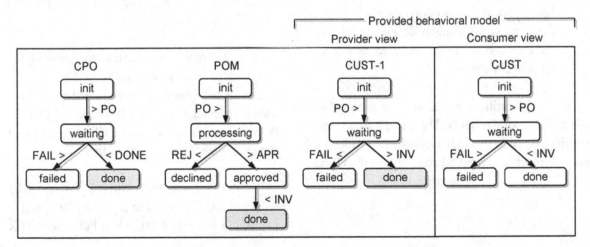

Figure 19.

$$c_1 = (\{ (\text{CPO, waiting}), (\text{POM, approved}), (\text{CUST}^{-1}, \text{done}) \},$$
$$\{ ((\text{CUST}^{-1}, \text{INV}), (\text{POM, INV})), ((\text{POM, APR}), (\text{CPO, DONE})) \})$$
$$c_2 = (\{ (\text{CPO, waiting}), (\text{POM, approved}), (\text{CUST}^{-1}, \text{init}) \},$$
$$\{ ((\text{CPO, PO}), (\text{CUST}^{-1}, \text{PO})) \})$$
$$c_3 = (\{ (\text{CPO, waiting}), (\text{POM, init}), (\text{CUST}^{-1}, \text{init}) \},$$
$$\{ ((\text{CPO, PO}), (\text{POM, PO})) \})$$
$$c_4 = (\{ (\text{CPO, waiting}), (\text{POM, declined}), (\text{CUST}^{-1}, \text{init}) \},$$
$$\{ ((\text{POM, REJ}), (\text{CPO, FAIL})) \})$$
$$c_5 = (\{ (\text{CPO, waiting}), (\text{POM, approved}), (\text{CUST}^{-1}, \text{failed}) \},$$
$$\{ ((\text{CUST}^{-1}, \text{FAIL}), (\text{CPO, FAIL})) \})$$

Figure 20.

$$((\text{SELR}^{-1}, \text{PO}), (\text{SOM, PO})), \qquad ((\text{SOM, SO}), (\text{PROD, SO})),$$
$$((\text{PROD, DEL}), (\text{FIN, DEL})), \qquad ((\text{PROD, INV}), (\text{FIN, INV})),$$
$$((\text{PROD, DEL}), (\text{SOM, DEL})), \qquad ((\text{FIN, INV}), (\text{SELR}^{-1}, \text{INV})),$$
$$((\text{FIN, INV}), (\text{SOM, INV}))$$

- PROD sent DEL and INV. (see Figure 21)

The copy rules shown in Figure 22 constitute a correct concrete integration of the components.

Execution Semantics of Integration

As denoted, the execution of a copy rule corresponds to changing the states of the variables involved. Since a copy rule contains multiple assignments of variables, it may trigger the further sending of multiple messages via the respective SEND ASMs. (see Figure 23)

We have presented mathematical models for behavioral models and their communication. An integration of behavioral models can be understood as a set of communications happening at specific time points. Therefore, we use copy rules to express an integration and complete the previous figure in Figure 24.

The execution of an integration consists of copying available variable values to their appro-

priate receivers at the right times and updating their belief models. (see Figure 25)

We assume that the state component of each copy rule of an integration contains an element for each participant behavioral model of the integration. The way the ADVANCEORCHESTRATION machine is defined, it implicitly, alternately triggers the SEND and RECEIVE abstract state machines of the participating behavioral models. Together with actually invoking Web services, we end up with the implementation of a process mediator between the participating Web services. (see Figure 26)

How Process Semantics Expresses Relevant Service Features

In this section, we show how specific recovery behavior of today's Web service implementations can be mapped to our formalization with behavioral models. (see Figure 27)

Figure 21.

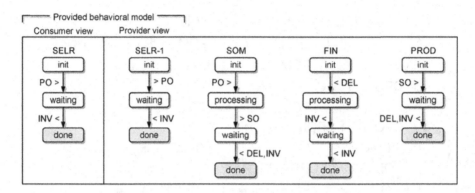

Figure 22.

$$c_6 = (\{(\text{SELR}^{-1}, \text{waiting}), (\text{SOM}, \text{waiting}), (\text{FIN}, \text{waiting}), (\text{PROD}, \text{done})\},$$
$$\{((\text{PROD}, \text{INV}), (\text{FIN}, \text{INV})), ((\text{PROD}, \text{DEL}), (\text{SOM}, \text{DEL})),$$
$$((\text{FIN}, \text{INV}), (\text{SOM}, \text{INV})), ((\text{FIN}, \text{INV}), (\text{SELR}^{-1}, \text{INV}))\})$$

$$c_7 = (\{(\text{SELR}^{-1}, \text{waiting}), (\text{SOM}, \text{waiting}), (\text{FIN}, \text{init}), (\text{PROD}, \text{done})\},$$
$$\{((\text{PROD}, \text{DEL}), (\text{FIN}, \text{DEL}))\})$$

$$c_8 = (\{(\text{SELR}^{-1}, \text{waiting}), (\text{SOM}, \text{waiting}), (\text{FIN}, \text{init}), (\text{PROD}, \text{init})\},$$
$$\{((\text{SOM}, \text{SO}), (\text{PROD}, \text{SO}))\})$$

$$c_9 = (\{(\text{SELR}^{-1}, \text{waiting}), (\text{SOM}, \text{init}), (\text{FIN}, \text{init}), (\text{PROD}, \text{init})\},$$
$$\{((\text{SELR}^{-1}, \text{PO}), (\text{SOM}, \text{PO}))\})$$

- **One-shot transactions.** A Web service provider may have decided to not provide any resolution mechanism for a transactional Web service operation. Thus, once a one-shot transaction has started, it cannot be undone any more. An example is provided on the left hand side of Figure 27. The respective, successful, final states are represented by a bold border. Please note that there is no successful, final state defined directly behind the input transition. Thus, an integrated process may either execute the full transition or not at all in order to reach a primary goal.

- **Canceling transactions.** One way to recover from a started transaction is to provide a cancellation feature. A Web service with cancellation feature usually does not return a booking confirmation in the first place. It will rather provide an offer that the invoker can accept or reject later on. The rejection thereby cancels the transaction.

- **Rolling back transactions.** Another way to recover from a started transaction is to roll back after its completion. The model for this looks very similar to the model for one-shot Web services. First, some transaction completes. The Web service now should be in a primary goal state. Afterwards, the system accepts a roll back message that puts the Web service to a recovery state. An example of the roll-back feature is shown on the right hand side of Figure 27.

Figure 23.

$$
\begin{aligned}
\text{COPY} \equiv \quad &\textbf{do forall } (\ states, varAss\ ) \in \text{Rules} \\
&\textbf{if } \text{bmState}(bm_1) = s_1 \textbf{ and } \ldots \\
&\qquad \textbf{and } \text{bmState}(bm_{|states|}) = s_{|states|} \\
&\qquad \textbf{and } \text{varState}(bm_{\text{out}_1}, o_1) = \text{initialized } \textbf{and } \ldots \\
&\qquad \textbf{and } \text{varState}(bm_{\text{out}_{|varAss|}}, o_{|varAss|}) = \text{initialized} \\
&\qquad \textbf{and } \text{varState}(bm_{\text{in}_1}, i_1) = \text{undef } \textbf{and } \ldots \\
&\qquad \textbf{and } \text{varState}(bm_{\text{in}_{|varAss|}}, i_{|varAss|}) = \text{undef } \textbf{then} \\
&\quad \textbf{do forall } (\ (\ bm_{\text{out}}, o\ ), (\ bm_{\text{in}}, i\ )\ ) \in varAss \\
&\qquad \text{varState}(bm_{\text{in}}, i) := \text{initialized} \\
&\textbf{where} \\
&\qquad (\ bm_k, s_k\ ) \in states, \quad k = 1 \, .. \, |states| \\
&\qquad (\ (\ bm_{\text{out}_n}, o_n\ ), (\ bm_{\text{in}_n}, i_n\ )\ ) \in varAss, \quad n = 1 \, .. \, |varAss|
\end{aligned}
$$

Figure 24.

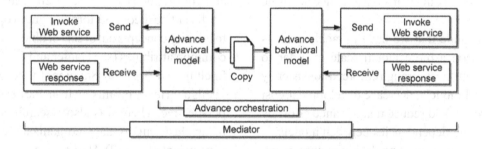

CURRENT APPROACH TO PROCESS INTEGRATION

After providing our view on issues in business process management in the previous sections, we now review existing approaches to the issues, show where they fall short and position our solution in the domain. In particular, we review research for:

- message alignment and
- process design.

Process design is currently approached as the problem to create an explicit model of the collaboration of the participants from scratch. In this chapter we take a declarative approach and follow the vision of model-driven software development that propagates a heavy use of models, model-to-model and model-to-code transformations. The more automated the transformations are, the less error prone the resulting software is. However, many models that are currently used in the model-driven research with respect to behavioral aspects, such as UML activity diagrams, BPMN, or BPEL lack formal semantics as part of their specification. Model-theoretic semantics have been proposed for each of the named types of diagrams. Unfortunately, a multitude of semantic definitions for the same diagram type still raise the question which of these definitions to use for a particular tool to interpret a specific diagram.

Figure 25.

ADVANCEORCHESTRATION(*IDs*) ≡
  choose { *M* : *M* ≡ ADVANCEBM(*bm*) ∨ *M* ≡ COPY, *bm* ∈ *IDs* }
  M

Figure 26.

MEDIATOR ≡
  choose { *M* : *M* ≡ ADVANCEORCHESTRATION(ID) ∨
      M ≡ SEND(*bm*) ∨ *M* ≡ RECEIVE(*bm*), *bm* ∈ ID }
  M

In our view presented above, we gave model-theoretic semantics to artifacts that are relevant to process integration. However, we do not allow the user to directly access the internal models. We restrict the user's influence to specifying properties of the transformations between the models. This avoids the well-known problem of model-driven approaches that models or code which become altered after they were generated from other models are inconsistent, thus out of synch with the rest of the models and thus no assertions can be made about their conformance with the models any more.

We conclude that we have to tackle process integration on a more global scale in order to increase robustness through enforced consistency with related models, decrease development cost through reuse, and reduce maintenance effort by understanding dependencies between models.

Although not providing the big picture, many proposals have been made for parts of our big picture by recent research. We review these existing approaches in order to reuse some and put

them together to create semantic business process management.

Message Alignment

Identifying promising groups of semantically equivalent or similar message types among a set of given message types can be seen as formal concept analysis. In the field of software restructuring and refactoring, formal concept analysis is used for the mining of redundancies in data types (see Mens and Tourw, 2004). Formal concept analysis bases on the lattice theory performing graph operations to identify concepts out of sets of objects that share common attributes (see Ganter and Godin, 2005, Snelting and Tip, 1998, Stumme et al., 2002). Work in this area looks promising from the performance perspective. There was also research performed using clustering for data reorganization (see Mc-Cormick et al., 1972). However, as concluded in a more recent work, clustering is different from frequent itemset mining and less appropriate for the task of concept analysis or semantic message

Figure 27.

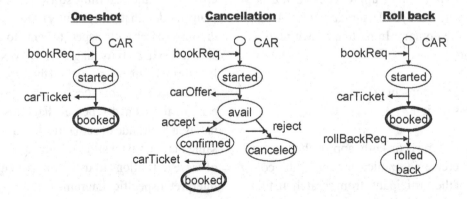

similarity (see van Deursen and Kuipers, 1999).

In the area of data mining, the task of concept analysis can be seen as closed frequent itemset mining. There exists work for the explicit mining of XML schema definitions (see Dong, 2005, Termier, 2004). However, the mining focuses on the tree structure of XML which is too strict for identifying semantic similarity in message formats that use completely incompatible complex structuring types to differently organize equivalent information. Similar approaches can be found for Web service mining. These approaches are either based on some distance calculation (see Wang and Stroulia, 2003), thus rather belong to the clustering domain, or perform an analysis of operation and parameter names (see Dong et al., 2004) without considering the data structures.

We highlight the task of closed frequent itemset mining here because there exists a linear time and space implementation by Uno et al. (2004a;b) which we are going to extend in this chapter for semantic message alignment.

Closed Frequent Itemset Mining

The closed frequent itemset mining problem is defined as follows.

- **Transactions and items.** A set of transactions P and a set of items A are given.
- **Itemsets.** Each transaction $p \in P$ is defined as a subset of A. A subset of A is also called an itemset.
- **Occurrences.** Every transaction p containing the itemset a is called an occurrence of a. The set of occurrences of a is denoted by $P(a)$.
- **Frequency and support.** An itemset $a \subseteq A$ is frequent, if the are at least φ transactions in P that subsume a. We call φ the minimum support.
- **Closed frequent itemset.** An itemset $a \subseteq A$ is a frequent closed itemset if there is no other a' with $P(a) = P(a')$ and $a \subset a'$

- **Closed frequent itemset mining.** Closed frequent itemset mining discovers all closed frequent itemsets of a given set of transactions P.

However, the traditional closed frequent itemset mining does not exactly meet the requirement. Part of the reason is that it evolved for the purpose of market basket analysis. Market basket analysis mines the selling transactions of a retail store. It reports patterns in the purchasing behavior of the store's customers. A result of market basket analysis might for example be that 70% of the customers have bought bread, butter and cheese together. If there was an online store of this company, it could use this information by proposing a customer to add butter to their cart, if the cart just contained bread and cheese. This application is much targeted and does for example neglect structured transactions and surely does not support the check whether a pattern was known upfront.

Fortunately, closed frequent itemset mining was deeply studied during the Internet boom in the early 2000s and an abstract description can be found in several textbooks Berry and Linoff (2004), Han and Kamber (2006), Petersohn (2005), Witten and Frank (2005). The naming of its elements as transactions and items still reminds of its origin.

Efficient algorithms exist for the mining of closed frequent itemsets. For example, formal concept analysis uses lattice theory, a special graph theory, for the representation of common attributes of objects. It has led to the development of efficient closed frequent itemset mining algorithms (Zaki et al., 2005; Uno et al., 2004a;b).

Process Design

Different approaches have been proposed to support procedural interoperability. The approaches range from providing no automation at all to being able to cope with complex services with complex goal requirements (see Rao and Su 2004).

For dealing with recovery goals, three systems

have been proposed in the literature. Berardi et al. (2005) propose a complex-goal-based Web service composition that allows a rich description of the participating components including internal state transition of components in addition to the globally observable behavior. In addition, a building block principle is incorporated that allows building a behavioral model out of common atomic services. Due to the complex description of services and integration requirements, the composer described by Berardi et al. (2005) runs in exponential time. As we seek for a scalable solution, we abandon the approach of Berardi et al. (2005).

A second composition approach was developed by Pistore et al. (2004; 2005a;b;d), Trainotti et al. (2005), Traverso and Pistore (2004) whose evaluations suggest running in polynomial time. This work expects initial process descriptions to exist which need to be created from scratch in reality although 80% of the behavioral information is already known in these settings. As these descriptions do not exist, we would have to use the work's input and output. As abstract BPEL does not have a formal semantics, different users of the models could have different interpretations of their meaning. Therefore, the work cannot be directly applied in our solution as we argue to reuse behavioral information from an earlier development phase, and only a view of the process exists at the time the integration is build. An executable integration must be mapped back to the earlier models which needs additional information and cannot be done by the solution of Pistore et al. (2004; 2005a;b;d), Trainotti et al. (2005), Traverso and Pistore (2004).

In addition to the practical constraints named above, the way the existing approach describes behavior is rather complex which results in a slower run time of that approach compared to the solution that was described in Lemcke and Friesen (2007a;b;2008). The third solution from Lemcke and Friesen (2007a;b;2008) assumes the behavior of a set of roles given via the state transition system introduced in the sections above. It is capable to

generate a correct integration with respect to a goal definition as described above. We use the approach of Lemcke and Friesen (2007a, 2007b, 2008) in this chapter to build semantic process design on top of that approach.

ARCHITECTURE FOR SEMANTIC PROCESS INTEGRATION

After having stated issues and of process integration and shortcomings of existing approaches, we provide our solutions that respect semantics for process integration. We begin with an architectural overview of our solution and then cover its parts individually, which are:

- semantic message alignment,
- semantic process design, and
- semantic process execution.

We understand establishing collaboration between enterprises as a two-step procedure as depicted on the right-hand side of Figure 28. First, a company needs to define their local procedures (2.2). Second, the companies combine their intra-enterprise business processes to a cross-enterprise business process (2.3). We introduce this principle to reduce the complexity of the whole integration problem. We assume that it is easier to separate thinking of local business processes and integration requirements rather than thinking of local business processes plus caring for consistent alignment with other participants' business processes at the same time. Our formal approach allows for the initial separation of the aspects in the design phase and their later joining in the execution phase.

A prerequisite to both steps is the semantic alignment of messages. Therefore, establishing integration starts with our CFIM of hierarchical types (1. in Figure 28).

As for the semantic process design (2. in Figure 28), only the local, intra-enterprise business processes are directly dependent on the components' capabilities. We provide an interactive model-to-model transformation that transforms a component model to a role model (2.1). As each participant performs a business transaction as their part of the collaborative business process, we employ the existing complex-goal-based Web service composition to create the partial business process of each participant (2.2). The composition needs knowledge of potential communication which was identified by the CFIM before and can now be further restricted. Restricting the potential to allowable communications is a model-to-model transformation. The composition is a model-to-code transformation because the result is a concrete, semantically executable integration of the company's components. What is missing now is the cross-enterprise integration.

As described in the sections before, the definition of a provided interface may be a special role when building a concrete integration in step 2.2. Thus, each intra-enterprise business process needs to define a provided interface that is used for interaction with the other companies to be integrated. As denoted before, there are two differ-ent views of the provided model: the provider and the consumer view. We provide a model-to-model transformation to convert between the two.

The provided interface now acts as the role model for cross-enterprise integration (2.3). Again, the cross-enterprise integration must be consistent among all participants. Therefore, we again allow for the restriction of the potential cross-enterprise communication and employ the complex-goal-based composition to create the cross-enterprise integration.

We finally need to provide a means to jointly execute the concrete integrations on the intra-enterprise and the cross-enterprise level. The formal behavioral descriptions introduced in the previous sections are a major enabler for this. However, the joining was not defined yet which will follow in the subsequent sections.

Example

Our example so far was used to compile the intra-enterprise business processes. We now advance our example to depict the cross-enterprise integration. The behavioral models to integrate are now the

Figure 28.

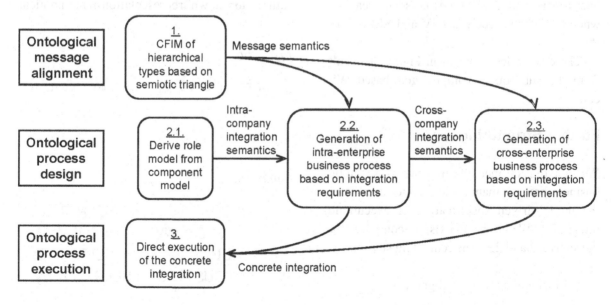

consumer views of the provided behavioral models of the customer (CUST) and the seller (SELR).

In our cross-company-code sales order processing scenario, the customer possesses non-deterministic behavior. The first time, non-determinism occurs when the purchase order management component may approve or decline the purchase order. The second time, the provided behavioral model may not be able to deliver the requested purchase order and answer with a failure notification. Whereas this appears as non-deterministic behavior to the customer, the opposite behavioral model in the cross-enterprise integration is deterministic. Namely, the concrete cross-enterprise integration can determine whether to send an invoice or a failure notification to the customer. The customer can cope with both answers.

However, in our example, the seller always succeeds and thus never sends a failure notification. Consequently, only one branch of the customer's provided behavioral model will be used. As the branching decision is deterministic, we need not connect variable assignments to the unused branch. The complex-goal-based WS composition would never visit that branch.

Finally, the integration expert defines the variable assignments shown in Figure 29.

The integration requirement consists of only one primary goal. The desired final state is reached when CUST has received INV and SELR sent INV.

The copy rules depicted in Figure 30 result from the subsequent complex-goal-based WS composition.

Further Structuring

We have thus defined a framework for semantic business process management which facilitates the model-driven specification of executable integration. We utilize an existing composer for the steps 2.2 and 2.3. The remaining steps

- 1 (semantic message alignment),

- 2.1 (derive role model from component model),
- the linkage between 2.2 and 2.3 (convert provided behavioral model from consumer to provider view), and
- 3 (semantic process execution)

are developed in the following.

SEMANTIC MESSAGE ALIGNMENT

In this section, we reduce the problem to detect redundant messages to CFIM of hierarchical types. In particular, we adopt the LCM algorithm from Uno et al. (2004a;b). The problem reduction consists of the three steps

1. create itemsets from structural types,
2. identify semantic similarities using CFIM, and
3. interpret the mining result.

Create Itemsets from Structural Types

For creating itemsets from structural types, the transformation mainly consists of reverting the natural "top-down" representation of hierarchical

Figure 29.

$$((\text{CUST, PO}), (\text{SELR, PO})), \quad ((\text{SELR, INV}), (\text{CUST, INV}))$$

Figure 30.

$$c_{10} = (\ \{(\text{CUST, waiting}), (\text{SELR, done})\}, \\ \{((\text{SELR, INV}), (\text{CUST, INV}))\}\ )$$

$$c_{11} = (\ \{(\text{CUST, waiting}), (\text{SELR, init})\}, \\ \{((\text{CUST, PO}), (\text{SELR, PO}))\}\ )$$

types to the inverse "bottom-up" representation of the vertical itemset mining format. We start with the basic transformation and handle further aspects thereafter.

Basic Transformation

The vertical data structure for a structured XSD element e containing the child elements $c_1, ..., c_i, ..., c_n$, where $1 < i < n$, is shown in Figure 31.

where e^T denotes the *transaction* that corresponds to element e and c^I denotes the *item* that corresponds to element c. If another XSD element f becomes added to the same vertical data structure with the child elements $c_i, ..., c_n, ..., c_m$, where $n < m$, the data structure is shown in Figure 32.

In addition to the basic transformation presented, the further aspects

* mapping between elements, items, and transactions,
* domain of analysis, and
* analysis range need to be considered.

Mapping Between Elements, Items, and Transactions

For the basic transformation presented above, we have neglected the question of how exactly an element relates to an item or a transaction. This question is important, because elements have both a name and a type. Let n_x be the name, and t_x the type of e_x. There are obviously three ways to map a complex element e_x to mining items or transactions. If e_x appears as item, the item may be defined as

1. the name: $e_x^I = n_x$,
2. the type: $e_x^I = t_x$, or
3. a combination of name and type: $e_x^I = \left(n_x, t_x \right)$ of the corresponding element.

Likewise, if e_x appears as transaction, the transaction may be defined as the name, the type, or a combination of both. However, in our solution we restrict the mapping of elements to transactions to only using the element's type to define the transaction. We pose this restriction because the other mappings for transactions are unsuited for the analysis we perform in our solution.

To give an example, a complex XML schema element e named n of type t may contain the sub elements $c_1, c_2, ..., c_i$, where c_x, named n_x, is of complex type t_x for $x = 1, ..., i$. The corresponding vertical data structures are shown in Figure 33.

The choice above determines when the miner would treat two elements appearing as items to be equal. The most precise estimation is surely performed by alternative 3, because the most information is used for the determination of equality. Therefore, alternative 3 might be a good choice in an already very much aligned repository. Contrarily, alternative 1 may even find matches in not so much aligned repositories as just names, which may be given arbitrarily by a human, are considered for matching. The precision of alternative 2 lies in between the ones of alternative 1 and 3, because elements of the same type are equal per definition. However, they may be used in different contexts which may be differentiated by the elements' names, which is not considered in alternative 2.

Figure 31.

$$(c_1^I, \{e^T\}), ..., (c_i^I, \{e^T\}), ..., (c_n^I, \{e^T\}),$$

Figure 32.

$$(c_1^I, \{e^T\}), ..., (c_{i-1}^I, \{e^T\}),$$
$$(c_i^I, \{e^T, f^T\}), ..., (c_n^I, \{e^T, f^T\}),$$
$$(c_{n+1}^I, \{f^T\}), ..., (c_m^I, \{f^T\})$$

Figure 33.

$$(n_1, \{t\}), (n_2, \{t\}), \ldots, (n_i, \{t\}) \quad \text{for alternative 1,}$$
$$(t_1, \{t\}), (t_2, \{t\}), \ldots, (t_i, \{t\}) \quad \text{for alternative 2, and}$$
$$((n_1, t_1), \{t\}), ((n_2, t_2), \{t\}), \ldots, ((n_i, t_i), \{t\}) \quad \text{for alternative 3.}$$

Analysis Range

In the paragraphs above, we have explained how a single complex type may be transformed to the vertical data structure. One more decision needs to be taken about the set of types to be analyzed—the analysis range. The alternatives are whether to consider

1. only the complex top-level elements of the given XML schemas, or
2. the top-level plus all contained complex elements.

The rationale for the first option is to only compare the given types. The rationale for the second is that it may detect similar complex types that were used to build up the given XML schemas. We call the second option for this reason **building block analysis**.

Let's consider the complex type s consisting of the complex elements e_1 and e_2, where e_1 and e_2 are complex, and e_1 consists of c_1 and c_2, and e_2 consists of c_3 and c_4. Let's further consider that another complex type t consists of c_1, c_3, and c_4. Building the vertical data structure for option 1 yields the results shown in Figure 34.

Since no two pairs contain s and t together, the miner will not discover that related complex types were used to construct the both—as long as e_1, e_2, c_1, c_3, and c_4 have different types and names. In contrast, the vertical data structure for option 2 is shown in Figure 35.

In this case, the miner will discover that both e_2 and t share c_3 and c_4 and thus are related.

The miner will also conclude that e_1 and t are related as they share c_1.

Domain of Analysis

Another variation of transforming multiple complex element definitions to the vertical data structure is the completeness their substructure is being considered—the domain of the analysis. The two options are to consider

1. just the directly contained subelements, and
2. all directly and indirectly contained subelements.

The rationale for the first option is, again, to only consider the given types for analysis. The rationale for the second is that it may detect complex type definitions with different granularity. We therefore call the second option granularity-agnostic analysis.

Let's consider the same example as before. The vertical data structure for option 1 is shown in (6.1). In contrast, the structure for option 2—without building block analysis—is shown in Figure 36.

In this case, the miner would determine that schema s and t are similar as they share c_1, c_3, and c_4.

Figure 34.

$$(e_1^I, \{s^T\}), (e_2^I, \{s^T\}), (c_1^I, \{t^T\}), (c_3^I, \{t^T\}), (c_4^I, \{t^T\})$$

Figure 35.

$$(e_1^I, \{s^T\}), (e_2^I, \{s^T\}), (c_1^I, \{e_1^T, t^T\}), (c_2^I, \{e_1^T\}), (c_3^I, \{e_2^T, t^T\}), (c_4^I, \{e_2^T, t^T\})$$

The granularity-agnostic analysis is especially useful when different partners have used different approaches to structure the same kind of data. For example, one partner may have chosen to create a type "purchase order" that contains ordered goods, taxable and total gross amounts, contact and delivery addresses without any substructure directly below the top-level element. Another partner may have chosen to create a similar type "order" with the same data, but grouped the data into the complex subelements "goods", "amounts", and "addresses". Using granularity-agnostic analysis, "purchase order" and "order" can be determined to be similar.

Identify Semantic Similarities using CFIM

In the realm of closed frequent itemset mining,

- a transaction is a denotation and
- the items of a transaction are a materialization.

When comparing transactions in the mining database, a transaction and its items can be understood as an observation of a denotation and a materialization in terms of the semiotic triangle. Therefore, the cases depicted in Figure 5 can be applied to every two transactions in the mining database. The different cases of misalignment are all handled by the way closed frequent itemset mining is applied on hierarchical types

- during populating the mining database and
- during performing the mining.

Figure 36.

$$(e_1^1, \{s^T\}), (e_2^1, \{s^T\}), (c_1^1, \{s^T, t^T\}), (c_2^1, \{s^T\}), (c_3^1, \{s^T, t^T\}), (c_4^1, \{s^T, t^T\})$$

Populating the Mining Database

When types are going to be analyzed, they are first loaded to the mining database. Now we focus on cases of existing alignment, or misalignment.

During population, more and more transactions are loaded to the mining database. A case of existing alignment or misalignment is observed when a transaction to be loaded is already contained in the mining repository. Therefore, the cases with similar denotations, i.e.,

- clean repetition (a),
- inconsistency (b),
- illusive friend (e), and
- false friend (f),

can be addressed during the population of the mining database (left-hand side of Figure 5).

To determine one of the above cases, we only need to compare the name of the new transaction to the names of existing transactions. As the transactions in the mining database are per definition organized as a set, the addition of an existing transaction is actually a violation to the definition of the closed frequent itemset mining.

For the resolution of these cases, it is important to differentiate based on the origins of two transactions with similar denotations, that is, complex types with same names.

- **Same partner.** In the case the conflicting types stem from the same partner, we assume that the one partner always uses the same denotation (term) to refer to the same concept (upper left part of Figure 5). In this case, only one version should be kept in the data structure, because either
  1. the structure of both types is equal (clean repetition, a), or
  2. an inconsistency in the partner's own data model was discovered (inconsistency, b).

In the first case, it is irrelevant which type is added to the structure. In the second case, the partner should first resolve their inconsistency internally, before trying to align with other partners.

- **Different partners.** In the case the conflicting types s and s' stem from different partners, we have to assume that same denotations (terms) are potentially used for different things (lower left part of Figure 5). Both types should be added to the structure, as the mining procedure should determine whether both schemas are really already aligned, or actually different. Therefore, we transform the case
- illusive friend (e) to parallel (g) and
- false friend (f) to clean distinction (h).

In other words, the equal transaction representations s^T and s'^T need to be made unequal to be added to the structure. We propose to add a unique distinguisher to s'^T and to perform the transformation to the item representation as described in the previous sections afterwards.

It is to be noted that this procedure only applies to conflicting transactions, not to their constituents with equal item representation, as equal item representations are used to determine the similarity of the transactions.

After populating the mining database, it only contains the cases of the right-hand side of Figure 5, i.e.,

- redundancy / synonym (c),
- heterogeneity (d),
- parallel (g), and
- clean distinction (h).

Performing the Mining

The closed frequent itemset mining determines the similarity of materializations in the mining database. A redundancy group stands for a set of mutually similar types. According to Figure 5, two observations may differ in the concepts they belong to. This distinction must clearly be made by a human utilizing the closed frequent itemset mining.

1. **Same concept.** That is, the observations have the same semantic meaning (redundancy / synonym, c).

Same concepts. In the first case, it is advisable that the differently named but structurally similar types become named the same. In addition, it should be a goal to not only homogenize the names but also make both types use the same complex type definition. As the miner detects overlap, this has not to be the case for the redundancy group. In order to support the homogenization, further closed frequent itemset mining runs can be applied on only the members of the redundancy group. This serves two purposes.

- First, further detection of semantically equivalent types that appear as sub types in the elements of the redundancy group.
- Second, if no more types are semantically equivalent, technically equivalent types can be identified.

The first case would facilitate the alignment of terms and thus bring forward a common understanding. The second case would foster the alignment of type structures and therefore lower efforts for later maintenance.

2. **Distinct concepts.** That is, the similar structures are used to denominate semantically different things (parallel, g). In this case the analysis revealed that although being semantically distinct, the materializations have some commonality. By further closed frequent itemset mining runs on the members of the redundancy group, it should be

determined, whether more similar subtypes of the members can be identified whose definitions can be merged.

The remaining cases of misalignment in Figure 5

1. heterogeneity (d) and
2. clean distinction (h).

are not detected by the closed frequent itemset mining. For the second case this is perfectly fine as a clean distinction (h) actually contains no redundancy. Thus, the only case which can not correctly be handled is heterogeneity (d). The reason is that there is no information at all that a machine could use in order to draw any conclusions on the potential similarity in this case. This is the spot where always human intelligence is needed in alignment. Due to this finding, a solution using closed frequent itemset mining to detect redundant interface objects should always allow a human in the loop to manually point out similarity. We facilitate this in our solution as the closed frequent itemset mining only supports the human analysis of the type repository. Our solution seeks to point out the most that could be possibly done automatically and always leaves room for human adaptation.

Interpret the Mining Result

The result of the mining is a set of redundancy groups. Each redundancy group consists of a set of types that have some overlap. After mining, the computer has to present the redundancy groups to the user. As there are more interesting and less interesting results, we introduce a generic rank that gives a measure for the confidence that can be derived from the overlap that a specific redundancy group contains redundant types. The generic rank contains weights which can be used to derive a domain-specific rank.

Rank

We now develop a rank that takes into account properties of a redundancy group that make it likely to contain redundant elements. It follows from the definition of redundancy that we are looking for a redundancy group that at the same time is large in the number of types $\tau = |T(A)|$ as well as in the number of common attributes $\kappa = |A|$. Let's consider two redundancy groups g_1 and g_2 with equal number of types and common attributes $\tau_{g_1} = 10$, $\kappa_{g_1} = 20$, and $\tau_{g_2} = 10$, $\kappa_{g_2} = 20$. Both have the same rank. However, if every type of g_1 contains more attributes than every type of g_2, we would like to rank g_2 higher, because its ratio of potentially redundant to potentially unique attributes is higher. For comparing redundancy groups' sizes, we look at the average number of attributes of all types of $T(A)$, denoted by $\alpha = \|T(A)\|$. Putting κ in relation to α yields the ratio of common attributes to the average number of attributes $\upsilon = \frac{\kappa}{\alpha}$.

We define a set of redundancy groups $G_1 = \{g_{1,1}, ..., g_{1,n_1}\}$ to be a more interesting redundancy group than $G_2 = \{g_{2,1}, ..., g_{2,n_2}\}$ if

1. G_1 is larger than G_2, $\tau_1 > \tau_2$
2. G_1's messages have absolutely more common constituents, $\kappa_1 > \kappa_2$; and
3. G_1's redundancy groups contain a higher average percentage of common constituents, $\upsilon_1 > \upsilon_2$.

We calculate an redundancy group's rank ρ as a combination of the three components $\tau, \kappa,$ and υ. To be comparable, we normalize each component by its maximum value among all redundancy groups, respectively denoted by $\hat{\tau}, \hat{\kappa},$ and $\hat{\upsilon}$. It follows that each component $\frac{\tau}{\hat{\tau}}, \frac{\kappa}{\hat{\kappa}}$ and $\frac{\upsilon}{\hat{\upsilon}}$ is in range [0; 1]. For combining the components, we use the product operation which produces a higher rank the more the components' values are balanced as opposed to the sum operation. Let's consider the two redundancy groups g_1 with $\frac{\tau}{\hat{\tau}} = \frac{10}{10}$, $\frac{\kappa}{\hat{\kappa}} = \frac{2}{10}$, $\frac{\upsilon}{\hat{\upsilon}} = \frac{3}{10}$, and g_2 with $\frac{\tau}{\hat{\tau}} = \frac{5}{10}$, $\frac{\kappa}{\hat{\kappa}} = \frac{5}{10}$, $\frac{\upsilon}{\hat{\upsilon}} = \frac{5}{10}$. Both would be treated the same using the sum operation, viz. $\frac{10+2+3}{10} = \frac{5+5+5}{10} = \frac{15}{10}$. However, g_1 is a rather large group with a relatively and absolutely rather small number of common attributes. On the other hand, g_2 is not as large as g_1, but has a relatively and absolutely larger core than g_1 which makes it more likely to contain redundancy. Combining the components of the rank via a product, we boost g_2 over g_1, as $\frac{10}{10} \cdot \frac{2}{10} \cdot \frac{3}{10} = \frac{60}{1000} < \frac{5}{10} \cdot \frac{5}{10} \cdot \frac{5}{10} = \frac{125}{1000}$. After scaling the product of the components by factor σ, rank ρ is in range $\left[0, \sigma\right]$. (see Figure 37)

The formula for ρ produces a larger rank for a redundancy group G_1 than for G_2 if G_1 is more interesting than G_2.

Proof. We must prove $\sigma\left(\frac{\tau_1}{\hat{\tau}} \cdot \frac{\kappa_1}{\hat{\kappa}} \cdot \frac{\upsilon_1}{\hat{\upsilon}}\right) > \sigma\left(\frac{\tau_2}{\hat{\tau}} \cdot \frac{\kappa_2}{\hat{\kappa}} \cdot \frac{\upsilon_2}{\hat{\upsilon}}\right)$, which is equivalent to $\frac{\tau_1}{\tau_2} \cdot \frac{\kappa_1}{\kappa_2} \cdot \frac{\upsilon_1}{\upsilon_2} > 1$. This is true when $\tau_1 > \tau_2$, $\kappa_1 > \kappa_2$, and $\upsilon_1 > \upsilon_2$, which is the definition of a more interesting redundancy group.

Determining the Redundancy

In principle, redundancy can be determined by analyzing the

- common, and the
- uncommon items in a redundancy group.

Obviously, the common elements identified by the miner point out some definite redundancy of the elements of the redundancy group.

But also the uncommon elements of a redundancy group provide an interesting insight. Let's assume that two business partners are willing to agree on common data types to exchange. In this setting, both business partners may contribute some kind of a business partner type to the community. If these partners worked together before, some of the nested data will already be aligned. Consequently, the miner will be able to determine this match based on the common, already aligned, elements. As, in this setting, both partners really talk about the same kind of business partner type, the field for the miner not known to be common may indeed be just different representations of the same things. Therefore, it might be interesting for the human integration experts to also look at the uncommon elements as these may contain matching pairs.

Discussion

In order for the algorithm to find redundancy groups, we assume that the data types fed to the miner are aligned to a certain extent already. This means that two conceptually equivalent data types also carry the same label. This assumption can be made because, when acting in the realm of a single company, at least some basic data types will be consistent with a common model that other data types are built upon. In SAP, e. g., data type labels conform to the naming conventions of the CCTS. Figure 38 show the recall and precision evolution along the ranked results when mining the message types exposed by SAP's standard software components. The left side (recall) shows that our mining is capable to recall more than 80% of actually semantically equivalent messages in SAP's repository. The right side (precision) shows that our rank shifts groups with better results to the front of the result list.

The assumption of a global naming convention might be a difficult one when dealing with multiple companies in a community. However, we

Figure 37.

$$\rho = \sigma\left(\frac{\tau}{\hat{\tau}} \cdot \frac{\kappa}{\hat{\kappa}} \cdot \frac{\upsilon}{\hat{\upsilon}}\right)$$

Figure 38.

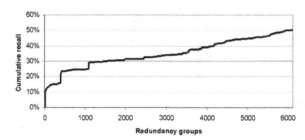 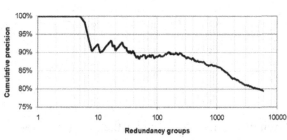

can still support the process of aligning the technical structures of multiple companies by hinting at definitions that have been manually aligned to a certain extend, but need further alignment work. Such a situation is actually likely to be found as communities form in order to perform similar tasks, for example shippers and carriers will probably talk about location, package types, and dates. If some members of a community already worked together, they might even have aligned their types with existing standards for communication, such as RosettaNet or CIDX. However, a well-known difficulty with such industry standards is the high degree of freedom the standards allow for. That means that although two partners implement, for example, RosettaNet, they may still have different custom extensions of the standard. In this very common situation, the algorithm is expected to perform well due to the existing alignment.

SEMANTIC PROCESS DESIGN

The open activities in semantic process design are the derivation of a role model from a component model and converting a provided behavioral model from the provider to the consumer view. Examples have been provided in the former sections.

Derive Role Model from Component Model

The component model describes

- the potential operations the component may perform,
- potential alternative outcomes of an operation invocation, and
- sequencing constraints that are required for a successful operation invocation.

However, the operations are general and need to be applied in the context of a business process in order to perform some meaningful task. For this purpose, a business process expert may define a view of the components to participate in a collaborative business process. As not the full functionality of the components may be needed in the context of the business process, the business process expert first needs to define the relevant fragment of the component models. The relevant fragment must be in concordance with the component models. Therefore, we define a relation between states of a component model C and states of a fragment F as follows.

We denote the originating component model state q^C for a fragment state q^F as shown in Figure 39.

We pose the further restriction on fragment behavioral models that for every fragment F, δ^F forms a rooted tree. Thus, we can uniquely name

Figure 39.

$$q^C = \sigma(q^F)$$

Figure 40.

$$\langle \sigma(\phi_{o1}), \sigma(\phi_{o2}) \rangle \in T(\delta^C) \rightarrow \langle \phi_{o1}, \phi_{o2} \rangle \in T(\delta^{\mathcal{F}})$$

Figure 41.

$$\sigma(s) = \sigma(\phi_{o^F})$$

the enabling state φ_{a^F} at which the specific operation a^F can be invoked.

In the following, we describe an algorithm to be performed by a business process expert that allows the excerption of a fragment from a behavioral model whose behavior is still in accordance with the component model. Being in accordance means that we want to preserve the knowledge of proper operation sequencing regarding one object instance which we define below.

Whenever we observe two operations o_1, o_2 on any path in a fragment F, calculated using the transitive closure *(T)* of all edges $\langle o_1, o_2 \rangle \in T(\delta^F)$; which also appear in the respective component model C on a common path; then the respective enabling states should be in the same order. Thus, Figure 40 should hold at all times.

We now present the excerption.

1. An excerption step begins with picking an operation o^C from C.
2. (a) If F does not contain any states yet, the new state o^F with $o^C = o(o^F)$ becomes the first operation in F.
   (b) i. If F already contains operations, the new state o^F with $o^C = o(o^F)$ becomes integrated into F. This is done by unifying o^F's enabling state

φ_{o^F} with an existing state s in F that has the same origin in C as φ_{o^F} (see Figure 41)

ii. If the former step is not possible, o^C cannot be added at this time.

Whenever an operation o^C is added to a fragment F, o^C becomes unfolded. That means, that the state o^F and all states that o^F's output transitions directly link to are new, separate states in F.

The described construction procedure only produces trees which are in accordance with their respective component model.

Proof of trees. It is exactly one tree generated due to two reasons. First, the enabling state φ_{o^F} of a newly added operation o^F unifies with an existing state in F if o^F is not the first operation. Second, all states except for φ_{o^F} are new states that were not present in F before.

Proof of accordance. Let's assume $\langle \sigma(\varphi_{o_2}), \sigma(\varphi_{o_1}) \rangle \in T(\delta^C)$, but $\langle \varphi_{o_2}, \varphi_{o_1} \rangle \notin T(\delta^F)$. That means there is no state q with $\langle \varphi_{o_2}, q \rangle \in T(\delta^F) \wedge \langle q, \varphi_{o_1} \rangle \notin T(\delta^F)$. From the algorithm follows that since o_1 was added, there must be some state q with $\langle \sigma(\varphi_{o_2}), \sigma(q) \rangle \in T(\delta^C), q = \varphi_{o_1}$, and

Figure 42.

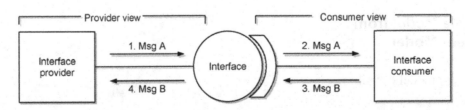

$\sigma\left(q\right) = \sigma\left(\varphi_{o_1}\right)$. By contradiction we have shown that our algorithm preserves operation order.

Convert Provided Behavioral Model from Consumer to Provider View

As depicted in Figure 42, every interface can in general be seen from:

- The consumer view, and
- The provider view.

The peer implementing an interface takes the provider view and a peer using an interface takes the consumer view. For example, if a piece of software makes use of an interface by reading information from the interface (consumer view), and then some piece of software implementing the interface must send that information to the interface (provider view). Vice versa, if a piece of software makes use of an interface by writing data to the interface (consumer view), then some piece of software implementing the interface must be ready to absorb and process the data (provider view). In that sense, the consumer view of an interface is the opposite of the provider view.

In other words, the concept of the opposite of an interface allows us to connect the consumer and the provider view. The opposite on an interface acts as a gateway between the implementation of the provider and the consumer. This is the key idea of for combining intra-enterprise and cross-enterprise integration.

We define the opposite behavioral model BM^{-1} of an original behavioral model $BM = \langle \Sigma, Z, Q, q_0, \delta \rangle$ as shown in Figure 43.

Figure 43.

$$BM^{-1} := \langle Z, \Sigma, Q, q_0, \delta \rangle$$

Please note that the only change is the mutual substitution of inputs and outputs.

Two operations that appear in a behavioral model BM appear in the same order in the opposite behavioral model BM^{-1}.

Proof. This is trivial because $Q^{BM} = Q^{BM^{-1}}$.

We have now arrived at intra-enterprise and cross-enterprise integrations in a model-driven manner. In the subsequent section, we jointly execute the generated integrations without having to write any implementation for the integration.

SEMANTIC PROCESS EXECUTION

Let's assume that there is a concrete cross-enterprise integration O_{ebus}. Let the set of identifiers of behavioral models in O_{ebus} be PID. Let's further assume that for each behavioral model BM in O_{ebus} with identifier bm there exists a concrete intra-enterprise integration O_{bm} that contains BM^{-1}. In order to deliver on the promise to track behavioral information through software design phases, we have to define a composition of integrations. We define the joint integration O_{join} of O_{ebus} and all O_{bm} by joining their copy rules. (see Figure 44)

The execution semantics of the joint integration illustrated in Figure 45 is a slight modification to the MEDIATOR ASM.

MEDIATOR* differs from MEDIATOR in the parameters of ADVANCEORCHESTRATION. In the joint integration, the behavioral models of all Web services and all behavioral models in the concrete cross-enterprise integration have to be advanced.

Lemma. Let o be an integration consisting of a set of copy rules C. Let o' be an integration that consists of two sets of copy rules C' and C'' that are joined by C. Let o'' be an integration consisting of C'. Two operations that are triggered to be executed in a sequence by advancement of C' through o' can also be triggered in sequence by o''.

Proof. As we have defined, each copy rule c of

Figure 44.

$$O_{\text{join}} := \text{Rules}^{O_{\text{ebus}}} \cup \bigcup_{bm \in \text{PID}} \text{Rules}^{O_{bm}}$$

Figure 45.

$$\begin{aligned}
&\text{MEDIATOR}^* \equiv \\
&\quad \text{choose} \{ M : M \equiv \text{ADVANCEORCHESTRATION}(\text{ID} \cup \text{PID}) \vee \\
&\qquad M \equiv \text{SEND}(bm) \vee M \equiv \text{RECEIVE}(bm), bm \in \text{ID} \} \\
&\qquad M
\end{aligned}$$

an integration p contains only states of behavioral models that participate in p and for each behavioral model that participates in p, there is exactly one state in the state component of c. Further, two integrations p and p0 are joined when they share exactly one participating behavioral model.

The COPY ASM performing o' from the lemma executes C', which is contained in o', as if C' was the single set of copy rules of an integration, such as in o''. Thus, every pair of operations triggered in a sequence by o' would also be triggered in the same sequence by o''. From the perspective of C', the joining integration o just appears as a participant of o''.

EXAMPLE

We can now jointly execute the intra-enterprise and cross-enterprise integrations by merging their copy rules. In this section, we walk through the copy rules in the natural order of their execution. But

before we start, let's have a closer investigation of the MEDIATOR* ASM that defines the execution semantics of a set of joined copy rules.

The definition of the MEDIATOR* ASM contains two sets of identifiers.

1. **ID.** This set contains the identifiers of component models. That is, CPO and POM from the customer and SOM, FIN, and PROD from the seller.
2. **PID.** This set contains the identifiers of the concrete intra-enterprise integration. That is, CUST and SELR.

The execution of MEDIATOR* triggers in alternation

- ADVANCEBM through ADVANCEORCHESTRATION for the members of PID $\cup$ ID and
- SEND and RECEIVE for the members of ID.

Figure 46.

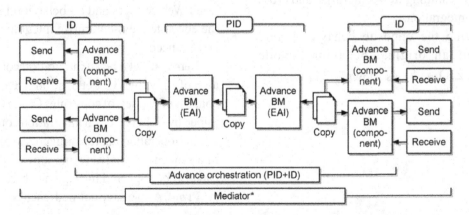

Figure 47.

Prev. No	No	Cp. rule	CPO	POM	CUST	SELR	SOM	FIN	PROD
	0		waiting	init	init	init	init	init	init
0	1	c_3	waiting	declined	init	init	init	init	init
1	2	c_4	failed	declined	init	init	init	init	init
0	3	c_3	waiting	approved	init	init	init	init	init
3	4	c_2	waiting	approved	waiting	init	init	init	init
4	5	c_{11}	waiting	approved	waiting	waiting	init	init	init
5	6	c_9	waiting	approved	waiting	waiting	waiting	init	init
6	7	c_8	waiting	approved	waiting	waiting	waiting	init	done
7	8	c_7	waiting	approved	waiting	waiting	waiting	waiting	done
8	9	c_6	waiting	approved	waiting	done	done	done	done
9	10	c_{10}	waiting	approved	done	done	done	done	done
10	11	c_1	done	done	done	done	done	done	done

As CUST = CUST^{-1} and SELR = SELR^{-1}, we can treat CUST and CUST^{-1} as well as SELR and SELR^{-1} the same in the joint integration and when given as an argument to an ASM. These behavioral models act as the synchronizing interfaces between the concrete intra-enterprise and the concrete cross-enterprise integration. To illustrate this, we walk through the execution of the joined copy rules in the following.

Figure 47 shows the states of all participating behavioral models during the execution of the joined integration.

Initially, all behavioral models are in their initial state. CPO initiates the collaboration by sending a PO. This happens non-deterministically from the perspective of the integration totally depending on the underlying Web service performing this operation. The receipt of the PO by the RECEIVE(CPO) ASM allows ADVANCEBM(CPO) to set CPO's state to waiting. This triggers the first copy rule. (see Figure 48)

Forwarding the PO to POM triggers SEND(POM) to invoke the underlying implementation of POM. As the implementation is known to be non-deterministic, RECEIVE(POM) may trigger ADVANCEBM(POM) to set POM's state to either declined or approved.

In the first case, the copy rule shown in Figure 49 is triggered which generates a failure notification from REJ and forwards it to CPO.

The receipt of FAIL by CPO triggers CPO's state to be changed to failed. This is an acceptable recovery goal. Thus, the execution came to a consistent end.

In the case that POM's state was set to approved by the non-deterministic implementation, the copy rule depicted in Figure 50 is triggered.

Thus, the approved PO is now forwarded to the external interface of CUST.

The receipt of PO triggers ADVANCEBM(CUST) to set CUST's state to waiting. We switch now from the customer's perspective to the cross-enterprise integration as the state change is recognized by the copy rule in Figure 51.

Executing the copy rule triggers SELR's state to change from init to waiting which is recognized by the rule from the seller's intra-enterprise integration. (see Figure 52)

Figure 48.

$$c_3 = (\; \{(\, \mathsf{CPO}, \text{waiting}\,), (\,\mathsf{POM}, \text{init}\,), (\,\mathsf{CUST}^{-1}, \text{init}\,)\},$$
$$\{((\,\mathsf{CPO}, \mathsf{PO}\,), (\,\mathsf{POM}, \mathsf{PO}\,))\}\,)$$

Figure 49.

$$c_4 = (\{ (\text{CPO, waiting}), (\text{POM, declined}), (\text{CUST}^{-1}, \text{init}) \}, \\ \{ ((\text{POM, REJ}), (\text{CPO, FAIL})) \})$$

Figure 50.

$$c_2 = (\{ (\text{CPO, waiting}), (\text{POM, approved}), (\text{CUST}^{-1}, \text{init}) \}, \\ \{ ((\text{CPO, PO}), (\text{CUST}^{-1}, \text{PO})) \})$$

Figure 51.

$$c_{11} = (\{ (\text{CUST, waiting}), (\text{SELR, init}) \}, \\ \{ ((\text{CUST, PO}), (\text{SELR, PO})) \})$$

Figure 52.

$$c_9 = (\{ (\text{SELR}^{-1}, \text{waiting}), (\text{SOM, init}), (\text{FIN, init}), (\text{PROD, init}) \}, \\ \{ ((\text{SELR}^{-1}, \text{PO}), (\text{SOM, PO})) \})$$

Figure 53.

$$c_8 = (\{ (\text{SELR}^{-1}, \text{waiting}), (\text{SOM, waiting}), (\text{FIN, init}), (\text{PROD, init}) \}, \\ \{ ((\text{SOM, SO}), (\text{PROD, SO})) \})$$

$$c_7 = (\{ (\text{SELR}^{-1}, \text{waiting}), (\text{SOM, waiting}), (\text{FIN, init}), (\text{PROD, done}) \}, \\ \{ ((\text{PROD, DEL}), (\text{FIN, DEL})) \})$$

$$c_6 = (\{ (\text{SELR}^{-1}, \text{waiting}), (\text{SOM, waiting}), (\text{FIN, waiting}), (\text{PROD, done}) \}, \\ \{ ((\text{PROD, INV}), (\text{FIN, INV})), ((\text{PROD, DEL}), (\text{SOM, DEL})), \\ ((\text{FIN, INV}), (\text{SOM, INV})), ((\text{FIN, INV}), (\text{SELR}^{-1}, \text{INV})) \})$$

Figure 54.

$$c_{10} = (\{ (\text{CUST, waiting}), (\text{SELR, done}) \}, \\ \{ ((\text{SELR, INV}), (\text{CUST, INV})) \})$$

Figure 55.

$$c_1 = (\{ (\text{CPO, waiting}), (\text{POM, approved}), (\text{CUST}^{-1}, \text{done}) \}, \\ \{ ((\text{CUST}^{-1}, \text{INV}), (\text{POM, INV})), ((\text{POM, APR}), (\text{CPO, DONE})) \})$$

The seller's components' states are subsequently advanced by the copy rules shown in Figure 53.

The latter copy rule triggers SELR's state to be set to done. This triggers the copy rule from the cross-enterprise integration. (see Figure 54)

After performing the previous copy rule, ADVANCEBM(CUST) sets CUST's state to done. This triggers the final copy rule (Figure 55).

Finally, ADVANCEBM(CPO) sets CPO's state to done. Now, the primary goal is achieved. Our exemplary execution ended successfully and consistently.

Please note that the copy rule c_5 was never triggered. The reason is that the seller acts deterministically in our example and never responds to a purchase order with a failure notification.

SUMMARY

We have shown in this chapter how our formal behavioral models are capable to store and reuse process semantics at run time and integration design time which was gathered at component design time.

Current approaches to store behavioral information such as UML activity diagrams, OWL-S, BPEL, and BPMN lack formal semantics as part of their specification. This implies that the models are not exchangeable across multiple tools making use of them. In particular, model-to-model and model-to-code transformations are essential in a model-driven approach. Without proper semantics, there is a risk to loose or falsify behavioral information throughout the transformations.

Our holistic approach takes message semantics into account which is an essential prerequisite for process integration. Process semantics is uniformly represented throughout the software life cycle. Due to the uniform representation and the

Table 1.

43From artifact	To artifact	Specification given as...
Communication data types	Potential communication	Subset of CFIM result
Component model	Role model	Restriction of component behavior by subset of operations and restricted sequencing
Role model & potential intra-enterprise communication	Intra-enterprise business process	Allowable communication & composition goal
Intra-enterprise business process & potential cross-enterprise communication	Cross-enterprise business process	Allowable communication & composition goal
Cross-enterprise business process	*Business process execution*	Formal integration models

execution semantics given via ASM, our behavioral models can interact with concrete integrations generated by our approach at run time. When the complex-goal-based WS composition is used to generate the integrations, a transactionally correct execution of a cross-enterprise scenario can be guaranteed by construction.

Finally, our model-driven approach allows defining the semantics of integration rather than explicitly coding integration as done in contemporary orchestration languages. Table 1 summarizes the specifications that guide the single transformations. In our approach, integration is rather generated instead of coded. A change is never being done to the concrete integration itself but always to the specification. A new integration globally consistent with the integration requirements can be generated at any time.

REFERENCES

Berardi, D., Calvanese, D., Giacomo, G. D., Hull, R., & Mecella, M. (2005). Automatic composition of transition-based Semantic Web services with messaging. In K. Böhm, C. S. Jensen, L. M. Haas, M. L. Kersten, P.-Å. Larson & B. C. Ooi (Eds.), *VLDB* (pp. 613–624). ACM. ISBN 1-59593-154-6, 1-59593-177-5

Bernstein, A., Klein, M., & Malone, T. W. (1999). The process recombinator: A tool for generating new business process ideas. *ICIS*, 178–192.

Berry, M. J. A., & Linoff, G. S. (2004). *Data mining techniques*. Wiley Publishing, Inc., second edition.

Börger, E. (2003). The ASM refinement method. *Formal Aspects of Computing, 15*, 237–257. doi:10.1007/s00165-003-0012-7

Börger, E., & Stärk, R. F. (2003). *Abstract state machines. A method for high-level system design and analysis*. Springer.

Christensen, E., Curbera, F., Meredith, G., & Weerawarana, S. (2001). Web services description language (wsdl) 1.1. Tech. Rep. W3C. Retrieved from http://www.w3.org/TR/wsdl

Dong, A. (2005). *XML tree finder system: A first step towards XML data mining–final report*. Tech. Rep. CS Department, University of Calgary.

Dong, X., Halevy, A., Madhavan, J., Nemes, E., & Zhang, J. (2004). Similarity search for Web services. In *30th VLDB*.

Fensel, D., & Bussler, C. (2002). The Web service modeling framework WSMF. *Electronic Commerce Research and Applications, 1*(2), 113–137. doi:10.1016/S1567-4223(02)00015-7

Friesen, A., & Lemcke, J. (2007). Composing Web-servicelike abstract state machines (ASM). In J. Koehler, M. Pistore, A. P. Sheth, P. Traverso & M. Wirsing (Eds.), *Autonomous and adaptive Web services, Dagstuhl Seminar Proceedings* (Vol. 07061). Internationales Begegnungs-und Forschungszentrum fuer Informatik (IBFI), Schloss Dagstuhl, Germany.

Ganter, B., & Godin, R. (2005). *Formal concept analysis*. Springer.

Gruber, T. R. (1995). Toward principles for the design of ontologies used for knowledge sharing? *International Journal of Human-Computer Studies*, *43*(5-6), 907–928. doi:10.1006/ijhc.1995.1081

Han, J., & Kamber, M. (2006). *Data mining. Concepts and techniques*. Morgan Kaufmann Publishers. ISBN 1558609016

Kastner, P. S., & Saia, R. (2006). The composite applications benchmark report. Tech. Rep. Aberdeen Group.

Krafzig, D., Banke, K., & Slama, D. (2004). *Enterprise SOA: Service-oriented architecture best practices (the coad series)*. Prentice Hall PTR. ISBN 0131465759

Küster, J. M., Ryndina, K., & Gall, H. (2007). Generation of business process models for object life cycle compliance. In G. Alonso, P. Dadam & M. Rosemann (Eds.), *BPM*. (LNCS 4714, pages 165–181). Springer. ISBN 978-3-540-75182-3

Lemcke, J., & Friesen, A. (2007a). Composing Web-servicelike abstract state machines (ASMs). In *IEEE SCW* (pp. 262–269). IEEE Computer Society.

Lemcke, J., & Friesen, A. (2007b). Considering realistic Web service features for semiautomatic composition. In *SEEFM'07*. Springer.

Lemcke, J., & Friesen, A. (2008). (To appear). Considering realistic Web service features for semiautomatic composition. [AMCT]. *Annals of Mathematics, Computing, and Teleinformatics*.

McCormick, W. T., Schweitzer, P. J., & White, T. W. (1972). Problem decomposition and data reorganization by a clustering technique. *Operations Research*, *20*(5), 993–1009. doi:10.1287/opre.20.5.993

Mens, T., & Tourw, T. (2004). A survey of software refactoring. In *IEEE Transactions on Software Engineering*.

Ogden, C. K., & Richards, I. A. (1923). The meaning of meaning: A study of the influence of language upon thought and of the science of symbolism. London: Routledge & Kegan Paul.

Papazoglou, M. P., & Ribbers, P. (2006). *E-Business: Organizational and technical foundations*. Wiley. ISBN 0470843764

Petersohn, H. (2005). *Data mining–Verfahren, prozesse, anwendungsarchitektur*. Oldenbourg Wissenschaftsverlag.

Pistore, M., Barbon, F., Bertoli, P., Shaparau, D., & Traverso, P. (2004). Planning and monitoring Web service composition. In C. Bussler & D. Fensel (Eds.), *AIMSA*. (LNCS 3192, pages 106–115). Springer. ISBN 3-540-22959-0

Pistore, M., Marconi, A., Bertoli, P., & Traverso, P. (2005a). Automated composition of Web services by planning at the knowledge level. In L. P. Kaelbling & A. Saffiotti (Eds.), *IJCAI*, 1252–1259. Professional Book Center. ISBN 0938075934

Pistore, M., Roberti, P., & Traverso, P. (2005b). Process-level composition of executable Web services: "on-the-fly" vs. "once-for-all" composition. In A. Gómez-Pérez & J. Euzenat (Eds.), *ESWC*. (LNCS 3532, pages 62–77). Springer. ISBN 3-540-26124-9

Pistore, M., Traverso, P., & Bertoli, P. (2005c). Automated composition of Web services by planning in asynchronous domains. In S. Biundo, K. L. Myers & K. Rajan (Eds.), *ICAPS* (pp. 2–11). AAAI. ISBN 1-57735-220-3

Pistore, M., Traverso, P., Bertoli, P., & Marconi, A. (2005d). Automated synthesis of executable Web service compositions from bpel4ws processes. In A. Ellis & T. Hagino (Eds.), *WWW (special interest tracks and posters)* (pp. 1186–1187). ACM. ISBN 1-59593-051-5

Rao, J., & Su, X. (2004). A survey of automated Web service composition methods. In J. Cardoso & A. P. Sheth (Eds.), *SWSWPC*. (LNCS 3387, pp. 43–54). Springer. ISBN 3-540-24328-3

Rosenkrantz, G. (1998). The science of being. *Erkenntnis, 48*(5), 251–255. doi:10.1023/A:1005489810828

Snelting, G., & Tip, F. (1998). Reengineering class hierarchies using concept analysis. *Foundations of Software Engineering*, 99–110.

Staab, S., & Studer, R. (Eds.). (2004). *Handbook on ontologies*. Springer. ISBN 3-540-40834-7

Stachowiak, H. (1973). Allgemeine modelltheorie. New York: Springer-Verlag, Wien.

Stumme, G., Taouil, R., Bastide, Y., Pasquier, N., & Lakhal, L. (2002). Computing iceberg concept lattices with Titanic. *Data & Knowledge Engineering, 42*, 189–222. doi:10.1016/S0169-023X(02)00057-5

Termier, A. (2004). *Extraction of frequent trees in an heterogeneous corpus of semistructured data: Application to XML documents mining*. Unpublished doctoral dissertation, Paris-South University.

Trainotti, M., Pistore, M., Calabrese, G., Zacco, G., Lucchese, G., et al. (2005). Astro: Supporting composition and execution of Web services. In B. Benatallah, F. Casati & P. Traverso (Eds.), *ICSOC*. (LNCS 3826, pp. 495–501). Springer. ISBN 3-540-30817-2

Traverso, P., & Pistore, M. (2004). Automated composition of semantic Web services into executable processes. In S. A. McIlraith, D. Plexousakis & F. van Harmelen (Eds.), *International Semantic Web Conference*. (LNCS 3298, pp. 380–394). Springer. ISBN 3-540-23798-4

Uno, T., Asai, T., Uchida, Y., & Arimura, H. (2004a). An efficient algorithm for enumerating closed patterns in transaction databases. *Discovery Science*, 16–31.

Uno, T., Kiyomi, M., & Arimura, H. (2004b). Lcm ver. 2: Efficient mining algorithms for frequent/closed/maximal itemsets. *FIMI*.

van Deursen, A., & Kuipers, T. (1999). Identifying objects using cluster and concept analysis. In *21ˢᵗ International Conference on Software Engineering* (pp. 246–255).

Wang, Y., & Stroulia, E. (2003). Semantic structure matching for assessing Web service similarity. In *Service-Oriented Computing-ICSOC*. (LNCS 2910, pp. 194–207). Springer. Witten, I. H., & Frank, E. (2005). *Data mining*. Elsevier Inc., second edition.

Zaki, M. J., Parimi, N., De, N., Gao, F., Phoophakdee, B., et al. (2005). Towards generic pattern mining. In *Formal Concept Analysis*.

Chapter 8
Business Rules Enabled Semantic Service Discovery and Selection for B2B Integration

Andreas Friesen
SAP Research, Germany

ABSTRACT

In service-oriented business applications, B2B integration happens when a service requester invokes services of one or more service providers. Typically, there are several candidate services with similar capabilities that can be chosen by a requester in order to serve his business needs. The selection of the service to be invoked may depend on different functional and non-functional properties. The non-functional properties usually address security, reliability, performance, and so forth. The functional properties address the business process interplay at the level of the technical Web service interface and the message choreography associated with it. At the technical integration level, the description of functional and non-functional service properties has been exhaustively addressed in the scientific literature in the past. The business level however, namely, the requester's business need, the business meaning of an offered service, and the capability of a service provider to successfully perform the requested business transaction, has been rather ignored. This chapter describes a solution for service discovery and selection at the business level, that is, at the level of offered business capability of a service provider and the ability to serve a concrete requested business transaction. The proposed solution is based on semantic interpretation of offered service capabilities, contractual restrictions, business rules of the requestor specifying selection preferences, and the parameters of the run-time service request. The applicability of the proposed solution is demonstrated on a shipper-carrier integration scenario.

DOI: 10.4018/978-1-60566-804-8.ch008

INTRODUCTION

The advent of Service-oriented Architecture (SOA) and Web Services (WS) opened new possibilities for smooth Enterprise Application Integration (EAI) in intra- and inter-enterprise scenarios in a loosely-coupled manner. In principle, Web Services enabled enterprise systems can be used by anyone, from anywhere, at any time, and on any type of platform. The providers can offer their business functionality deployed as Web Services on a Web Server and publish their specifications to a repository offering them to potential users (requesters). A potential requester can discover, select, compose, bind and invoke the offered Web Services in order to achieve its business goals.

The traditional Web Services technology stack comprises at least the following core technologies: Simple Object Access Protocol (SOAP), Web Service Description Language (WSDL) and Universal, Description, Discovery and Integration (UDDI). SOAP is used for communication with a Web Service. WSDL describes the Web Service interface. UDDI provides publishing and discovery functionality for Web Service specifications and capabilities. Additionally, mainly industry-driven, a large set of WS-* standards emerged during the last years and covers in the meantime near to any functional and non-functional property or extensibility mechanism associated with Web Services technology (Krafzig, 2005).

However, the lack of formally represented semantic meaning in this technology stack causes the tasks of discovering, selecting, composing, and binding Web Services being considered as manual steps performed by a human.

On the other hand, Semantic Web and Semantic Web Services (SWS), mainly driven by the academic community, promises new standardized means to formally capture the representation of the semantic meaning of data and interfaces. This enables the machines to automatically reason and to draw conclusions about the "intended meaning".

The so-called Semantic Web Services promise a higher degree on automation concerning discovery, composition, invocation, and monitoring of Web Services. Several logical languages, ontologies, and frameworks for semantic annotation or description of Web Services have been proposed, e.g., OWL, OWL-S, WSMO and SA-WSDL (McGuinness, 2004; Martin, 2004; Fensel, 2006; Farrell, 2007). All of the proposed Semantic Web Services Frameworks conceptually support, or at least provide, a vision concerning the lifecycle phases of the Web Service usage process. However, also all of them are, in a sense, rather meta-frameworks since they fall short in describing the exact realization of the single phases. This becomes obvious, if use case dependent requirements have to be taken into account, e.g., association of the single phases of the Web Service usage process with design, configuration or run-time of a an integration scenario. The concrete realization of one phase influences the sub-sequent phases.

Furthermore, the distinction of functional and non-functional properties describing service capabilities becomes very important for the realization of single service usage phases finally leading to the selection of the preferred service to be invoked.

The non-functional properties usually address service usage aspects concerned with security, trustworthiness, reliability, performance, etc. The non-functional properties are, of course, inevitably important in open environments like SOA and B2B and are often even mission-critical for successful business transactions. Nevertheless, by their nature they play a supportive role and come into play only after functional requirements could be met at a satisfactory level.

The functional properties address the business process interplay at the level of the technical web service interface and valid message choreography behind it. Furthermore, service properties and capabilities at the business level, i.e., the *"business meaning"* and *"business level semantics"* of a provided service and the capability of a service provider to successfully perform a concrete requested business transaction, need to be covered. Additionally, special conditions on service usage, the parameters of a request for a business transaction at run-time, and business preferences of the requester need to be addressed at the business level, too. Special conditions on service usage are either contractually agreed between requester and provider or specified by the requester without the knowledge of the provider.

We do not further elaborate on the nonfunctional and functional properties dealing with integration issues at the pure technical interface level as far as they are not absolutely necessary for understanding of the main topic of this chapter. Those aspects have been exhaustively addressed in the scientific literature for virtually any of the technologies and frameworks in the area of (Semantic) Web Services mentioned above.

In the following, we focus on the *"business level"* interdependency between business processes of a service requester and service provider. In a SOA-based environment the interfaces of business processes for enterprise collaboration or integration have to be encapsulated and exposed as Web Services providing at least de-facto standardized technical integration means for a defined class of business process integration scenarios. From the technical integration perspective, this leads to a dramatic reduction of the process integration efforts (in terms of time and money) between a specific requester and a specific provider. Therefore, the main focus and effort during the enterprise integration process is not anymore on how the enterprises have to collaborate in the technical sense by aligning and adapting their business process workflows.

The remaining challenge is to address flexibility and agility in a business value network with many competing participants, i.e., to figure out the business goal, value, and the result of a collaboration under specific business requirements and constraints. This challenge can be approached as a service discovery and selection problem.

We concentrate on the service discovery and negotiation phase based on business capabilities at the configuration time. The service selection phase is based on requester's preferences in the form of business rules and the parameters of a concrete service request at the run-time. Hence, we focus on B2B scenarios requiring a run-time decision concerning invocation of a web service from a set of available services selected at the configuration time.

Section 2 describes the impact of SOA on Enterprise Application Integration with respect to business process integration across different applications and identifies SOA is an important precondition and driver for realization of more dynamic business integration scenarios. Section 3 describes the lifecycle phases in the web service usage process and introduces different notions of service, service capability and service goal important to understand and differentiate their meaning in the different phases of the web service usage process. Section 4 introduces different kinds of B2B Integration Scenarios and their characteristics from web service discovery perspective. B2B Integration Scenarios amenable for dynamic business integration are identified, analyzed, and characterized according to the web service usage process introduced in section 3. Section 5 provides set-theoretic semantics behind web service capabilities, service discovery goals, service contracts, and introduces business rules as means to express requester's selection preferences in the form of conditional implications. Section 6 develops a new business rules enabled solution on top of the *contract-based solution* for dynamic semantic service discovery and selection for B2B integration introduced in (Friesen, 2006). For the sake of completeness we provide an overview of theoretical foundations behind the contract-based solution illustrated on simple "shipper-carrier" examples from the logistics domain. The proposed business rules framework extends the ontology of the contract-based solution and explains rules ordering strategies as well as definition, and evaluation of business rules. Finally, the stepwise-introduced algorithms developed within this framework establish a connection to the concepts of the ontology and define reasoning algorithms over them.

IMPACT OF SOA ON ENTERPRISE INTEGRATION

Enterprise Application Integration (EAI) is a process of integration of various enterprise computer applications so that they share processes and information in an interoperable way. One of the main applications for EAI is business process integration across applications and corporate boundaries. From the technical perspective, successful business process integration implies structural interoperability of the exchanged data/ messages, functional interoperability, i.e., the granularity and the functional coverage of the interfaces, and process interoperability, i.e., the sequencing of tasks in the participating workflows (incl. fault and compensation handling).

Service-oriented architecture (SOA) is a paradigm for development and integration of systems by grouping functionality around business processes and packaging it as *services*. The loose coupling of services with technologies of underlying applications that are running business processes enables their combination into new (more complex) composite business applications. SOA can therefore be seen as an IT infrastructure that enables business processes running in different applications to exchange messages with one another in a standardized (interoperable) way.

Applying SOA to EAI means that the interfaces of business processes for enterprise collaboration or integration have to be grouped, encapsulated and exposed as Web Services at the enterprise level which provide standardized technical integration means for a defined class of business process integration scenarios. The degree of reusability of Web Services defined in this way is considered

to increase significantly compared to a "simple" Web Services enabling of enterprise applications without any guidance with respect to the business meaning, scope, and semantics of the provided interface within an EAI scenario. The standardized integration interfaces and their high degree of reusability lead to a dramatic reduction of process integration efforts for SOA-enabled business applications for a concrete EAI project. The basic concepts realizing the above mentioned integration approach have been described in (Greiner, 2006). These concepts have been adopted and developed towards aligning data, functionality, and processes within a frame of multi-level community ontology and even further increasing the automation degree of the enterprise integration process (Alazeib, 2007; Lemcke, 2007).

Figure 1 shows the orchestration-based (left side) and choreography-based (right side) integration approach behind those concepts. The first two steps, namely a) web services enablement of the interfaces to the Private Business Processes running in enterprise applications, and b) creation of Public Business Process (Composite Application) layer that hides internal details of the private business process and mediates data/messages, functionality, and process workflow in order to expose externally observable process behavior available for integration as a set of interoperable Web Services. The last step, namely the integration of the Public Business Processes through modeling of a Collaborative (cross-organizational) Business Process results in orchestration-based integration scenarios in a creation of an executable business process instance orchestrating Public Business Processes. In choreography-based scenarios, the workflow constraints imposed by the Collaborative Business Process model are added to the Public Business Processes so that they can communicate directly to one another in the specified way. At least, the result of the first two steps, namely externally observable behavior of the Public Business Process exposed as a set of interoperable Web Services, is obviously reusable.

Figure 1. SOA-based enterprise business process integration

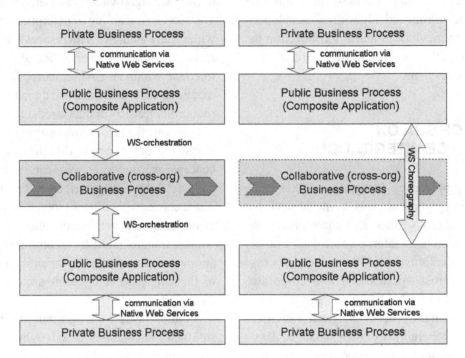

As a consequence of integration effort reduction (in terms of time and money), there is a shift in scope of the enterprise integration from "point-to-point process" integration scenarios (fixed at the design time) to more flexible "one requester-multiple providers" process composition scenarios (able to address changing business requirements and capabilities at configuration time and to react to business selection rules at run time, Figure 2). We assume that services shown in Figure 2 expose complex behavior, i.e., each service, besides other things, exposes Public Business Process interface required for the integration with the Public Business Process interface of the requester (as sketched in Figure 1).

In such "one-to-many" process composition scenarios, the main focus and effort during an enterprise integration project shifts from technical alignment and adaptation of business process workflows of the participants towards more abstract business-oriented requirements like "what is the business goal, value, and the result of a potential collaboration under specific business requirements and constraints" and "what service/provider can serve best my current service request". These questions have to be answered in SOA-context during Web Service Discovery and Selection phase which build a crucial part of the Web Service Usage Lifecycle which is the topic of the next chapter.

WEB SERVICE USAGE

The most general notion of the web service usage process consists of the following three phases: web service discovery, web service selection, and web service invocation (Booth, 2004). We argue that this approach is too straightforward since it does not take into account several additional aspects associated with the web service usage. Two of them are discussed in the following.

The first aspect, and in our view the most important one, is the differentiation between the

Figure 2. Dynamic one-to-many process composition scenarios

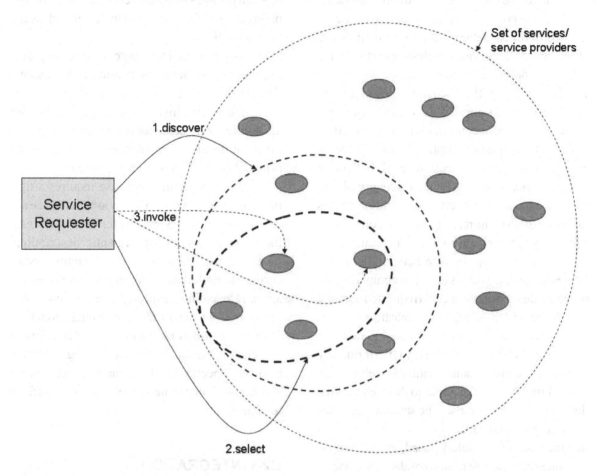

"abstract" and "concrete" service. According to (Preist, 2004), an abstract service is distinguished from a concrete service in that the former abstracts from the concrete service parameters which determine the latter. Thus, an abstract service describes a class of service parameter configurations that is associated with the web service capability. A concrete service describes a concrete service parameter configuration as it is delivered by the invocation of a web service. Hence, the web service capability description does not contain complete information about every possible concrete service that can be delivered. Since the ultimate goal of a potential requester is to find and select a concrete service that optimally serves its needs, the selection and invocation steps inevitably overlap.

The second aspect concerns the possible negotiation of service parameters between requester and provider, and thus, once again the inevitable invocations of the web service interface. Besides the obvious overlap of the conceptually seen different phases, successful service discovery does not necessarily lead to successful delivery of a service, since in the set of potential service candidates there might be no one that is finally able to define a concrete service on which both the requester and provider agree.

A more sophisticated web service usage process addressing the above aspects is described in (Preist, 2004). The relationship between a requester and a provider party goes through three different phases: a service discovery phase, in which potential providers are discovered; a service definition phase, in which the concrete service to be carried out is defined in all its details; and a service delivery phase, in which the value of this concrete service is actually delivered to the requester.

The lifecycle of the discovery phase presented in (Keller, 2004) consists of a goal discovery phase, taking into account that it needs some effort to come to a "goal description" which properly expresses the service request, a Web Service discovery phase and a service discovery phase, which map to the discovery and definition phases in (Preist, 2004). The result of the goal definition is a formally specified abstract goal that can be used as a search criterion for Web Service discovery. Web Service discovery is based on comparing the semantic description of a goal (requested abstract service) against those of provided abstract services (web service capability descriptions) in terms of relevance. Web Service discovery is performed by matching the goal against available web service capabilities. Notice that input to the Web Service discovery phase comprises the semantic descriptions of goals and capabilities only. This implies that the matching is solely based on information contained in these descriptions of abstract services. A selection of a service due to concrete parameter information, which possibly requires invocation of the service's interface, is in the scope of the subsequent service definition phase. A concrete example of a semantic web service discovery framework specification for WSMO that follows the web service usage phases described in (Preist, 2004) has been developed in (Grimm, 2005).

Service Definition starts from an already identified set of potential web service candidates which have been identified as relevant for a goal in the service discovery phase. It potentially involves negotiation of service parameters, and thus, invocation of the candidates Web Service interface. In general, figuring out which service to finally choose is beyond the information contained in the semantic descriptions of a goal and web services. In this phase, the generalization to abstract services

is given up and a concrete service with a concrete parameter configuration has to be defined, as it is later on delivered.

Finally, Service Delivery comprises any steps required for the actual invocation and consumption of the concrete service selected for execution. This involves the invocation of the Web Service according to its behavioral interface as well as different forms of mediations concerning the protocol or the data to be transmitted.

The service definition phase requires a tight integration with work on behavioral interface and invocation of Web Service interfaces and breaks the scope of processing semantic descriptions. Ideas that include negotiation of parameters according to preference information would require an extra encoding of preferences which is currently not present in the conceptual models of SWS frameworks or semantic service descriptions in general. Furthermore, such a negotiation is also very specific for the domain of value of the service, such that generic tool support is difficult to achieve.

B2B INTEGRATION

The SWS usage process relies in the service discovery phase on the descriptions of abstract service capabilities of the provided Web Services, i.e., it enables a potential service requester to find a set of potential web service candidates that can probably serve its requests. The offered web service capability descriptions are equal for all potential requesters. The choice (selection) of one web service from the set of potential candidates is left to the service definition phase. There are several possible use-case dependent scenarios. The following scenarios are taken into consideration (without pretending to be exhaustive):

Scenario 1: Service request takes place sporadically and has a "low value", e.g., flight or hotel reservations from private persons, i.e., neither requester nor provider are interested to negotiate on requester-specific service conditions. Hence, the requester has to accept the service conditions (general terms) of the provider. This case fits perfectly into the introduced SWS usage process, so we do not elaborate on it further.

Scenario 2: Service request takes place sporadically but has a very high „value", e.g., imagine you are going to order an aircraft at AIRBUS. The negotiations in this case definitely require very complex human interaction. The service capability is described on a very high level of abstraction leaving a lot of space for configuration of concrete parameters. In principle, the requester has to negotiate with all potential providers anyway. Therefore, we do not consider this case either.

Scenario 3: There are several possible scenarios somewhere in the middle of the two extremes described previously. Such scenarios can be characterized by frequently occurring requests for a standardized service over a period of time. However, the number of requests may justify the efforts to negotiate about requester-specific conditions for service usage for a requester as well as for a provider. The requester-specific conditions can be seen as constraints on the web service capability and must be consistently applied on the requester as well as on the provider side. These constraints cannot be part of the published web service capability since they are requester-specific, i.e., in general, for each requester different.

Scenario 4: The last scenario under consideration is similar to Scenario 3 but in this case the requester sets constraints on the service capability usage according to its own preferences. However, service requester does not negotiate with the provider on requester-specific conditions, i.e., accepts the general terms of the provider. This type of constraints defines business rules of the requester.

We claim that the web service usage process for:

- Scenario 3 can be characterized by a negotiation phase that results in a "service contract" or "service agreement" restricting the

usage of the "static part" of the web service capability and potentially influencing the "dynamic part" of the web service capability. "Static part" means here the declaratively described and published parameters of a WS capability. "Dynamic part" comprises the parameters of the WS capability that can only be accessed through the invocation of the WS interface. The contract can be used for automatic pre-selection of a suitable WS during subsequent concrete service requests. The pre-selection criteria apply to concrete service requests as long as the respective contract remains unchanged.

- Scenario 4 can be characterized by a configuration phase that results in a set of declaratively-described requestor-specific business rules. Similarly to a contract, the rules can be used for automatic pre-selection of a suitable WS at run time. The pre-selection criteria apply to concrete service requests as long as the respective set business rules remains unchanged.

Obviously, Scenarios 3 and 4 cannot be always strictly separated. Hence, ideally a combined usage of contracts and sets of business rules must be possible within the same framework without a break in technology.

WS CAPABILITIES, CONTRACTS AND BUSINESS RULES

This section introduces set-theoretic semantics of the concepts "web service capability", "contract", and "goal" that have been introduced in section 3 and elaborate on the relationships among them. Furthermore, we show that introduction of business selection rules as conditional implications needs further consideration in order to create a consistent model without to cause break in technology.

Figure 3. Set-based view on WS capability and contract

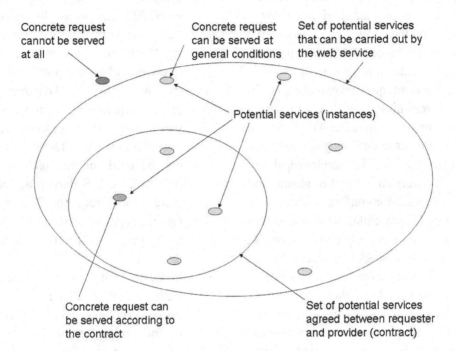

Web Service Capabilities, Contracts and Discovery Goals

A web service capability can be described as a set of service instances that can be delivered by invoking the web service. A contract between a requester and provider can be seen as a subset of this set. A concrete request during the invocation of the web service can be seen as an instance of the contract, the capability or some more general set. Figure 3 illustrates this relationship.

Furthermore, the result of the discovery phase based on the abstract (discovery) goal describing the set of all potentially intended concrete requests is a list of web services that can completely or partially serve this goal (Figure 4). The web service capabilities may overlap. Hence, the result of the negotiation phase is a set of contracts that are subsets of the respective service capabilities at the one hand and subsets of the abstract goal at the other.

The introduction of contracts provides an elegant way for service pre-selection. The usage of semantic techniques based on description logics derived from the approach for semantic web service discovery introduced by Li&Horrocks provides a compact solution that is completely configurable in declarative way (Li, 2003). The semantic modeling of web service capabilities and contracts will be shortly introduced in the next chapter. For more detailed information about this solution see (Friesen, 2006). However, similarly to WS capabilities, the contracts may also overlap and eventually do not cover the abstract goal completely (Figure 5).

Therefore, at runtime, additional WS selection criteria (requestor's preferences) may be required if a concrete request is within the scope of overlapping web service capabilities or contracts. It may also happen that some concrete requests cannot be served at all, especially, if the abstract goal has not been completely covered by the set of available contracts or web service capabilities.

Figure 4. WS capabilities and abstract goals

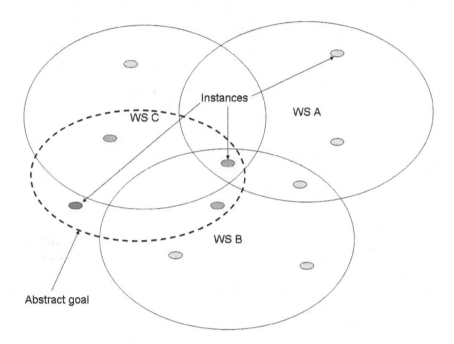

Business Rules as Requester's Preferences

Additional WS selection criteria (requestor's preferences) are required if web service capabilities or contracts overlap for a concrete service request. The definition of requester's preferences concerning the selection of services may be expressed as a set of business rules of the form: IF condition = true THEN action.

The definition of requester's preferences in the form of business rules is essential for the realisation of the above described B2B integration scenarios. However, the application of declarative semantic web services discovery solutions based on the principles described in (Li, 2003) together with existing business rules engines, or individually developed one-off efforts, causes a break in the technological realisation of the overall solution, prevents (or at least significantly complicates) consistency checks and is a non-straightforward, complex, error-prone, and therefore, costly

procedure. This is because semantic discovery engine and business rules engine would have to be integrated. That leads to complex, error-prone, and costly integration efforts, requires modelling of contracts and rules in two different languages, manual checks for consistency between contracts and rules etc. In the following we introduce a declarative solution seamlessly integrating the business rules into the semantic selection engine without a break in technology.

BUSINESS RULES FOR DYNAMIC DISCOVERY AND SELECTION

The solution described in the following relies only on the expressivity and reasoning support provided by Description Logics (DL) (Baader, 2003), i.e., the mathematical and logical foundations used in (Li, 2003) and further extended in (Friesen, 2006). Furthermore, it further extends (Friesen, 2006) in a way that enables full business

Figure 5. Overlapping contracts require selection

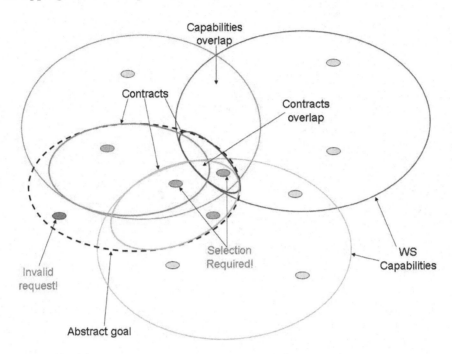

rules support for the formulation of requester's preferences as well as the automatic inference of the actions to be performed according to the conditions specified in the requester's preferences using a DL reasoner.

In the following, in order to make this contribution self-contained, we recap the contract-based solution described in (Friesen, 2006) and describe the general idea of business rules enablement in the proposed business rules framework.

Overview of the Contract-Based Solution

Applying the contract-based solution to the discovery and selection problem requires a domain model formalized in Description Logics (also called *ontology* in the following). An abstract service capability has to be built based on the domain ontology. The abstract service capability is provider-independent and covers all possible service capabilities within the business domain

of the integration scenario.

Web Service (WS) capabilities of the service providers and the abstract request of a service requester can be modeled as sub-concepts of the abstract WS capability. The abstract request and WS capabilities are then used in the discovery phase in order to identify potential providers to negotiate with. There are different possible degrees concerning the quality of the semantic match: exact, plug-in, subsume, intersection, and disjoint.

In the case of successful negotiations, the contract between a requester and service provider has to be modeled as a sub-concept of the WS capability. The concrete request is then described either as an instance or as a most specific sub-concept of the abstract WS capability according to the used ontology. Figure 6 illustrates these dependencies. This means, a concrete request can be served by a Web Service if the subsumption test between the concrete request and the contract associated with a WS capability is successful. If several contracts

Figure 6. Inheritance relations between introduced concepts

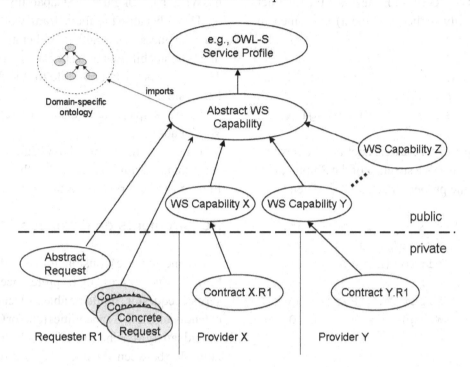

match the concrete request a second selection step is required in order to choose between the remaining Web Services. This step usually requires invocation of the matching Web Services in order to get information (for instance pricing) necessary for the final selection according to the goals of the requester (e.g., for requesters goal "take the cheapest service"). The concrete selection goals are in general domain- and requester-specific making a generic solution complicated or even impossible.

In DL terms a concrete run-time request of a requester R1 can be potentially served by service WSCapabilityX of a provider X if the one of the following DL subsumption expressions is true:

(1) ConcreteRequest.R1 ⊑ Con-
tractX.R1 ⊑ WSCapabilityX ⊑ AbstractWSCapability
(2) ConcreteRequest.R1 ⊑ WSCapabilityX ⊑ AbstractWSCapability

According to the contract-based approach, the expression (1) has higher selection priority than (2), i.e., the expression (2) is only checked if (1) is false for all available contracts. However, as illustrated in Figure 4, a requestor may possess more than one contract that may satisfy (1). In this case, it isn't possible neither to declaratively express selection priorities among the matching contracts nor to take into account additional selection criteria (preferences) of a requestor that are not part of the declarative specification of a contract. The same is obviously true also for the WS Capabilities in (2).

The requester's needs for the specification of business rules for the partially-ordered pre-selection of service capabilities are manifold. The conditions used in the definitions of the business rules may rely on the criteria available from the declarative specifications of service capabilities but may also be requester-specific.

Let us consider the CARRIER-SHIPPER use case from (Friesen, 2006) as a running example.

In the CARRIER-SHIPPER use case the Abstract WS Capability (called Shipment) is defined in DL as follows:

```
Shipment ⊑ (=1 shipFrom.Location)
   ⊓ (=1 shipTo.Location)
   ⊓ (=1 shipItem.ShippingItem)
```

Consequently, a Carrier X defines the capability of its service as a subclass of the Shipment by restricting the property ranges of Shipment:

```
WSCapabilityX ⊑ (=1 shipFrom.
(Europe ⊔ NorthAmerica))
   ⊓ (=1 shipTo.(Europe ⊔
NorthAmerica)
   ⊓ (=1 shipItem.((Parcel ⊓
Parcel.hasWeight <=70kg) ⊔ Doc-
ument))
```

Analogously, a contract between a shipper and carrier X would further restrict the WSCapabilityX by building a subclass of WSCapabilityX that further restricts the ranges of WSCapabilityX properties (some example contracts are provided in (Friesen, 2006)).

A concrete shipment request at run-time is also described as a sub-concept of Shipment:

```
RequestA ⊑ (=1 shipFrom.Frankfurt)
   ⊓ (=1 shipTo.NewYork)
   ⊓ (=1 shipItem.Parcel)
```

This means, the selection of a service capable to serve RequestA can be decided using (1) or (2). In an ideal case, the shipper would like to express something like the two rules below. However, in the framework described in (Friesen, 2006), a shipper cannot (in a consistent way) express such selection criteria.

Rule1: "For all shipment requests from Europe to US or China with shipItem.Document use WSCapabilityX".

Rule2: "For all shipment requests with Parcel. hasWeight >=10kg use WSCapabilityX".

This is because the above framework requires that a business rule is defined either as a subclass of a WSCapability or as a subclass of a Contract. This is obviously not possible for the Rule1 and Rule2 since:

Rule1: shipTo.China cannot be satisfied by WSCapabilityX

Rule2: Neither Parcel.hasWeight >70kg nor shipFrom and shipTo outside NorthAmerica and Europe can be served by WSCapabilityX

Requirements on Business Rules

The requestor is responsible for the definition of business rules expressing its preferences, i.e., the service requestor should be able to decide to what extent available WS capabilities (and/or Contracts) should satisfy a business rule. The subsumption relationship between a business rule and a capability (i.e., if the business rule triggers then the capability will definitely serve the request) is too strong and inflexible. On the other hand, if a business rule cannot be satisfied by a service capability at all then any request triggering this rule will result in an invalid service invocation. Therefore, there must be at least a potential (theoretical) overlap between the condition of the business rule and assigned capability (i.e., at least a part of requests triggering the business rule may be served by this capability). Furthermore, for consistency reasons, it must be possible to figure out at run-time if the request will be served by the service (according to the declarative description of the service capability) prior to its invocation.

Additionally, if considering a set of business rules, some extra criteria for the consistency analysis of a set of defined business rules can be defined:

1. A set of business rules can be (is usually) partially or totally ordered
   a. Total ordering (Match First Rule Selection Strategy)

b. Partial ordering (Match All Rules Selection Strategy)
2. The conditions in the business rules may overlap or one rule may be even more specific that another rule. Consistency checks supporting the requester by the definition of the correct ordering of rules would be extremely useful (e.g., a more specific rule will never trigger if it is ordered after the more general rule)
3. More than one capability may be assigned to (associated with) a rule. This can be interpreted as a specific case of partial ordering, i.e., the final selection of the service capability will take place at run time according to the specified selection strategy (e.g., take the cheapest service) after the invocation of the web services,)

Business Rules Framework

The proposed business rules framework enables business rules to be completely described in DL. The triggering of the rules (the evaluation of the rules' conditions) can be derived using a DL reasoner.

Ordering of Rules

The framework supports total and partial rules ordering strategies, i.e.,:

```
BROrder = Seq(
   {Rule} or {Par(Set of Rules)}
   {Rule} or {Par(Set of Rules)}
...)
```

Seq (for sequential) expresses the global ordering, i.e., the first rule in the sequence that triggers has the highest priority. The optional construct Par (for parallel) expresses partial ordering for a set of rules within Par. This means all rules triggering within the Par have the same priority.

Note: The curly braces indicate that an element is optional.

Definition of Business Rules

The business rules are defined in four steps:

1. Define the condition part of a business rule and set its order in BROrder
2. Check order consistency of the rule condition against already defined rule conditions
3. Match the condition part against all available WS Capabilities (Contracts). The complete set of potential business rules is created (stored to LocalStore)
4. Select and assign one or more business rules from the LocalStore, i.e., store them to the requestor's ontology.

Step 1

a) Definition of the condition

```
ruleCondition ≡ (somePropertyX.
RangeRestriction ⊓ someProp-
ertyY.RangeRestriction ⊓ ...) ∈
RuleConditions
```

b) Set order
Add ruleCondition to BROrder

Step 2

Check consistency of the rule condition against all already defined rule conditions.

We assume here that the already defined rule conditions are correctly ordered. Hence, we examine rule conditions (ruleConditionOld ∈ BROrder) in BROrder one by one according to their order (starting with the lowest order):

```
If (ruleConditionNew ⊑ ruleCon-
ditionOld) and (ruleConditionNew
```

```
≠ ruleConditionOld) then
If order(ruleConditionOld) <
order(ruleConditionNew) then
Insert ruleConditionNew in
BROrder directly before ruleCon-
ditionOld
```

Step 3

Match the condition part defined in Step1 against all available WS Capabilities

```
ruleCondition ∈ RuleConditions
FORALL wsCapability ∈ WSCap-
ability in ontology {
IF (IsConsistent (ruleCondition
⊓ wsCapability)) then add to
LocalStore
}
```

"add to LocalStore" means introducing a new rule as follows:

```
ruleCondition_wsCapability ≡
(ruleCondition ⊓ wsCapability)
∈ Rules
```

Step 4

Select from LocalStore one or more rules and store (assign) the selected rule(s) to the ontology of the requester

```
FORALL rule_wsCapability ∈
Rules
If selected(rule_wsCapability)
then add to ontology rule_wsCap-
ability ∈ AssignedRules
```

Evaluation of Business Rules

The evaluation of the business rules happens at run time when a concrete service request is issued. The evaluation takes the following 3 steps:

Step 1

Check if the current request triggers one or more rules via a subsumption check:
  Initialize TriggeredRules:= ∅

```
FORALL rule ∈ AssignedRules in
ontology {
If Request ⊑ rule then rule ∈
TriggeredRules
}
```

Step 2

Select all rules from TriggeredRules with the same lowest ordering number according to the specified ordering of rules in BROrder.

Step 3

Proceed with the run time selection according to the specified run-time selection strategy (e.g., cheapest, fastest, etc.)

CONCLUSION

While the most of the work in the area of Semantic Web Services focuses on the technical interoperability, i.e., the interoperability of the interfaces (inputs, outputs, preconditions, effects, ordering of the exchanged messages, etc.) the proposed approach concentrates on the business compatibility, i.e., how to ensure the consistency of business requirements in B2B integration context under the assumption that systems can be technically connected in an interoperable way using Web

Service interfaces. The proposed approach relies on the phases of the Semantic Web Service Usage process. While in the related state-of-the-art negotiation and selection are recognized as important steps for the usage of Semantic Web Services, the exact definition and implementation of these phases remains an open research question.

In this chapter we focused on selected B2B integration scenarios and provided a precise definition and formalization of the web service negotiation and selection phases. The introduced business rules framework enables full business rules support for the formulation of requester's preferences in DL-based semantic service discovery engines relying on (Li, 2003). The automatic inference of the actions to be performed according to the conditions specified in the requester's preferences is achieved through a DL reasoner. This approach avoids the break in the technological realisation and additional integration efforts that would be introduced in solutions like (Friesen, 2006) through usage of business rules engines or other alternative solutions like logic programming or one-off development efforts.

The described solution has been applied to the SHIPPER-CARRIER use case in order to demonstrate the feasibility of the approach. Finally, the described solution can be applied in a similar way also to Enterprise Application Integration scenarios in other business domains, e.g., Supply Chain Management (SCM), by exchanging the business domain ontology that serves as anchor for the description of service capabilities and discovery goals

REFERENCES

Alazeib, A. (Ed.). (2007). *D1.2 The FUSION approach (FUSION)*. Retrieved on December 8, 2008, from http://www.fusionweb.org/Fusion/download/download.asp

Baader, F., Calvanese, D., McGuinnes, D., Nardi, D., & Patel-Schneider, P. (2003). *The description logic handbook: Theory, implementation, and applications*. Cambridge University Press.

Booth, D., Haas, H., & McCabe, F. (2004). *Web services architecture. W3C note*. Retrieved on December 8, 2008, from http://www.w3.org/TR/ws-arch/

Farrell, J., & Lausen, H. (Eds.). (2007). *Semantic annotations for WSDL and XML schema*. Retrieved on December 8, from http://www.w3.org/TR/sawsdl/

Fensel, D., Lausen, H., Polleres, A., de Bruijn, J., Stollberg, M., Roman, D., & Domingue, J. (2006). *Enabling Semantic Web services: The Web service modeling ontology*. Springer.

Friesen, A., & Namiri, K. (2006, July). Towards semantic service selection for B2B integration. In *Proceedings of the 6th International Conference on Web Engineering (ICWE 2006)*, Menlo Park, CA

Greiner, U., Lippe, S., Kahl, T., Ziemann, J., & Jäkel, F. W. (2006). A multilevel modeling framework for designing and implementing cross-organizational business processes. *Technologies for Collaborative Business Process Management*, 13-23.

Grimm, S., & Friesen, A. (2005). *D4.8 Discovery specification (DIP deliverable)*. Retrieved on December 8, 2008, from http://dip.semanticweb.org/documents/D4.8Final.pdf

Keller, U., Lara, R., & Polleres, A. (Eds.). (2004). *D5.1 WSMO Web service discovery*. Retrieved on December 8, 2008, from http://www.wsmo.org/TR/d5/d5.1

Krafzig, D., Banke, K., & Slama, D. (2005). *Enterprise SOA: Service oriented architecture best practices*. Prentice Hall.

Lemcke, J., & Friesen, A. (2007). Composing Web-servicelike abstract state machines (ASMs). In *Proceedings of IEEE International Conference on Services Computing (SCW 2007)* (pp. 262-269).

Li, L., & Horrocks, I. (2003). A software framework for matchmaking based on Semantic Web technology. In *Proceedings of the Twelfth World Wide Web Conference (WWW 2003)*.

Martin, D. (Ed.). (2004). *OWL-S: Semantic markup for Web services*. Retrieved on December 8, 2008, from http://www.w3.org/Submission/2004/SUBM-OWL-S-20041122/

McGuinness, D. L., & van Harmelen, F. (2004). *OWL Web ontology language overview. W3C recommendation*. Retrieved on December 8, 2008, from http://www.w3.org/TR/owl-features/

Preist, C. (2004). A conceptual architecture for Semantic Web services. In *Proceedings of the 3rd International Semantic Web Services Conference (ISWC 2004)*.

Chapter 9
A Semantic Web Service Based Middleware for the Tourism Industry

Yildiray Kabak
Development and Consultancy Ltd., Turkey

Mehmet Olduz
Development and Consultancy Ltd., Turkey

Gokce B. Laleci
Development and Consultancy Ltd., Turkey

Tuncay Namli
Development and Consultancy Ltd., Turkey

Veli Bicer
Middle East Technical University, Turkey

Nikola Radic
European Dynamics, Greece

George Milis
European Dynamics, Greece

Asuman Dogac
Development and Consultancy Ltd., Turkey

ABSTRACT

Currently in the travel domain, most of the travel products are sold through global distribution aystems (GDSs). Since only major airline companies or hotel chains can afford to join GDSs, it is difficult for small and medium enterprises to market their travel products. In this chapter, we describe a middleware, called SATINE, to address this problem. In the SATINE middleware, existing travel applications are wrapped as Web services. Web services, as such, is of limited use because the service consumer must know all the details of the Web service like the functionality of the Web service (what it does) and the

DOI: 10.4018/978-1-60566-804-8.ch009

content and the structure of input and output messages. Therefore, we annotate both the service func-tionality and the service messages with Web ontology language (OWL) ontologies. Service functionality ontology is obtained from the "Open Travel Alliance (OTA)" specifications. Service message ontologies are automatically generated from the XML schema definitions of the messages. These local message ontologies are mapped into one or more global message ontologies through an ontology mapping tool developed, called OWLmt. The mapping definitions thus obtained are used to automatically map heterogeneous message instances used by the Web service provider and the consumer using a global ontology as a common denominator. This architecture is complemented by a peer-to-peer network which uses the introduced semantics for the discovery of Web services. Through the SATINE middleware, the travel parties can expose their existing applications as semantic Web services either to their Web site or to Web service registries they maintain. SATINE middleware facilitates the discovery and execution of these services seamlessly to the user.

INTRODUCTION

The tourism industry today is the second largest economic sector, after manufacturing in the world. Tourism industry embarked on e-Business earlier than in other sectors as evident in several online travel e-Commerce sites.

Currently, travel information services are domi-nantly provided by Global Distribution Systems (GDSs) such as Galileo (Galileo, 2007), Sabre (Sabre, 2005) and Amadeus (Amadeus, 2007). Major airline companies, many hotel chains and car rental companies list their inventories with major GDSs. A GDS gives its subscribers pricing and availability information for multiple travel products such as flights, hotel rooms and car rentals. Travel agents, corporate travel departments, and even Internet travel services, subscribe to one or more GDSs. However, small and medium sized enterprises cannot participate to GDS-based e-Business activities since selling their products through GDSs is too expensive for them. Furthermore, GDSs are legacy systems that mostly rely on private networks. They are mainly for human use and have difficult to use cryptic interfaces, have limited search capabilities, and

are difficult to inter-operate with other systems and data sources.

In order to facilitate eBusiness, the travel industry has formed a consortium called the Open Travel Alliance (OTA) (OTA, 2005), and OTA has produced XML schemas of message specifications to be exchanged between the trad-ing partners, including availability checking, booking, rental, reservation, query services, and insurance. However, not all travel applications can be expected to produce and consume OTA compliant messages.

In this paper, we describe a middleware to fa-cilitate eBusiness for all the involved parties in the travel domain which has been implemented within the scope of the SATINE Project (Satine, 2007). The main idea is to expose existing travel applica-tions as Web services and facilitate the discovery of and execution of Web services through semantic mediation and peer-to-peer (P2P) networks. The use of P2P technology facilitates the discovery of the services of small and medium size enterprises (SMEs) to enable them to easily sell their services over the Internet. Web service technology together with travel domain specific ontologies allow the parties consume heterogeneous messages.

The technology of the middleware is as follows:

- The existing travel domain applications are wrapped as Web services. Web services, as such, is of limited use because the service consumer must know all the details of the Web service like the functionality of the Web service (what it does) and the content and the structure of input and output messages. Although there are efforts to standardize the messages exchanged in the travel domain such as Open Travel Alliance, not every travel application can be OTA compliant. Furthermore, the GDSs must be a part of the system since today an important part of the travel information comes through them. Therefore, we handle the interoperability of Web service messages through semantic mediation.

- The main mechanism to discover Web services is the Web service registries. We show how to use the semantic annotation of Web services in the UDDI and ebXML registries to facilitate Web service discovery.

- There could be Web services not registered to any service registry but simply made available through a Web site. This may be preferable especially by SMEs which may not wish to have extra overhead of maintaining Web service registries. To facilitate the discovery of Web services, SATINE middleware uses peer-to-peer network which exploits the defined semantics. We show how to handle semantic routing for Web service discovery and how to invoke Web services over the P2P networks.

- In the SATINE middleware, the technical details are hidden behind user friendly graphical interfaces. This is essential to facilitate the usage of the system and to help with its take-up.

The paper is organized as follows: The "System Architecture Overview" Section gives a brief introduction to the SATINE system architecture. The "Semantic Infrastructure" Section, elaborates the underlying semantic mechanisms of SATINE architecture including the functionality ontologies and the message ontologies together with their utilization for semantic annotation of the Web services. The "Semantic Mediation" Section provides the details of the ontology mapping and the normalization components. The "SATINE P2P Network" Section covers the "Semantic Service Advertisement" and the "Semantic Service Discovery in SATINE" architecture. The role of service registries and how they are semantically enriched are given in the "Enhanced Service Registries" Section. In the "Experimental Results" Section, the performance results of the system prototype are described. In the "Related Work" Section, similar works in the literature are elaborated by comparing them with the work presented in this paper. Finally, the conclusions about the work is presented in the "Conclusion" Section.

SYSTEM ARCHITECTURE OVERVIEW

The overall architecture of the SATINE middleware is presented in Figure 1. The Web service providers and service requesters are represented as "edge peers" in the "Peer Network". The parties can advertise their existing tourism Web services to the "SATINE P2P network" as well as the new Web services which are created by wrapping existing tourism applications including the services of the GDSs. These services can either be hosted by the edge peers themselves, or in a service registry connected to the rest of the P2P network through the edge peers. In this way, the outmost layer of "P2P Network" contains the set of wrapped sources which are either the service registries or Web Services themselves.

Figure 1. The architecture of the SATINE middleware

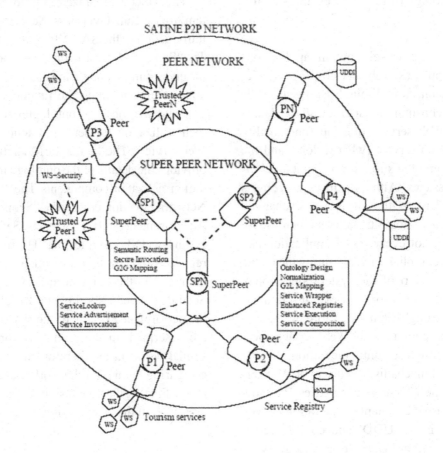

SATINE uses super peer - peer architecture. It has been observed that P2P networks can lead to an efficient network architecture when a small subset of peers, called super-peers, takes over specific responsibilities for peer aggregation, query routing, and mediation. Super-peer based P2P infrastructures are usually based on a two-phase routing architecture, which routes queries first in the super-peer backbone, and then distributes them to the peers connected to the super-peers (Nejdl, Wolpers, Siberski, Schmitz, Schlosser, Brunkhorst, & Loser, 2002).

In the SATINE middleware, the super peers store the global semantic knowledge, that is, one or more global message ontologies and their mappings to local ontologies which are then used for semantic mediation of the messages exchanged.

Peers interact with their super peers to advertise their services and also for Web service discovery and invocation. Furthermore, the super peers facilitate the semantic routing of messages between the edge peers by the use of indices. By means of semantic routing, the messages between peers do not have to be routed by flooding the messages to all of the peers; instead the messages are routed only to the related peers based on the semantics of the content of the messages and using the routing indices.

In order to facilitate the discovery of the advertised Web services in the P2P network, we annotate the functionality of Web services through SATINE Tourism functionality ontologies. The SATINE Semantic Infrastructure is elaborated in detail in Section III.

Figure 2. An example OTA compliant functionality ontology

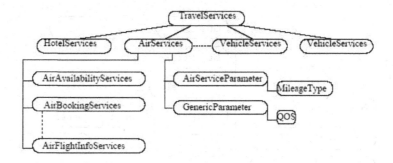

Another characteristic of SATINE P2P architecture is the semantic mediation of exchanged messages between the parties involved. There are many different message formats and contents in the travel domain and if the sender and the consumer use different messages, they need to be semantically mediated to be of any use at the receiving end. For example, one may wish to invoke a Web service to reserve a flight by using Amadeus GDS (Amadeus, 2007) but the consumer of this Web service may not be aware of the content of Amadeus messages.

SATINE allows automatic creation of local message ontologies in Web Ontology Language (OWL) (OWL, 2005) from the XML message schemas that the parties are already using. These local message ontologies are manually mapped to the global ontology with the help of SATINE ontology mapping tool, namely, OWLmt (OWLmt, 2005). Once this mapping is defined, message instances are automatically converted one into other by using the mapping definition produced. SATINE Semantic mediation component is detailed in Section IV.

Annotating the services through ontologies enables us to query the P2P network semantically to locate the services requested. The SATINE peer-to-peer network is enhanced with indices for semantically publishing and discovering Web services. In order to increase scalability, the queries are routed only to the peers that are hosting the requested services based on the semantics

presented in the query message. The SATINE P2P architecture is elaborated in detail in Section V.

In SATINE, the tourism service provider peers may introduce service registries to the SATINE P2P network to publish their Web services. To enable semantic service discovery in SATINE P2P network, semantically enriched UDDI and ebXML service registries are integrated to the SATINE architecture as detailed in Section VI.

SEMANTIC INFRASTRUCTURE

In the SATINE middleware, the domain specific semantics is necessary for the Web services in the following respects:

• *For describing service functionality semantics*: In order to facilitate the discovery of the Web services, there is a need for semantics to describe what the service does. In other words, the service requestor should be able to locate a Web service which meets his needs in terms of its functionality. Note that, the naming of services performing the same kind of operation varies for different providers and languages. In SATINE, we have utilized OTA (OTA, 2005) specifications to construct a Service Functionality Ontology. OTA specifications expose significant domain knowledge in developing a global Web service functionality ontology since the OTA request/response pairs can be arranged into a class hierarchy to define operation semantics of travel

Figure 3. An example OTA compliant message ontology part for AirAvailability request

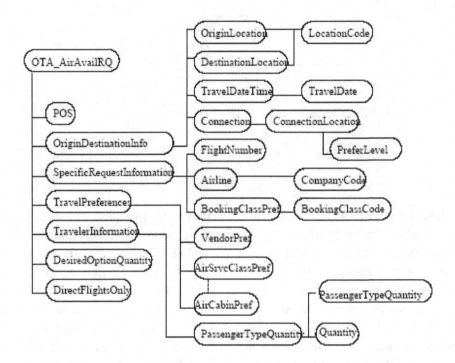

Web services. An example OTA compliant travel functionality ontology is presented in Figure 2. Using this ontology, not only the functionality of a service (i.e. "AirAvailabilityServices") but also some of the service properties bounded to that functionality (i.e. "Quality of Service") can be specified.

• Service functionality semantics enables us to discover the Web services based on their semantics. However in order to execute the discovered Web services, message level interoperability is necessary. Service functionality semantics may suffice to achieve interoperability only when all the Web services use the same message standards. However, it is not realistic to expect all the travel service providers to comply with the same message structure and content. Hence, there is a need to transform one message content and structure into another. In order to facilitate message transformation, SATINE utilizes semantic mediation. Currently the tourism application messages are usually in XML. In the SATINE middleware, the travel service providers and requesters express the

semantics of the Web service messages through local ontologies in OWL. However it may not be straight forward for travel service providers to create Web services exchanging OWL instances. Hence there is a need for automatic bidirectional transformation of XML message instances to OWL message instances. To be able to realize this, automatic generation of OWL Schemas from XML Schema Definitions (XSDs) is needed. Such transformations, called Normalization, have been realized within the scope of the Harmonise project (Harmonise, 2005). This normalization tool is enhanced to cover OWL concepts instead of RDFS in SATINE infrastructure. The local message ontologies generated from XSD schemas are mapped into the Global message ontology. Currently, SATINE uses more than one global message ontology one of which is based on the OTA specifications. It should be noted that our aim is not to propose ontologies for travel domain but to show how such ontologies, once developed, can be used for the semantic interoperability.

Figure 4. Relating service functionality and service message ontologies with OWL-S

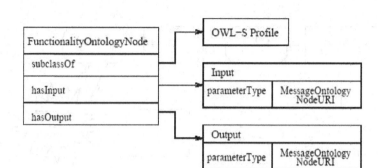

Annotating Web Service Functionality and Messages through Ontologies

Each Web service provider is expected to map their local semantics to a global ontology once at the conceptual level with the help of the semantic mapping tool SATINE provides. The automatic translation of the messages at the instance level is performed through the ontology mapping component presented in Section IV. A part of an example OTA message ontology for the input messages of Air Availability services is given in Figure 3.

In the SATINE middleware, for semantic description of Web services the "Web Ontology Language for Services (OWLS)" (OWL-S, 2005) is used. OWL-S provides an upper ontology which defines a top level "Service" class with some generic properties common to most of the services. The "Service" class has the following three properties:

- *presents*: The range of this property is ServiceProfile class. That is, the class Service presents a ServiceProfile to specify what the service provides for its users as well as what the service requires from its users.
- *describedBy*: The range of this property is ServiceModel class. That is, the class Service is describedBy a ServiceModel to specify how it works.
- *supports*: The range of this property is ServiceGrounding. That is, the class Service supports a ServiceGrounding to specify how it is used.

Based on the service functionality and service message ontologies, Web services are annotated in SATINE architecture through OWL-S as depicted in Figure 4:

- Each node in the functionality ontology is created as a subclass of OWL-S Profile class. For each Web service, an OWL-S definition is created as an instance of the related functionality ontology node. In this way, the functionality of the Web services is annotated through the service functionality ontology.
- In the OWL-S, Profile class has properties called "hasInput" and "hasOutput" whose ranges are "Input" and "Output" classes. These classes, in return have a property, namely, "parameterType". The value of this property is set to a node in the SATINE local message ontology. In this way the service's input and output parameters are annotated with the service message ontologies.

Figure 5. Normalization process in SATINE architecture

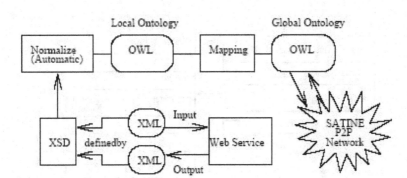

SATINE provides graphical user interfaces (GUI) to guide a user to create semantic annotation of the Web services. The GUI tool produces semantic definitions in terms of OWL-S files automatically where the message semantics are annotated with the "local message ontologies".

SEMANTIC MEDIATION

SATINE architecture enables the semantic mediation through an OWL ontology mapping component, namely, OWLmt. OWLmt allows the design of mappings between two ontologies that are syntactically different but semantically equivalent and the automatic translation of the OWL instances based on the mapping definitions. However, since most of the Web services exchange XML messages defined by an XML Schema Definition (XSD) (XML Schema, 2007), a normalization tool is integrated to the SATINE system. The normalization tool enables the conversion of OWL instances to XML messages and vice versa as well as the automatic creation of local message ontologies from XSD schemas.

In the following sections, the normalization and the ontology mapping processes are detailed emphasizing how they are utilized in the SATINE architecture.

Normalization

Normalization tool enables the creation of OWL ontologies from a set of XML Schema Definitions (XSDs) of the services. This is very suitable for the creation of the local ontologies of travel service providers. Once a travel service provider has the XSDs of its services, the only process needed in order to communicate through SATINE network is the creation of local OWL ontologies from these schemas automatically, and the definition of the mappings between this local ontology and one of the global ontologies available in the system.

It is clear that when an OWL ontology is created from an XML Schema (XSD), it is not possible to extract some of the OWL specific semantics such as class expressions or various types of properties. Yet, it is still possible to obtain the class hierarchies and the properties of classes and this information proves useful in ontology mapping.

The integration of the normalization process in SATINE infrastructure is presented in Figure 5. In this way, it becomes possible for tourism Web services to consume XML messages in SATINE architecture. Whenever a local ontology is automatically created from an XSD file, a normalization map is created automatically and stored in the peer. This normalization map is used by the Normalization tool to convert the OWL instance in local ontology provided as an input to

Figure 6. Architecture of OWLmt

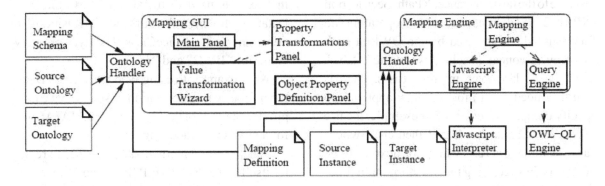

the Web service to an XML message. The output of the Web service provided as an XML message is denormalized to OWL and continues its journey in the SATINE P2P network as presented in Section IV-B.

Ontology Mapping

Ontology Mapping is the process where two ontologies with an overlapping content are related at the conceptual level, and the source ontology instances are transformed into the target ontology instances according to those relations. In the SATINE architecture, an OWL mapping tool is developed, called OWLmt (OWL-mt, 2005) which is used to handle ontology mediation. OWLmt provides two key components which are the mapping GUI and the mapping engine as shown in Figure 6.

The mapping GUI provides a user-friendly environment, which enables the designer to define the relations among the similar entities based on the overlapping content in the source and target ontologies. As a result of this "matching" process, the "mapping definition" is constructed which stores the relations between the two ontologies. The representation of the matching between the entities of the two ontologies and all the information related to it are defined as mapping patterns in the mapping definition. Mapping definition

is also represented in OWL. Mapping patterns mainly involve the following:

- *Matching the source ontology classes to target ontology classes*: Four mapping patterns namely, "EquivalentTo", "SimilarTo", "IntersectionOf" and "UnionOf" are used to represent the matching between the classes of source and target ontologies.
- *Matching the source ontology Object Properties to target ontology Object Properties*: "ObjectPropertyTransform" pattern is used to represent the path of classes connected with object properties in order to map one or more object properties in the source ontology with one or more object properties in the target ontology.
- *Matching the source ontology Data Properties to target ontology Data Properties*: Datatype properties of an instance in the source ontology are transformed to the target ontology instance datatype properties by specifying a "DatatypePropertyTransform".

OWLmt provides a powerful translation mechanism for the datatype properties, because the datatype properties may be structurally different in source and target ontologies. As a result, more complex transformation operations may be necessary than copying the data in the source instance to the target instance. XPath specification (XPath, 2005) defines a set of basic operators and functions which are used by the OWLmt such as "copy", "concat", "split", "substring", "abs", and "floor". However, in some cases, there is a further need for a programmatic approach to specify complex functions. For example, the use of conditional branches (e.g. if-then-else, switch-case) or iterations (e.g. while, for-next) may be necessary in specifying the transformation functions. To handle this kind of data transformation, OWLmt is supported by JavaScript statements. By specifying the JavaScript to be used in the "DatatypePropertyTransform" pattern, the complex functions can also be applied to the data as well as the basic functions and the operators. Similarly, the data transformation can also be performed by invoking a Web service by providing its WSDL. The Web service support is important for the use of data dictionaries to lookup the corresponding data values.

In Figure 7, an example mapping definition between OTA global ontology (Figure 3) and a local ontology for AirAvailability request message

is presented. In this example, the Javascript shown in Box 1 is used to transform "AirCabinPref" Datatype property values of "First", "Business" or "Economy" to "ServiceClass" Datatype property values of "1", "2" and "3".

As an example to using Web services for DatatypeProperty transformation, a Web service may provide the code of the airport once the IATA Code for a city is provided (Figure 7).

When a tourism organization wishes to register itself to the SATINE P2P Network, or wants to add a new Web service that is conformant to a new Local Message Ontology, two mapping definitions need to be defined for its local message ontology: local-to-global and global-to-local. This is necessary because the communication language in the Super Peer Network (Figure 1) is the global ontologies. Whenever a peer sends a message to its super-peer it has to be translated to the global ontology from the local ontology, and whenever a super-peer sends a message to its peer, it is translated to the local ontology of the peer. Each edge peer provides the OWLmt mapping GUI to the user to define these mapping definitions and these are stored in the peer and its

Figure 7. Example mapping for AirAvailability request message

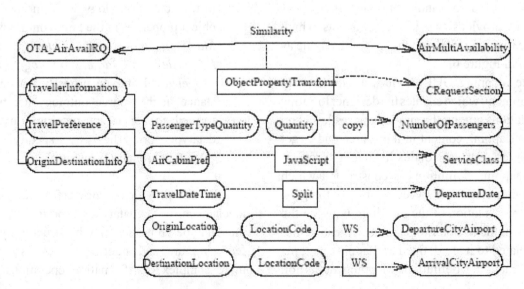

Box 1. An example Javascript for DatatypeProperty transformation

```
if(x==null){
 return "";}
var str=new java.lang.String(x);
if(str.equals("First")){
 return "1";
}else if(str.equals("Business")){
 return "2";
}else if(str.equals("Economy")){
 return "3";
}else{ return "";}}
```

super peer. The edge peer also enables the user to update available mapping definitions through the OWLmt mapping GUI, and the updated mappings between local ontologies and global ontologies are informed to the peer and its super peer. The global ontologies and the mapping definitions between global ontologies, can only be updated by domain experts, again through the OWLmt mapping GUI, and these updated mapping definitions are flooded between the Super-Peer Network.

The mapping engine is responsible for creating the target ontology instances using the mapping patterns stored in the mapping definitions and the instances of the source ontology. It uses OWL Query Language (OWL-QL) (OWL-QL, 2005) to retrieve required data from the source ontology instances. The mapping engine first executes the class mapping patterns. Then, the property mapping patterns are executed. Similar to the class mapping patterns, OWL-QL queries are used to locate the data.

The use of the OWL-QL enables OWLmt to have reasoning capabilities. In order to perform value transformations, the mapping engine uses the JavaScripts or Web services in the "DatatypePropertyTransform" pattern.

Once the mapping definitions are prepared and stored in peers and its super-peer; the mapping engine works seamlessly to the user at the service invocation phase. In order to enable semantic interoperability, the travel services are not invoked directly by the peer; the service requester sends a

service invocation request to its super peer. The service requestor does not have to know the local semantics of the services provided by different parties. Hence, the input message is translated to the global semantics automatically by the peer using the mapping engine and sent to the super-peer of the service requester. Once the service provider gets the input message from its super-peer, it is translated to the local semantics of the service provider automatically and given as an input to the service to be invoked. The invocation result is also mediated to the service requestor in the same manner.

SATINE P2P NETWORK

One of the major aims of developing a semantically enriched P2P network infrastructure for SATINE is to provide a scalable distributed architecture for the currently centralized service discovery and invocation mechanisms in the tourism domain. The available Service Registry Based architectures are also centralized. This P2P architecture enables the user to query multiple Service Registries in a seamless manner. In addition to this, this architecture enables the SMEs who may not have the ability of maintaining a Service Registry to advertise their Web services in their Web Sites through the P2P Network. One of the major drawbacks of P2P networks is flooding of all the query messages over the whole P2P network; in SATINE we address this problem by developing a semantic routing mechanism which enables the routing of query messages only to the relevant peers based on the semantics of the query message.

One of the major aims of developing a semantically enriched P2P network infrastructure for SATINE is to provide a scalable distributed architecture for the currently centralized Service Registry based service discovery and invocation mechanisms in the tourism domain. In addition to this, this architecture enables the SMEs to advertise their Web services that have not been registered to any Service Registry. One of the major drawbacks of P2P networks is flooding of all the query messages over the whole P2P network; in SATINE we address this problem by developing a semantic routing mechanism which enables the routing of query messages only to the relevant peers based on the semantics of the query message.

SATINE P2P architecture is implemented based on the JXTA platform (JXTA, 2005). JXTA is an Open Source project supported and managed by Sun Microsystems. JXTA provides discovery mechanisms for the resources owned by the peers. SATINE Peer-to-Peer architecture has enhanced JXTA capabilities for publishing, discovering and invoking semantically enriched Web services. It facilitates the discovery of Web services both from the individual peers in the SATINE network and also from the public service registries that are a part of the P2P Network. In SATINE, the edge peers can wrap UDDI and ebXML service registries and provide functionalities for publishing semantically enriched web services to service registries and semantic querying of the service registries as presented in Section VI. This facilitates the semantic discovery of web services from several service registries in a P2P environment.

Semantic Service Advertisement in SATINE P2P Network

SATINE provides user interfaces which guide the user to create semantic annotation of the Web services. As presented in Section III, in SATINE, Web service's semantic definition is represented as an OWL-S file where the functionality ontology nodes are referred for annotating service functionality, and message ontology nodes are referred for annotating the semantics of service parameters.

Each SATINE edge peer provides a graphical interface to the user for advertising its services to the SATINE P2P network. In order to advertise a Web service to the system, the technical description (WSDL), semantic description (OWL-S)

is provided to the system through the "Service Advertisement" component. While advertising the Web service, the user also indicates whether he wishes the Web service to be published to a service registry. In this case, the access information for the Web service registries is also provided. The edge peer processes this information, and if a registry is selected, the service is semantically published to the selected registry seamlessly to the user using the methods described in Section VI.

To enable semantic message routing and semantic query mechanisms based on service advertisements, the service semantics are processed by the P2P network accordingly. A service advertisement triggers the interaction of the edge peer with the SATINE super peer network: the peer sends the OWL-S file of the service to its super peer. SATINE super peer network handles the semantic routing of the queries to the appropriate peers by establishing routing indices based on the semantics of the services advertised. First, for a given peer its super peer processes the semantic definition of the service, and updates its indices to indicate that the peer has a service with the specified semantics. The functionality semantics of the service from the OWL-S file is extracted and it is added to the index table of the Super Peer as an entry pointing the peer that sends the advertisement. Then the super peer informs other super peers about the semantics of the web service advertised, their routing indices are also updated by adding the functionality semantics pointing the sender Super Peer, or updating the functionality semantics entry to add a new pointer to this sender super peer so that the queries can be correctly routed.

Semantic Service Discovery in SATINE P2P Network

In order to handle the semantic querying, SATINE provides each peer a query formulation and a query interpretation component, namely "Service Lookup" component as presented in Figure

8. The query formulation tool parses the travel functionality ontology and presents it through a graphical interface to the user for specifying the query parameters so that a user can easily search for the services he is looking for. As presented in Figure 8, on the left hand side panel, the functionality ontology nodes are presented. Whenever the user selects one of the nodes in this panel, the properties of this functionality ontology node and its possible values are presented on the right hand side panel. Based on the user input, the OWL-QL query is constructed at the backend. For example, if the user selects "AirAvailabilityServices" as a functionality ontology node, and "QualityRatingExcellent" as the value of "QOS" property, the OWL-QL query presented in Box 2 is generated automatically by the SATINE Lookup interface.

Afterwards, the query is sent to the SATINE P2P network. The super-peers semantically route the query only to the related peers by checking their indices. While the query is being routed in the SATINE P2P network, the query is mapped from one global ontology to another whenever necessary based on the mapping definitions available at the super peers. For example, in Figure 9, Web service Peer 1 (WSP1) issues a query to find a service with the functionality of "AirAvailabilityServices". The service lookup query is sent to the super peer of WSP1, which is Super Peer 1 (SP1). SP1 resolves the query and checks its indices. As a result, it discovers that there exists a path to a service provider with "AirAvalabilityServices" from SP2 and SP3 routes. Then, the query is forwarded to the corresponding super peers. Note that by such semantic routing, the flooding of the messages is highly reduced. Additionally, in the topology presented in Figure 9, the lookup messages may go in a loop between SP2 and SP3 since their indices points at each other. This looping is prevented in the SATINE architecture by attaching the route that the query passed to the message.

Figure 8. SATINE service lookup interface

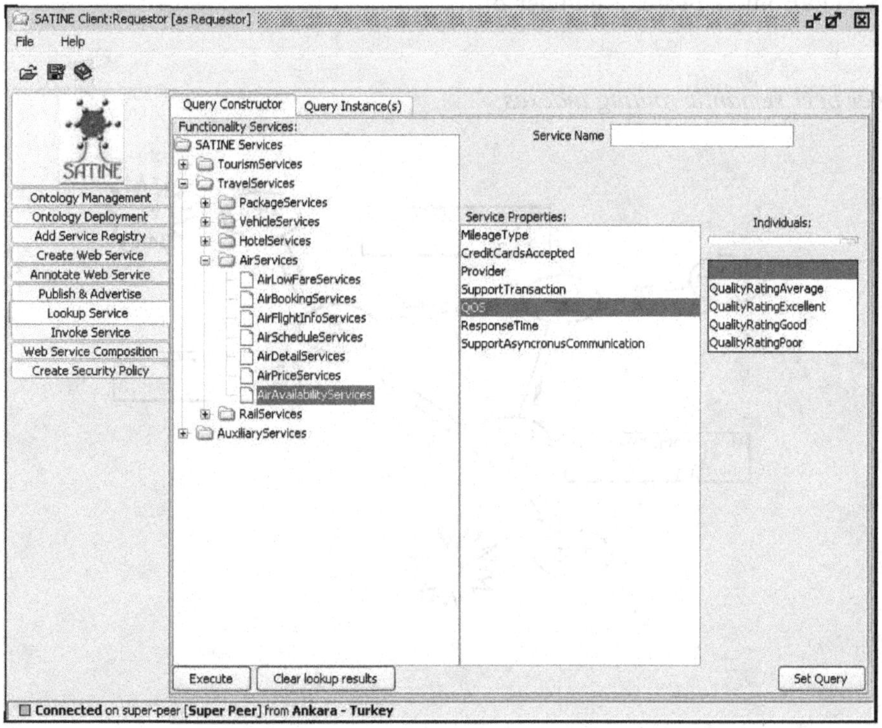

When the lookup message arrives at the service provider, the OWL-QL query is executed on the semantic definitions of its services. If it is an edge peer wrapping a service registry, the mechanisms for semantically querying the UDDI and ebXML registries, which are elaborated in Section VI, are exploited automatically. As a response to the query, there may be a set of "AirAvailabilityServices" that match the query requirements. All the available "AirAvailabilityServices" found in the SATINE network are accumulated in the service requestor and displayed to the user through a graphical interface by presenting the service name, service provider and service description so that the user can select the preferred ones and continue with invoking them.

ENHANCED SERVICE REGISTRIES

The SATINE System supports both ebXML (ebXML, 2007) and the UDDI (UDDI, 2005) registries, to store and discover semantically enriched travel Web services. In order to exploit the service registries in SATINE middleware, a number of

Box 2. An example OWL-QL query generated by SATINE lookup interface

```
(and (|http://www.w3.org/1999/02/22-rdf-syntax-ns#|:type ?x
|http://144.122.230.177:8080/satine/TravelFunctionality
Ontology.owl#|:|AirAvailabilityServices|)
(|http://www.w3.org/1999/02/22-rdf-syntax-ns#|:type ?p
|http://144.122.230.177:8080/satine/TravelFunctionality
Ontology.owl#|:|QOS|)
(|http://144.122.230.177:8080/satine/Profile.owl#
|:|sParameter| ?p
|http://144.122.230.177:8080/satine/TravelFunctionality
Ontology.owl#|:|QualityRatingExcellent|))
```

mechanisms are developed to relate the semantics of the Web services with the registries.

The Web services are discovered in the SATINE network based on their functional properties which are specified according to a functionality ontology. Hence, the functionality ontologies have to be stored in the service registries to query the services published to the registry. After storing the functionality ontologies to service registries, it is necessary to relate the services advertised in the registry with the semantics defined through the ontology.

UDDI registries do not provide a mechanism

Figure 9. Super peer semantic routing indexes

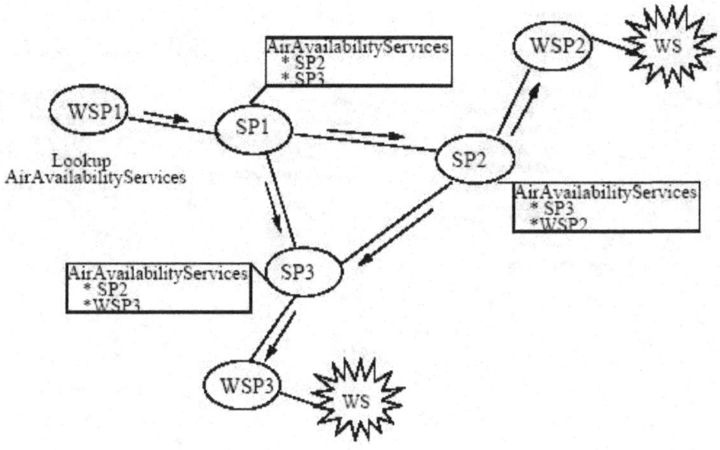

to store an ontology internal to the registry. The mechanism to relate semantics with services advertised in the UDDI registries are the tModel keys and the category bags of registry entries. tModel keys provide the ability to describe compliance with taxonomies, ontologies or controlled vocabularies. Therefore if tModel keys are assigned to the nodes of the ontology and if the corresponding tModel keys are put in the category bags of the services, it is possible to locate services conforming to the semantic given in a particular node of the ontology. This issue is elaborated in (Dogac, Laleci, Kabak, & Cingil, 2002) and (Dogac, Cingil, Laleci, & Kabak, 2002), where the mechanisms are introduced to store and relate DAML-S (earlier version of OWL-S) ontologies with services advertised in the UDDI registries.

An ebXML registry, on the other hand, allows to define semantics basically through two mechanisms: first, it allows properties of registry objects to be defined through "slots" and, secondly, metadata can be stored in the registry through a "ClassificationScheme". Furthermore, "Classification" objects explicitly link the services advertised with the nodes of a "Classification-Scheme". This information can then be used to discover the services by exploiting the ebXML query mechanisms. How to store OWL ontologies into ebXML registries and how to associate these ontologies with Web services are described

in (Dogac, Kabak, & Laleci, 2004) and (Dogac, Kabak, Laleci, Mattocks, Najmi, & Pollock, 2005), respectively.

Within the SATINE P2P Network, ebXML and UDDI registries are connected to the "Registry Peer". "Registry Peers" can be thought of as wrappers for registries: they facilitate the communication between the service registries and the rest of the P2P network. The requests for storing ontologies, and storing or searching for Web services are realized by the registry peer in terms of JXTA messages. The registry peer processes these JXTA messages and creates the necessary communication with the registries based on the types of the registries. In SATINE, the registry peer communicates with the UDDI registry through the UDDI4J API (UDDI4J, 2005). For ebXML registries, we adapted the freebXML which is the OASIS ebXML Registry Reference Implementation Project (ebxmlrr 2.1) (freebXML Registry, 2007). With this adapted ebXML registry, SATINE System has the capability of storing and discovering the technical (WSDL) and semantic (OWL-S) information of the semantically enriched travel Web Services. The registry peer converts the JXTA messages to the related ebXML SOAP Messages, which are then translated to the SQL statements before being sent to the ebXML Registry as presented in Figure 10.

The ebXML registry implementation consists

Figure 10. SATINE ebXML integration

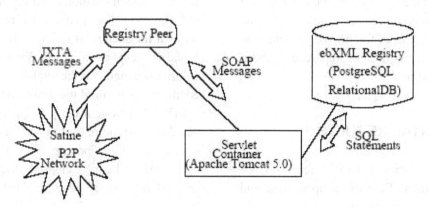

basically of three parts; the client, the servlet container and the relational database. The relational database constitutes the main ebXML registry; in other words, it holds tables to store all the registry data. The freebXML implementation allows various relational database products such as Oracle, PostgreSQL, and MSSQL to be used as the database. In the SATINE middleware, the PostgreSQL Relational Database (PostgreSQL, 2005), which is an open source database, is used as the registry part of the SATINE ebXML Wrapper.

The general overview of the SATINE ebXML Registry structure is presented in Figure 10. As a middle layer, a servlet container is used to interconnect the client and the registry. The servlet container is required for the SATINE ebXML Wrapper because all the messages sent to and received from the client are the SOAP Messages. The servlet container makes the necessary conversions from SOAP messages to SQL statements which are consumable by the registry in the relational database. freebXML implementation essentially supports the Apache Tomcat 4.0.4 or above. For the SATINE middleware, we set up the version of 5.0 for the Apache Tomcat servlet container. The client side, which is the registry peer in the SATINE middleware, constitutes the other end point.

The registry peer submits its request to the ebXML Registry with SOAP Messages through the servlet container. These requests can be: deploying an ontology schema, publishing a Web Service with its semantics or querying the registry. For all these requests, client prepares a SOAP message with the core request in it. The classes and packages of freebXML implementation are used and modified to prepare and submit the SOAP messages.

EXPERIMENTAL RESULTS

There are two metrics that will effect SATINE system deployment: Ease of set up and use and the performance of the system.

To facilitate system set up for the end users, we have developed an automatic installer as presented in Figure 12. Also we have developed viewlets explaining the set up, discovery, and invocation steps in SATINE environment. These viewlets are available at (Satine Viewlets, 2005).

In order to evaluate SATINE system's performance in real life settings, we identified sample usage scenarios and the factors that may affect the system performance in these scenarios.

We believe that SATINE system functionality can better be exploited as a middleware running behind a tourism portal.

Currently most of the tourism portals communicate with GDSs in the backend to accomplish the requests of the end users. We have integrated SATINE functionalities to the prototype version of a tourism portal that is currently being used in Turkey as presented in Figure 13.

A typical transaction in this portal can be summarized as follows: the end user issues a search request to the portal for example to find the flights available from Istanbul to Rome. Under normal circumstances, the portal communicates with the GDSs it has alliance with and as a response receives the available flight information along with the prices. In SATINE architecture this transaction is performed in two steps: first the available "FlightAvailability" services in the P2P network are discovered through a semantic query, then the discovered services are invoked, and the results of the web service invocations are presented to the user when the invocation of all services are finalized. Based on this scenario, we have identified a typical transaction as (a query service plus the invoke service) operation pair. We set the primary performance metric as the total time elapsed from issuing the query until the results are returned.

In SATINE system, the queries are semantically routed only to the relevant peers in the network, hence the number of peers providing the requested service affect the total elapsed time, rather than the total number of peers in the SATINE P2P network.

Figure 11. A tourism portal using SATINE middleware

Figure 12. SATINE installer

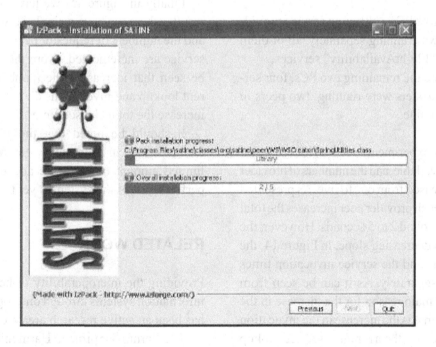

SATINE system is implemented in Java and includes around 127,000 lines of code. The test-bed contained eight Pentium 4 PCs running at 1.8 GHz with 2GB of memory. The experimental set up can be summarized as follows:

Figure 13. Results for one service requestor, multiple provider peers

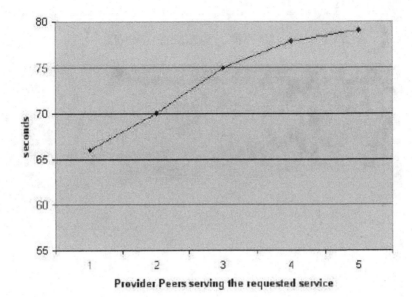

- One super peer, one trusted peer and one ontology manager peer running in one of the PCs,
- In each five PCs, a different service provider peer was running separately, all of them serving "FlightAvailability" services,
- Finally on the remaining two PCs, four service requesters were running, two peers in each machine.

In the first experiment, one service requestor peer is made available, and the numbers of provider peers are increased from one to five. As presented in Figure 15, each provider peer increases the total elapsed time around 2 to 5 seconds. However, the increase has a decreasing slope. In Figure 14, the discovery time and the service invocation times are depicted separately. As it can be seen from the figure the main reason for the increase in the total elapsed time is the increase in the invocation time. However, on the average a service lookup plus invocation transaction takes not more than one and a half minute which is an acceptable response time given that this includes all hetero-geneous message translations plus semantic Web service discovery.

Finally in Figure 15, we have presented the results where we have a single service provider, and the numbers of requestor peers querying this service are incremented. From the results it can be seen that increasing the number of concurrent lookup and invocations do not dramatically increase the total elapsed time.

It should be noted that these experiments are performed in a laboratory environment with limited amount of hardware and the industrial performance of the system is yet to be tested.

RELATED WORK

Providing the interoperability of heterogeneous information systems through ontology mediation has been an active research area recently.

The Harmonise project (Harmonise, 2005) developed a harmonization network for the tourism industry to allow participating tourism organizations to keep their proprietary data format and use

Figure 14. Discovery and invocation times for one requestor, multiple provider peers

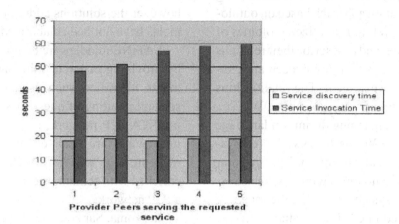

Figure 15. Results for one service provider, multiple requestor peers

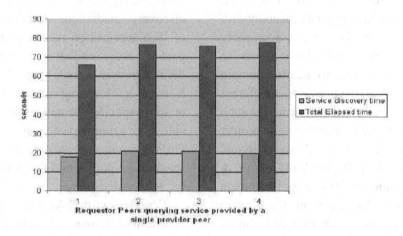

ontology mediation while exchanging information in a seamless manner. For this purpose they have defined a Interoperability Minimum Harmonization Ontology (IMHO) and an interchange format for the tourism industry. The MAFRA tool is used for ontology mediation (Maedche, Motik, Silva, & Volz, 2002). MAFRA uses a component that defines the relations and transformations between RDF ontologies. For representing the similarities in a formal way, MAFRA provides a meta-ontology called Semantic Bridge Ontology (SBO).

SATINE middleware has both benefited and extended the Harmonise framework as follows:

- Existing applications are wrapped as semantically enriched Web services to facilitate service discovery and to provide semantic interoperability.
- Ontology mediation is based on OWL ontologies and an OWL mapping tool is developed for this purpose.
- To facilitate the discovery of Web services and to provide scalability a peer-to-peer architecture is developed.

(Suwanmannee, Benslimane, & Thiran, 2005) also focuses on integration of heterogeneous data sources in the Semantic Web context using a semantic mediation approach based on ontologies. They use OWL to formalize ontologies of different resources and to describe their relations and correspondences to allow the semantic interoperability between them. The relationships between local ontologies are defined in OWL, i.e., OWL is used as a mapping definition language exploiting native OWL constructs such as equivalantClass and equivalentProperty. The mediator queries the local ontologies wrapping the back-end information systems by using the mapping definition defined in OWL to mediate between heterogeneous local data representations. This approach is limited to the mapping definition capabilities of native OWL constructs. SATINE middleware extends this mapping especially with various different tools for Datatype property transformation mechanisms which proves to be essential for the tourism application domain since the parties in years have developed different formats for expressing similar information such as hotel rates and flight classes. Edutella project (Nejdl, Wolf, Qu, Decker, Sintek, Naeve, Nilsson, Palmr, & Risch, 2002), (Nejdl, Wolf, Staab, & Tane, 2002) provides an RDF-based metadata infrastructure for P2P applications, building on the JXTA Framework for sharing educational resources. In (Nejdl, Wolpers, Siberski, Schmitz, Schlosser, Brunkhorst, & Loser, 2003), a super peer based routing strategy is described for RDF based peerto-peer networks.

SATINE middleware semantic routing framework benefited from this work and has extended it for semantic Web services. In (Ding, Solvberg, & Lin, 2004) a vision on Semantic Retrieval in a P2P network is presented. The authors identified the requirements of the system based on a scenario in tourism domain. Avoiding query flooding in P2P network based on semantics, addressing semantic mismatches between the nodes in the P2P network, and using local repositories enriched with semantics for publishing information are among the identified requirements. Being a vision paper,

(Ding, Solvberg, & Lin, 2004) presents the needs, however the solutions addressing these requirements have not been elaborated.

SATINE middleware complements this work by providing concrete solutions to the requirements identified such as demonstrating how semantic routing of query messages is achieved in JXTA P2P network, showing how semantic mismatches are resolved through an ontology mapping tool, and how Web service registries enriched with semantics can be exploited within a P2P network.

In (Toma, Sapkota, Scicluna, Gomez, Roman & Fensel, 2005), the Web Services Execution Environment (WSMX) is described. WSMX functionality can be summarized as performing discovery, mediation, selection and invocation of Web services on receiving a user goal. The goal discovery is about discovering abstract, predefined, reusable goals given the input provided by the user. This input can be in natural language or some specific formalism. In the SATINE architecture a more practical approach is taken and the Web services are annotated with travel domain specific ontologies and this information is used for service discovery.

(Vu, Hauswirth & Aberer, 2006) introduces an approach for semantic discovery of web services in P2P-based registries taking into account quality of service (QoS) characteristics. Query results can be ranked and users can provide feedbacks on the actual QoS provided by a service. We plan to adopt a similar QoS feature in the future releases of the SATINE architecture.

(Xu, Chen 2007) describes a P2P architecture for the discovery of semantic Web services which are published and deployed on same the Web server to guarantee the availability. In this approach the Web Services having similar properties are published to the same Web Server which serves as a peer. SATINE differs from this approach in that, the end users are free to publish their Web Services to any Web Service Registry, or Web Server they wish, through the semantic advertising and routing mechanisms proposed. We enable the discovery of these Web services through a hybrid architecture that contains both Web Service Registries and individual Web Servers as peers. In addition to this, SATINE complements (Xu, Chen 2007) by providing a semantic mediation mechanism; the peers in the network do not have to use the same ontology.

(Maedche, & Staab, 2004) provides a vision on building "fully-enabled service driven systems" by the use of the following enabling technologies: Semantic Web, Web services and P2P architectures. The authors highlight the importance of semantic mediation, ontology based service discovery, and semantically enriched P2P networks for achieving this vision. Scenarios involving knowledge exchange between tourism enterprises and on the fly discovery and invocation of tourism services are presented as motivating scenarios. As in (Ding, Solvberg, & Lin, 2004), this paper is also a visionary paper: it identifies the requirements and enabling technologies.

SATINE middleware complements these visions by providing a prototype implementation demonstrating how these technologies can be exploited together to achieve a semantic interoperability platform in the tourism domain. Finally, in (Dogac, Kabak, Laleci, Sinir, Yildiz, Kirbas, & Gurcan, 2004), the initial ideas on the use of semantically enriched Web services in the travel domain are presented.

CONCLUSION

Web services have become a prominent technology for providing syntactic interoperability. However, in order to fully exploit their potential, it is necessary to introduce semantics. Semantics is domain specific knowledge. Within the scope of the SATINE Project, we have demonstrated how semantically enriched Web services can be used to enhance eBusiness in the travel domain.

In the SATINE middleware, the tourism orga-

nizations do not have to advertise their services through Global Distribution Systems. SATINE allows tourism organizations to advertise their services by themselves to the rest of the P2P network. Therefore especially for SMEs, it is advantageous to be a part of the SATINE network which enables their services to be discovered by a wider community without the cost and overhead of connecting to Global Distribution Systems.

Furthermore, in the SATINE middleware, to provide semantic mediation of the exchanged messages, ontologies are derived from the existing local message schemas. These local ontologies are mapped into one another through global ontologies and mapping definitions thus created are used in mapping message instances automatically. Through this mechanism tourism parties exchange messages conforming to their own message schema with the rest of the peers.

The performance evaluation of the prototype system in laboratory environment with limited amount of hardware is promising: the results indicate that the response time is within acceptable levels although the Web services invoked are first discovered by using semantic information and their messages are translated back and forth.

ACKNOWLEDGMENT

This work is supported by the European Commission, DG Information Society and Media, eBusiness Unit through IST-1-002104-STP SATINE project and in part by the Scientific and Technical Research Council of Turkey, Project No: EEEAG 102E035

REFERENCES

Algorithm, R. S. A. (2005). Retrieved from http://en.wikipedia.org/wiki/RSA

Amadeus. (2007). Retrieved from http://www.amadeus.com/

Ding, H., Solvberg, I., & Lin, Y. (2004, March). A vision on semantic retrieval in P2P network. In *the International Conference on Advanced Information Networking and Applications (AINA 2004)*, Fukuoka, Japan.

Dogac, A., Cingil, I., Laleci, G. B., & Kabak, Y. (2002, August 23-24). Improving the functionality of UDDI registries through Web service semantics. *3rd VLDB Workshop on Technologies for E-Services (TES-02)*, Hong Kong, China.

Dogac, A., Kabak, Y., & Laleci, G. B. (2004, March). Enriching ebXML registries with OWL ontologies for efficient service discovery. In *Proc. of RIDE'04*, Boston.

Dogac, A., Kabak, Y., Laleci, G. B., Mattocks, C., Najmi, F., & Pollock, J. (2005). Enhancing ebXML registries to make them OWL aware. [Springer.]. *Distributed and Parallel Databases Journal*, *18*(1), 9–36. doi:10.1007/s10619-005-1072-x

Dogac, A., Kabak, Y., Laleci, G. B., Sinir, S., Yildiz, A., Kirbas, S., & Gurcan, Y. (2004). Semantically enriched Web services for travel industry. *ACM Sigmod Record*, *33*(3). ebXML. (2007). Retrieved from http://www.ebxml.org/

Dogac, A., Laleci, G. B., Kabak, Y., & Cingil, I. (2002). Exploiting Web service semantics: Taxonomies vs. ontologies. *A Quarterly Bulletin of the Computer Society of the IEEE Technical Committee on Data Engineering*, *25*(4).

ebRIM, ebXML Registry Information Model v2.5. (2007). Retrieved from http://www.oasis-open.org/committees/regrep/documents/2.5/specs/ebRIM.pdf

ebXML Registry Services Specification v2.5. (2007). Retrieved from http://www.oasis-open.org/committees/regrep/documents/2.5/specs/ebRIM.pdf

freebXML Registry Open Source Project. (2007). Retrieved from http://ebxmlrr.sourceforge.net

Galileo. (2007). Retrieved from http://www.cendanttds.com/galileo/

Harmonise, IST200029329. (2005). *Tourism harmonisation network. Deliverable 3.2 semantic mapping and reconciliation engine subsystems.*

IBM UDDI Registry. (2005). Retrieved from http://www-3.ibm.com/services/uddi/find

Jena2 Semantic Web Toolkit. (2005). Retrieved from http://www.hpl.hp.com/semweb/jena2.htm

Maedche, A., Motik, D., Silva, N., & Volz, R. (2002). MAFRA-A MApping FRamework for distributed ontologies. In *Proc. of the 13th European Conf. on Knowledge Engineering and Knowledge Management EKAW2002*, Madrid, Spain.

Maedche, A., & Staab, S. (2003). Services on the move-towards P2P-enabled Semantic Web services. *Proceedings of the Tenth International Conference on Information Technology and Travel and Tourism, ENTER 2003*, Helsinki.

Nejdl, W., Wolf, B., Qu, C., Decker, S., Sintek, M., Naeve, A., et al. (2002). EDUTELLA: A P2P networking infrastructure based on RDF. In *Proc. of the 11th Intl. World Wide Web Conf.*

Nejdl, W., Wolf, B., Staab, S., & Tane, J. (2002). Edutella: Searching and annotating resources within an RDF-based P2P network. In *Proc. of the Semantic Web Workshop, 11th Intl. World Wide Web Conf.*

Nejdl, W., Wolpers, M., Siberski, W., Schmitz, C., Schlosser, M., Brunkhorst, I., & Loser, A. (2003). Super-peer-based routing and clustering strategies for RDF-based peer-to-peer networks. In *Proc. of the Intl. World Wide Web Conf.*

Open Travel Alliance. (2005). Retrieved from http://www.opentravel.org/

OWL-mt. OWL Mapping Tool. (2005). Retrieved from http://www.srdc.metu.edu.tr/artemis/owlmt/

OWL-QL. OWL Query Language. (2005). Retrieved from http://ksl.stanford.edu/projects/owl-ql/

OWL-S. (2005). Retrieved from http://www.daml.org/services/daml-s/0.9/

Postgre, S. Q. L. An Open-Source Object Relational Database Management System (ORDBMS). (2005). Retrieved from http://www.paragoncorporation.com/ArticleDetail.aspx?ArticleID=11

Project, J. X. T. A. (2005). Retrieved from http://www.jxta.org/

Sabre. (2005). Retrieved from http://www.sabre.com/

SATINE Project. (2007). Retrieved from http://www.srdc.metu.edu.tr/webpage/projects/satine

Schema, R. D. F. (1999). *Resource description framework schema specification. W3C proposed recommendation.* Retrieved from http://www.w3.org/TR/PRrdfschema

Schema, X. M. L. (2007). Retrieved from http://www.w3.org/XML/Schema

Simple Object Access Protocol (SOAP). (2005). Retrieved from http://www.w3.org/TR/SOAP/

Suwanmannee, S., Benslimane, D., & Thiran, P. (2005, March). OWL-based approach for semantic interoperability. In *the Proceedings of AINA, IEEE Computer Science Press.*

Toma, I., Sapkota, B., Scicluna, J., Gomez, J.-M., Roman, D., & Fensel, D. (2005). *A P2P discovery mechanism for Web service execution environment.* Retrieved from http://dip.semanticweb.org/documents/ p2pDiscovery.pdf

Tomcat. (2005). Retrieved from http://jakarta.apache.org/

Triple, D. E. S. Algorithm. (2005). Retrieved from http://csrc.nist.gov/publications/fips/fips463/fips46-3.pdf

UDDI4J Java API. (2005). Retrieved from http://uddi4j.sourceforge.net/

Universal Description Discovery and Integration (UDDI). (2005). Retrieved from http://www.uddi.org

Viewlets, S. A. T. I. N. E. (2005). Retrieved from http://www.srdc.metu.edu.tr/webpage/projects/satine/viewlet/

Vu, L.-H., Hauswirth, M., & Aberer, K. (2006). *Towards P2P-based Semantic Web service discovery with QoS support.* Retrieved from http://infoscience.epfl.ch/record/97742/files/?ln=fr

Web Ontology Language, O. W. L. 1.0 Reference. (2005). Retrieved from http://www.w3.org/TR/2002/WD-owl-ref-20020729/ref-daml

Web Service Description Language (WSDL). (2005). Retrieved from http://www.w3.org/TR/wsdl

Web Services Policy Framework (WS-Policy). (2005). Retrieved from http://www128.ibm.com/developerworks/library/specification/ws-polfram/

XPath. XML Path Language. (2005). Retrieved from http://www.w3.org/TR/xpath

Xu, B., & Chen, D. (2007). Semantic Web services discovery in P2P environment. Retrieved from http://ieeexplore.ieee.org/stamp/stamp.jsp?arnumber=4346418&isnumber=4346351

Chapter 10
Application of the FUSION Approach for Tool Assisted Composition of Web Services in Cross Organisational Environments

Alexakis Spiros
CAS Software AG, Germany

Balogh Andras
CAS Software AG, Germany

Bauer Markus
CAS Software AG, Germany

Kiss Akos
InfomatiX, Hungary

ABSTRACT

*The research project FUSION aims at supporting collaboration and interconnection between enterprises with technologies that allow for the semantic fusion of heterogeneous service-oriented business applications. The resulting FUSION approach is an **enterprise application integration (EAI)** conceptual framework proposing a system architecture that supports the composition of business processes using semantically annotated **Web services** as building blocks. The approach has been validated in the frame of three collaborative commercial proof-of-concept pilots. The chapter provides an overview on the FUSION approach and summarises our integration experiences with the application of the FUSION approach and tools during the implementation of transnational career and human resource management services.*

DOI: 10.4018/978-1-60566-804-8.ch010

APPLICATION FOR A JOB INTRODUCTION

Small and medium enterprises (SMEs) cooperating with international partners in the **Enlarged Europe** need holistic **Enterprise Applications Integration (EAI)** solutions in order to operate effectively. The project FUSION (Business process fusion based on Semantically-enabled Service-oriented Business Applications, IST-027385) corresponded to this need: it aimed at supporting collaboration and interconnection between commercial enterprises by developing a framework and technologies that allow for the semantic fusion of heterogeneous service-oriented business applications.

FUSION results are based on **Service Oriented Architectures (SOA).** In **SOA** services are described using formal definitions such as WSDL. High level languages such as BPEL allow us to define the orchestration for the fine grained services exposed by different systems which then can be incorporated into workflows and business processes implemented in composite applications.

These standards however, can't overcome inconsistencies at the data and functional level. FUSION has addressed these **interoperability** issues by developing a conceptual framework, system architecture and a toolset that supports semantically enhanced business processes deploying of semantic Web service annotations.

FUSION has facilitated three trans-national **business cases**, typical examples of cross-organizational collaboration in the '**Enlarged Europe**'. The first is the integration of transactions of a franchising firm (Greece, Poland, Romania, Bulgaria, Ukraine, Cyprus and FYROM); the second pilot deals with the collaboration of companies in a chain of schools of foreign languages and computing (Bulgaria, FYROM, Albania); the final example is the automation of international career and human resource management services (Hungary and Germany).

Since the authors of this chapter are practitioners (working at CAS Software and InfomatiX), this chapter is based on their experiences made in the process of applying the FUSION solution from the integrator's perspective. Accordingly, it intends to provide a proof of concept of the outcomes of the project FUSION, but does not follow an academic approach. After an overview of the FUSION approach and methodology and a short presentation of the FUSION **business cases** we will concentrate on our integration experiences gained within the InterJob pilot, a HR scenario between Hungary and Germany.

FUSION APPROACH AND METHODOLOGY OVERVIEW

Fusion Approach

The project FUSION has proposed a Global Architecture and a **Reference Framework** including an appropriate toolset that facilitate effective **Enterprise Application Integration (EAI)**, by offering semi-automated search and discovery of services, dynamic data mediation and semantically-assisted manual and semi-automatic business process composition. FUSION has utilised Semantic **Web Services** by uplifting traditional **Web Services** to semantically annotated services and deploying a common reference conceptual model. FUSION has realised a conceptual architecture adopting widely accepted Web Service industry standards, in combination with the most promising Semantic **Web Services** standardization efforts, i.e. SA-WSDL, OWL-S and WSMO (Friesen, 2007).

The FUSION approach consists of the following phases:

1. Web Service Enablement and System Installation: expose the functionality required for implementation of the business processes as **Web Services**

2. **Ontology Engineering** Phase: extensions and instantiations to customise the FUSION EAI Ontology
3. **Semantic Uplifting** Phase: semantic annotation of Enterprise Services and publication of Semantic Profiles
4. Process Design Phase: semi-automatic composition of Enterprise Services into Business Processes.

The users involved in the phases above are:

- IT Consultants, responsible for extending the ontology with necessary concepts and annotating the **Web services** with FUSION ontology concepts, or
- Business Consultants (Business Process expert), for creating generic processes that can be customized for more specific installations.

In order to facilitate the resolution of structural and semantic differences of the input and output messages exchanged between interoperable **Web services** of a defined process, a multi-layered and multi-faceted FUSION Ontology has been introduced. Layering defines the level of abstraction and the level of exposure of the Ontology whereas the facets represent the role of the concepts within the solution. The ontology provides a common reference for data semantics through the data facet, enables search and discovery of **Web Services** through the functional facet and enables process composition in the process facet. The ontology also introduces an upper layer covering domain independent concepts, the domain dependent extensions are then expressed in the facets (Bouras, 2007).

The **FUSION architecture** is made up of:

- the FUSION Semantic Analyzer, a design time environment,
- the FUSION Ontology Repository,

- the FUSION Integration Mechanism, a runtime execution environment .

The components that build up the **FUSION architecture** are described below.

Semantic Analyzer: Concepts Designer

The Concepts Designer is responsible for handling and managing the multi-layered, multifaceted FUSION Ontology during each phase of the ontology lifecycle. The tool supports and facilitates the creation, development and maintenance the FUSION Ontology, which constitutes a well-defined representation and concept model of business applications and services and is stored in the Ontology Repository.

Semantic Analyzer: Semantic Profiler

Semantic Profiler is a graphical environment that allows the user to create the semantic profiles of the available **Web Services** that represent business services. It is an editor for adding annotations utilizing classes and instances of all the developed facets of the FUSION Ontology through SAWSDL (Semantically Annotated Web Service Description Language). It also generates XSLT transformations for up and down-casting functionality, i.e. it provides a mapping from concrete system dependent data types into ontology concepts and vice versa.

Semantic Analyzer: Process Designer

The Process Designer enables the user to reuse Abstract Process Models, search and discover candidate services automatically, check for and resolve data incompatibilities and, finally, ground the Abstract Process Models to executable BPEL process code using the previously discovered services.

Two tools assist manual process design and

semi-automatic process design respectively. The semantical manual process designer allows for customising an Abstract Process Model (abstract BPEL), invoke discovery and grounding and deploy it on a BPEL engine. The semi-automatic designer generates the orchestration out of a list of **Web services** and a composition goal, consisting of the primary goal and the recovery goal. From these a composition plan is created, containing the control and data flow of the process. This composition is then transformed to executable BPEL.

Ontology Repository

The Ontology Repository module constitutes a fully functional file system, where concepts, classes and instances of the facets of the FUSION Ontology are stored.

Integration Mechanism

The integration mechanism is the execution environment of the FUSION system. It supports registration and publication of semantically annotated **Web Services**, semantically-enriched categorization, search in the services registry and the deployment and the execution of the grounded business process models. The integration mechanism includes a) a Semantic Registry, b) a native BPEL engine and c) a generic deployment and administration component (Bouras, 2006).

FUSION Methodology

As the deployment and applicability of the FUSION system and solution over a collaborative, enterprise systemic environment requires a set of conditions and prerequisites, including the exposure of **Web Services** and the creation of the semantic profiles of the exposed enterprise services, the FUSION IT Consultant, who is responsible for the FUSION-enablement of the given business applications, should perform the service-oriented semantic analysis of the preselected scenarios. The term "service-oriented semantic analysis" has been selected for this process, because of the fact that it involves:

a)   the **semantic uplifting** of **Web Services** (constituting the key implementation technology for **service-oriented architectures**), which are exposed from the installed enterprise applications, realizing a variety of supported business functionality;

b)   the creation and publication of the **semantic** (SA-WSDL compatible) profiles of the given enterprise services, based on the utilization of concepts and classes existing, restricting or extending the multi-faceted FUSION EAI Ontology, which serves as a common reference model; and

c)   the in-depth **ontological analysis** of the respective use cases, with regard to all the ontological facets that are applied in the specific collaborative business scenario.

More specifically, the proposed methodology for service-oriented semantic analysis of collaborative business scenarios includes:

1.   the **data space semantic analysis**, with respect to the objects exchanged among the heterogeneous enterprise applications (existing in the respective use case), involving
     a.   **Identification of the Exchangeable Object**; where the FUSION IT Consultant specifies in detail (including involved systems, workflow analysis, contingency actions, etc.) the given business scenario, so as to identify the objects, i.e. the electronic documents, to be exchanged among the several heterogeneous systems.
     b.   **Definition of the Exchangeable Object**; where the FUSION IT Consultant specifies the objects to be exchanged between two systems, by

providing a table with the structural elements of the object and a brief description of each one of them.

c. **Structural Elements Semantic Mapping**, where the FUSION IT Consultant either enriches the second (2nd) layer of the Data facet of the FUSION EAI Ontology or applies restrictions to specific data-related ontological concepts, in order to provide mappings among the structural elements of the exchangeable objects to classes of the Data facet of the FUSION EAI Ontology.

2. the **semantic analysis of the business functionality**, with respect to the functionality supported and realized by the **Web Services** that are exposed from enterprise applications (existing in the respective use case), involving:

   a. the identification and the description of the supported functionality of the related *wsdl:portType* existing in the given **Web Services**; and

   b. the mapping and semantic categorization of the identified business functionality supported by the exposed **Web Services**, either by extending the functional facet of the FUSION EAI Ontology (in case the respective ontological concept has not been included in the classification taxonomy), and/or by applying annotations that point on the respective ontological terms of the functional facet.

3. the **semantic analysis of the collaborative business processes**, describing what to consider with respect to the ontology when creating a process model for manual composition and what ontological concepts are of importance and how they are related to the process model. This process semantic analysis includes the following steps:

a. **process model creation**; A process model is made up of several activities including inbound or outbound messages (receive, reply), two way operations (invoke) and variable assignments (assign). These activities could be contained in several BPEL containers such as sequence, flow, switch etc. A process model normally starts with a receive activity, a one way operation that starts the process, and ends with a reply activity. The first receive and last reply use the same parnerLink, since the final message goes back to the same entity that started the process.

b. **Non-deterministic activities definition**; As **Web Services** return a failure message when something has gone wrong, it is therefore necessary to be prepared to receive such information in a process. In BPEL it is possible to detect if a variable has been instantiated. In this case we want to detect whether variable profile or variable failure was instantiated, in order to know how to proceed. A switch statement in this situation could direct the control flow in two different ways: 1) If failure message is initiated, rollback and reply, and 2) Otherwise, process normally.

c. **Process model annotation**; The only annotations in a process model are references to Functional Facet entities. Ontology classes in the Functional Facet have object properties that describe their inputs and outputs from the Data Facet of the ontology therefore it is superfluous to annotate the variables in the model with Data Facet Entities (DFEs).

d. **Publishing a process model**; the model itself (abstract BPEL process) is classified under a Process concept in the ontology. A Process concept has to be created and its data type property hasProcessModel set to contain the URI of the BPEL process model location.

e. **Customizing a process model**; First, a process model has to be looked up in the ontology editor. Afterwards, the remaining steps are straightforward: enabling/disabling optional tasks, discovery, grounding and deployment.

4. the **semantic state space analysis**, which includes the identification and the in-detail analysis of the state space of the given collaborative business scenarios, and the definition, in semantic terms and relations, of the possible states involved.

PILOT USE CASES OVERVIEW

FUSION has applied the developed concepts and tools in the frame of three different "**Enlarged Europe**" scenarios. They have been driven by organisations that need to facilitate the globalization of their operations enhancing the **interoperability** of their business applications.

Each use case includes operations spanning the **Enlarged Europe**, in particular:

- **Germanos:** integration of transactions of a franchising firm (Greece, Poland, Romania, Bulgaria, Ukraine, Cyprus and FYROM)
- **Interjob:** provision of career and human resource management services (Hungary and Germany)
- **Pharos:** collaboration of companies in a chain of schools (Bulgaria, FYROM, Albania).

Pharos is a chain of schools of Foreign Languages and Computing. From its headquarters in Sofia the network's Regional Directorate monitors and coordinates all activities. In each country, the Country Headquarters supervise and coordinate educational and business activities of the chain of schools at national level.

Germanos is a franchising company operating a chain of retail stores for telecommunication goods and services. In each country the company has established one national headquarter to coordinate the logistics and retail activity at the national level. Their IT landscape consists of different IT systems, as for instance Web Map Service (WMS), Enterprise Resource Planning (ERP) and Customer Relationship Management (CRM), delivered from different vendors and on different platforms.

Interjob is a network of SMEs active in the provision of executive search services. The members of the network are acting as typical human resource (HR) consultants in their regional markets. For international requests, i.e. recruiting skilled engineers from new member states for vacancies in old member states, they co-operate acting like a single entity. Each network member is independently operating CRM and HR systems that suit his needs.

For each pilot we have executed the following steps of the FUSION Approach:

- first, we have extended existing software with a Web Service layer,
- second, we have installed the FUSION system software components at the participating sites,
- third, we have engineered the FUSION EAI ontology for the specific domain,
- fourth, for selected use cases we have designed the processes using the FUSION process designer.

The pilots represent different **interoperability** aspects. While in the Pharos use case all systems have been individually tailored, Germanos deploys only standard software. Processes at Germanos are already automated while the international operations of Pharos are performed by mail, phone or fax. Other aspects of use case complementarity are complexity and intercultural focus: Germanos processes are rather complex, while the exchange of HR information in the Interjob case needs harmonisation due to intercultural differences.

In the next sections, we will present our integration experiences with the Interjob case in more detail.

APPLICATION OF THE FUSION APPROACH IN THE FRAME OF THE INTERJOB USE CASE

InterJob is a network of Small and Medium sized Enterprises (SMEs) active in the provision of executive search services with clients in sectors such as banking, insurance, oil, public utilities, etc. The network includes more than 10 SMEs in Germany, Hungary, Russia and Poland. Members of the network are HR consultants in their regional markets. For international requests, i.e. recruiting skilled engineers from new member states for vacancies in old member states, they co-operate like a single entity. InterJob expects concrete benefits from applying FUSION, i.e. to be able to share profiles among the branch offices without double administration, to save working time for the employees and response time for the customer, and decrease the cost of the communication.

Interjob has several branch offices all over Europe operating similar but separated HR systems. Candidate profiles belonging to the different branch offices are locally stored and clients can maintain them using their own interfaces. For sharing candidate profiles within the network InterJob uses a system called the HR Pool which is available from all offices via web based user interface.

In the candidate selection process communication via telephone or e-mail among the Interjob offices and manual pre-selecting of candidates are real drawbacks considering the time consumption to provide high quality matching services. In addition, the costs of human workforce have been

risen (meaning the manual selection of potential candidates) and Interjob has been searching for new methods to automate the pre-selection of candidates in order to decrease transaction costs and use precise results to enhance its services.

IT INFRASTRUCTURE OF INTERJOB BEFORE FUSION INTEGRATION

The Interjob technical environment consists either of CRM or dedicated HR systems from different vendors and on different platforms. They support operations in the single entities and are not interconnected. They are used for:

- description of job vacancies,
- description of profiles,
- management of documentation,
- scheduling,
- accounting,
- promotion activities.

The main systems involved in the selected use case, CAS genesisWorld and HR Pool, will be presented in the following.

Each branch office works with the CRM system CAS genesisWorld, developed by CAS Software. This software is basically a CRM groupware application server providing Web and desktop clients. Therefore, each office has a CAS genesisWorld application server and several client machines. Candidate profiles are stored on the local CRM server which is available for the employees of the branch office. They perform different operations on the candidate profiles, including adding a new profile, removing it or searching candidate profiles based on various retrieval conditions.

For the needs of the Interjob pilot, the CAS genesisWorld system has been customized on server as well as on client level. It was necessary to introduce new database schemes at the backend, as well as a new graphical user interface in the client layer.

Interjob has developed a system for sharing the profiles amongst the branch offices: the HR Pool is a central storage (and matching) server. Branch offices can upload their profiles to this central server, or search for suitable candidates provided by other offices. Since the central HR pool stores anonymous candidate profiles, the branch offices are not able to directly contact the retrieved candidates without paying the providing office for the full profile (containing the contact details).

There is only one instance of the HR Pool installed at InterJob headquarters. Users can connect to it using a Web based user interface. HR Pool uses the HR-XML standard for the data structure. Using this standardized data structure HR Pool is a completely generic solution for storing HR related data and data exchange can be accomplished among different systems easily trough its web service interface.

Both, CAS genesisWorld and HR Pool, provide web service interfaces. Genesis World publishes its interface for participation in office-boundary-crossing processes and HR Pool publishes the interface in order to communicate with web applications.

FUSION INTEGRATION PROCESS

The Interjob pilot has two integrator partner companies: the genesisWorld systems have been integrated by CAS Software AG and the HR Pool's integrator is InfomatiX Ltd.

According to the specifications, the fully integrated process is "Candidate Search". A recruiter may submit a job profile using his genesisWorld system to the HR Pool to find a suitable candidate. The matching algorithm is executed in the HR pool. The process makes use of the linking capability in genesisWorld: the local (onymous) and the partners' (anonymous) CVs (Candidate Profiles) for which the matching was successful get linked locally with the job profile initiating the matching.

After the process has been executed, a recruiter can see the list of candidates in the customized CAS genesisWorld Client program.

Figure 1 depicts the Candidate search use case. The swimlanes represent the three roles present in the scenario. The dashed lines and the artefacts stand for data communication and data objects while continuous arches show the control flow.

First, a job description is added to an Interjob office's local system, and then the job description is matched with the candidate profiles of the same Interjob office by the HR Pool's service. The match results are then linked with the job description stored in the local system. Next, a matching with candidate profiles of other providers is executed in the HR Pool, and the anonym results are stored and linked in the local system again.

The JobDescription object initiating the whole process is used in all operations afterwards.

DATA-LEVEL SEMANTIC ANALYSIS

This section describes the steps we have followed for the data-level semantic analysis of the "Candidate Search" use case.

Step 1: Identification of the Exchangeable Objects

The first step includes an analysis of the given collaborative business scenario, emphasizing at the identification of the objects, i.e. electronic business documents, exchanged among the involved enterprise applications.

The Exchangeable Objects of this scenario are *Candidate Profile* and *Job Description*.

Step 2: Definition of the Exchangeable Object

As basis for the definition of the exchangeable Objects *Candidate Profile* and *Job Description* HR-XML has been chosen. HR-XML contains a

Figure 1. Candidate search BPMN

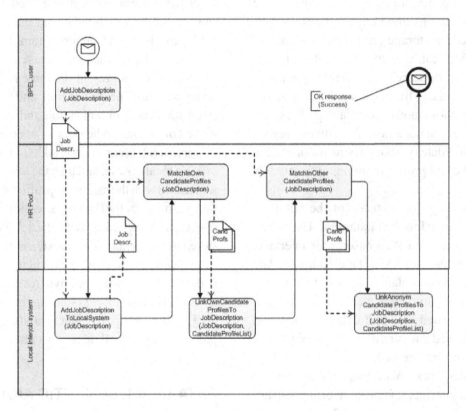

variety of objects of different facets in the domain of human resources. For the identified objects the Staffing Exchange Protocol (SEP) and Cross-Process Objects (CPO) facets were utilised.

The two entities to start definition with are *Resume* and *Candidate*. Three XSD files were created (with the help of domain experts from Interjob) in which the definition of "Job Description" and

"Candidate Profile" is placed; these are based on the definitions of the two objects from the SEP. The third XSD file contains common data type definitions that are referenced SEP and CPO.

The Table 2 depicts the textual description of the exchangeable objects

Table 1.

Workflow Title	Candidate Search
Involved Systems	CAS genesisWorld (CRM), HR Pool (Directory service)
Description	This process undertakes the task of inserting a new Job Description in the corporate CRM system and executing a search in the HR Pool Candidate Profile Storage system.
Workflow Analysis	1. The user stores the Job Description in the local system 2. The user initiates a matching procedure in the HR Pool to find matching locally stored Candidate Profiles 3. The user links the results with the Job Description provided 4. The user initiates a matching procedure in the HR Pool to find matching Candidate Profiles published by other Interjob agents 5. The user creates new (anonymous) Candidate Profile entries and links the results with the Job Description provided 6. Process ends

Table 2.

I. Indicative Item structure	II. Description
Candidate_Record_Info	Identification tag for the data object
Candidate_Supplier	Information about the supplier, that is about the (Interjob) HR Office/ Agent who published the object
Personal_Data	Personal details about the candidate
Objective	The objective of the candidate
Executive_Summary	An overall description, summary about the candidate
Preferred_Position	Detailed description about the position the candidate intends to find
Employment_History*	Information about a concrete employment of the candidate (more occurrences are possible)
Education_History*	Information about a concrete education period of the candidate (more occurrences are possible)
Qualification*	Description of a concrete qualification of the candidate
Language*	Information about language knowledge (more occurrences are possible)
Revision_Date	Date of publishing/saving

III. Indicative Item structure	IV. Description
Profile_Record_Info	Identification tag for the data object
Profile_Supplier	Information about the supplier, that is about the (Interjob) HR Office/ Agent who published the object
Position_Dateinfo	Start/End date of the offered position
Organization	Description of the organization
Position_Detail	Detailed information about the offered position
Formatted_Position_Detail	Further details about the position, ordered in key-value pairs
How_To_Apply	Description about the application method for the job
Revision_Date	Date of publishing/aving

Step 3: Structural Elements Semantic Mapping

The main objective of this final step of the Data Space Semantic Analysis procedure is to provide semantic mappings of each structural element of the exchangeable objects to the concepts of the second (2nd) layer of the Data facet of the FUSION EAI Ontology. In principle, we had two possibilities: either looking for suitable classes for reuse or defining new ones.

After an examination of the FUSION ontology, we implied that the main classes regarding the HR domain are generally missing and, in consequence, most of the classes of the Interjob pilot had to be newly created. Some properties and general classes could still be reused though, like start/end date properties, and Person and Contact details classes.

Figure 2 shows the objects we have created for the Interjob pilot. The list of objects can be seen on the left, with a darker disk before them and without a prefix. As an example, details of the Candidate Profile class are shown in the right part of the window.

Figure 2. Newly created objects in the ontology for the Interjob pilot

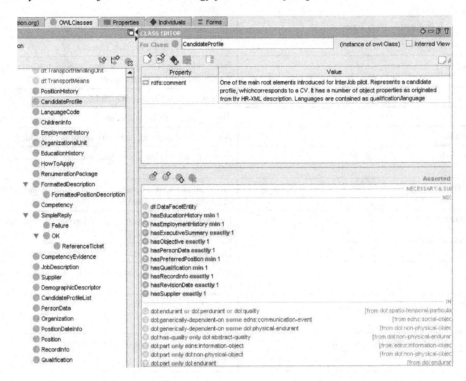

SERVICE-LEVEL SEMANTIC ANALYSIS

This section describes the steps we have followed for the service-level semantic analysis of the "Candidate Search" use case.

Step 1: Identification of Services Involved in the Process

The HR Pool is offering two match functions that accept a job description and return a set of matching candidate profiles. One function is responsible for searching for candidate profiles that originated from the office itself (local) and the other searches for candidates that have been submitted to the pool by other members.

GenesisWorld is offering a service for saving a job description in the CRM system and a service for linking a candidate profile to a job description.

Step 2: Semantic Modelling of Service Classification

Though the FUSION ontology was including several CRM taxonomy concepts, we had to develop extensions around a HumanResources concept. It's functions and their suitable taxonomy classes are listed in Table 3.

Table 3.

V. WSDL portType	VI. Service Classification Taxonomy concept
GW_JobProfileManager	Opportunity_Manager
GW_AnonymCVsManager	Short_Listing
GW_LocalCVsManager	Short_Listing
HRPool_LocalMatchManager	Recruitment
HRPool_PoolMatchManager	Recruitment

Step 3: Semantic Annotation of Web Service Interfaces

In a next step, we have annotated the WSDLs using the Semantic Profiler tool. The tool has proven to be user friendly, allowing for intuitive definition of the references from the WSDL elements to the FUSION Ontology. The Data Facet Entities used in the pilot's use cases are modelled in OWL, a screenshot is shown in Figure 3.

WSDLs contain Data Facet (at the element level) and Functional Facet (at the port type level) annotations. The Data Facet annotations describe the inputs and outputs of the operations. The Functional Facet annotations describe the functionality and purpose of the operations.

In total, we have published eight services to the Semantic Registry: two for the HR Pool (matching within own Candidate Profiles and matching within other agents' profiles) and three for each InterJob office (entering a Job description, linking it with local Candidate Profiles, linking with other agents' Candidate Profiles).

PROCESS-LEVEL SEMANTIC ANALYSIS

For the Semantic Analysis at process level, we have followed the two steps explained below.

Step 1: Design Activities for Manual Process Composition

Abstract BPEL process models contain invoke activities without end point references. In the

Figure 3. Data facet entities created for the pilot, Protégé screenshot

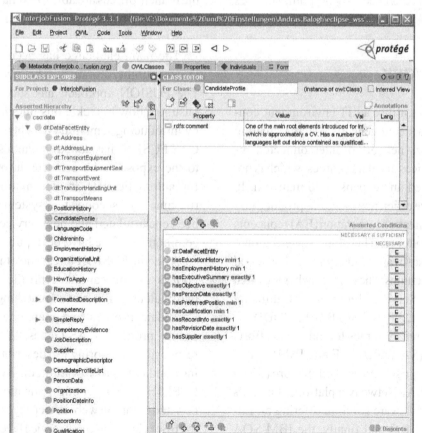

following, we have annotated these activities with Functional Facet Entities from the ENIO ontology to provide a description of their purpose and functionality. These annotations provide the necessary information for the semantic registry to perform discovery.

The process model serves as a template for multiple composition scenarios using the rules that can be defined on BPEL activities. The rule we have employed is an "AtLeastRule", allowing either matching among own candidates of a recruiter agent only, matching among other agents' candidates only, or matching among both kinds.

Step 2: Grounded Process Models (manual composition)

An abstract process model has been grounded after discovery is performed, so that it can be executed on the BPEL engine. When grounded, the process model contains references to end point services that it can invoke.

RELATED WORK

Most enterprises utilise an IT environment consisting of several heterogeneous systems, creating a complex, fuzzy network of interconnected applications, services and data sources, which is not well documented and expensive to maintain. In order to improve efficiency as well as productivity Enterprise Application Integration (EAI) concepts have to be introduced. Therefore, several global players of the software industry have developed EAI-implementations. These approaches are often based on Web Services Technologies, utilising standards like SOAP, WDSL, BPEL, UDDI).

There are three examples for industrial efforts of big players (SAP, ORACLE and IBM) in this area. SAP Enterprise Service Architecture (ESA) is based on the SAP Netweaver platform, Oracle's Fusion is a middleware solution offering an Enterprise Service Bus and finally, the IBM SOA

patterns allow for reusing experience collected in past integration projects.

However, for successful EAI integration it is indispensable that the semantics of different systems have to be formally defined and integrated at one point. Semantic Web Services are the topic of many European Research projects: DIP, ATHENA, SEKT, INTEROP, SUPER, GENESIS, ASG, ASTRO. Their outcomes and lessons learnt have influenced the results of FUSION.

RESULTS AND CONCLUSIONS

FUSION Integration Results

The aim of the integration at InterJob was to make sharing candidate profiles easier and replace the inefficient 'via email or phone' method to a faster and more reliable solution. After the integration, the branch-offices are able to exchange candidate profiles in a more convenient and cost effective way.

The main challenge has been the data-level incompatibility among the two involved systems. The FUSION approach has successfully demonstrated how to tackle this integration problem by introducing semantic concepts. In a first step, CAS FUSION has added semantics as meta-data to the exposed **web services** in order to allow for automatic data transformation in process run-time. In a second step, system services have been encapsulated and new services that apply a common interface have been published.

After the FUSION integration the Interjob HR Pool is storing candidate profiles and offering two matching functions (matching within own Candidate Profiles and matching within other agents' profiles). CAS GenesisWorld (CRM) is responsible for storing job descriptions and linking candidate profiles to them. By applying the FUSION approach, both applications employed a new and common web service layer, the Mediated **Web Services**. This new service layer encapsulates

Figure 4. InterJob environment after integration

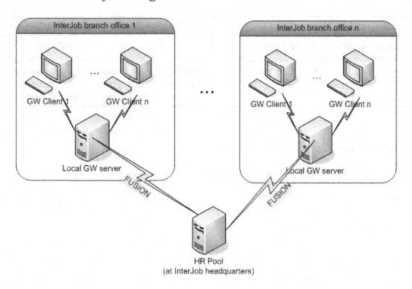

the native services and provides data transformations for them, exposing services that are ready for interconnection.

The main drawback of the legacy Interjob environment was the complete separation of both IT systems. Therefore, all data had to be entered twice, which was an error-prone and time-consuming process. After the application of the FUSION Approach, the communication between the applications is now automated, while the algorithmized matching of the HR Pool is still available.

Description of Interjob Collaborative Processes before Fusion and with Fusion.

Three typical processes carried out at Interjob have been subject of FUSION. They handle the

processing of job applications and searching for suitable candidates for particular jobs. The impact of FUSION to these processes is described in Table 4, Table 5, Figure 5 and Table 6.

Summary of Experiences, Benefits Achieved, Need for Improvement

Applying the Fusion approach was a compelling challenge for the integrator companies. However, we gained a lot of benefits. We got familiar with **semantic technologies** and developed close relationships with the participating research organizations. FUSION results will lead to short term improvement of the current solution portfolio of the integrators and to more interoperable solutions in the future in the areas of Customer Relationship Management (CRM), Sales Force Automation (SFA), **Management Information**

Table 4. Application for a job

Before FUSION	After FUSION
Candidates submit their CV to InterJob via e-mail or fax and profiles are created manually by an InterJob employee. The employee has to create this manual step twice as there are two systems, the local CRM and the HR Pool.	Candidates interested in a job can submit their CV including contact details to a central portal. The portal fires a BPEL process, which enters the data into the local Interjob Partner gW systems and the HR Pool. There is no matching algorithm implemented in gW, therefore there is no automatic local matching executed.

Table 5. Candidate search

Before FUSION	After FUSION
There is no unified matching algorithm used at InterJob. Employees do the matching of profiles manually. If they do not have own profiles they can search for matching profiles of other offices using the HR Pool. Searching within Interjob network is very slow.	A recruiter may submit a job profile to the system to find a suitable candidate. A matching algorithm is executed in the HR pool. The process makes use of the linking capability in genesisWorld: the local (onymous) and the partners' (anonymous) CVs get linked with the job profile for which the matching was successful.

Figure 5. Resulted candidate search BPMN

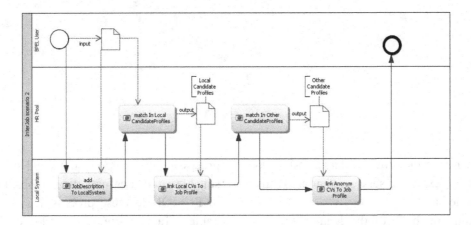

Systems (MIS) and Professional Services Automation (PSA).

As Interjob was the first integration project with the newly conceived FUSION-approach we encountered initial difficulties in understanding the concept behind the process steps. The necessary extension of the ontology and the creation of a process model template had been difficult tasks and the most time-consuming parts of the integration. Therefore, a goal for further projects should be not to reuse existing templates, if possible.

The Interjob pilot is ideal for demonstrating the difference between traditional BPEL processing and the FUSION approach. Using BPEL, the integrator IT specialist (IT Consultant) together with the Business Consultant would have to be present at each step of the composition and the data-level incompatibilities would have to be solved from scenario to scenario in a different manner. At the same time, the FUSION approach allows for using the Process Model template and the predefined Data-level ontology concepts; and the weaving of new InterJob or other HR offices in the "HRPool's FUSION-enabled network" to participate in the shared Candidate Profile searching process is rather quick and straightforward.

The HR XML standard was introduced into the CRM data model. HR-XML makes it possible to

Table 6. Successful placement

Before FUSION	After FUSION
Once a candidate is selected for a job, his status is updated in the local system unless the profile belongs to another branch. Then the offices have to communicate via e-mail or phone.	Once a candidate is selected for a job, his status is automatically updated in the system.

build a bridge between the national differences of CV-s and job descriptions. The basic idea of connecting different systems via FUSION was validated and the developed scenario became technologically realizable. Interjob is now in the position to deploy the Semantic Web concept, Interjob offices save transaction costs and time by using a common HR-XML compatible, FUSION-enabled portal (Kiss, 2008).

An important asset of FUSION is keeping the chance of preserving the productive legacy systems and the compatibility with applications using the native services in other integration scenarios. A restriction is that only systems with a **SOA** interface can be considered. Concluding, we believe that the FUSION approach is perfectly applicable for companies having heterogeneous systems that lack a common interface and we expect further exploitation of the approach in near future.

REFERENCES

W3C. (2006). *Semantic annotations for Web services description language working group.* Retrieved on January 15, 2009, from http://www.w3.org/2002/ws/sawsdl

Bouras, A., Gouvas, P., & Mentzas, G. (2007, September). *ENIO: An enterprise application integration ontology.* Paper presented at the 1st International Workshop on Semantic Web Architectures for Enterprises (SWAE), Regensburg, Germany.

DERI Innsbruck at the Leopold-Franzens-University Innsbruck. Austria, DERI Galway at the National University of Ireland, Galway, Ireland, BT, The Open University, and SAP AG. (2005, June 3). *Web service modeling ontology (WSMO). W3C member submission.* Retrieved on January 15, 2009, from http://www.w3.org/Submission/WSMO/

France Telecom, Maryland Information and Network Dynamics Lab at the University of Maryland, National Institute of Standards and Technology (NIST), Network Inference, Nokia, SRI International, Stanford University, Toshiba Corporation, & University of Southampton. (2004, November 22). OWL-S: Semantic markup for Web services. W3C member submission. Retrieved on January 15, 2009, from http://www.w3.org/Submission/OWL-S/

Friesen, A., Alazeib, A., Balogh, A., Bauer, M., Bouras, A., Gouvas, P., et al. (2007, July). *Towards semantically-assisted design of collaborative business processes in EAI scenarios.* Paper presented at the 5th IEEE International Conference on Industrial Informatics, INDIN, Vienna, Austria.

HR-XML Consortium. (2008). *About HR-XML Consortium, Inc.* Retrieved on January 15, 2009, from http://www.hr-xml.org/

Kiss, A., Martinek, P., & Czilik, I. (2008, October). Integrating HR offices over semantically enriched SOA. Paper presented at the Conference for Information Security Solutions Europe (ISSE), Madrid, Spain.

OASIS. (1993-2009). *OASIS Web services business execution language (WSBPEL) TC.* Retrieved on January 15, 2009, from http://www.oasis-open.org/committees/tc_home.php?wg_abbrev=wsbpel

Steinbeis Foundation (StW). (n.d.). *Project information about FUSION.* Retrieved on January 15, 2009, from http://www.fusionweb.org

Chapter 11
Semantic Business Process Management:
A Case Study

Sebastian Stein
IDS Scheer AG Altenkesseler, Germany

Christian Stamber
IDS Scheer AG Altenkesseler, Germany

Marwane El Kharbili
IDS Scheer AG Altenkesseler, Germany

Pawel Rubach
Telekomunikacja Polska S.A., Poland

ABSTRACT

The application of semantic technologies promises boosting business process management because semantic integration of business and IT is achieved. To enable the vision of semantic business process management, semantic technologies like ontologies, reasoners, and semantic Web services must be integrated in BPM tools. We extended a professional BPM tool to allow semantic business process modelling using the EPC notation. In addition, we adapted the tool's EPC to BPEL transformation to preserve the semantic annotations. By introducing a proxy service, we are able to perform Semantic Web service discovery on a standard BPEL engine. We evaluated our approach in an empirical case study, which was replicated 13 times by 17 participants from 8 different organisations. We received valuable feedback, which is interesting for researchers and practitioners trying to bring semantic technologies to end-users with no or only limited background knowledge about semantics.

DOI: 10.4018/978-1-60566-804-8.ch011

INTRODUCTION

Business processes are a core asset of every company. They govern how employees, departments, and resources collaborate to create business value and to adapt to changing market conditions. Today, business processes are often supported or even automated by a combination of IT systems. The IT implementation of business processes is hindered due to the business-IT divide (Smith & Fingar, 2003; Dehnert & van der Aalst, 2004; Koehler, Hauser, Sendal, & Wahler, 2005). Business processes are designed by business experts with no IT knowledge. On the other hand, IT implementation is done by IT experts, who do not have the necessary business knowledge to correctly interpret the business process models. To overcome this business-IT divide it is suggested to use semantic technologies like ontologies, reasoners, and semantic web services (Hepp, Leymann, Domingue, Wahler, & Fensel, 2005).

Even though the use of semantics in business process management (BPM) promises many advantages, an empirical evaluation is still missing. Therefore, we[1] first created a semantic business process management (sBPM) prototype to allow using semantics while implementing business processes. Afterwards, we conducted an empirical case study with participants from industry and research to evaluate this prototype.

In this chapter, we report on the technical details of the sBPM prototype as well as on the empirical evaluation. The chapter is structured as follows: First, we[1] provide background information by explaining the basic concepts of BPM and sBPM in section 2. Section 3 describes the research design and the research question. The case study is based on a sBPM prototype. The two parts of it are described in section 4 and section 5. Section 6 introduces the different parts of the case study like the real-world business process used, the participants involved, and the interviews conducted. The results of the case study are presented and

discussed in section 7. The chapter is concluded with a summary.

BACKGROUND

Business Process Management

In general system theory (von Bertalanffy, 1976) a system is defined by its border, by its goal or purpose, by its elements, and by the relations between those elements. An enterprise is such a system, because it fulfils all those characteristics. An enterprise has a border to the environment (customers, competitors, market). It also has a goal like creating a high return on investment or maximizing the shareholder value. An enterprise consists of many elements and the relations between those elements. During its lifetime, the enterprise is restructuring itself in order to adapt itself to a changing environment. An enterprise model captures all relevant aspects of the enterprise. It is created to document the structural and dynamic aspects of the enterprise, but also to plan and communicate possible changes internally and externally. The structural elements of the enterprise model are grouped according to their nature into different dimensions like organisational elements, functional elements, data elements, etc. Different diagram types are used to model the static relations between elements of the same dimension. For example, an organisational chart is used to model the formal hierarchy within the enterprise. In contrast, dynamic models define how the different system elements of the enterprise work together to achieve the enterprise's goals. Those dynamic models are called business processes, workflow processes or executable processes depending on their purpose and level of abstraction. The enterprise model is usually structured according to an enterprise architecture framework like Zachman[2], ArchiMate[3] or ARIS (Scheer, 2002; Scheer, Thomas, & Adam, 2005). Such an enterprise architecture framework defines the dimensions, abstraction levels, possible element types, and relation types.

The enterprise as a system changes during its lifetime to adapt to the continuously changing business environment. Changes are initiated unconsciously or consciously. In the first case, system elements like employees react spontaneously e. g. by providing a discount on a partly damaged product. In the second case, changes are carefully planned, implemented, evaluated, and adjusted in a change program. This cyclic approach of process improvement is known as Deming cycle (Deming, 1982).

BPM as defined by Schmelzer and Sesselmann (2008) comprises all tasks related to the elements and models of the enterprise model. However, often the term BPM is used in a narrower meaning (see e. g. Weske (2007)) focusing only on the process dimension of the enterprise model. In that case, BPM comprises tasks like documenting as-is processes, planning to-be processes, implementing processes, executing processes, and monitoring and controlling executed processes. Here, also enterprise application integration (EAI) is important. Technical process descriptions are used to describe the integration between different applications. Parties have to agree on the interaction between them, but also on the data messages exchanged. Creating a shared understanding about the integration effort is still challenging and some possible solutions are presented throughout this book. A common approach for describing integration scenarios is using a graphical process modelling language.

There are different graphical notations available for documenting business processes like Event-driven Process Chains (EPC) (Scheer, Thomas, & Adam, 2005) or Business Process Modeling Notation (BPMN) (OMG, 2006). Those notations are used by business experts to capture the tacit knowledge of process owners by making it explicit. The business process models created are also the source for process implementation.

During business process automation, IT experts either generate or manually define an executable process model based on the business process model. For automated refinement, various transformation algorithms and frameworks are available. A detailed literature overview can be found in (Stein, Kühne, & Ivanov 2008).

Transforming business processes into executable ones is hindered due to the fact that IT experts do not have the necessary skills to correctly interpret the business process models created by business experts. This gap between business and IT is known as business-IT divide (Smith & Fingar, 2003; Dehnert & van der Aalst, 2004; Koehler, Hauser, Sendal, & Wahler, 2005). To overcome this problem, Hepp, Leymann, Domingue, Wahler, & Fensel (2005) suggest using semantic technologies like ontologies, reasoners, and semantic web services in BPM. Such an approach is known as semantic business process management (sBPM). The next section documents the current state of sBPM research.

Semantic Business Process Management

In sBPM, an enterprise model is based on semantic technologies so that it can be processed and "understood" by machines. This is achieved by providing ontologies for the different aspects of an enterprise model. Having a machine-processable enterprise model enables two major use-cases:

1. Semantic reasoning can be used to reveal so far unknown facts from the enterprise model. For example, an enterprise model can be analysed if it complies with a new government regulation.
2. Semantic technologies can be used to derive new parts of the enterprise model. For example, by analysing a semantic business process it might be possible to derive an executable process automatically.

In order to enable this vision of sBPM, a stack of ontologies to represent the various aspects of an enterprise model is introduced (Hepp & Roman, 2007; Pedrinaci, Brelage, van Lessen, Domingue, Karastoyanova, & Leymann, 2008). However, sBPM will only be adopted in industry if it builds on existing models and languages allowing an easy transition. Following this idea, Abramowicz, Filipowska, Kaczmarek, & Kaczmarek (2007) create a semantic representation of the BPMN modelling language, which allows relating BPMN activities to WSMO goals (Fensel, Lausen, Polleres, de Bruijn, Stollberg, Roman, & Domingue, 2006). WSMO goals are used to describe the capabilities required by a function. This semantic description can be used to discover semantic web services able to support the annotated function. Similar work is available for the EPC notation (Filipowska, Kaczmarek, & Stein, 2008). Nitzsche, Wutke, & van Lessen (2007) provide an ontologized version of BPEL. Again, BPEL activities can be related to WSMO goals enabling semantic web service discovery during process execution. Other authors like Markovic and Kowalkiewicz (2008) focus on other aspects of process models like semantically capturing goals to be achieved by a business process.

In a related effort, Bouras, Gouvas, Kourtesis, & Mentzas (2007) show how semantics can be applied to solve the challenge of enterprise application integration. Here, the Enterprise Interoperability Ontology (EnIO) (Bouras, Gouvas, & Mentzas, 2007) is proposed to represent the common understanding of data, services, and processes within EAI scenarios. This work enables e. g. assisted composition for web services (Alexakis, Bauer, Pace, Schumacher, Friesen, Bouras, & Kourtesis, 2007) so that developing an integration solution is accelerated and quality of the found solution is improved.

Besides defining the necessary ontologies, also new or extended tools are needed to support end-users in creating semantic business process models and executing them. Dimitrov, Simov, Stein, & Konstantinov (2007) provide a semantic business process modeling tool based on WSMO Studio[4], which allows modeling semantic business processes using semantic BPMN. The software design of a semantic process execution engine based on semantic BPEL is outlined in (van Lessen, Nitzsche, Dimitrov, Konstantinov, Karastoyanova, & Cekov, 2007).

Besides process design and execution, semantics are also used for process analysis (Celino, Alves de Medeiros, Zeissler, Oppitz, Facca, & Zoeller, 2007) and process mining (Alves de Medeiros, Pedrinaci, van der Aalst, Domingue, Song, Rozinat, Norton, & Cabral, 2007). Semantic compliance management as defined by El Kharbili, Stein, Markovic, & Pulvermüller (2008) is a more holistic approach ensuring compliance of semantic enterprise models with laws and regulations.

This overview shows that sBPM is an actively researched area. So far, most efforts are fundamental research either defining the necessary languages (Hepp & Roman, 2007; Pedrinaci, Brelage, van Lessen, Domingue, Karastoyanova, & Leymann, 2008; Abramowicz, Filipowska, Kaczmarek, & Kaczmarek, 2007; Filipowska, Kaczmarek, & Stein; 2008; Nitzsche, Wutke, & van Lessen, 2007; Markovic & Kowalkiewicz, 2008; Bouras, Gouvas, & Mentzas, 2007), some preliminary tools (Dimitrov, Simov, Stein, & Konstantinov, 2007; van Lessen, Nitzsche, Dimitrov, Konstantinov, Karastoyanova, & Cekov, 2007; Alexakis, Bauer, Pace, Schumacher, Friesen, Bouras, & Kourtesis, 2007) or overall approaches and methodologies (Hepp, Leymann, Domingue, Wahler, & Fensel, 2005; Celino, Alves de Medeiros, Zeissler, Oppitz, Facca, & Zoeller, 2007; Alves de Medeiros, Pedrinaci, van der Aalst, Domingue, Song, Rozinat, Norton, & Cabral, 2007; El Kharbili, Stein, Markovic, & Pulvermüller, 2008; Bouras, Gouvas, Kourtesis, & Mentzas, 2007). However, empirical evaluation of the proposed technologies to validate the practical relevance of sBPM is still missing. Such work would provide feedback, which could be incorporated in research agendas to realign the research efforts with requirements from the industrial field. We tackle this problem in this chapter by first introducing a sBPM prototype and afterwards evaluating it in an empirical case study. The following section gives a detailed description of the research design applied and the research question answered.

RESEARCH DESIGN

Scientific rigour requires first defining the research question to be answered (Creswell, 2002). Afterwards, a research design is created facilitating the answering of the research question. As shown in the previous section, introducing semantic technologies in BPM promises many advantages, but an empirical evaluation of sBPM is still missing. Therefore, we formulate the following research question: How does BPM benefit from introducing semantic technologies and how is the adoption in industry of sBPM hindered?

Our research interests are of explorative nature. According to Yin (2003), controlled experiments as well as case studies are research methods able to answer such how and why questions. Kitchenham, Pickard, & Peeger (1995) add that experiments are usually applied for "research-in-the-small" and case studies for "research-in-the-typical". We are clearly focused on "research-in-the-typical", since our intention is to investigate the usage of sBPM in a real-world setting. Kitchenham, Pickard, & Peeger (1995) also state that case study research is often used to evaluate new technologies. This also applies in our case.

Therefore, we conduct an empirical case study following the case study research methodology defined by Yin (2003). We augment Yin's methodology with ideas taken from Kitchenham, Pickard, & Peeger (1995), because they describe specific practices for case study research in software engineering, which are applicable in our case as well.

As we aim at evaluating sBPM "in-the-typical", we want participants to use the tools they also use in BPM. Therefore, we do not use the sBPM modelling tool by Dimitrov, Simov, Stein, & Konstantinov (2008), because it is a research prototype and not used in industry. Instead, we extend the existing BPM tool ARIS, which has according to market research reports from Gartner (Blechar, 2007) and Forrester (Peyret, 2007) a leading market position. We also use Oracle BPEL Process Manager for process execution, which is also a well established commercial software product.

From a more abstract point of view, we are following design science in business information systems research as described by Hevner, March, Park, & Ram (2004). We design a sBPM prototype based on existing software. Prototyping is an accepted research method in business information systems research Wilde and Hess (2007). According to the guidelines defined by Hevner, March, Park, & Ram (2004) for business information systems research, an evaluation step is necessary. This evaluation step must be based on an accepted evaluation method. We adhere to this point by evaluating the sBPM prototype in an empirical case study following an accepted case study research methodology (Yin, 2003). The case study is using a sBPM software prototype, which is described in the following section.

SEMANTIC BUSINESS PROCESS MODELLING PROTOTYPE

Overview

The case study is based on a sBPM prototype. This prototype consists of two parts:

1. An extension of the business process modelling tool ARIS to support semantic annotations of business processes. This

prototype generates an executable process based on BPEL. This part is described in this section.

2. An execution environment based on Oracle BPEL Process Server to execute the generated BPEL code. The execution environment also supports semantic web service discovery during run-time based on semantic annotations injected in the generated BPEL code. This part of the prototype is described in the following section 5.

Representation of Semantics in ARIS

The semantic web community develops and supports different semantic formalisms like OWL-S (Martin, Burstein, Hobbs, Lassila, McDermott, McIlraith, Narayanan, Paolucci, Parsia, Payne, Sirin, Srinivasan, & Sycara, 2004) and WSMO (Fensel, Lausen, Polleres, de Bruijn, Stollberg, Roman, & Domingue, 2006). Therefore, an ARIS extension for sBPM must not be bound to a specific semantic formalism, but instead be as independent as possible. This means, the way semantic descriptions are represented in ARIS must be the same for different semantic formalisms if possible. In an ideal case, this allows exchanging the semantic formalism without having to change the semantically annotated process models. Also, the user interface to select or create a semantic description must be identical, because the semantic formalism used does not matter for a business expert. The sBPM prototype supports semantic annotations based on WSMO. Nevertheless, the general modelling principle used in the prototype can be straightforwardly transferred to other formalisms like OWL-S.

Describing the functionality of (IT) systems is not a completely new approach and it has been used in IT architecture management for several years. However, the semantic community proposes a much more formal approach, which is harder to understand by people with no background

in logic, mathematics or computer science, but which, on the other hand, is expressive enough to use automated reasoning. In the past, so called "Information System Functions" were used in ARIS to describe IT systems. We reuse this object to annotate a function in an EPC process model.

Figure 1 shows a part of an EPC process model with the function "Verify Formal Requirements". In a complete EPC process model, this function would be related to other functions or events. The semantic description "Formal Verification" is represented by an "Information System Function", which is connected to the function. The "Information System Function" was created by importing a WSMO goal description as described in the next sub-section. As the semantic description is represented by a separate modelling object and not stored as an attribute value of the function, it can be reused to annotate different functions or IT systems. For example, if the semantic description is changed, only this object and its attributes must be updated. All other objects like functions related to it will have the updated semantic description as well. This ensures that semantic descriptions stay consistent and prevents redundancy, because each semantic description is only stored once in the modelling repository. Figure 1 also shows the ontological input/output instances defined by the WSMO goals. They are represented by a separate object and connected to the function as well.

Selecting a WSMO Goal in ARIS

Functions of an EPC process model can be annotated with semantic descriptions to describe their functionality. In our prototypical extension of ARIS, we support the annotation with the graphical user interface shown in Figure 2. The dialog is presented when the user selects the function in the EPC model, which should be annotated.

As a first step, the user selects a folder on the local hard drive, where WSMO goal descriptions as WSML files are stored. The dialog lists all files found in the selected folder on the left side

Figure 1. A Function Annotated with a WSMO Goal

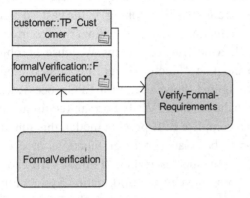

of the dialog. When the user clicks on an entry in the list, the content of the file is shown on the right side of the dialog. At this stage, the content of the WSML file is shown without any syntax highlighting or other visual support.

The user evaluates the applicability of a WSMO goal based on the WSML code. Finally, the user confirms the selection of a WSMO goal by clicking the "OK" button. An "Information System Function" object is created and automatically related to the function as shown in Figure 1 and discussed before.

We provide a small support functionality to remove a semantic description from a function,

too. The dialog to select a WSMO goal and the support functionality to remove a WSMO goal are implemented in ARIS' internal scripting engine. The scripts are available to the users and can be changed by them if necessary.

Completing the Data Flow

By selecting a WSMO goal to annotate a function, the WSMO goal and the ontological input/output instances are added to the EPC. In the next step, the user completes the data flow by relating an ontological output instance of a function to an ontological input instance of a later function. This mapping is later used during execution to do automated lifting and lowering of data schemas. This is illustrated in Figure 3. We provide supporting functionality to help users in creating the necessary modelling artefacts.

Injecting Semantic Annotations in BPEL

Besides user interface extensions enabling semantic annotation of business process models, we also provide an adapted version of ARIS' EPC to BPEL transformation. This adapted transformation

Figure 2. Graphical User Interface to Select a WSMO Goal in ARIS

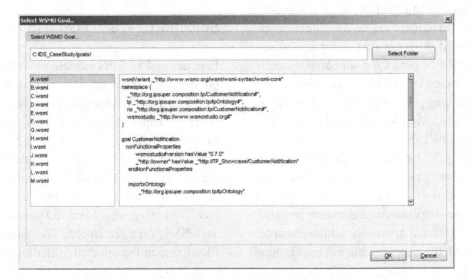

Figure 3. Completing the Data Flow in the EPC

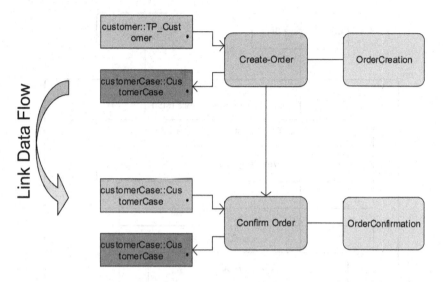

preserves the semantic annotations by generating a special invoke for each function, which is annotated semantically. A detailed description of the mechanism used follows in the next section.

SEMANTIC BUSINESS PROCESS EXECUTION PROTOTYPE

Overview

We use the BPEL language version 1.1 as format for executable business processes. BPEL allows orchestrating a set of web services and there are many middleware products delivered by various vendors supporting this standard. BPEL itself has a mechanism to support dynamic binding at runtime. Each web service is represented as a partnerlink in BPEL. The partnerlinks are special kinds of variables specifying the web service to be called. It is possible to exchange the content of a partnerlink during runtime by assigning a new value to it. However, it can only be exchanged with content of the same partnerlink type. Because of this limitation, we decided not to use this mechanism of BPEL. Instead, we introduce the semantic invocation service (SISi). Each time a web service

should be discovered at runtime, SISi is called. The following sub-section explains in detail the architecture and interface design of SISi.

Semantic Invocation Service (SISi)

A central component of our solution to semantic web service discovery during process execution is the semantic invocation service (SISi). Figure 4 sketches its software architecture. It can be seen that we use a classical layered software architecture (see e. g. Hofmeister, Nord, & Soni, 2000) consisting of three layers. We provide a reference implementation of SISi as Open Source (Stamber, Stein, & El Kharbili, 2008).

The top layer consists of the External Interface Component exposing SISi' functionality to external users. Currently, we only provide a Web Service Interface Module. This module consists primarily of code generated with the Apache Axis2 web service framework. The web service interface is used by the BPEL process server to invoke SISi. SISi itself uses the web service interface module to invoke the discovered web service.

The actual application logic of SISi is available in the Core Component. The central Controller Module receives the semantic service discovery

Figure 4. Architecture of the semantic invocation service (SISi)

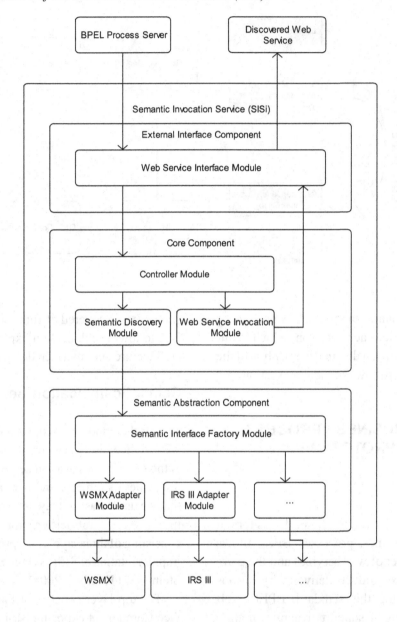

request and uses the Semantic Discovery Module to initiate the discovery. In a second step, the controller module uses the Web Service Invocation Module to call the discovered web service. Both modules used by the controller are rather small in the current implementation. They mainly forward the requests to the other components of SISi. However, we decided to include the modules anyway to ensure extensibility to full future

requirements. For example, if data mediation is required in a future version, this can be added to the semantic discovery module without having to change the controller.

The bottom layer called Semantic Abstraction Component provides access to the semantic discovery components. Even though there are preliminary efforts[5] to standardise such components in a reference architecture, we are not aware of any widely accepted standard. Therefore, an individual adapter module is required for each semantic discovery component to be supported. The current implementation contains only an adapter module for WSMX. All adapter modules must implement the same set of interface operations so that they can be used transparently through the Semantic Interface Factory Module. This approach gives us great flexibility, because any specifics of the different semantic discovery components to be supported are implemented in a single module.

Figure 5 shows the input consumed and the output produced by SISi. In order to perform its task, SISi needs the semantic description, which is a WSMO goal in our case, and it needs the input message for the web service to be invoked. As a result, SISi returns the message it received from the invoked web service. As SISi cannot foresee which web service will be found and invoked, it cannot provide an operation with parameters as the discovered web service has.

The code snippet in Figure 6 shows the WSDL definition of SISi and Figure 7 shows the belonging data definition of the different message parts. It can be seen that the input message consists of two parts {the semantic description and the message to be forwarded to the discovered web service). Currently, the type of the message part for the semantic description is just a plain string. On the other hand, we do not know what type is required for the input message of the discovered web service. Therefore, we use a hash map, which

can contain objects of any type. The output message of SISi consists only of one message part. This message part transports the message received from the discovered and invoked web service back to the calling BPEL process. Again, as we do not know the format of this message, we also use a hash map able to store a collection of objects of any type.

Execution Principle

In order to execute the generated process, a special execution environment is required, in which SISi is just one part of it. Additionally, the landscape includes an orchestration engine for executing the generated BPEL process, as well as a web service engine hosting the involved web services. Furthermore, also a semantic reasoner is needed for discovering the web services based on the given semantic descriptions. The overall system landscape and the underlying execution principle can be found in Figure 8. The execution of the BPEL process works as follows:

1. The BPEL process is executed on a standard orchestration engine. Whenever a semantically annotated function is found, the request is forwarded to SISi.

2. SISi receives the semantic discovery request. Besides the semantic description, SISi also takes the needed input parameters. SISi passes the semantic description to the semantic reasoner.

Figure 5. Input consumed and output produced by SISi

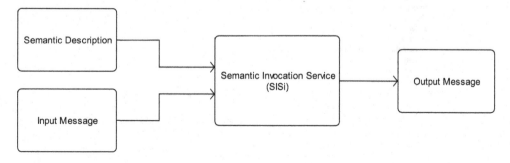

Figure 6. WSDL definition of the semantic invocation service (SISi)

```
<?xml version="1.0" encoding="utf-8"?>
<wsdl:definitions name="WebServiceInterfaceWS"
targetNamespace="http://sisi.externalinterface/"
 xmlns:wsdl="http://schemas.xmlsoap.org/wsdl/"
 xmlns:tns="http://sisi.externalinterface/"
 xmlns:dataNs="http://sisi.externalinterface/dataTypes"
 xmlns:xsd="http://www.w3.org/2001/XMLSchema">
 <wsdl:types>
  <schema xmlns="http://www.w3.org/2001/XMLSchema">
   <import namespace="http://sisi.externalinterface/dataTypes"
    schemaLocation="SISi_WebServiceInterface_dataTypes.xsd"/>
  </schema>
 </wsdl:types>
 <wsdl:message name="invokeSemanticWebServiceRequest">
  <wsdl:part name="semanticDescription" element="xsd:string"/>
  <wsdl:part name="parameters" element="dataNs:hashMap"/>
 </wsdl:message>
 <wsdl:message name="invokeSemanticWebServiceResponse">
  <wsdl:part name="parameters" element="dataNs:hashMap"/>
 </wsdl:message>
 <wsdl:portType name="WebServiceInterfaceWS">
  <wsdl:operation name="invokeSemanticWebService">
   <wsdl:input message="invokeSemanticWebServiceRequest"/>
   <wsdl:output message="invokeSemanticWebServiceResponse"/>
  </wsdl:operation>
 </wsdl:portType>
</wsdl:definitions>
```

3. The reasoner uses semantic discovery algorithms to find matching semantic web service descriptions. The best fitting web service description is selected and passed back to SISi

4. SISi uses the semantic web service description and finds through the included grounding information the underlying concrete web service implementation. Then, this web service is invoked with the input parameters received in the second step.

Figure 7. Data definition of the semantic invocation service (SISi)

```
<xsd:schema xmlns:xsd="http://www.w3.org/2001/XMLSchema"
 xmlns:tns="http://sisi.externalinterface/dataTypes">
 <xsd:complexType name="hashMap">
  <xsd:complexContent>
   <xsd:extension base="map">
    <xsd:sequence/>
   </xsd:extension>
  </xsd:complexContent>
 </xsd:complexType>
 <xsd:complexType name="map">
  <xsd:sequence>
   <xsd:element name="mapEntry" type="mapEntry" minOccurs="0"
    maxOccurs="unbounded"/>
  </xsd:sequence>
 </xsd:complexType>
 <xsd:complexType name="mapEntry">
  <xsd:sequence>
   <xsd:element name="key" type="xsd:anyType"/>
   <xsd:element name="value" type="xsd:anyType"/>
  </xsd:sequence>
 </xsd:complexType>
</xsd:schema>
```

5. The web service is executed and the output data returned to SISi.
6. SISi forwards the output back to the BPEL process.

CASE STUDY

Overview

It is the aim of the case study to evaluate sBPM in a real-world setting. Therefore, the prototype described in the previous sections together with a business process model taken from an existing company is used. The business process used is introduced in the following sub-section. A tutorial explaining the necessary steps was provided to the participants. This semantic tutorial is described in sub-section 6.3. The case study was conducted by 17 individuals from 8 different organisations. A description of the participants can be found in sub-section 6.4.

After the participants conducted the tutorial using the sBPM prototype, they were interviewed. Details about those interviews along with the questionnaire used can be found in sub-section 6.5.

VoIP Activation Process at Telekomunikacja Polska

The business process used in the semantic tutorial was contributed by Telekomunikacja Polska (TP - http://www.tp.pl/). Telekomunikacja Polska Group is the dominant player in the Polish telecommunications market serving 10.6 million fixed-line subscribers and over 12 million mobile customers, as of Q1/2007, employing about 28.000 people.

The voice-over-IP (VoIP) ordering business process was used in the tutorial, because it is a rather complex one involving internal and external parties. The business process is illustrated in Figure 9 using a simplified EPC notation. Most events and all semantic annotations were removed from the process model so that it fits on one page.

The VoIP ordering process allows TP's customers to order the VoIP service for an existing contract. The ordering process is initiated by the customer through TP's web portal. After identifying the customer, the process first checks if all technical and formal requirements are fulfilled. A new order is created, which must be confirmed by

Figure 8. System architecture

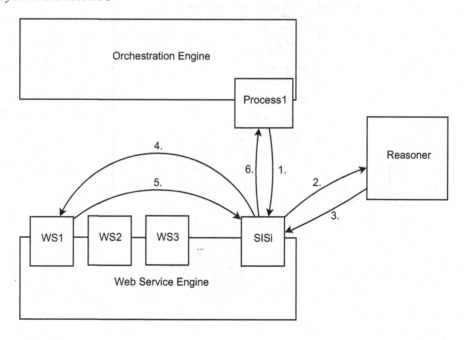

Figure 9. VoIP ordering process at Telekomunikacja Polska

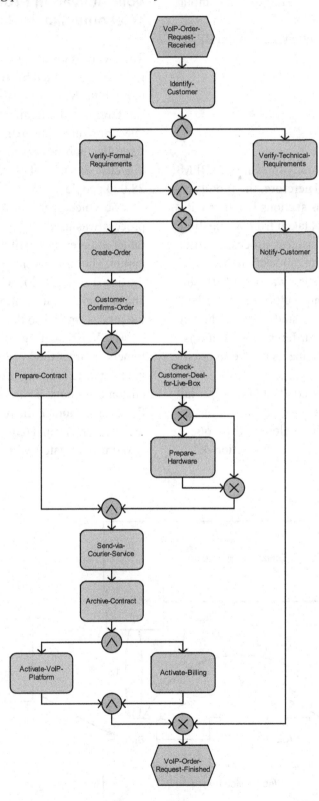

the customer. A check is run to see if the customer already has the necessary hardware. If not, the hardware is sent together with the contract to the customer. After TP receives the signed contract, the contract is archived, the billing system is activated, and finally the VoIP service is activated.

Semantic Tutorial

A tutorial describing the necessary steps using the prototype was provided to the participants. This tutorial is a written document and a modelling database for ARIS. The tutorial starts with describing the domain ontology and the business process to be annotated semantically. Afterwards, it provides a step-by-step instruction to first annotate the business process with WSMO goals, second to complete the data flow, third to transform the business process into an executable one, and finally how the business process is executed. Each part of the tutorial is illustrated by one example, i. e. it is explained how to annotate the first function in the business process. Annotating the remaining functions is the task of the participant and no further guidance is available in the tutorial. The tutorial does not include any descriptions about semantics.

Participants

There are participants from different organisations. Table 1 shows the different types of organisations, how many organisations of each type participated, how often the case study was done, and how many people took part. Research consulting institutes are research institutes, which are not solely enhanced through the public, but also other commercial consulting services.

A typical example is the German Fraunhofer institutes. We distinguish between university and university of applied sciences, because the latter one focuses on practical application in contrast to theoretical education. None of the participants took part in preparing any parts of the technologies

used in this case study. We provided no additional material for background reading to the participants besides the semantic tutorial. We paid special attention that participants do not get aware of our own preconception of sBPM and the case study propositions. The questionnaire used is discussed in the following sub-section.

Questionnaire

After the participants conducted the tutorial, we gathered their experience through semi-structured interviews with 18 open-ended questions. The interviewees were asked to describe what they have done, how non-semantic and semantic approach differ, and to reflect on the usage of semantics. At the beginning of each interview, we elaborated on the background of our research effort and explained that the interview results are made anonymous and not publicly available assuring privacy. We emphasised that we are not trying to prove or disprove semantics as beneficial. We encouraged participants to ask questions. The interviews were not recorded but instead conducted by two researchers. One researcher led the interview and the other researcher focused on taking notes. Each interviewer wrote a small summary immediately after the interview and both summaries were then exchanged. We also collected work artefacts such as the semantically annotated business process models so that we have multiple sources of evidence Yin (2003). Some interviews were conducted as group interviews with two or three participants. Therefore, there is a higher number of participants than interviews.

The questionnaire is shown below. Questions were rephrased if necessary. Also, we skipped questions if the interviewee already provided an answer earlier during the interview.

1. Do you have any questions how the interview is conducted or about the background of the research?

Table 1. Participants

Type of Organisation	Organisations	Interviews	Participants
Research Consulting Institute	2	2	3
University	1	2	2
University of Applied Sciences	2	4	4
Company	3	5	8
Sum	8	13	17

2. To start with, we like to ask you to describe briefly what you did in the tutorial.

3. You mentioned the term semantic description. How do you understand this term?

4. How do you define the term ontology?

5. During the tutorial a domain ontology is provided. Did you use the domain ontology while conducting the tutorial?

6. The domain ontology is available in the tutorial in different representations. Which representation did you use and why?

7. How does assigning a service for a function work in the tutorial?

8. How is a semantic description represented in the tutorial? (or: What is a goal and what does it comprises?)

9. During the tutorial you had to select a semantic description to annotate the functions in the business process. Where you confident to have selected the correct semantic description?

10. Did you made use of the pre-/post-conditions defined while selecting a semantic description?

11. In a first step during the tutorial you did something about data. Can you explain what you have done there and why?

12. If you take a look at the overall semantic approach, what is in your opinion the main different between the semantic approach and the non-semantic approach embedded in ARIS?

13. Can you motivate dynamic service binding? Is it relevant in industry?

14. Do you think that the semantic approach has any advantages compared to a non-semantic approach? Why?

15. Do you think the semantic approach is feasible for a business analyst used to EPC modelling?

16. How long did you need to conduct the semantic tutorial?

17. Where you able to follow the descriptions in the tutorial or was something missing?

18. Thank you for participating in the tutorial. We would like to take a look at the modelling database used during the tutorial. Would you please be so kind to send us this database?

RESULTS AND DISCUSSION

Overview

This section presents the case study results and a discussion of the outcomes. The results are not just observed facts, but also a summary of the discussions with the participants. This section is structured around the main interview points and the most interesting discussions we had. The answers between participants from the different types of organisation were consistent if not discussed otherwise. Before the results are presented, a discussion on the general limitations of the study is done first.

Limitations of Study

Scientific rigor requires openly discussing the limitations of the research done. For example, we have only done one particular study in one particular domain. Therefore, we cannot claim that the results found are also valid for other domains, where sBPM can be applied to. Therefore, the results presented in the following sub-sections are meant as research hypothesis, which must be investigated in detail with further research. Creating new research hypothesis is a typical outcome of explorative studies as done here.

Another limitation of the study is related to the sBPM prototype. Of course this sBPM prototype only has limited functionality and therefore no general evaluation of sBPM is possible. For example, participants have to specify the mapping between ontological input and output instances. In a more advanced solution, semantic data mediation could be used freeing the participants from this task. A similar limitation is related to the business process used in the case study. It can be questioned if implementing this business process requires dynamic service binding during process execution. We tried to overcome such limitations by asking participants to focus on the underlying principle of sBPM and to not focus too much on the specifics of the prototype and example business process. We are convinced that our case study reveals some interesting insights, which might inspire new research studies.

Understanding Semantics

At the beginning of each interview, we asked participants to summarise the different steps of the tutorial. Most participants were able to name the steps and their order. During this summary, most of them used the word "semantic". We asked them how they understand semantics and how they define the term ontology.

All participants said a semantic description is not a technical one, but instead business oriented.

Interestingly, some of the participants said that a semantic description defines only what needs to be done but not how to achieve it. None of the participants provided one of the popular definitions of ontology like "shared conceptualisation". Instead, all participants tried to describe what an ontology is. Almost all participants pointed out that an ontology is a collection of terms, concepts or classes. Some of them used the term "glossary" or "taxonomy", but only a few called an ontology a "namespace", a "domain", a "classification" or a "domain specific language". Some participants pointed out that an ontology not only defines terms, but also relations between them. For example, one participant said an ontology describes "what exists and how everything is related to each other" and another said it is a "model of the world". One participant pointed out that an ontology standardises the vocabulary used. Interestingly, some participants also talked about "business cases" while actually referring to concepts. However, only a few pointed out that an ontology is processable by machines.

None of the participants seemed to be comfortable with the term "ontology", because the term is not known from daily language usage, and seems artificial to them. We therefore conclude that one should not use the term ontology while talking to business experts, but instead, should talk about "semantics" or "semantic descriptions". To give a more detailed definition, one should talk about a glossary of business terms, which also has detailed relations between terms in contrast to ordinary glossaries. One should also point out that semantic descriptions of services are business oriented, processable by computers, and used to describe what needs to be done, and not how it should be implemented.

Getting Familiar with the Domain

At the beginning of the semantic tutorial, the domain ontology developed by TP was presented to the reader. All participants confirmed to have studied the domain ontology at the beginning of the tutorial, but only a few of them used it later. The example process was still simple enough to understand and the terminology used was also known to the participants, who proved to be experienced in BPM, because they were familiar with similar business processes. Many participants pointed out that it is unclear where the domain ontology comes from and who creates it. The domain ontology was only available in the printed tutorial, but it was not part of the tool. This was confusing for some participants, because they expected the ontology to be present in the tool, too. Many of them pointed out that for more complex ontologies an "ontology browser" is required to allow easy navigation between the different concepts. We conclude that having a domain ontology is useful even if no other semantic technologies are used. Such an ontology must be integrated in the business process modelling tool allowing easy usage and navigation.

Visualisation of Ontologies

The domain ontology was presented in three different ways to the participants: first a "star" of the main concepts generated by WSMO Studio, second a UML class diagram with a class for each concept plus the belonging attributes and the main relations, and third the WSML code.

If participants were familiar with UML modelling like the participants not working in a company, they found the UML class diagram most useful. Participants said that the UML class diagram contains far more information compared to the star diagram. If participants were not familiar with UML, they preferred the star, because it provides an easy to understand overview of the domain ontology. All participants said the WSML code is not useful and readable. Some of them noted that it might be possible to understand the WSML syntax after training, but that it is definitely not useful for business experts. One participating business

expert confirmed that by saying he refuses to look at "something" like the WSML code.

We conclude that a graphical representation along with a textual description of a domain ontology is required. Probably several graphical representations are necessary allowing the user to select the preferred one. Again, the graphical visualisation of the domain ontology should be part of the business process modelling tool.

Selecting WSMO Goals

One important step of the tutorial was selecting a goal for each function. For this purpose, we provided the prototypical goal selection dialog shown in Figure 2. It turned out that all participants just identified the name of the WSMO goal in the WSML code and based their decision mostly on the name. Only a few of them looked at additional details of the goal description such as pre-/post-conditions. However, most participants recognised they must use the pre-/post-conditions when goal selection is ambiguous.

Most participants were not satisfied with goal selection. Many pointed out that browsing a list of goals does not scale and more advanced search mechanisms are required. A participant suggested that it must be possible to filter the list of goals based on concepts taken from the ontology. Another participant proposed using the pre-/post-conditions as filter criteria, e. g. just showing those goals able to produce a defined state (i. e. post-condition). It was also suggested to add a graphical representation for each goal. One participant suggested the visualisation shown in Figure 10. According to this participant, it is important to include the different description parts such as capabilities and conditions always in the same place so that necessary information can be identified quickly.

We conclude that goal selection is an important part and must be supported by a sophisticated tool. This requirement is amplified, because some participants pointed out that they cannot see any advantage compared to selecting a web service directly. Therefore, research should focus on ways to graphically visualise goals and semantic description and evaluate the usefulness through empirical experiments.

Completing the Data Flow

After selecting a goal, participants completed the data flow by mapping output instances of a function to input instances of a later function. Even though all participants were able to complete this step, some concerns were raised. Participants pointed out that input/output instances are similar to technical data descriptions, whereas business objects are used in business process modelling, which is a conceptual data definition. According to participants, those two concepts are not interchangeable, because a business object is expected to be always persistent whereas a variable must be stored in a data store explicitly. Both concepts are not on the same level of abstraction, because business objects are a more abstract (i. e. conceptual) view on data in contrast to ontological input/output instances. This is an interesting point, which must be further investigated. It seems that ontological instances defined by WSMO goals are not abstract enough to be useful in business process modelling.

Motivating Service Binding During Runtime

We asked participants to motivate dynamic service binding during process execution. We received a diverse set of answers with no clear conclusion. However, some answers proved that in contrast to our case study proposition some participants were able to motivate service binding during runtime. We explicitly asked participants for an economic motivation. If they provided such a motivation, they often mentioned failover scenarios. In our opinion, this problem can be already solved today

with enterprise service bus (ESB) platforms, but we did not confront participants with our point of view. Participants said that instead of hard coding an endpoint URL into the executable process, only the service name is added to the process. This helps in case the service is moved to another server. Again, this seems to be a case where today's technologies such as service registries (e. g. based on UDDI) can be applied.

Some participants noted dynamic service binding only makes sense if there are several services for each goal. If there is only a 1:1 relation between service and goal, participants were not able to justify dynamic service binding. Participants with research background also pointed out that dynamic service binding in a company might not be as relevant as e. g. in ubiquitous computing, because a company is able to better control and govern the portfolio of services. Other participants mentioned dynamic service binding is dangerous, because it adds a new error source and increases the complexity of the enterprise computing stack. This shows there is no consensus whether dynamic service binding is necessary in business process automation.

Advantages and Disadvantages of Semantic Approach

We asked participants about advantages and disadvantages of the semantic approach. Surprisingly, most of them mentioned a better separation of business and IT as the main advantage of the semantic approach, because the business process model is not polluted with technical details such as web service descriptions. Instead, the business expert only specifies the required capabilities. This helps business experts to concentrate on the business relevant part of process modelling instead of dealing with implementation details. It also allows using not yet existing services. In addition, technical service descriptions (WSDL) do not have to be available in the business process modelling tool, which prevents redundancy. Participants

Figure 10. Participant contribution: graphical representation of a WSMO goal

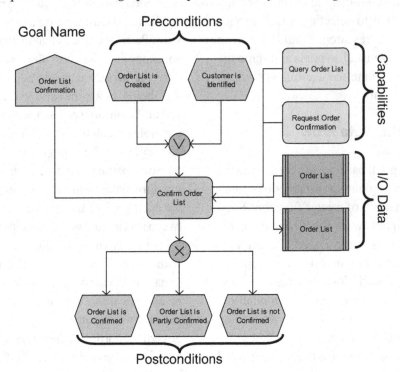

characterised the semantic approach as creating a process template, which can be flexibly enacted, because the business process model only specifies what has to be done but not how to do it. Some participants mentioned the possibility of dynamic service binding as an advantage, but there was no consensus about that as discussed before.

A significant problem is the conceptual mismatch between business objects and ontological input/output instances. Besides, several participants were not convinced that the investment in semantics will pay off, because ontologies must be defined and maintained. Some participants were reluctant about ontology modelling, because in their opinion similar efforts such as establishing an enterprise data model failed in the past. Such concerns are also raised by Hepp (2007) and must be taken into account. All participants agreed that business experts are not able to create ontologies and goals. Graphical tools are required to overcome hurdles like WSML syntax and logical expressions. Using semantics might require

having ontology engineers, which is a specific qualification. In general, the learning curve is increased, because semantics bring their own set of technologies, methods, and methodologies along. Also, the complexity of the enterprise computing stack is increased, which augments the probability of introducing errors and integration problems. Many participants pointed to the unbalanced distribution of efforts and benefits for using semantics as another major disadvantage. Ontologies, goals, and semantic descriptions must be defined by IT after consulting business experts, but those artefacts mainly help business people. This discrepancy must be carefully managed to ensure close cooperation between all involved parties.

Feasibility of Semantic Approach for Business Experts

We asked participants whether the semantic approach is possible to follow for business experts.

Most of them agreed that it is feasible, but they also mentioned potential problems. Currently, technology is still too visible. For example, WSML code should not be shown and ontological input/output instances must be lifted to a more abstract level. Ontologies and goals used must exist upfront, because currently it is impossible for business experts to define and modify them on their own. Besides the tooling issues, a solution must be found to provide incentives to those who have to create the semantic descriptions.

Some participants were surprised that they were asked to annotate functions with semantic descriptions. They believed that a business process model already contains enough information. Those participants envisioned a more advanced way of using semantics in BPM. For example, one participant desired to have a repository of semantically described process fragments. Instead of defining the control flow of the business process, the participant expected to just define the pre- and post-conditions as well as constraints and the control flow would be automatically created by an "intelligent component". This vision of sBPM seems to be similar with what van der Aalst and Pesic (van der Aalst & Pesic, 2006) propose as Declarative Service Flow (DecSerFlow) language. Instead of defining a fixed control flow, the flow is declaratively defined allowing a more flexible enactment. It will be interesting to see if such visionary approaches to sBPM will gain momentum.

SUMMARY

This chapter presented the evaluation of semantic business process management through an empirical case study. First, sBPM was introduced and it was shown how semantics might improve BPM. The literature review conducted showed that most sBPM research focuses on designing new representational formalisms and overall approaches. However, empirical evaluation of the new concepts introduced by sBPM has been largely ignored until

now. A research design was presented, seeking to overcome this lack of evaluation by conducting an empirical case study. The case study is based on a sBPM prototype, which builds on the combination of a semantic extension of a leading business process modelling tool and a semantic business process execution environment. After describing the prototype, the case study using this prototype was described and a discussion of the results was presented.

The case study shows that practitioners see advantages in sBPM. However, many obstacles have been identified that still need to be overcome such as having better tool support for the individual steps involved in an sBPM initiative, but also solving some conceptual problems. The results cannot be generalised, because only one single case study with one specific business process was conducted. Still, the work presented reveals first problems, which must be tackled in order to pass initial acceptance barriers and make sBPM successful. We encourage other researchers to support this research work by further investigating the found issues to make sBPM successful.

REFERENCES

Abramowicz, W., Filipowska, A., Kaczmarek, M., & Kaczmarek, T. (2007). Semantically enhanced business process modelling notation. In M. Hepp, K. Hinkelmann, D. Karagiannis, R. Klein & N. Stojanovic (Eds.), *Workshop on semantic business process and product lifecycle management (SBPM)* (Vol. 251, pp. 88-91). CEUR Workshop Proceedings, Innsbruck, Austria.

Alexakis, S., Bauer, M., Pace, A., Schumacher, A., Friesen, A., Bouras, A., & Kourtesis, D. (2007). Application of the fusion approach for assisted composition of Web services. In *8th IFIP Working Conference on Virtual Enterprises (PRO-VE)* (Vol. 243/2007, pp. 531-538). IFIP International Federation for Information Processing, Guimarães, Portugal. Springer.

Alves de Medeiros, A. K., Pedrinaci, C., van der Aalst, W. M. P., Domingue, J., Song, M., Rozinat, A., et al. (2007). An outlook on semantic business process mining and monitoring. In *On the Move to Meaningful Internet Systems 2007: OTM 2007 Workshops*. (LNCS 4806, pp. 1244-1255). Vilamoura, Portugal: Springer.

Blechar, M. (2007). *Magic quadrant for business process analysis market*. Gartner.

Bouras, A., Gouvas, P., Kourtesis, D., & Mentzas, G. (2007). Semantic integration of business applications across collaborative value networks. In *8th IFIP Working Conference on Virtual Enterprises (PRO-VE)* (Vol. 243/2007, pp. 539-546). IFIP International Federation for Information Processing, Guimarães, Portugal. Springer.

Bouras, A., Gouvas, P., & Mentzas, G. (2007). ENIO: An enterprise application integration ontology. In *1st International Workshop on Semantic Web Architectures for Enterprises in conjunction with 18th International Conference on Database and Expert Systems Applications (DEXA)* (pp. 419-423). Regensburg, Germany.

Celino, I., Alves de Medeiros, A. K., Zeissler, G., Oppitz, M., Facca, F., & Zoeller, S. (2007). Semantic business process analysis. In M. Hepp, K. Hinkelmann, D. Karagiannis, R. Klein & N. Stojanovic (Eds.), *Workshop on Semantic Business Process and Product Lifecycle Management (SBPM)* (Vol. 251, pp. 44-47). CEUR Workshop Proceedings, Innsbruck, Austria.

Creswell, J. W. (2002). *Research design: Qualitative, quantitative, and mixed method approaches* (2nd ed.). Thousand Oaks: Sage Publications.

Dehnert, J., & van der Aalst, W. M. P. (2004). Bridging the gap between business models and workflow specifications. *International Journal of Cooperative Information Systems, 13*(3), 289–332. doi:10.1142/S0218843004000973

Deming, W. E. (1982). *Out of the crisis*. MIT Press.

Dimitrov, M., Simov, A., Stein, S., & Konstantinov, M. (2007). A BPMO based semantic business process modelling environment. In M. Hepp, K. Hinkelmann, D. Karagiannis, R. Klein & N. Stojanovic (Eds.), *Workshop on Semantic Business Process and Product Lifecycle Management (SBPM)* (Vol. 251, pp. 101-104). CEUR Workshop Proceedings, Innsbruck, Austria.

El Kharbili, M., Stein, S., Markovic, I., & Pulvermüller, E. (2008). Towards a framework for semantic business process compliance management. In *The Impact of Governance, Risk, and Compliance on Information Systems (GRCIS)* (Vol. 339, pp. 1-15). CEUR Workshop Proceedings, Montpellier, France.

Fensel, D., Lausen, H., Polleres, A., de Bruijn, J., Stollberg, M., Roman, D., & Domingue, J. (2006). *Enabling Semantic Web services: The Web service modeling ontology*. Springer.

Filipowska, A., Kaczmarek, M., & Stein, S. (2008). Semantically annotated EPC within semantic business process management. In *Workshop on Advances in Semantics for Web Services (semantics4ws)*. Milan, Italy.

Hepp, M. (2007). Possible ontologies: How reality constrains the development of relevant ontologies. *IEEE Internet Computing, 11*(1), 90–96. doi:10.1109/MIC.2007.20

Hepp, M., Leymann, F., Domingue, J., Wahler, A., & Fensel, D. (2005). Semantic business process management: A vision towards using Semantic Web services for business process management. In *IEEE International Conference on e-Business Engineering (ICEBE)* (pp. 535-540). Beijing, China.

Hepp, M., & Roman, D. (2007). An ontology framework for semantic business process management. In *8th International Conference Wirtschaftsinformatik* (pp. 423-440). Karlsruhe, Germany.

Hevner, A. R., March, S. T., Park, J., & Ram, S. (2004). Design science in information systems research. *MIS Quarterly, 28*(1), 75–105.

Hofmeister, C., Nord, R., & Soni, D. (2000). *Applied software architecture* (2nd ed.). MA: Addison-Wesley.

Kitchenham, B., Pickard, L., & Peeger, S. L. (1995). Case studies for method and tool evaluation. *IEEE Software, 12*(4), 52–62. doi:10.1109/52.391832

Koehler, J., Hauser, R., Sendall, S., & Wahler, M. (2005). Declarative techniques for model-driven business process integration. *IBM Systems Journal, 44*(1), 47–65.

Markovic, I., & Kowalkiewicz, M. (2008). Linking business goals to process models in semantic business process modeling. In *12th IEEE International EDOC Conference*. Munich, Germany.

Martin, D., Burstein, M., Hobbs, J., Lassila, O., McDermott, D., McIlraith, S., Narayanan, S., Paolucci, M., Parsia, B., Payne, T., Sirin, E., Srinivasan, N., & Sycara, K. (2004). *OWL-S: Semantic markup for Web services. World Wide Web Consortium (W3C)*.

Nitzsche, J., Wutke, D., & van Lessen, T. (2007). An ontology for executable business processes. In M. Hepp, K. Hinkelmann, D. Karagiannis, R. Klein & N. Stojanovic (Eds.), *Workshop on Semantic Business Process and Product Lifecycle Management (SBPM)* (Vol. 251, pp. 52-63). CEUR Workshop Proceedings, Innsbruck, Austria.

OMG. (2006, February). *Business process modeling notation (BPMN) specification*. Object Management Group (OMG).

Pedrinaci, C., Brelage, C., van Lessen, T., Domingue, J., Karastoyanova, D., & Leymann, F. (2008). Semantic business process management: Scaling up the management of business processes. In *2nd IEEE International Conference on Semantic Computing (ICSC)*, Santa Clara, CA.

Peyret, H. (2007). *The Forrester wave: Enterprise architecture tools, Q2*. Forrester.

Scheer, A. W. (2002). *ARIS-Vom geschäftsprozess zum anwendungssystem*. Berlin: Springer.

Scheer, A. W., Thomas, O., & Adam, O. (2005). Process modelling using event-driven process chains. In M. Dumas, W. M. P. van der Aalst & A. H. M. ter Hofstede (Eds.), *Process-Aware Information Systems* (pp. 119-146). NJ: Wiley.

Schmelzer, H. J., & Sesselmann, W. (2008). Geschäftsprozessm in der praxis (6th ed.). München: Carl Hanser Verlag.

Smith, H., & Fingar, P. (2003). Business process management: The third wave (1st ed.). Tampa, FL: Meghan-Kiffer Press.

Stamber, C., Stein, S., & El Kharbili, M. (2008). Prototypical implementation of a pragmatic approach to Semantic Web service discovery during process execution. In W. Abramowicz & D. Fensel (Eds.), *11th International Conference on Business Information Systems (BIS)* (Vol. 7, pp. 201-212). LNBIP, Innsbruck, Austria.

Stein, S., Kühne, S., & Ivanov, K. (2008). Business to IT transformations revisited. In *1st International Workshop on Model-Driven Engineering for Business Process Management (MDE4BPM)*, Milan, Italy.

van der Aalst, W. M. P., & Pesic, M. (2006). Decserflow: Towards a truly declarative service flow language. Eindhoven, The Netherlands: BPM-06-21, BPM Center.

van Lessen, T., Nitzsche, J., Dimitrov, M., Konstantinov, M., Karastoyanova, D., & Cekov, L. (2007). An execution engine for semantic business processes. In *2nd International Workshop on Business Oriented Aspects concerning Semantics and Methodologies in Service oriented Computing (SeMSoC)*.

von Bertalanffy, L. (1976). *General system theory*. New York: Braziller Inc.

Weske, M. (2007). *Business process management: Concepts, languages, architectures*. Berlin: Springer.

Wilde, T., & Hess, T. (2007). Forschungsmethoden der wirtschaftsinformatik-eine empirische untersuchung. *Wirtschaftsinformatik, 49*(4), 280–287. doi:10.1007/s11576-007-0064-z

Yin, R. K. (2003). Case study research: Design and methods (3rd ed.). London: Sage Publications.

ENDNOTES

[1] The work published in this chapter was partially done within the SUPER research project (http://www.ip-super.org/) under the 6th EU Framework Programme Information Society Technologies Objective (contract no. FP6-026850).

[2] http://www.zifa.com and http://www.zachmaninternational.com.

3http://www.archimate.org/.

[4] http://www.wsmostudio.org/.

[5] http://www.oasis-open.org/committees/tchome.php?wg abbrev=semantic-ex

Compilation of References

Aalst, W. M. P., Beisiegel, M., Hee, K. M. V., Konig, D., & Stahl, C. (2007). An SOA-based architecture framework. *International Journal of Business Process Integration and Management, 2*(2), 91–101. doi:10.1504/IJBPIM.2007.015132

Aalst, W. M. P., Hofstede, A. H. M., Kiepusze-wski, B., & Barros, A. P. (2003). Workflow patterns. *Distributed and Parallel Databases, 14*(1), 5–51. doi:10.1023/A:1022883727209

Abramowicz, W., Filipowska, A., Kaczmarek, M., & Kaczmarek, T. (2007). Semantically enhanced business process modelling notation. In M. Hepp, K. Hinkelmann, D. Karagiannis, R. Klein & N. Stojanovic (Eds.), *Workshop on semantic business process and product lifecycle management (SBPM)* (Vol. 251, pp. 88-91). CEUR Workshop Proceedings, Innsbruck, Austria.

Akkiraju, R., Farrell, J., Miller, J., Nagarajan, M., Schmidt, M., Sheth, A., et al. (2005). *WSDL-S: Web service semantics. W3C member submission.*

Akkiraju, R., Goodwin, R., Doshi, P., & Roeder, S. (2003). A method for semantically enhancing the service discovery capabilities of UDDI. *Workshop on Information Integration on the Web,* Acapulco, Mexico.

Alazeib, A. (Ed.). (2007). *D1.2 The FUSION approach (FUSION).* Retrieved on December 8, 2008, from http://www.fusionweb.org/Fusion/download/download.asp

Alazeib, A., Balogh, A., Bauer, M., Bouras, A., Friesen, A., Gouvas, P., et al. (2007). Towards semantically-assisted design of collaborative business processes in EAI scenarios. *5th IEEE International Conference on Industrial Informatics (INDIN 2007)* (pp. 779-784). Vienna, Austria.

Alexakis, S., Bauer, M., Pace, A., Schumacher, A., Friesen, A., Bouras, A., & Kourtesis, D. (2007). Application of the fusion approach for assisted composition of Web services. In *8th IFIP Working Conference on Virtual Enterprises (PRO-VE)* (Vol. 243/2007, pp. 531-538). IFIP International Federation for Information Processing, Guimarães, Portugal. Springer.

Allen, R., & Garlan, D. (1997). A formal basis for architectural connection. *ACM Transactions on Software Engineering and Methodology, 6*(3), 213–249. doi:10.1145/258077.258078

Alonso, G., Casati, F., Kuno, H., & Machiraju, V. (2004). *Web services–concepts, architectures, and applications.* Berlin, Germany: Springer-Verlag.

Alves de Medeiros, A. K., Pedrinaci, C., van der Aalst, W. M. P., Domingue, J., Song, M., Rozinat, A., et al. (2007). An outlook on semantic business process mining and monitoring. In *On the Move to Meaningful Internet Systems 2007: OTM 2007 Workshops.* (LNCS 4806, pp. 1244-1255). Vilamoura, Portugal: Springer.

Alves, A., Arkin, A., Askary, S., Barreto, C., Bloch, B., Curbera, F., et al. (2007). *Web services business process execution language version 2.0.* OASIS Standard.

Amadeus. (2007). Retrieved from http://www.amadeus.com/

Anicic, N., Ivezic, N., & Jones, A. (2006). An architecture for semantic enterprise application integration standards. In D. Konstantas, J. P. Bourrières, M. Léonard & N. Boudjlida (Eds.), *Interoperability of enterprise software and applications* (pp. 25-34). London: Springer-Verlag.

Anicic, N., Marjanovic, Z., Ivezic, N., & Jones, A. (2006, December 28). An Aarchitecture for Ssemantic eEnterprise Aapplication Iintegration Sstandards. *International Journal of Manufacturing Technology and Management, Volume 10*, Numbers (2-3), 28 December 2006, pp. 205-226(22).

ATHENA. (2004). Advanced technologies for interoperability of heterogeneous enterprises networks and their applications. *FP6-2002-IST-1, Integrated Project Description of Work.*

Baader, F., Calvanese, D., McGuinnes, D., Nardi, D., & Patel-Schneider, P. (2003). *The description logic handbook: Theory, implementation, and applications.* Cambridge University Press.

Baresi, L., Heckel, R., Thöne, S., & Varro, D. (2006). Style-based modeling and refinement of service-oriented architectures. *Software and Systems Modeling, 5*(2), 187–207. doi:10.1007/s10270-006-0001-4

Barrett, R., Patcas, L. M., Murphy, J., & Pahl, C. (2006). Model driven distribution pattern design for dynamic Web service compositions. In *International Conference on Web Engineering ICWE06* (pp. 129-136). Palo Alto: ACM Press.

Bass, L., Clements, P., & Kazman, R. (2003). *Software architecture in practice* (2nd edition). *SEI Series in Software Engineering*. Boston, MA: Addison-Wesley.

Bellifemine, F., Bergenti, F., Caire, G., & Poggi, A. (2005). JADE-a java agent development framework. In R. Bordini, M. Dastani, D. J., & A. El Fallah Seghrouchni (Eds.), *Multiagent programming: Languages, platforms, and applications, volume 15 of multiagent aystems, artificial societies, and simulated organizations* (pp. 125–147). Berlin, et al.: Springer.

Benatallah, B., Casati, F., Grigori, D., Motahari-Nezhad, H., & Toumani, F. (2005). Developing adapters for Web services integration. In *Proceedings of the International Conference on Advanced Information Systems Engineering (CAiSE)*, Porto, Portugal (pp. 415-429). Springer Verlag.

Benguria, G., Larrucea, X., Elvesæter, B., Neple, T., Beardsmore, A., & Friess, M. (2006). A platform independent model for service oriented architectures. In *2nd International Conference on Interoperability of Enterprise Software and Applications (I-ESA 2006)*.

Bennett, K. (1995, January). Legacy systems. *IEEE Software*, 19–73. doi:10.1109/52.363157

Berardi, D., Calvanese, D., Giacomo, G. D., Hull, R., & Mecella, M. (2005). Automatic composition of transition-based Semantic Web services with messaging. In K. Böhm, C. S. Jensen, L. M. Haas, M. L. Kersten, P.-Å. Larson & B. C. Ooi (Eds.), *VLDB* (pp. 613–624). ACM. ISBN 1-59593-154-6, 1-59593-177-5

Bernstein, A., Klein, M., & Malone, T. W. (1999). The process recombinator: A tool for generating new business process ideas. *ICIS*, 178–192.

Bernus, P., Nemes, R., & Schmidt, G. (2003). *Handbook on enterprise architecture (international handbooks on information systems)*. Heidelberg, Germany: Springer-Verlag.

Berry, M. J. A., & Linoff, G. S. (2004). *Data mining techniques*. Wiley Publishing, Inc., second edition.

Beyer, D., Chakrabarti, A., & Henzinger, T. (2005). Web service interfaces. *14th International Word Wide Web Conference (WWW 2005)* (pp. 148-159), Chiba, Japan.

Bisbal, J., Lawless, D., Wu, B., & Grimson, J. (1999). Legacy information systems: Issues and directions. *IEEE Software, 16*, 103–111. doi:10.1109/52.795108

Blake, M. B., & Gomaa, H. (2005, July). Agent-oriented compositional approaches to services-based cross-organizational workflow. *Decision Support Systems, 40*(1), 31–50. doi:10.1016/j.dss.2004.04.003

Blechar, M. (2007). *Magic quadrant for business process analysis market*. Gartner.

Bohring, H., & Auer, S. (2005). Mapping XML to OWL ontologies. *13th Leipziger Informatik-Tage Conference (LIT 2005)* (pp. 147-156).

Booth, D., Haas, H., & McCabe, F. (2004). *Web services architecture. W3C note.* Retrieved on December 8, 2008, from http://www.w3.org/TR/ws-arch/

Börger, E. (2003). The ASM refinement method. *Formal Aspects of Computing, 15,* 237–257. doi:10.1007/s00165-003-0012-7

Börger, E., & Stärk, R. F. (2003). *Abstract state machines. A method for high-level system design and analysis.* Springer.

Bouras, A., & Gouvas, P. P., & G. Mentzas, G. (2007, September 3-7). ENIO: An Eenterprise Aapplication Iintegration Oontology. In the *pProceedings of the 18th International Conference on Database and Expert Systems Applications (DEXA 2007),* 3-7 September, 2007, Regensburg, Germany, (pp. 419-423).

Bouras, A., Gouvas, P., & Mentzas, G. (2007, September). *ENIO: An enterprise application integration ontology.* Paper presented at the 1st International Workshop on Semantic Web Architectures for Enterprises (SWAE), Regensburg, Germany.

Bouras, A., Gouvas, P., Kourtesis, D., & Mentzas, G. (2007). Semantic integration of business applications across collaborative value networks. In *8th IFIP Working Conference on Virtual Enterprises (PRO-VE)* (Vol. 243/2007, pp. 539-546). IFIP International Federation for Information Processing, Guimarães, Portugal. Springer.

Bouras, T., Gouvas, P., & Mentzas, G. (2008). Dynamic data mediation in enterprise application integration. In O. Cunnigham & M. Cunnigham (Eds.), *Collaboration and the knowledge economy: Issues, applications, and case studies, e-challenges e-2008 conference* (pp. 917-924), Stockholm, Sweden.

Brodie, M., & Stonebraker, M. (1995). *Migrating legacy systems: Gateways, interfaces, and the incremental approach.* San Francisco: Morgan Kaufmann.

Bruijn, J., Bussler, C., Domingue, J., Fensel, D., Hepp, M., Keller, U., et al. (2005). *Web service modeling ontology (WSMO).* W3C member submission.

Buhler, P., & Vidal, J. M. (2005). Towards adaptive workflow enactment using multiagent systems. *Information Technology and Management Journal, Special Issue on Universal Enterprise Integration,* 61–87.

Bussler, C. (2003). The role of Semantic Web technology in enterprise application integration. *A Quarterly Bulletin of the Computer Society of the IEEE Technical Committee on Data Engineering, 26*(4), 62–68.

Buzan, B. T. (2005). *Definition of mind maps.* New York: St. Martin's Press.

Cabri, G., Leonardi, L., & Puviani, M. (2007). Service-Oriented Agent Methodologies. In *5th IEEE International Workshop on Agent-Based Computing for Enterprise Collaboration (ACEC-07).*

Casola, V., Fasolino, A. R., & Mazzocca, T. (2007). A policy-based evaluation framework for quality and security in service oriented architectures. In *Proceedings of the IEEE Conference on Web Services,* (ICWS 2007).

Celino, I., Alves de Medeiros, A. K., Zeissler, G., Oppitz, M., Facca, F., & Zoeller, S. (2007). Semantic business process analysis. In M. Hepp, K. Hinkelmann, D. Karagiannis, R. Klein & N. Stojanovic (Eds.), *Workshop on Semantic Business Process and Product Lifecycle Management (SBPM)* (Vol. 251, pp. 44-47). CEUR Workshop Proceedings, Innsbruck, Austria.

Christensen, E., Curbera, F., Meredith, G., & Weerawarana, S. (2001). *Web services description language (WSDL) version 1.1. W3C note.*

Christiaens, S., De Leenheer, P., de Moor, A., & Meersman, R. (2008). Business use case: Ontologising competencies in an interorganisational setting. In M. Hepp, P. De Leenheer, A. de Moor & Y. Sure (Eds.), *Ontology management for the Semantic Web, Semantic Web services, and business applications, from Semantic Web and beyond: Computing for human experience.* Springer.

Clement, L., Hately, A., von Riegen, C., & Rogers, T. (2004). *Universal description, discovery, and integration version 3.0.2.* OASIS Standard.

Colgrave, J., & Januszewski, K. (2004). *Using WSDL in a UDDI registry version 2.0.2. OASIS UDDI specification TC technical note.*

Colgrave, J., Akkiraju, R., & Goodwin, R. (2004). External matching in UDDI. *2004 IEEE International Conference on Web Services (ICWS'04)* (pp. 226 - 233), San Diego, CA.

Creswell, J. W. (2002). *Research design: Qualitative, quantitative, and mixed method approaches* (2nd ed.). Thousand Oaks: Sage Publications.

Curtis, B., Krasner, H., & Iscoe, N. (1988). A field study of the software design process for large systems. *Communications of the ACM, 31*(11), 1268–1287. doi:10.1145/50087.50089

Daconta, M. C., Obrst, L. J., & Smith, K. T. (2003). *The Semantic Web.* New York: Wiley.

de Bruijn, J., Bussler, C., Domingue, J., Fensel, D., Hepp, M., Keller, U., et al. (2005). *Web service modeling ontology (WSMO). W3C member submission.* Retrieved on June 3, 2005, from http://www.w3.org/Submission/WSMO/

De Leenheer, P., & Christiaens, S. (2007). Mind the gap: Transcending the tunnel vision on ontology engineering. In *Proceedings of the 2nd International Conference on the Pragmatic Web,* Tilburg, The Netherlands. ACM DL.

De Leenheer, P., & Christiaens, S. (2008). Challenges and opportunities for more meaningful and sustainable Internet systems. In *Proceedings of the First Future of the Internet Symposium,* Vienna, Austria. (LNCS). Springer-Verlag.

De Leenheer, P., & Meersman., R. (2007). Towards community-based evolution of knowledge-intensive systems. In *Proc. on the Move Federated Conferences: ODBASE (OTM 2007),* Vilamoura, Portugal. (LNCS 4803, pp. 989-1006). Springer.

De Leenheer, P., & Mens, T. (2008). Ontology evolution: State of the art and future directions. In Hepp, et al.

De Leenheer, P., De Moor, A., & Meersman, R. (2007). Context dependency management in ontology engineering: A formal approach. *Journal on Data Semantics VIII.* ([]. Springer.]. *LNCS, 4380,* 26–56.

De Moor, A., De Leenheer, P., & Meersman, R. (2006). DOGMA-MESS: A meaning evolution support system for interorganizational ontology engineering. In *Proc. of the 14th International Conference on Conceptual Structures, (ICCS 2006),* Aalborg, Denmark. (LNCS). Springer-Verlag.

Dehnert, J., & van der Aalst, W. M. P. (2004). Bridging the gap between business models and workflow specifications. *International Journal of Cooperative Information Systems, 13*(3), 289–332. doi:10.1142/S0218843004000973

Deming, W. E. (1982). *Out of the crisis.* MIT Press.

DERI Innsbruck at the Leopold-Franzens-University Innsbruck. Austria, DERI Galway at the National University of Ireland, Galway, Ireland, BT, The Open University, and SAP AG. (2005, June 3). *Web service modeling ontology (WSMO). W3C member submission.* Retrieved on January 15, 2009, from http://www.w3.org/Submission/WSMO/

Dickinson, I., & Wooldridge, M. (2005). Agents are not (just) Web services: Considering BDI agents and Web services. In *AAMAS 2005 Workshop on Service-Oriented Computing and Agent-Based Engineering (SOCABE),* 2005.

Diehl, V. (1987). Productivity loss in brainstorming groups: Toward the solution of a riddle. *Journal of Personality and Social Psychology, 53,* 497–509. doi:10.1037/0022-3514.53.3.497

Dijkman, R. M., & Dumas, M. (2004). Service-oriented design: A multiviewpoint approach. *International Journal of Cooperative Information Systems (IJCIS). Special Issue on Service Oriented Modeling, 13*(4), 337–368.

Dimitrov, M., Simov, A., Stein, S., & Konstantinov, M. (2007). A BPMO based semantic business process modelling environment. In M. Hepp, K. Hinkelmann, D. Karagiannis, R. Klein & N. Stojanovic (Eds.), *Workshop on Semantic Business Process and Product Lifecycle Management (SBPM)* (Vol. 251, pp. 101-104). CEUR Workshop Proceedings, Innsbruck, Austria.

Ding, H., Solvberg, I., & Lin, Y. (2004, March). A vision on semantic retrieval in P2P network. In *the International Conference on Advanced Information Networking and Applications (AINA 2004),* Fukuoka, Japan.

Djurić, D. (2004). MDA-based ontology infrastructure. [ComSIS]. *Computer Science and Information Systems, 1*(1), 91–116. doi:10.2298/CSIS0401091D

Dogac, A., Cingil, I., Laleci, G. B., & Kabak, Y. (2002, August 23-24). Improving the functionality of UDDI registries through Web service semantics. *3rd VLDB Workshop on Technologies for E-Services (TES-02),* Hong Kong, China.

Dogac, A., Kabak, Y., & Laleci, G. B. (2004, March). Enriching ebXML registries with OWL ontologies for efficient service discovery. In *Proc. of RIDE'04,* Boston.

Dogac, A., Kabak, Y., Laleci, G. B., Mattocks, C., Najmi, F., & Pollock, J. (2005). Enhancing ebXML registries to make them OWL aware. [Springer.]. *Distributed and Parallel Databases Journal, 18*(1), 9–36. doi:10.1007/s10619-005-1072-x

Dogac, A., Kabak, Y., Laleci, G. B., Sinir, S., Yildiz, A., Kirbas, S., & Gurcan, Y. (2004). Semantically enriched Web services for travel industry. *ACM Sigmod Record, 33*(3). ebXML. (2007). Retrieved from http://www.ebxml.org/

Dogac, A., Laleci, G. B., Kabak, Y., & Cingil, I. (2002). Exploiting Web service semantics: Taxonomies vs. ontologies. *A Quarterly Bulletin of the Computer Society of the IEEE Technical Committee on Data Engineering, 25*(4).

Dong, A. (2005). *XML tree finder system: A first step towards XML data mining–final report.* Tech. Rep. CS Department, University of Calgary.

Dong, X., Halevy, A., Madhavan, J., Nemes, E., & Zhang, J. (2004). Similarity search for Web services. In *30th VLDB.*

ebRIM, ebXML Registry Information Model v2.5. (2007). Retrieved from http://www.oasis-open.org/committees/regrep/documents/2.5/specs/ebRIM.pdf

ebXML Registry Services Specification v2.5. (2007). Retrieved from http://www.oasis-open.org/committees/regrep/documents/2.5/specs/ebRIM.pdf

El Kharbili, M., Stein, S., Markovic, I., & Pulvermüller, E. (2008). Towards a framework for semantic business process compliance management. In *The Impact of Governance, Risk, and Compliance on Information Systems (GRCIS)* (Vol. 339, pp. 1-15). CEUR Workshop Proceedings, Montpellier, France.

Endert, H., Hirsch, B., Küster, T., & Albayrak, S. (2007, May 14). Towards a mapping from BPMN to agents. In J. Huang, R. Kowalczyk, Z. Maamar, D. L. Martin, I. Müller, S. Stoutenburg, & K. Sycara (Eds.), *Service-oriented computing: Agents, semantics, and engineering. AAMAS 2007 International Workshop, SOCASE 2007,* Honolulu, HI (pp. 92-106).

Erl, T. (2004). *Service-oriented architecture: Concepts, technology, and design.* Upper Saddle River, NJ: Prentice Hall.

Erradi, A., Anand, S., & Kulkarni, N. (2006). SOAF: An architectural framework for service definition and realization. *Proceedings of the IEEE International Conference on Services Computing* (pp. 151-158). IEEE Computer Society.

European Commission. (2006). *Enterprise interoperability research roadmap.*

Farrell, J., & Lausen, H. (2007). *Semantic annotations for WSDL and XML schema. W3C recommendation.*

Farrell, J., & Lausen, H. (Eds.). (2007). *Semantic annotations for WSDL and XML schema.* Retrieved on December 8, from http://www.w3.org/TR/sawsdl/

Fensel, D., & Bussler, C. (2002). The Web service modeling framework WSMF. *Electronic Commerce Research and Applications*, *1*(2), 113–137. doi:10.1016/S1567-4223(02)00015-7

Fensel, D., Ding, Y., Omelayenko, B., Schulten, E., Botquin, G., Brown, M., & Flett, A. (2001). Product data integration for B2B e-commerce. *IEEE Intelligent Systems*, *16*(4), 54–59. doi:10.1109/5254.941358

Fensel, D., Lausen, H., Polleres, A., de Bruijn, J., Stollberg, M., Roman, D., & Domingue, J. (2006). *Enabling Semantic Web services: The Web service modeling ontology*. Springer.

Fettke, P., & Loos, P. (2006). *Reference modeling for business systems analysis*. Hershey, PA: IGI Publishing.

Filipowska, A., Kaczmarek, M., & Stein, S. (2008). Semantically annotated EPC within semantic business process management. In *Workshop on Advances in Semantics for Web Services (semantics4ws)*. Milan, Italy.

FIPA. (2000). *FIPA communicative act library specification. Specification, Foundation for Intelligent Physical Agents*. Retrieved from www.fipa.org

Fischer, K., Hahn, C., & Madrigal-Mora, C. (2007). Agent-oriented software engineering: A model-driven approach. *International Journal of Agent-Oriented Software Engineering*, *1*(3/4), 334–369. doi:10.1504/IJAOSE.2007.016265

Foster, H., Mukhija, A., Uchitel, S., & Rosenblum, D. (2008). A model-driven approach to dynamic and adaptive service brokering using modes. *Proceedings of 6th International Conference on Service Oriented Computing ICSOC 2008* (pp. 558-564).

France Telecom, Maryland Information and Network Dynamics Lab at the University of Maryland, National Institute of Standards and Technology (NIST), Network Inference, Nokia, SRI International, Stanford University, Toshiba Corporation, & University of Southampton. (2004, November 22). OWL-S: Semantic markup for Web services. W3C member submission. Retrieved on January 15, 2009, from http://www.w3.org/Submission/OWL-S/

freebXML Registry Open Source Project. (2007). Retrieved from http://ebxmlrr.sourceforge.net

Friesen, A., & Alazeib, A. A., Balogh, A., M. Bauer, M., A. Bouras, A., P. Gouvas, P., G. Mentzas, G., & A. Pace, A. (2007, July 23-27). Towards semantically-assisted design of collaborative business processes in EAI scenarios. In the *pProceedings of the 5th IEEE International Conference on Industrial Informatics*, July 23-27 2007, Vienna, WF-006149, (Vol.ume 2, Pagep. 779).

Friesen, A., & Lemcke, J. (2007). Composing Web-servicelike abstract state machines (ASM). In J. Koehler, M. Pistore, A. P. Sheth, P. Traverso & M. Wirsing (Eds.), *Autonomous and adaptive Web services, Dagstuhl Seminar Proceedings* (Vol. 07061). Internationales Begegnungs-und Forschungszentrum fuer Informatik (IBFI), Schloss Dagstuhl, Germany.

Friesen, A., & Namiri, K. (2006, July). Towards semantic service selection for B2B integration. In *Proceedings of the 6th International Conference on Web Engineering (ICWE 2006)*, Menlo Park, CA

Frost, R. (2007). Jazz and the eclipse way of collaboration. *IEEE Software*, *24*(6), 114–117. doi:10.1109/MS.2007.170

Gacitua-Decar, V., & Pahl, C. (2008). Pattern-based business-driven analysis and design of service architectures. *Proceedings of the 3rd International Conference on Software and Data Technologies* (pp. 252-257).

Gacitua-Decar, V., & Pahl, C. (2008). Service architecture design for e-businesses: A pattern based approach. *Proceedings of the 9th International Conference on Electronic Commerce and Web Technologies EC-Web08*. (LNCS 5183, pp. 41-50). Berlin, Germany: Springer-Verlag.

Galileo. (2007). Retrieved from http://www.cendanttds.com/galileo/

Gamma, E., Helm, R., Johnson, R. E., & Vlissides, J. M. (1993). Design patterns: Abstraction and reuse of object-oriented design. *Proceedings of the 7th European Conference on Object-Oriented Programming* (pp. 406-431). Berlin, Germany: Springer-Verlag.

Ganter, B., & Godin, R. (2005). *Formal concept analysis.* Springer.

Garcia, R., & Gil, R. (2007). Facilitating business interoperability from the Semantic Web. In W. Abramowicz (Ed.), *BIS 2007.* (LNCS 4439, pp. 220-232). Berlin/Heidelberg: Springer.

Garlan, D., & Schmerl, B. (2006). Architecture-driven modelling and analysis. *Proceedings of the Eleventh Australian Workshop on Safety Critical Systems and Software-SCS '06* (pp. 3-17). Melbourne, Australia: Australian Computer Society, Inc.

Gašević, D., Devedžić, V., & Djurić, D. (2004). MDA standards for ontology development–tutorial. In *4th International Conference on Web Engineering ICWE2004,* Galway, Ireland. Retrieved on December 9, 2008, from http://afrodita.rcub.bg.ac.yu/~gasevic/tutorials/ICWE2004/

Grasso, A., Meunier, J., Pagani, D., & Pareschi, R. (1997, May). Distributed coordination and workflow on the World Wide Web. *Computer Supported Cooperative Work, 6*(2-3), 175–200. doi:10.1023/A:1008652312739

Greenwood, D., & Calisti, M. (2004). Engineering Web service-agent integration. *2004 IEEE International Conference on Systems, Man and Cybernetics, 2,* 1918–1925.

Greiner, U., Lippe, S., Kahl, T., Ziemann, J., & Jäkel, F. W. (2006). A multilevel modeling framework for designing and implementing cross-organizational business processes. *Technologies for Collaborative Business Process Management,* 13-23.

Grimm, S., & Friesen, A. (2005). *D4.8 Discovery specification (DIP deliverable).* Retrieved on December 8, 2008, from http://dip.semanticweb.org/documents/D4.8Final.pdf

Grønmo, R., Jaeger, M. C., & Hoff, H. (2005). Transformations between UML and OWLS. In A. Hartman & D. Kreische (Eds.), *Model-driven architecture–foundations and applications.* (LNCS 3748, pp. 269–283). Berlin, Germany: Springer-Verlag.

Gruber, T. R. (1995). Toward principles for the design of ontologies used for knowledge sharing? *International Journal of Human-Computer Studies, 43*(5-6), 907–928. doi:10.1006/ijhc.1995.1081

Hahn, C. (2008). A platform independent agent-based modeling language. In *Proceedings of the Seventh International Conference on Autonomous Agents and Multiagent Systems (AAMAS)* (pp. 233-240).

Hahn, C., Madrigal-Mora, C., & Fischer, K. (2008). A platform-independent metamodel for multiagent systems. *International Journal on Autonomous Agents and Multi-Agent Systems.* The Netherlands: Springer.

Hahn, C., Madrigal-Mora, C., Fischer, K., Elvesæter, B., Berre, A. J., & Zinnikus, I. (2006, September 19-20). Metamodels, models, and model transformations: Towards interoperable agents. *Multiagent System Technologies, 4th German Conference, MATES 2006,* Erfurt, Germany. (LNCS 4196, pp. 123-134). Springer.

Haller, A., Gomez, J., & Bussler, C. (2005). Exposing Semantic Web Sservice principles in SOA to solve EAI scenarios. iIn *Workshop on Web Service Semantics, in, WWW2005.*

Halpin, T. (2001). *Information modeling and relational databases: From conceptual analysis to logical design.* Morgan Kaufmann

Han, J., & Kamber, M. (2006). *Data mining. Concepts and techniques.* Morgan Kaufmann Publishers. ISBN 1558609016

Harmonise, IST200029329. (2005). *Tourism harmonisation network. Deliverable 3.2 semantic mapping and reconciliation engine subsystems.*

Hauguel, P. E., & Viardot, E. (2001). De la supply chain au réseau industriel. *L'expension. Management Review,* 94–100.

Hendler, J. (2001). Agents and the Semantic Web. *IEEE Intelligent Systems, 16*(2), 30–37. doi:10.1109/5254.920597

Hepp, M. (2007). Possible ontologies: How reality constrains the development of relevant ontologies. *IEEE Internet Computing, 11*(1), 90–96. doi:10.1109/MIC.2007.20

Hepp, M., & Roman, D. (2007). An ontology framework for semantic business process management. In *8th International Conference Wirtschaftsinformatik* (pp. 423-440). Karlsruhe, Germany.

Hepp, M., De Leenheer, P., de Moor, A., & Sure, Y. (Eds.). (2008). *Ontology management for the Semantic Web, Semantic Web Services, and business applications.* Springer-Verlag.

Hepp, M., Leymann, F., Domingue, J., Wahler, A., & Fensel, D. (2005). Semantic business process management: A vision towards using Semantic Web services for business process management. In *IEEE International Conference on e-Business Engineering (ICEBE)* (pp. 535-540). Beijing, China.

Hevner, A. R., March, S. T., Park, J., & Ram, S. (2004). Design science in information systems research. *MIS Quarterly, 28*(1), 75–105.

Hofmeister, C., Nord, R., & Soni, D. (2000). *Applied software architecture* (2nd ed.). MA: Addison-Wesley.

HR-XML Consortium. (2008). *About HR-XML Consortium, Inc.* Retrieved on January 15, 2009, from http://www.hr-xml.org/

IBM UDDI Registry. (2005). Retrieved from http://www-3.ibm.com/services/uddi/find

IDEAS. (2003). *Project deliverable (WP1-WP7). Public reports.* Retrieved from www.ideas-roadmap.net

Intelligent Agents, J. A. C. K. (2006). *The agent oriented software group (AOS).* Retrieved from http://www.agent-software.com/shared/home/

INTEROP. (2003). Interoperability research for networked enterprises applications and software. Network of excellence, annex 1-description of work.

Izza, S., & Vincent, L. Burlat, P., Lebrun, P., & Solignac, H. (2006). Extending OWL-S to solve enterprise application integration issues. *Interoperability for Enterprise Software and Applications Conference (I-ESA'06),* Bordeaux, France.

Izza, S., Vincent, L., & Burlat, P. (2005). A framework for semantic enterprise integration. In *Proceedings of INTEROP-ESA'05*, Geneva, Switzerland (pp. 78-89).

Izza, S., Vincent, L., & Burlat, P. (2006). A framework for Semantic enterprise integration. In D. Konstantas, J. P. Bourrières, M. Léonard, & N. Boudjlida (Eds.), *Interoperability of enterprise software and applications* (pp. 75-86). London: Springer-Verlag.

Jarrar, R., & Meersman, R. (2007). Ontology engineering-the DOGMA approach. In E. Chang, T. Dillon, R. Meersman & K. Sycara (Eds.), *Advances in Web Semantic, volume 1, a state-of-the art Semantic Web advances in Web Semantics IFIP2.12.* Springer.

Jena2 Semantic Web Toolkit. (2005). Retrieved from http://www.hpl.hp.com/semweb/jena2.htm

Jennings, N. R., Faratin, P., Norman, T. J., O'Brien, P., Odgers, B., & Alty, J. L. (2000). Implementing a business process management system using ADEPT: A real-world case study. *Int. Journal of Applied Artificial Intelligence, 14*(5), 421–465. doi:10.1080/088395100403379

Jouault, F., & Kurtev, I. (2006). Transforming models with ATL. In *Satellite Events at the MoDELS 2005 Conference.* (LNCS 3844, pp. 128–138). Springer.

Kahl, T., Vanderhaeghen, D., Ziemann, J., Zinnikus, I., Loos, P., & Fischer, K. (2006). Agent-supported cross-organizational business process management and implementation. *International Transactions on Systems Science and Applications, 1*(4), 369–374.

Kaiser, M. (2007). Toward the realization of policy-oriented enterprise management. *IEEE Computer, 40*(11), 57–63.

Kastner, P. S., & Saia, R. (2006). The composite applications benchmark report. Tech. Rep. Aberdeen Group.

Kaufer, F., & Klusch, M. (2006). WSMO-MX: A logic programming based hybrid service matchmaker. In *4th European Conference on Web Services (ECOWS '06)* (pp. 161–170).

Keller, U., Lara, R., Polleres, A., Toma, I., Kifer, M., & Fensel, D. (2004). *WSMO D5.1-WSMO Web service discovery (v0.1). WSML working draft.*

Kendall, E. (2006). The ontology definition metamodel-an MDA-based framework for semantic interoperability. *Semantic Technology Conference*, San Jose, CA.

Kiss, A., Martinek, P., & Czilik, I. (2008, October). Integrating HR offices over semantically enriched SOA. Paper presented at the Conference for Information Security Solutions Europe (ISSE), Madrid, Spain.

Kitchenham, B., Pickard, L., & Peeger, S. L. (1995). Case studies for method and tool evaluation. *IEEE Software, 12*(4), 52–62. doi:10.1109/52.391832

Klein, M. (1999). Towards a systematic repository of knowledge about managing collaborative design conflicts. In *Working Paper Series 210*. MIT Center for Coordination Science.

Kleppe, A., Warmer, J. B., & Bast, W. (2003). *MDA explained—the model driven architecture: Practice and promise.* Addison-Wesley.

Klusch, M. (2008). Semantic Web service coordination. In M. Schumacher, H. Helin, & H. Schuldt (Eds.), *CASCOM-intelligent service coordination in the Semantic Web.* Birkhäuser: Verlag, Springer.

Klusch, M., Fries, B., & Sycara, K. (2006). Automated Semantic Web service discovery with OWLS-MX. In *AAMAS '06: Proceedings of the Fifth International Joint Conference on Autonomous Agents and Multiagent Systems* (pp. 915–922). New York:ACM Press.

Koehler, J., Hauser, R., Küster, J., Ryndina, K., Vanhatalo, J., & Wahler, M. (2006). The role of visual modeling and model transformations in business-driven development. In *Fifth International Workshop on Graph Transformation and Visual Modeling Techniques.*

Koehler, J., Hauser, R., Sendall, S., & Wahler, M. (2005). Declarative techniques for model-driven business process integration. *IBM Systems Journal, 44*(1), 47–65.

Kourtesis, D., & Paraskakis, I. (2008). Combining SAWS-DL, OWL-DL, and UDDI for semantically enhanced Web service discovery. In S. Bechhofer, M. Hauswirth, J. Hoffmann & M. Koubarakis (Eds.), *ESWC 2008.* (LNCS 5021, pp. 614-628). Berlin/Heidelberg: Springer.

Kourtesis, D., & Paraskakis, I. (2008). Web service discovery in the FUSION semantic registry. In W. Abramowicz & D. Fensel (Eds.), *BIS 2008.* (LNBIP 7, pp. 285-296). Berlin/Heidelberg: Springer.

Kourtesis, D., Ramollari, E., Dranidis, D., & Paraskakis, I. (2008). Discovery and selection of certified Web services through registry-based testing and verification. In L. Camarinha-Matos & W. Pickard (Eds.), *Pervasive collaborative networks, IFIP 283/2008* (pp. 473-482). Boston: Springer.

Kozen, D., & Tiuryn, J. (1990). Logics of programs. In J. van Leeuwen (Ed.), *Handbook of theoretical computer science, vol. b* (pp. 789–840). Amsterdam, The Netherlands: Elsevier Science Publishers.

Krafzig, D., Banke, K., & Slama, D. (2004). *Enterprise SOA: Service-oriented architecture best practices (the coad series).* Prentice Hall PTR. ISBN 0131465759

Krafzig, D., Banke, K., & Slama, D. (2005). *Enterprise SOA: Service oriented architecture best practices.* Prentice Hall.

Küster, J. M., Ryndina, K., & Gall, H. (2007). Generation of business process models for object life cycle compliance. In G. Alonso, P. Dadam & M. Rosemann (Eds.), *BPM.* (LNCS 4714, pages 165–181). Springer. ISBN 978-3-540-75182-3

Lara, R., Stollberg, M., Polleres, A., Feier, C., Bussler, C., & Fensel, D. (2005). Web service modeling ontology. *Applied Ontology, 1*(1), 77–106.

Lécue, F., Salibi, S., Bron, P., & Moreau, A. (2008). Semantic and syntactic data flow in Web service composition. *2008 IEEE International Conference on Web Services (ICWS '08)* (pp. 211-218), Beijing, China.

Lemcke, J., & Friesen, A. (2007). Composing Web-servicelike abstract state machines (ASMs). In *Proceedings of IEEE International Conference on Services Computing (SCW 2007)* (pp. 262-269).

Lemcke, J., & Friesen, A. (2007). Considering realistic Web service features for semiautomatic composition. In *SEEFM'07*. Springer.

Lemcke, J., & Friesen, A. (2008). (To appear). Considering realistic Web service features for semiautomatic composition. [AMCT]. *Annals of Mathematics, Computing, and Teleinformatics*.

Lenzerini, M. (2002). Data integration: a theoretical perspective. In *PODS '02: Proceedings of the Twenty-first ACM SIGMOD-SIGACT-SIGART Symposium on Principles of Database Systems* (pp. 233–246). New York: ACM Press.

Li, K., Verma, K., Mulye, R., Rabbani, R., Miller, J., & Sheth, A. (2006). Designing Semantic Web processes: The WSDL-S approach. In J. Cardoso & A. Sheth (Eds.), *Semantic Web services, processes, and applications* (pp. 161-193). Springer.

Li, L., & Horrocks, I. (2003). A software framework for matchmaking based on Semantic Web technology. In *Proceedings of the Twelfth World Wide Web Conference (WWW 2003)*.

Liapis, A. (2007). Computer mediated collaborative design environments. Published doctoral dissertation, The Robert Gordon University, Aberdeen, UK.

Liapis, A. (2007). The designer's toolkit: A collaborative design environment to support virtual teams. In *the Proceedings of IASK International Conference*, Oporto, Portugal.

Liapis, A. (2008). Synergy: A prototype collaborative environment to support the conceptual stages of the design process. In *Proceedings of the International Conference on Digital Interactive Media in Entertainment and Arts, DIMEA 2008*, Athens, Greece. ACM/IEEE Digital Library.

Liapis, A., Christiaens, S., & DeLeenheer, P. (2008). Collaboration across the enterprise: An approach for enterprise interoperability. *International Conference on Enterprise Information, ICEIS 2008*, Barcelona, Spain.

Luo, J., Montrose, B., Kim, A., Khashnobish, A., & Kang, M. (2006). Adding OWL-S support to the existing UDDI infrastructure. *2006 IEEE International Conference on Web Services (ICWS'06)*, Chicago, IL.

Maedche, A., & Staab, S. (2003). Services on the move-towards P2P-enabled Semantic Web services. *Proceedings of the Tenth International Conference on Information Technology and Travel and Tourism, ENTER 2003*, Helsinki.

Maedche, A., Motik, D., Silva, N., & Volz, R. (2002). MAFRA-A MApping FRAmework for distributed ontologies. In *Proc. of the 13th European Conf. on Knowledge Engineering and Knowledge Management EKAW2002*, Madrid, Spain.

Malins, J., & Liapis, A. (2007). The design educator's toolkit. *Virtual Environments in Art, Design, and Education*. Dublin Institute of Technology, Dublin, Ireland.

Malins, J., Watt, S., Liapis, A., & McKillop, C. (2006). Tools and technology to support creativity in virtual teams. In S. MacGregor & T. Torres (Eds.), *Virtual teams and creativity: Managing virtual teams effectively for higher creativity*. Hershey, PA: IGI Global.

Malone, T. W. Crowston., K., & Herman, G. A. (2003). *Organizing Bbusiness kKnowledge: The MIT pProcess Hhandbook*. Cambridge, MA: MIT Press, 2003. [14]

Markovic, I., & Kowalkiewicz, M. (2008). Linking business goals to process models in semantic business process modeling. In *12th IEEE International EDOC Conference*. Munich, Germany.

Martin, D. (Ed.). (2004). *OWL-S: Semantic markup for Web services*. Retrieved on December 8, 2008, from http://www.w3.org/Submission/2004/SUBM-OWL-S-20041122/

Martin, D., Burstein, M., Hobbs, J., Lassila, O., McDermott, D., McIlraith, S., et al. (2004). OWL-S: Semantic markup for Web services. W3C member submission. Retrieved on November 22, 2004, from http://www.w3.org/Submission/OWL-S/

Martin, D., Domingue, J., Brodie, M., & Leymann, F. (2007). Semantic Web services, part 1. *IEEE Intelligent Systems, 22*(5), 12–17. doi:10.1109/MIS.2007.4338488

Martin, D., Domingue, J., Sheth, A., Battle, S., Sycara, K., & Fensel, D. (2007). Semantic Web services, part 2. *IEEE Intelligent Systems, 22*(6), 8–15. doi:10.1109/MIS.2007.118

Masolo, C., Borgo, et al. (2002, August). *The W Wonder-Web L library of F foundational o Ontologies. WonderWeb D deliverable D17*, August 2002.

McCormick, W. T., Schweitzer, P. J., & White, T. W. (1972). Problem decomposition and data reorganization by a clustering technique. *Operations Research, 20*(5), 993–1009. doi:10.1287/opre.20.5.993

McGuinness, D. L., & van Harmelen, F. (2004). *OWL Web ontology language overview. W3C recommendation*. Retrieved on December 8, 2008, from http://www.w3.org/TR/owl-features/

McGuinness, D., & van Harmelen, F. (2004). *OWL Web ontology language overview. W3C recommendation*.

McIlraith, S., & Martin, D. (2003). Bringing semantics to Web services. *IEEE Intelligent Systems, 18*(1), 90–93. doi:10.1109/MIS.2003.1179199

McIlraith, S., & Son, T. C. (2002). Adapting golog for composition of Semantic Web services. *Proceedings of the Eighth International Conference on Principles of Knowledge Representation and Reasoning* (pp. 482-493).

McIlraith, S., Son, T., & Zeng, H. (2001). Semantic Web services. *IEEE Intelligent Systems, 16*(2), 46–53. doi:10.1109/5254.920599

Meersman, R. (1999). The use of lexicons and other computer-linguistic tools in semantics, design, and cooperation of database systems. In Y. Zhang, M. Rusinkiewicz & Y. Kambayashi (Eds.), *Proceedings of the Conference on Cooperative Database Systems (CODAS 99)*. (pp. 1-14). Springer-Verlag.

Meersman, R. (2001). Ontologies and databases: More than a fleeting resemblance. In A. d'Atri & M. Missikoff (Eds.), *OES/SEO 2001 Rome Workshop*. Luiss Publications.

Meersman, R. (2002). Web and ontologies: Playtime or business at the last frontier in computing? In *Proceedings of the NSF-EU Workshop on Database and Information Systems Research for Semantic Web and Enterprises* (pp. 61-67).

Mellor, S. J., Scott, K., Uhl, A., & Weise, D. (2004). *MDA distilled*. Addison-Wesley.

Mendling, J., Lassen, K., & Zdun, U. (2005). *Transformation strategies between block-oriented and graph-oriented process modelling languages*. Tech. Rep. JM-200510 -10. TU Vienna.

Mens, T., & Tourw, T. (2004). A survey of software refactoring. In *IEEE Transactions on Software Engineering*.

Nagarajan, M., Verma, K., Sheth, A., Miller, J., & Lathem, J. (2006). Semantic i Interoperability of Web S services - C challenges and E experiences. *2006 IEEE International Conference on Web Services (ICWS 2006)*.

Nejdl, W., Wolf, B., Qu, C., Decker, S., Sintek, M., Naeve, A., et al. (2002). EDUTELLA: A P2P networking infrastructure based on RDF. In *Proc. of the 11th Intl. World Wide Web Conf.*

Nejdl, W., Wolf, B., Staab, S., & Tane, J. (2002). Edutella: Searching and annotating resources within an RDF-based P2P network. In *Proc. of the Semantic Web Workshop, 11th Intl. World Wide Web Conf.*

Nejdl, W., Wolpers, M., Siberski, W., Schmitz, C., Schlosser, M., Brunkhorst, I., & Loser, A. (2003). Super-peer-based routing and clustering strategies for RDF-based peer-to-peer networks. In *Proc. of the Intl. World Wide Web Conf.*

Newell, A. (1982). The knowledge level. *Journal of Artificial Intelligence, 18*(1), 87–127. doi:10.1016/0004-3702(82)90012-1

Nissen, M. E. (2000). Supply chain process and agent design for e-commerce. *33rd Hawaii International Conference on System Sciences*, Maui, HI.

Nitzsche, J., van Lessen, T., Karastoyanova, D., & Leymann, F. (2007). BPEL for Semantic Web services (BPEL4SWS). In *Proceedings of the 3rd International Workshop on Agents and Web Services in Distributed Environments AWeSome'07-On the Move to Meaningful Internet Systems, OTM 2007 Workshops.*

Nitzsche, J., Wutke, D., & van Lessen, T. (2007). An ontology for executable business processes. In M. Hepp, K. Hinkelmann, D. Karagiannis, R. Klein & N. Stojanovic (Eds.), *Workshop on Semantic Business Process and Product Lifecycle Management (SBPM)* (Vol. 251, pp. 52-63). CEUR Workshop Proceedings, Innsbruck, Austria.

Nonaka, I., & Takeuchi, H. (1995). *The knowledge-creating company: How Japanese companies create the dynamics of innovation.* Oxford University Press.

OASIS. (1993-2009). *OASIS Web services business execution language (WSBPEL) TC.* Retrieved on January 15, 2009, from http://www.oasis-open.org/committees/tc_home.php?wg_abbrev=wsbpel

Oasis. (2006, August 2). Reference model for service oriented architecture 1.0, committee specification 1. Retrieved from http://www.oasis-open.org

Oberle, D. (2006). *Semantic Mmanagement of Mmiddleware, volume I of Tthe Semantic Web and Bbeyond.* Springer, 2006.

Oberle, D., Ankolekar, et al. (2006, July). *DOLCE ergo SUMO: On Ffoundational and Ddomain Mmodels in SWIntO, AIFB,.* University of Karlsruhe. July 2006.

Object Management Group. (2003). *MDA model-driven architecture guide v1.0.1. OMG.* Retrieved on September 9, 2008, from www.omg.org/docs/omg/03-06-01.pdf

Object Management Group. (2003). *Ontology definition metamodel-request for proposal (OMG Document: as/2003-03-40). OMG.* Retrieved on September 9, 2008, from http://www.omg.org/docs/ad/03-03-40.pdf

Object Management Group. (2006). *MDA guide, Object Management Group, Inc., final adopted specification.*

Ogden, C. K., & Richards, I. A. (1923). The meaning of meaning: A study of the influence of language upon thought and of the science of symbolism. London: Routledge & Kegan Paul.

Omelayenko, B., & Fensel, D. (2001). A two-layered integration approach for product information in B2B e-commerce. In K. Madria & G. Pernul (Eds.), *Proceedings of the Second International Conference on Electronic Commerce and Web Technologies (EC WEB-2001).* (LNCS 2115, pp. 226–239). Springer-Verlag.

OMG. (2006, February). *Business process modeling notation (BPMN) specification.* Object Management Group (OMG).

Open Travel Alliance. (2005). Retrieved from http://www.opentravel.org/

Ouyang, C., Dumas, M., Breutel, S., & ter Hofstede, A. H. M. (2006, June 5-9). Translating standard process models to BPEL. In *Advanced Information Systems Engineering, 18th International Conference, CAiSE 2006,* Luxembourg (pp. 417–432). Springer.

Ouyang, C., Dumas, M., Hofstede, A. H. M., & Aalst, W. M. P. (2007). Pattern-based translation of BPMN process models to BPEL web services. [JWSR]. *International Journal of Web Services Research, 5*(1), 42–62.

OWL-mt. OWL Mapping Tool. (2005). Retrieved from http://www.srdc.metu.edu.tr/artemis/owlmt/

OWL-QL. OWL Query Language. (2005). Retrieved from http://ksl.stanford.edu/projects/owl-ql/

OWL-S. (2005). Retrieved from http://www.daml.org/services/daml-s/0.9/

Pahl, C. (2007). An ontology for software component matching. *International Journal on Software Tools for Technology Transfer (STTT). Special Edition on Foundations of Software Engineering, 9*(2), 169–178.

Pahl, C. (2008). Semantic model-driven development of Web service srchitectures. [IJWET]. *International Journal of Web Engineering and Technology, 4*(3), 386–404. doi:10.1504/IJWET.2008.019540

Pahl, C., Giesecke, S., & Hasselbring, W. (2007). An ontology-based approach for modelling architectural styles. *First European Conference on Software Architecture ECSA 2007* (pp. 60-75). Berlin, Germany: Springer-Verlag.

Paolucci, M., Kawamura, T., Payne, R. T., & Sycara, K. (2002). Semantic matching of Web service capabilities. In I. Horrocks & J. Hendler (Eds.), *The Semantic Web-ISWC 2002.* (LNCS 2342, pp. 333-347). Berlin/Heidelberg: Springer-Verlag.

Papazoglou, M. P., & Ribbers, P. (2006). *E-Business: Organizational and technical foundations.* Wiley. ISBN 0470843764

Papazoglou, M. P., & van den Heuvel, W. J. (2006). Service-oriented design and development methodology. *Int. J. of Web Engineering and Technology, 2*(4), 412–442. doi:10.1504/IJWET.2006.010423

Payne, T. R. (2008). Web services from an agent perspective. *IEEE Intelligent Systems, 23*(8).

Payne, T., & Lassila, O. (2004). Semantic Web services. *IEEE Intelligent Systems, 19*(4), 14–15. doi:10.1109/MIS.2004.29

Pedrinaci, C., Brelage, C., van Lessen, T., Domingue, J., Karastoyanova, D., & Leymann, F. (2008). Semantic business process management: Scaling up the management of business processes. In *2nd IEEE International Conference on Semantic Computing (ICSC)*, Santa Clara, CA.

Penserini, L., Perini, A., Susi, A., & Mylopoulos, J. (2006, June 5-9). From stakeholder intentions to software agent implementations. In *Advanced Information Systems Engineering, 18th International Conference, CAiSE 2006,* Luxembourg (pp. 465–479). Springer.

Petersohn, H. (2005). *Data mining–Verfahren, prozesse, anwendungsarchitektur.* Oldenbourg Wissenschaftsverlag.

Petrie, C., & Bussler, C. (2003). Service agents and virtual enterprises: A survey. *IEEE Internet Computing*, 58–78.

Peyret, H. (2007). *The Forrester wave: Enterprise architecture tools, Q2.* Forrester.

Pistore, M., Barbon, F., Bertoli, P., Shaparau, D., & Traverso, P. (2004). Planning and monitoring Web service composition. In C. Bussler & D. Fensel (Eds.), *AIMSA.* (LNCS 3192, pages 106–115). Springer. ISBN 3-540-22959-0

Pistore, M., Marconi, A., Bertoli, P., & Traverso, P. (2005). Automated composition of Web services by planning at the knowledge level. In L. P. Kaelbling & A. Saffiotti (Eds.), *IJCAI,* 1252–1259. Professional Book Center. ISBN 0938075934

Pistore, M., Roberti, P., & Traverso, P. (2005). Process-level composition of executable Web services: "on-the-fly" vs. "once-for-all" composition. In A. Gómez-Pérez & J. Euzenat (Eds.), *ESWC.* (LNCS 3532, pages 62–77). Springer. ISBN 3-540-26124-9

Pistore, M., Traverso, P., & Bertoli, P. (2005). Automated composition of Web services by planning in asynchronous domains. In S. Biundo, K. L. Myers & K. Rajan (Eds.), *ICAPS* (pp. 2–11). AAAI. ISBN 1-57735-220-3

Pistore, M., Traverso, P., Bertoli, P., & Marconi, A. (2005). Automated synthesis of executable Web service compositions from bpel4ws processes. In A. Ellis & T. Hagino (Eds.), *WWW (special interest tracks and posters)* (pp. 1186–1187). ACM. ISBN 1-59593-051-5

Plasil, F., & Visnovsky, S. (2002). Behavior protocols for software components. *ACM Transactions on Software Engineering, 28*(11), 1056–1075. doi:10.1109/TSE.2002.1049404

Pokraev, S., Koolwaaij, J., & Wibbels, W. (2003). Extending UDDI with context aware features based on semantic service descriptions. *2003 International Conference on Web Services (ICWS'03)* (pp. 184-190), Las Vegas, NV.

Postgre, S. Q. L. An Open-Source Object Relational Database Management System (ORDBMS). (2005). Retrieved from http://www.paragoncorporation.com/ArticleDetail.aspx?ArticleID=11

Preist, C. (2004). A conceptual architecture for Semantic Web services. In *Proceedings of the 3rd International Semantic Web Services Conference (ISWC 2004).*

Preist, C., Esplugas-Cuadrado, J., Battle, S. A., Grimm, S., & Williams, S. K. (2005). Automated business-to-business integration of a logistics supply chain using Semantic Web services technology. In Y. Sure, W. Nejdl, C. Goble, G. Antoniou, P. Haase, S. Staab, et al. (Eds.), *The Semantic Web–ISWC 2005* (pp. 987-1001). Berlin/Heidelberg: Springer.

Project, J. X. T. A. (2005). Retrieved from http://www.jxta.org/

Rao, A. S., & Georgeff, M. P. (1991). Modeling rational agents within a BDI architecture. In J. Allen, R. Fikes, & E. Sandewall (Eds.), *2nd International Conference on Principles of Knowledge Representation and Reasoning (KR91)* (pp. 473-484). San Mateo, CA: Morgan Kaufmann Publishers Inc.

Rao, J., & Su, X. (2004). A survey of automated Web service composition methods. In J. Cardoso & A. P. Sheth (Eds.), *SWSWPC.* (LNCS 3387, pp. 43–54). Springer. ISBN 3-540-24328-3

Richardson, T., Wood, R. K., & Hopper, A. (1988). Virtual network computing. *IEEE Internet Computing, 2*(1), 1–7.

Rosenkrantz, G. (1998). The science of being. *Erkenntnis, 48*(5), 251–255. doi:10.1023/A:1005489810828

Russell, S., & Norvig, P. (1995). *Artificial intelligence: A modern approach.* Upper Saddle River, NJ: Prentice Hall.

Rymer, J., M., Gilpin, M., & K., Volmer, K. (2004). *Market Ooverview: "Integration Llandscape 2005".* Forrester Research, Inc.

Sabre. (2005). Retrieved from http://www.sabre.com/

Salman, A. B., & Henning, S. (2004). *An analysis of the skype peer-to-peer Internet telephony protocol.* New York: Columbia University, Department of Computer Science.

SATINE Project. (2007). Retrieved from http://www.srdc.metu.edu.tr/webpage/projects/satine

Savarimuthu, B. T. R., Purvis, M., Purvis, M. K., & Cranefield, S. (2005). Integrating Web services with agent based workflow management system (WfMS). *IEEE/WIC/ACM International Conference on Web Intelligence,* 471- 474

Scheer, A. W. (2002). *ARIS-Vom geschäftsprozess zum anwendungssystem.* Berlin: Springer.

Scheer, A. W., Thomas, O., & Adam, O. (2005). Process modelling using event-driven process chains. In M. Dumas, W. M. P. van der Aalst & A. H. M. ter Hofstede (Eds.), *Process-Aware Information Systems* (pp. 119-146). NJ: Wiley.

Schema, R. D. F. (1999). *Resource description framework schema specification. W3C proposed recommendation.* Retrieved from http://www.w3.org/TR/PRrdfschema

Schema, X. M. L. (2007). Retrieved from http://www.w3.org/XML/Schema

Schmelzer, H. J., & Sesselmann, W. (2008). Geschäftsprozessm in der praxis (6th ed.). München: Carl Hanser Verlag.

Schulz, K., & Orlowska, A. (n.d.). Facilitating cross-organisational workflows with a workflow view approach. *Data & Knowledge Engineering, 51*(1), 109–147. doi:10.1016/j.datak.2004.03.008

Searle, J. R. (1969). *Speech acts.* Cambridge, UK: Cambridge University Press.

Semantic Web Services Language (SWSL) Committee. (2006). *Semantic Web services framework (SWSF).* Retrieved on September 9, 2008, from http://www.daml.org/services/swsf/1.0/

Sheth, A. (1998). Changing focus on interoperability in information systems: From system, syntax, structure to semantics. In M. F. Goodchild, M. J. Egenhofer, R. Fegeas & C. A. Kottman (Eds.), *Interoperating geographic information systems* (pp. 5-30). Kluwer Academic Publishers.

Simons, A. J. (2002, November-December). The theory of classification, part 4: Object types and subtyping. In R. Wiener (Ed.), *Journal of Object Technology,* 27-35.

Simple Object Access Protocol (SOAP). (2005). Retrieved from http://www.w3.org/TR/SOAP/

Singh, M. P. (2004). Business process management: A killer app for agents? In *Proceedings of the Third International Joint Conference on Autonomous Agents & Multiagent Systems (AAMAS) 2004* (p. 26).

Singh, M. P., & Huhns, M. N. (1999). Multiagent systems for workflow. *International Journal of Intelligent Systems in Accounting Finance & Management, 8,* 105–117. doi:10.1002/(SICI)1099-1174(199906)8:2<105::AID-ISAF163>3.0.CO;2-#

Singh, M. P., & Huhns, M. N. (2005). *Service-oriented computing-semantics, processes, agents.* John Wiley & Sons, Ltd.

Sirin, E., Parsia, B., Wu, D., Hendler, J., & Nau, D. (2004). HTN planning for Web service composition using SHOP2. *International Semantic Web Conference 2003, 1,* 377–396.

Sivashanmugam, K., Verma, K., Sheth, A., & Miller, J. (2003). Adding semantics to Web services standards. *2003 International Conference on Web Services (ICWS'03)* (pp. 395-401), Las Vegas, NV.

Smith, H., & Fingar, P. (2003). Business process management: The third wave (1st ed.). Tampa, FL: Meghan-Kiffer Press.

Snelting, G., & Tip, F. (1998). Reengineering class hierarchies using concept analysis. *Foundations of Software Engineering,* 99–110.

Spyns, P., Meersman, R., & Jarrar, M. (1998). Data modelling versus ontology engineering. *SIGMOD Record, 31*(4), 12–17. doi:10.1145/637411.637413

Srinivasan, N., Paolucci, M., & Sycara, K. (2005). An efficient algorithm for OWL-S based semantic search in UDDI. In J. Cardoso & A. Sheth (Eds.), *Semantic Web services and Web process composition.* (LNCS 3387, pp. 96-110). Berlin/Heidelberg: Springer-Verlag.

Staab, S., & Studer, R. (Eds.). (2004). *Handbook on ontologies.* Springer. ISBN 3-540-40834-7

Stachowiak, H. (1973). Allgemeine modelltheorie. New York: Springer-Verlag, Wien.

Stamber, C., Stein, S., & El Kharbili, M. (2008). Prototypical implementation of a pragmatic approach to Semantic Web service discovery during process execution. In W. Abramowicz & D. Fensel (Eds.), *11th International Conference on Business Information Systems (BIS)* (Vol. 7, pp. 201-212). LNBIP, Innsbruck, Austria.

Steen, M. W. A., Strating, P., Lankhorst, M. M., Doest, H. W. L., & Iacob, M. E. (2005). In Z. Stojanovic & A. Dahanayake (Eds.), *Service-oriented enterprise architecture. Service-oriented software system engineering: Challenges and practices* (pp. 132-154). Hershey, PA: Idea Group.

Stein, S., Kühne, S., & Ivanov, K. (2008). Business to IT transformations revisited. In *1st International Workshop on Model-Driven Engineering for Business Process Management (MDE4BPM)*, Milan, Italy.

Steinbeis Foundation (StW). (n.d.). *Project information about FUSION*. Retrieved on January 15, 2009, from http://www.fusionweb.org

Stollberg, M., Cimpian, E., Mocan, A., & Fensel, D. (2006). A Semantic Web Mmediation aArchitecture. In *Proceedings of the 1st Canadian Semantic Web Working Symposium (CSWWS 2006)*.

Stormer, H., & Knorr, K. (2001). AWA-eine architektur eines agentbasierten workflow-systems. In H. H. Buhl, A. Huther & B. Reitwiesner (Eds.), *Tagungsband 5. Internationale Tagung Wirtschaftsinformatik (WI2001)* (pp. 147–160).

Studer, R., Grimm, S., & Abecker, A. (2007). *Semantic Web services: Concepts, technologies, and applications*. New York: Springer.

Stumme, G., Taouil, R., Bastide, Y., Pasquier, N., & Lakhal, L. (2002). Computing iceberg concept lattices with Titanic. *Data & Knowledge Engineering, 42*, 189–222. doi:10.1016/S0169-023X(02)00057-5

Suwanmannee, S., Benslimane, D., & Thiran, P. (2005, March). OWL-based approach for semantic interoperability. In *the Proceedings of AINA, IEEE Computer Science Press*.

Tektonidis., D., Bokma, A., Oatley, G., & Salampasis, M. (2005). ONAR: An oOntologies-based Sservice-Ooriented Aapplication Iintegration fFramework,. *I-ESA'05*, Geneva, Switzerland.

Termier, A. (2004). *Extraction of frequent trees in an heterogeneous corpus of semistructured data: Application to XML documents mining*. Unpublished doctoral dissertation, Paris-South University.

Toma, I., Sapkota, B., Scicluna, J., Gomez, J.-M., Roman, D., & Fensel, D. (2005). *A P2P discovery mechanism for Web service execution environment*. Retrieved from http://dip.semanticweb.org/documents/ p2pDiscovery.pdf

Tomcat. (2005). Retrieved from http://jakarta.apache.org/

Tomek, I., Shakshuki, E., Peng, A., Koo, A., & Prabhu, O. (2003). *FCVW-towards an eclipse-based CSCW framework*.

Trainotti, M., Pistore, M., Calabrese, G., Zacco, G., Lucchese, G., et al. (2005). Astro: Supporting composition and execution of Web services. In B. Benatallah, F. Casati & P. Traverso (Eds.), *ICSOC*. (LNCS 3826, pp. 495–501). Springer. ISBN 3-540-30817-2

Traverso, P., & Pistore, M. (2004). Automated composition of semantic Web services into executable processes. In S. A. McIlraith, D. Plexousakis & F. van Harmelen (Eds.), *International Semantic Web Conference*. (LNCS 3298, pp. 380–394). Springer. ISBN 3-540-23798-4

Triple, D. E. S. Algorithm. (2005). Retrieved from http://csrc.nist.gov/publications/fips/fips463/fips46-3.pdf

UDDI4J Java API. (2005). Retrieved from http://uddi4j.sourceforge.net/

Universal Description Discovery and Integration (UDDI). (2005). Retrieved from http://www.uddi.org

Uno, T., Asai, T., Uchida, Y., & Arimura, H. (2004a). An efficient algorithm for enumerating closed patterns in transaction databases. *Discovery Science, 16*–31.

Uno, T., Kiyomi, M., & Arimura, H. (2004b). Lcm ver. 2: Efficient mining algorithms for frequent/closed/maximal itemsets. *FIMI*.

van der Aalst, W. M. P., & Pesic, M. (2006). Decserflow: Towards a truly declarative service flow language. Eindhoven, The Netherlands: BPM-06-21, BPM Center.

van Deursen, A., & Kuipers, T. (1999). Identifying objects using cluster and concept analysis. In *21st International Conference on Software Engineering* (pp. 246–255).

van Lessen, T., Nitzsche, J., Dimitrov, M., Konstantinov, M., Karastoyanova, D., & Cekov, L. (2007). An execution engine for semantic business processes. In *2nd International Workshop on Business Oriented Aspects concerning Semantics and Methodologies in Service oriented Computing (SeMSoC)*.

Verma, K., Sivashanmugam, K., Sheth, A., Patil, A., Oundhakar, S., & Miller, J. (2005). METEOR-S WSDI: A scalable P2P infrastructure of registries for semantic publication and discovery of Web services. *Journal of Information Technology Management*, *6*(1), 17–39. doi:10.1007/s10799-004-7773-4

Vidal, J., Buhler, P., & Stahl, C. (2004). Multiagent systems with workflows. *IEEE Internet Computing*, *8*(1), 76–82. doi:10.1109/MIC.2004.1260707

Viewlets, S. A. T. I. N. E. (2005). Retrieved from http://www.srdc.metu.edu.tr/webpage/projects/satine/viewlet/

Vollmer, K., & H., Peyret, H. (2005). *Topic Ooverview: "Application Iintegration Ssolutions"*. Forrester Research, Inc.

von Bertalanffy, L. (1976). *General system theory*. New York: Braziller Inc.

Vu, L.-H., Hauswirth, M., & Aberer, K. (2006). *Towards P2P-based Semantic Web service discovery with QoS support*. Retrieved from http://infoscience.epfl.ch/record/97742/files/?ln=fr

W3C. (2006). *Semantic annotations for Web services description language working group*. Retrieved on January 15, 2009, from http://www.w3.org/2002/ws/sawsdl

Wang, Y., & Stroulia, E. (2003). Semantic structure matching for assessing Web service similarity. In *Service-Oriented Computing-ICSOC*. (LNCS 2910, pp. 194–207). Springer. Witten, I. H., & Frank, E. (2005). *Data mining*. Elsevier Inc., second edition.

Warwas, S., & Hahn, C. (2008). The concrete syntax of the platform independent modeling language for multiagent systems. In *Proceedings of the International Workshop on Agent-based Technologies and Applications for Enterprise Interoperability (ATOP 2008)*, Estoril, Portugal.

Web Ontology Language, O. W. L. 1.0 Reference. (2005). Retrieved from http://www.w3.org/TR/2002/WD-owl-ref-20020729/ref-daml

Web Service Description Language (WSDL). (2005). Retrieved from http://www.w3.org/TR/wsdl

Web Services Policy Framework (WS-Policy). (2005). Retrieved from http://www128.ibm.com/developerworks/library/specification/ws-polfram/

Weske, M. (2007). *Business process management: Concepts, languages, architectures*. Berlin: Springer.

Wilde, T., & Hess, T. (2007). Forschungsmethoden der wirtschaftsinformatik-eine empirische untersuchung. *Wirtschaftsinformatik*, *49*(4), 280–287. doi:10.1007/s11576-007-0064-z

Wooldridge, M. (1997). Agent-based software engineering. *IEE Proceedings. Software*, *144*(1), 26–37. doi:10.1049/ip-sen:19971026

XPath. XML Path Language. (2005). Retrieved from http://www.w3.org/TR/xpath

Xu, B., & Chen, D. (2007). Semantic Web services discovery in P2P environment. Retrieved from http://ieeexplore.ieee.org/stamp/stamp.jsp?arnumber=4346418&isnumber=4346351

Yang, J., Heuvel, W., & Papazoglou, M. (2002). Tackling the challenges of service composition in e-marketplaces. In *Proceedings of the 12th International Workshop on Research Issues on Data Engineering: Engineering E-Commerce/E-Business Systems (RIDE-2EC 2002)*, San Jose, CA.

Yin, R. K. (2003). Case study research: Design and methods (3rd ed.). London: Sage Publications.

Zaki, M. J., Parimi, N., De, N., Gao, F., Phoophakdee, B., et al. (2005). Towards generic pattern mining. In *Formal Concept Analysis*.

Zdun, U., & Dustdar, S. (2007). Model-driven and pattern-based integration of process-driven SOA models. *International Journal of Business Process Integration and Management*, *2*(2), 109–119. doi:10.1504/IJBPIM.2007.015135

Zeng, L., Ngu, A., Benatallah, B., & O'Dell, M. (2001, January 29-February 1). An agent-based approach for supporting cross-enterprise workflows. In *Proceedings of the 12th Australasian Database Conference,* Gold Coast, Queensland, Australia. *ACM International Conference Proceeding Series, 10,* 123-130. Washington, D.C.: IEEE Computer Society.

Zinnikus, I., Hahn, C., & Fischer, K. (2008). A model-driven agent-based approach for the integration of services into a collaborative business process. In *Proceedings of the Seventh International Conference on Autonomous Agents and Multiagent Systems (AAMAS)* (pp. 241-248).

About the Contributors

Gregoris Mentzas is Professor of Information Management at the School of Electrical and Computer Engineering of the National Technical University of Athens (NTUA) and Director of the Information Management Unit (IMU), a multidisciplinary research unit at the University. During the 2006-2009 period, he serves in the Board of Directors of the Institute of Communication and Computer Systems of NTUA. His area of expertise is information technology management and his research concerns the integration of knowledge management, semantic web and e-service technologies, collaboration and workflow management, corporate knowledge management in e-government and e-business settings. He has spoken at conferences and guest seminars worldwide, and is internationally known for his scholarly work in the area of knowledge management and e-government. Prof. Mentzas holds a Diploma Degree in Engineering (1984) and a Ph.D. in Operations Research and Information Systems (1988), both from NTUA. During 1996-1997 he was a Visiting Fellow in the UK, in the area of "Information Management Systems n Business Transformation".

Andreas Friesen is senior researcher and project manager at SAP Research. His research interests comprise for more than 4 years application of semantic technologies in software engineering. He is currently working on new technologies merging model-driven and ontology-driven software engineering methods. In this role he is shaping the vision of hybrid software engineering approach combining the benefits of the well established software modeling methodology with the expressive descriptive power of ontologies and logical reasoning and its application for SAP and partner ecosystem. Previously he was coordinating a project on semantic Business Process Fusion for heterogenious Enterprise Applications especially providing process-oriented interoperability solutions for cross-organizational application integration scenarios. Dr. Friesen is with SAP Research for over 4 years working on different research projects. He holds a Doctoral Degree from the University of Siegen and is author of around 30 articles and scientific papers.

***

Spiros Alexakis studied Computer Science at the University of Karlsruhe and visited a post graduate course in Economics. After two years at SIEMENS he joined CAS Software in 1992 as a software engineer. In the following he became System Engineer and Project Manager. Since 1996 he is in the position of Director Innovation & Business Development, in charge of innovation management, business development and research. Spiros has collected extensive experience in management of research initiatives. He has co-ordinated over 20 international research projects, that have delivered successful and exploitable results. He has published a number of papers on collaborative working, customer relationship management and enterprise application integration. Spiros has been a member of the FUSION management board, in charge of the validation pilots.

András Balogh was born in Tatabánya, Hungary on 15 October 1981. He started his studies at the Faculty of Electrical Engineering and Informatics at the Budapest University of Technology and Economics. He took part in several competitions during his university years (most significant results: 1ˢᵗ place: IBM 48 Hours Programming Contest, 2ⁿᵈ place: University Scientific Conference). Andras was awarded several scholarships, Marie Curie Fellowship being one. He has published articles on a variety of topics. His focus is on technical rather than on scientific issues, and he is experienced in a wide range of current technologies and tools. In the context of FUSION, Andras has developed a graphical tool for (semantic) process design, and was involved in the use case planning and implementation.

Markus Bauer started his career in 1998 as researcher at the research group Programmstrukturen at Forschungszentrum Informatik (FZI) in Karlsruhe. In 2003, he became manager of the research group Programmstrukturen leading nine full-time researchers. During his time at FZI, his work was focused on software architecture, software reengineering and software quality. In 2005, he joined CAS Software AG, where he is now leading the development of the company's next generation CRM software and the underlying software platform. In the frame of FUSION Markus worked on the implementation of cross organisational business processes using semantic web services. Markus Bauer has received a PhD from Universität Karlsruhe for his work on the analysis of subsystem structures in object-oriented software systems. He published approx. 15 research papers on software architecture, software reengineering and software quality.

Veli Bicer has worked in various projects at all stages of software development life-cycle. He has extensive experience in Business Process Management Systems, Semantic Web Technologies, Web Services, Ontologies, P2P networks, Agent Technologies, e-Health systems and Trust and Security Services. He has worked on several IST projects, namely IST-1-002104-STP SATINE, IST-1-002103-STP Artemis, IST-027074-STP SAPHIRE and IST-02765-STP RIDE.

Thanassis Bouras holds a Diploma from the School of Electrical and Computer Engineering of the National Technical University of Athens (Greece). His Thesis was in the area of System Analysis and Design for Knowledge Management Applications. In the past, he has worked on several ATHOC (ATHENS 2004 Olympic Games) projects. During the last 5 years, he has participated as research engineer in several EC and National co-funded projects in the areas of knowledge management (INKASS), business and semantic interoperability (FUSION, COMMIUS), assisted and independent living (SOPRANO) and e-learning (ELEVATE). He is currently a research engineer at the Institute of Communication and Computer Systems of NTUA. His current research interests include the emerging semantic web and business (re-) engineering of media that support knowledge distribution and transfer in an intra- and inter- organizational level and web services that implement e-Business and e-Government applications.

Stijn Christiaens is a researcher at the Semantics Technology and Applications Research Laboratory (STARLab) at the Vrije Universiteit Brussel in Brussels, Belgium. He is currently working on theories, methods and tools to support ontology creation and maintenance at the domain expert level.

Asuman Dogac is full professor in the Department of Computer Engineering of Middle East Technical University (METU). She is also the founder & director of Software Research and Development Center, METU and the general manager of the SRDC Ltd. Her expertise includes Internet Computing, semantic Web, agent technology, interoperability, e-Business, and eHealth. She has been consulting the industry and government organizations. In 2004, Dr. Dogac received IBM (USA) Faculty award. She is also the recipient of several local awards: 1991 Mustafa Parlar Research Award, 1994 Husamettin Tugac Research Award, 1999 METU Achievement Award, 2000 METU Tarik Somer Superior Achievement award, 2000 Mustafa Parlar Science award and 2001 Tarik Somer award. She has published more than 100 papers in refereed international conferences and journals including Communications of the ACM, IEEE Transactions on Software Engineering, IEEE Transactions on Information Technology in Biomedicine, Information Systems Journal (Elsevier), Journal of Parallel and Distributed Databases and the ACM Computing Surveys.

Marwane El Kharbili is working in the ARIS research department of IDS Scheer AG, working on IDS Scheer's business rules management solution for business process management (BPM). As part of his research activities, Marwane is involved in various research projects, such as the European project SUPER (www.ip-super.org). Marwane is also a PhD student currently working on his thesis tackling semantic compliance management issues in BPM. His topics of interest are business rule management, business process management, semantic web, compliance management, and complex event processing. Marwane has an engineering degree (Diplom-Inform. Eq. Master) from the university of Karlsruhe in Germany and a Masters degree of engineering (ingenieur informatique) from the ENSIMAG school of applied mathematics and informatics at the Grenoble INP university in France.

Catarina Ferreira da Silva is currently a post-doc research assistant at the Centre for Informatics and Systems of the University of Coimbra (CISUC) within the Information Systems Group. Previously she was a teaching and research assistant in computer science department of University of Lyon I and in the collaborative Information Systems research team of LIRIS UMR 5205 lab (Laboratory of Computer Graphics, Image and Information Systems). She holds a Ph.D. (2007) from the University of Lyon 1 and a M.Sc. (2003) from the French Institute of Applied Science (INSA) of Lyon, both in computer science. Her main research interests are Semantic Interoperability, Semantic Web, Information Systems Interoperability, Knowledge Representation and Reasoning.

Klaus Fischer is DFKI Research Fellow and head of the Multiagent System (MAS) Research Group at DFKI. He holds a diploma and doctoral degree from Technische Universität (TU) in München. In 1992 he joined the MAS Research Group at DFKI in Saarbrücken and assumed the responsibility of group leader in November 1993. He is deputy head of the department of Agents and Simulated Reality. In his work he has a long record of successfully managed projects for industrial partners as well as for public authorities.

Veronica Gacitua is a postgraduate research student at the School of Computing at Dublin City University. Previously, she has worked as an enterprise architect in a large size mining company for three years. The main projects during this period encompassed the creation of an architectural instrument to support IT planning within the company, and the initialisation of a long-term enterprise applications architecture migration project. The support to IT planning has been provided through the initial and incremental development of an enterprise architecture that relates IT assets, business processes and organizational units of the company. The architectural migration has considered the migration from a heterogeneous enterprise applications architecture toward a service-oriented architecture. She has graduated in Electronic Engineering and obtained a master degree in Electronic Engineering from the Universidad Técnica Federico Santa Maria, Chile.

Parisa Ghodous is currently full professor in computer science department of University of Lyon I. She is head of collaborative Information Systems team of LIRIS UMR 5205 (Laboratory of Computer Graphics, Images and Information Systems). Her research expertise is in the following areas: Interoperability, Semantic Web, Web services, Collaborative modeling, Product data exchange and modeling and Standards. She is in editorial boards of CERA, ICAE and IJAM journals and in the committees of many relevant international associations such as concurrent engineering, ISPE, Interoperability.

Panagiotis Gouvas graduated in 2004 from the School of Electrical and Computer Engineering of the National Technical University of Athens (NTUA). His Diploma Thesis was in the area of Mobile and Personal Communications (Location Based Services in Wireless LANs). During 2001-2009 period, he participated as software and research engineer in several research ICT, IST and e-Contect projects. At present, he is a PhD candidate in the School of Electrical & Computer Engineering at NTUA, as well as, a research associate in the Institute of Communication and Computer Systems of NTUA. His research interests lie in the field of Multi-Agent systems, Service Oriented Architectures, Knowledge Representation and Management, Semantic Web and Grid-based architectures.

Christian Hahn is a research scientist at the MAS research group at DFKI. He holds a Diploma in computer science from the University of Saarbrücken in 2004. He has been doing research and development on agent-based systems, model-driven systems engineering, and software development methodologies the last 4 years. He has experience from a number of IST projects including ATHENA and INTEROP in FP6, and SHAPE in FP7.

Yildiray Kabak has been working as a software engineer for research and industrial projects in eBusiness and eHealth domains since year 2000. Yildiray Kabak has extensive expertise on Internet Computing, Semantic Web Technologies, Agent Technology, Interoperability, e-Business, e-Health and IT Security & Privacy. Yildiray is a PhD candidate in METU Computer Engineering Department. He has developed middleware applications for eHealth and tourism systems including a ebXML and web based framework for the testing of Integrating Healthcare Enterprise (IHE) Profiles. He also has worked on several IST projects, namely IST-2000-26429 HERMES, IST-2000-31050 AgentAcademy, IST-2000-31046 HUMANTEC, IST-1999-20216 LEVER, INCO DC 97 2496 MARIFlow, MEDFORIST, IST-1-002104-STP SATINE, IST-1-002103-STP Artemis, IST-027074-STP SAPHIRE, IST-02765-STP RIDE, IST-213031 iSURF and IST-027306 ABILITIES.

Akos Kiss studied Electrical and Computer Engineering at Budapest University of Technology and Economics. Since September 2006 he is working as Java Developer and Project Manager at InfomatiX Ltd. In the frame of FUSION, he has developed the integration between CRM systems and HR databases.

Dimitrios Kourtesis is a Research Associate at the South East European Research Centre (SEERC) in Thessaloniki, Greece, and a PhD candidate in the Department of Computer Science at the University of Sheffield. He holds an MSc (Distinction) in Software Engineering and Telecommunications, and a BSc (Hons) in Computer Science, both from the University of Sheffield. His research interests are in the areas of Service Oriented Computing and Semantic Web Technologies, and he has worked in a number of research projects related to these areas. He is a professional member of the British Computer Society (BCS).

Gokce B. Laleci has been working as a software engineer for research and industrial projects in eBusiness and eHealth domains since year 2000. She has designed and developed service oriented middleware solutions for tourism domain, peer-to-peer semantic resource discovery mechanisms for eHealth and tourism domain, a semantic middleware for developing multi-agent based systems, clinical decision support systems for remote healthcare monitoring. Furthermore, he has worked on several IST projects, namely IST-2000-26429 HERMES, IST-2000-31050 AgentAcademy, IST-2000-31046 HUMANTEC, IST-1999-20216 LEVER, INCO DC 97 2496 MARIFlow, MEDFORIST, IST-1-002104-STP SATINE, IST-1-002103-STP Artemis, IST-027074-STP SAPHIRE, IST-213031 iSURF and IST-02765-STP RIDE. She got her PhD from METU Computer Engineering Department.

Jens Lemcke is both a Research Associate at SAP Research in Karlsruhe and an external Ph.D. student at the Forschungszentrum Informatik (FZI), where he is supervised by Prof. Rudi Studer. Jens' Ph.D. topic is scalable, ontological EAI and e-business integration. Prior to joining SAP, Jens received his Diploma in Computer Science from the University of Rostock. During his studies at Rostock University, Jens did an internship at the IBM Silicon Valley Lab in California, USA. While at SAP Research, Jens has contributed to the EU-funded research projects: DIP, FUSION, and MOST. Part of his time at SAP was also spent at the SAP Labs in Palo Alto, USA, where he collaborated with the Stanford Logic Group in the POEM project.

Aggelos Liapis is a senior researcher currently working on a Marie Curie supported programme at Vrije Universiteit Brussel, Brussels. He is a computer scientist whose particular specialism is the development of computer supported collaborative environments, semantics, ontologies, and computer graphics. While doing his PhD in Computer Mediated Collaborative Design Environments at The Robert Gordon University, Aberdeen, Scotland he developed a prototype collaborative environment focused to assist professional product designers when distributed during the early stages of the design process.

Cristina Martinez has a background in Science Philosophy (Cum laude), in Communication (Cum Laude and Major) and has an MSc in Telematics (Cum Laude) from the Université Libre de Bruxelles. She started her career with the United Nations working for an IT track and trace development project for Africa, Asia and Latin-America. She joined the Andersen Consulting company in 1998 to work for the eCommerce group of the Technology department as a solutions engineer. She became a member of the staff of the European Commission in 2002 and is currently Administrator for Research in the Enterprise Networking and RFID Unit of the Information Society and Media Directorate-General. In addition to her responsibility for research projects in the ICT area, she devotes part of her time on policy aspects related to the future of Business Collaboration and Interoperability. She is head of the Future Internet Enterprise Systems cluster responsible for giving research directions in the Enterprise Interoperability and Collaboration domain. Cristina Martinez is married and has two children.

Paulo Melo is an Assistant Professor in the Faculty of Economics of the University of Coimbra. He has received a B.Sc. in Computer Science (1990), a M.Sc. in Systems and Automation (1996) and a Ph.D. in Business Management (2006) from the University of Coimbra. He has been working in Research and Development for the last two decades, in management, research and support roles. He has articles published in several international journals and conference proceedings in Operations Research, Group Decision Support and Management.

George Milis is an experienced senior IT Consultant and Analyst and possesses an MSc in Advanced Computing with specialization in Artificial Intelligence from the Department of Computing, Imperial College London, and a Diploma from the Aristotle University of Thessaloniki, Greece, in Electrical and Computing Engineering. George is currently working as a Consultant and Project Manager at European Dynamics SA. He has contributed in many European research projects, as well as, commercial projects addressing real needs of the public sector. He poses great experience in project quality assurance and quality control, preparation of documentation, and design of advance software solutions. George also participates and contributes in many conferences and workshops, presenting and discussing new ideas according to the European research agenda. He is currently dedicated to the advancement of IT solutions in a way to become easily and efficiently adoptable by the foreseen end-users communities.

Mehmet Olduz received his MSc Degree from the Department of Computer Engineering at Middle East Technical University. He is senior software engineer at SRDC Limited where he has worked in various projects at all stages of software development life-cycle. He has extensive experience in Business Process Management Systems, Semantic Web Technologies, Web Services, Ontologies, P2P networks, Agent Technologies, e-Health systems and Trust and Security Services. He is recently working on industrial applications of high-performance computing and networking, and is one of the architects of tourism and eHealth solutions. He has worked on several IST projects, namely IST-1-002104-STP SATINE, IST-1-002103-STP Artemis, IST-027074-STP SAPHIRE, IST-213031 iSURF and IST-02765-STP RIDE.

Claus Pahl is a Senior Lecturer at Dublin City University's School of Computing, where he is the leader of the Software and Systems Engineering group. Claus has graduated from the Technical University of Braunschweig and has obtained a PhD from the University of Dortmund. He has published more than 170 papers in various journals, books, conference, and workshop proceedings. He is on the editorial board of the four journals and is a regular reviewer for journals and conferences in the area of Web and Software technologies and their applications. He is the principal investigator of several basic and applied research projects in software engineering. Claus' research interests cover a broad spectrum from service- and component technologies in software engineering to infrastructure and development technologies for Web applications such as e-business and e-learning.

Iraklis Paraskakis is a Senior Research Officer at the South East European Research Centre (SEERC) in Thessaloniki, Greece, Academic Director of the centre's Doctoral Programme, and coordinator of the Information & Knowledge Management research cluster. He is also Senior Lecturer in the Department of Computer Science at CITY College, Greece, and Associate Lecturer in the Department of Informatics at the Hellenic Open University. He holds a PhD in Information Technology and Education from the Open University (UK), and an MSc in Analysis, Design and Management of Information Systems from London School of Economics. His research interests are in the areas of educational informatics, information systems, and knowledge management. He has served as organising chair and program committee member in several international and regional conferences, and as a referee for several journals in the area of educational informatics. He is a member of BCS, IEEE, EARLI, AIED and AACE.

Nikola Radic is a senior Java software developer and analyst at European Dynamics SA, Athens, Greece. His major title is MSc in electronics and telecommunications with the emphasis on design of digital electronic systems. In the last 10 years he was actively working on many IST projects and leading many commercial ones, using the latest cutting-edge technologies. He is always looking for challenges and way to improve his knowledge and experience with the new technologies. His currently one of the leading software engineers at European Dynamics responsible for development and management of several EU enterprise applications.

Pawel Rubach earned an MSc degree in 2003 from the Warsaw School of Economics, where he specialized in Information Systems and Applied Computer Science. Since 2003, he has been employed at the Warsaw School of Economics where he participated in many research projects, the largest of them focusing on Computer-Based Assessment. He gathered also practical experience while working as a systems administrator, application architect, systems analyst, project manager, and IT architect in different environments, ranging from small IT solution providers to large corporations such as the PKO BP S.A. (the largest Polish bank). In the years 2007-2008 as IT Architect at the Polish Telecom, Research & Development Branch (TP R&D), he contributed to two EU-sponsored projects: SUPER (http://www. ip-super.org) and SPICE (http://www.ist-spice.org). He spent the academic year 2008-2009 working on his Ph.D. as a Fulbright Visiting Scholar at Texas Tech University in Lubbock, Texas.

Paulo Rupino da Cunha is an Assistant Professor at the University of Coimbra and the head of its Information Systems Group. He is a Visiting Associate at Brunel University, UK. He holds a Ph.D. and a M.Sc. in Informatics Engineering - Information Systems. His main research interests are Information Systems Design, Quality Management and Information Systems, Business Models and Strategy, and IT governance issues. For two terms he was the Vice-President of Instituto Pedro Nunes, an Innovation and Technology Transfer organization providing specialized consulting, training and business incubation. For a period of three years, he was the elected Coordinator of the Informatics Engineering Chapter for the centre region of Portugal of the Portuguese Engineering Association, and for a two year term he was a member of the Executive Committee of the Department of Informatics Engineering of the University of Coimbra.

Gérald Santucci has been working in the Information Society and Media Directorate-General of the European Commission since February 1986. In March 2007, he was appointed Head of the Unit Networked Enterprise & Radio Frequency Identification (RFID). The adoption by the European Commission, in March 2007, of a Communication on RFID has constituted a first milestone towards the achievement of a European policy framework regarding RFID. Work underway includes the follow-up of a Recommendation on the implementation of privacy and information security principles in RFID-enabled applications (adopted by the EC on 11 May 2009) and a new series of global consultations on the Internet of Things. Over the years, Mr Santucci has gained extensive experience in the activities of the Directorate-General through his involvement in research management, including heading the Unit

"Applications relating to Administrations" (i.e. eGovernment) 1999-2002, the Unit "Trust and Security" 2003, and "ICT for Enterprise Networking" 2004-2006. Mr Santucci was also the "father" of the AIM exploratory action (Advanced Informatics in Medicine), launched in 1989 under the RACE programme (R&D on Advanced Communications Technologies for Europe).

Christian Stamber is working as a Software Developer for SAP AG, Germany. He holds an engineering degree (Dipl.-Inf., comparable to M.Sc. in Computer Science) from University of Kaiserslautern, Germany. His diploma thesis was aligned to the European research project SUPER (www.ip-super.org) in cooperation with IDS Scheer AG. Christian researched how to use semantic technologies in business process management. The insights gained during accomplishment of the thesis were part of additional scientific publications.

Sebastian Stein is responsible at IDS Scheer, Germany for developing and maintaining the ARIS SOA modelling method. Besides, he is involved in standardisation efforts at OMG and OASIS. He participates in the BPMN standardisation process and he is an author of OMG's OCEB certification program. Besides those tasks, Sebastian contributes to different public research projects within ARIS Research like the SUPER project. He focuses on integrating business process management (BPM) and service oriented architectures (SOA). He has published several scientific and popular papers. Besides his work assignments, Sebastian is currently finishing his PhD thesis at University of Kiel, Germany. He holds a Master of Science in Software Engineering from Blekinge Institute of Technology, Sweden and a diploma in Business Information Systems from University of Applied Sciences Dresden, Germany.

Tuncay Namli has extensive expertise on context management and IT Security and Privacy in IT systems. He has developed privacy and security applications in eHealth systems. Furthermore, he has worked on several IST projects, namely IST-1-002104-STP SATINE, IST-1-002103-STP Artemis, IST-027074-STP SAPHIRE, IST-02765-STP RIDE, IST-213031 iSURF and IST-027306 ABILITIES. Tuncay is a PhD candidate in METU Computer Engineering Department.

Ingo Zinnikus graduated from Saarland University, Germany in 1998 and is since then working for DFKI. He has been working on the application of multiagent systems for a number of topics such as logistics, recommendation systems and business process execution. Besides numerous publications he has contributed to a number of successful national and European proposals. He served as program committee member for a number of international workshops. Fields of Interest: Multiagent systems, service-oriented architectures and Semantic Web services. Experience with projects: the German government funded project TeleTruck, the EU funded projects SAID (FP5), VITAL (FP6, Technical Coordination), ATHENA (FP 6), and COIN (FP7), as well as domestic industry projects in German.

Index

X